Using Strategy Analytics to Measure Corporate Performance and Business Value Creation

Sandeep Kautish
Lord Buddha Education Foundation, Nepal

A volume in the Advances in
Business Information Systems and
Analytics (ABISA) Book Series

Published in the United States of America by
    IGI Global
    Business Science Reference (an imprint of IGI Global)
    701 E. Chocolate Avenue
    Hershey PA, USA 17033
    Tel: 717-533-8845
    Fax: 717-533-8661
    E-mail: cust@igi-global.com
    Web site: http://www.igi-global.com

Library of Congress Cataloging-in-Publication Data

Names: Kautish, Sandeep Kumar, 1981- editor.
Title: Using strategy analytics to measure corporate performance and
    business value creation / Sandeep Kumar Kautish, editor.
Description: Hershey : Business Science Reference, 2021. | Includes
    bibliographical references and index. | Summary: "This book provides
    concepts of strategic analytics and strategic analytics applications in
    each area of management i.e. market dynamics, customer analysis,
    operations, and people management with the goal of presenting best
    industry practices for turning managers into quantitative analysts or
    quantitative analysts and finally into expert strategists"-- Provided by
    publisher.
Identifiers: LCCN 2021000190 (print) | LCCN 2021000191 (ebook) | ISBN
    9781799877165 (hardcover) | ISBN 9781799877172 (paperback) | ISBN
    9781799877189 (ebook)
Subjects: LCSH: Strategic planning. | Management information systems. |
    Personnel management. | Organizational effectiveness.
Classification: LCC HD30.28 .U5775 2021 (print) | LCC HD30.28 (ebook) |
    DDC 658.4/012--dc23
LC record available at https://lccn.loc.gov/2021000190
LC ebook record available at https://lccn.loc.gov/2021000191

This book is published in the IGI Global book series Advances in Business Information Systems
and Analytics (ABISA) (ISSN: 2327-3275; eISSN: 2327-3283)

British Cataloguing in Publication Data
A Cataloguing in Publication record for this book is available from the British Library.

All work contributed to this book is new, previously-unpublished material.
The views expressed in this book are those of the authors, but not necessarily of the publisher.

For electronic access to this publication, please contact: eresources@igi-global.com.

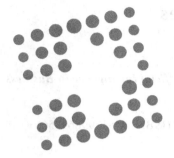

Advances in Business Information Systems and Analytics (ABISA) Book Series

ISSN:2327-3275
EISSN:2327-3283

Editor-in-Chief: Madjid Tavana, La Salle University, USA

MISSION

The successful development and management of information systems and business analytics is crucial to the success of an organization. New technological developments and methods for data analysis have allowed organizations to not only improve their processes and allow for greater productivity, but have also provided businesses with a venue through which to cut costs, plan for the future, and maintain competitive advantage in the information age.

The **Advances in Business Information Systems and Analytics (ABISA) Book Series** aims to present diverse and timely research in the development, deployment, and management of business information systems and business analytics for continued organizational development and improved business value.

COVERAGE

- Big Data
- Business Models
- Statistics
- Decision Support Systems
- Information Logistics
- Business Information Security
- Management Information Systems
- Geo-BIS
- Data Analytics
- Business Process Management

IGI Global is currently accepting manuscripts for publication within this series. To submit a proposal for a volume in this series, please contact our Acquisition Editors at Acquisitions@igi-global.com or visit: http://www.igi-global.com/publish/.

Titles in this Series

For a list of additional titles in this series, please visit: http://www.igi-global.com/book-series/

701 East Chocolate Avenue, Hershey, PA 17033, USA
Tel: 717-533-8845 x100 • Fax: 717-533-8661
E-Mail: cust@igi-global.com • www.igi-global.com

Editorial Advisory Board

Table of Contents

Detailed Table of Contents

    Shivani Agarwal, KIET School of Management, KIET Group of
        Institutions, Delhi, India
    Priyansh Teotia, KIET School of Management, KIET Group of
        Institutions, Delhi, India

Cold calling has been an essential tool for decades in marketing of goods and services. On the other hand, with time, recruitment and selection has become a hectic and hefty task for organizations. This report tries to highlight the scope and importance of cold calling in recruitment and selection. It also highlights the effectiveness and efficiency of recruitment agencies and their proficiency in finding the best possible candidate. It also tries to find the importance of various factors like company image, remuneration, job position, etc. that shape the attitude of a potential candidate towards a job offer. The chapter also puts focus on the skills of the sales representative that have an important effect in shaping the attitude of a prospect towards the job opening.

    Salha Ben Salem, University of Monastir, Tunisia
    Nadia Mansour, University of Sousse, Tunisia & University of
        Salamanca, Spain
    Moez Labidi, University of Monastir, Tunisia

This survey presented the various ways that are utilized in the literature to include financial market frictions in dynamic stochastic general equilibrium (DSGE) models. It focuses on the fundamental issue: to what extent the Taylor rules are optimal when the central bank introduces the goal of financial stability. Indeed, the latest financial crisis shows that the vulnerability of the credit cycle is considered the main source for the amplification of a small transitory shock. This conclusion changed the instrument that drives the transmission of monetary policy through the economy and pushed the policymakers to include financial stability as a second objective of the central bank.

Chapter 3

   Aizhan Tursunbayeva, University of Twente, The Netherlands
   Stefano Di Lauro, University of Sannio, Italy
   Gilda Antonelli, University of Sannio, Italy

A real-life case study presented in this chapter reports on how organizational network analysis approach was used in a medium-sized Italian company with circa 100 employees to examine how the company employees were connected by shared values at work, what these values are, and whether and how their value connectedness impacted the quality of their collaboration. The findings indicate that there was a positive correlation between shared work values and work collaboration, present benchmarks for network parameters, as well as propose macro-categories of work values. To the best of the authors' knowledge, this is the first study to use the network-analysis approach to explore shared values and employee collaboration at work. The chapter should be of substantial interest not only to academic scholars but also to organizational leaders and HR practitioners.

Chapter 4

   Rodrigo Marques de Almeida Guerra, Federal University of Santa
      Maria, Brazil
   Lídia Maria Begot Bento Cardoso, Federal University of Pará, Brazil
   Nathalia Maciel Nogueira, Federal University of Pará, Brazil
   Marcelo Pamplona Carneiro, Federal University of Pará, Brazil

Entrepreneurial resilience is a recent topic and is widespread in scientific research, especially when associated with periods of instability and crises. This chapter aims to analyze the relationship between the variables open-mindedness (OM), entrepreneurial resilience (ER), market turbulence (MT), and overall performance (OP) in SMEs located in the legal amazon. Data collection coincided with the pandemic of COVID-19, with 384 SME managers participating. The sample was analyzed using structural equation modeling (SEM). The results suggest mediation of the variable ER on the relationship between OM and OP, and moderation of the variable MT on OM and ER. The research's originality is attested by the model's empirical relationships, research context, and adverse scenario provided by the COVID-19 expansion. The practical implications indicate that managers should pay more attention to the variables investigated through the creation of new skills and competencies necessary for entrepreneurial activity in periods of economic crisis and market turbulence.

Samir Yerpude, Symbiosis Centre of Innovation and Research, Symbiosis International University (Deemed), India

Business strategy is all the actions and decisions taken by the management to achieve the business goals for sustaining the competitive edge. A successful business strategy determines the longevity of the organization. The strategists analyse the vision, mission, and values to frame and articulate the business strategy. Different tools such a Business Model Canvas, etc. are then used to create the business model. Once the business strategy is created, it is also equally critical to evaluate the same amidst the changing business environment. For the validation of strategies at all levels, data plays a vital role for the management to proceed with fact-based decision making. Informed decisions based on facts reduce the probability of erroneous results assisting the businesses align to the documented strategy. Strategic analytics practice creates the essential understanding about how the quantitative techniques and methods can be deployed using the structured and unstructured data that assists strategic decision making for the organization.

Guneet Kaur, University of Stirling Innovation Park Ltd, UK

The research work is focused on examining the role of business intelligence (BI) tools in strategic financial analysis. The effective utilization of data is essential in order to survive in today's competitive business environment. Traditionally, data analysis was performed manually by using a spreadsheet. However, due to big data proliferation at an unprecedented pace, it becomes difficult for the financial services industry to manage large datasets. Therefore, to address this issue, both academia and industry practitioners have come forward to meet the needs of a growing business with the help of BI tools. In this context, this chapter aims to assist the BI researchers and practitioners in the financial services industry to make fact-based decisions by using popular BI tools like Power BI, Tableau, and SAS analytics. Consequently, the chapter provides a detailed review of the applications of these BI tools in strategic financial analysis and to enhance overall corporate performance.

The research work is focused on examining the role of artificial intelligence (AI) in addressing challenges associated with cryptocurrencies like Bitcoin, Ethereum, etc. The popularity of Bitcoin has sparked the emergence of new alternative cryptocurrencies, commonly referred to as 'altcoins'. Simultaneously with its growing popularity and public awareness, the Bitcoin system has been branded as a haven for security breaches, selfish mining, money laundering, extreme volatility, and unpredictability of future prices. To address these challenges, stakeholders accepting cryptocurrencies must apply AI techniques to process and analyze large amounts of cryptocurrency data. In this context, this chapter discusses the recent research work to assist the researchers and practitioners in the cryptocurrency domain to make fact-based decisions by using AI techniques. Consequently, the chapter provides a detailed review of the background on fiat currencies, cryptocurrencies, challenges associated with cryptocurrencies, and the role of AI techniques in addressing those challenges.

Chapter 8

Deferred tax asset (DTA) is a tax/accounting concept that refers to an asset that may be used to reduce future tax liabilities of the holder. It usually refers to situations where a company has either overpaid taxes, paid taxes in advance, or has carry-over of losses (the latter being the most common situation). DTAs are thus contingent claims, whose underlying assets are the company's future profits. Consequently, the correct approach to value such rights implies the use of a contingent claim valuation framework. The purpose of this chapter is to propose a precise and conceptually sound mathematical approach to value DTAs, considering future projections of earnings and rates, alongside the DTA's legal time limit. The authors show that with the proposed evaluation techniques, the DTA's expected value will be much lower than the values normally used in today's practice, and the company's financial analysis will lead to much more sound and realistic results.

Chapter 9

Joao Carlos Silva, ISCTE, University Institute of Lisbon, Portugal
Nuno Souto, ISCTE, University Institute of Lisbon, Portugal
José Pereira, ISEG, Universidade de Lisboa, Portugal

Deferred tax asset (DTA) is a tax/accounting concept that refers to an asset that may be used to reduce future tax liabilities of the holder. In a company's balance, it usually refers to situations where it has either overpaid taxes, paid taxes in advance, or has carry-over of losses (the latter being the most common situation). In fact, accounting and tax losses may be used to shield future profits from taxation, through tax loss carry-forwards. The purpose of this chapter is to propose a precise and conceptually sound approach to value DTAs. For that purpose, making use of an adapted binomial CRR (Cox, Ross, and Rubinstein) algorithm, the authors derive a precise way to value DTAs. This way, the DTAs are valued in a similar way of the binomial options pricing model, and the subjectivity of its evaluation is greatly reduced. The authors show that with the proposed evaluation techniques, the DTA's expected value will be much lower than the values normally used in today's practice, and the bank's financial analysis will lead to much more sound and realistic results.

Chapter 10

Basil J. White, Independent Researcher, USA
Beth Archibald Martin, Maryland Institute College of Art, USA
Ryan J. Wold, Civic Studio, USA

The integrated value model (IVM) empowers analysis of the interdependent aspects of policies, plans, performance measures, priorities, and programs (P5). As organizations are holistic systems of processes and performance, knowing how P5 adds value becomes critical to success and achievement of internal goals and responses to external demands. Modeling these artifacts and mapping them to policies and practices allows analysts to measure the alignment to initiatives. The IVM supports efforts in strategic communications, change management, strategic planning, and decision support. Elements of P5 have explicit hierarchical and relational connections, but modeling the connections and developing logical inferences is an uncommon strategic business practice. This chapter describes how to use those goals to create a logical model for a public sector organization and how to use this model to identify, describe, and align business value. Further, this chapter demonstrates the model's capabilities and suggests future applications.

Vineet Chouhan, Sir Padampat Singhania Universit, Udaipur, India
Pranav Saraswat, MIT World Peace University, Pune, India

This case is related with the biggest 2020 scam by one of the major new private sector banks (i.e., YES bank). The case is related with the misuse of the power of banks in providing the benefits to one person, due to the power and influence granted by the political party leaders that influence providing unlimited loans to one person and further the acts of the bank officials that led to the partial breakdown of the banking system in India. Further, the case deals with the major accused and the shell company's creator as DHFL. The present analysis put lights on the future lessons to be learnt by various sectors in order to prevent heavy losses and loss of customer faith (being the most vital component). It starts by giving a background of the crisis that led the RBI to come into picture. It also shows the effectiveness of the actions of RBI for YES bank. At last, it points out the importance of independent management and the roles of auditors and other regulators in dealing with this crisis.

Foreword

Strategic analysis has the purpose of researching the business environment of an organization, as well as studying the organization itself in order to formulate decision-making strategies to achieve the proposed objectives.

To implement or maintain their business, companies must periodically carry out a strategic analysis, in order to determine what should be improved and what is already well underway in the organization, improving the company's effectiveness by increasing the capacity by continuously deploying resources intelligently and efficiently.

Strategic analysis is intended to help the company figure out how to start, where it wants to go and how far it can go. The main questions a company should ask when carrying out a strategic analysis: How is the competitive market composed? How do potential customers in this market behave? When carrying out a strategic analysis, the company must identify in the competitor market who the potential companies are and thus be able to define strategies that will keep it active and competitive in this market.

Strategic analysis should be a fundamental part of an organization's activities periodically, as part of the organization's PDCA cycle. Know what you are doing correctly and fight what is not working, in order to keep the organization running smoothly.

It is necessary to carry out an analysis of customers, listen to the customer: what are their expectations, needs and dissatisfactions. The strengths and weaknesses of the competition must also be identified, as well as evaluating the company's performance, in terms of its image, objectives, goals, strategies, structure and prospects for the future. One should be aware of market movement, changes in external factors that affect a company, as well as carry out an analysis of projected growth, trends, barriers, which are the threats, as well as focus on areas of opportunity and key factors for the success.

In this book you will find strategic analysis techniques in the form of chapters showing experiences that help the reader acquire knowledge to apply strategic management, serving as a bridge to elucidate some gaps that separate theoretical concepts from practice.

I congratulate Dr. Sandeep Kautish for bringing out with the idea of this book and producing an exemplary reference material for all readers.

Luis Felipe Dias Lopes
Departamento de Ciências Administrativas, Universidade Federal de Santa
Maria, Brazil

Preface

This book will be serving as a state-of-art documentation of Strategy Analytics, its present role around organizational outcomes and outlines the need of greater integration in organization strategy and analytics for better strategic decisions process to measure the corporate performance and business value creation.

Strategic Analytics is relatively new field in conjunction with Strategic Management and Business Intelligence. Generally Strategic Management field deals with enhancement of decision making capabilities of managers. Typically, such decision making processes are heavily dependent upon various internal and external reports. Managers need to develop their strategies using clear strategy processes supported by the increasing availability of data. This situation calls for a different approach to strategy, such as an integration with analytics, as the science of extracting value from data and structuring complex problems.

There are no sufficient literature (books, research articles) available on Strategic Analytics concepts and its applications. The proposed book will of one its kind which will not only cover introductory concepts of strategic analytics but also provides strategic analytics applications in each area of management i.e. market dynamics, customer analysis, operations and people management. Also, the book unveils best industry practices i.e. turning managers into quantitative analysts or quantitative analysts and finally into expert strategists. The proposed book will also provide a roadmap for business practitioners for tackling with complex business dynamics using optimization techniques and modern business analytics tools.

This book will be one contact reference to academic fraternity, management practitioners, business analysts and research students who are interesting in Strategic Analytics domain and using it in their research/practice work. The proposed book will open up a new direction for Strategic Analytics as this will be very second book on the given topic. The topics/chapters which have been covered in the book are never been covered in any other book.

Chapter 1 is about Cold calling which has been an essential tool for decades in marketing of goods and services. On the other hand, with time Recruitment and Selection has become a hectic and hefty task for organizations. This report tries to highlight the scope and importance of Cold Calling in recruitment and selection. It also highlights the Effectiveness and Efficiency of recruitment agencies and their proficiency in finding the best possible candidate. It also tries to find the importance of various factors like Company Image, Remuneration, Job Position etc. that shape the attitude of a potential candidate towards a job offer. The chapter also puts focus on the skills of the sales representative that have an important effect in shaping the attitude of a prospect towards the job opening.

Chapter 2 is a survey presented the ways, which are utilized in the literature to include financial market frictions in DSGE models. Besides, it focuses on the fundamental issue; to what extent the Taylor rules are optimal when the central bank introduces the goal of financial stability. Indeed, the latest financial crisis shows that the vulnerability of the credit cycle is considered as the main source for the amplification of a transitory shock. This conclusion changed the instrument that drives the transmission of monetary policy through the economy and pushed the policymakers to include financial stability as a second objective of the central bank.

Chapter 3 is a Case Study from Italy reports on a study in a medium-sized Italian company examining, with the help of an organizational network analysis approach, how company employees were connected by shared values at work. The findings of this chapter provide insights on this connectedness, present benchmarks for network parameters, and propose macro-categories of work values. Therefore, the chapter would be of substantial interest for scholars, organizational leaders, and Human Resource practitioners.

Chapter 4 reveals that little has been done to better understand entrepreneurial resilience, especially when associated with complex and difficult to measure variables. This chapter investigated the relationship between the constructs open mind, entrepreneurial resilience, overall performance and market turbulence. This research analyzed a sample of 384 small and medium- sized companies (SMEs) located in the Legal Amazon. The Legal Amazon covers a geographical area composed of nine states. Structural equation modeling was applied with the aid of statistical software, having confirmed all the hypotheses, including the moderation of the market turbulence in MA→RE and the mediation of RE over MA→DG.

Chapter 5 shows Business strategy is basically all the actions and decisions taken by the management to achieve the business goals for sustaining the competitive edge gained in the market. A successful business strategy determines the longevity of the organization. For the validation of strategies at all levels data plays a vital role for the management. Strategic Analytics creates the essential understanding about how quantitative techniques and methods can be deployed using the structured / unstructured data that supports strategic decision making for the organization. Successful implementation of Strategic analytics proves to be beneficial for the organization. The insights generated are in correlation with the business domain knowledge making it easier to take decision with a context.

Chapter 6 talks about data-intensive nature of the financial services industry, it faces issues while handling large data sets. Therefore, the financial services industry needs efficient tools to locate, collect, analyze, interpret, and document data. Business intelligence incorporates data mining, business analytics, data visualization, data infrastructure, and best workplace practices to help companies make more data-driven decisions. Therefore, the aim of this chapter is to help researchers and practitioners in the financial services industry make fact-based decisions using business intelligence (BI) tools such as Power BI, Tableau, and SAS analytics. As a result, the chapter offers a thorough examination of how these BI methods can be used in strategic financial analysis and improve overall corporate efficiency.

Chapter 7 is about the rise of new alternative Cryptocurrencies, also known as "altcoins," has been fueled by the success of Bitcoin. Despite this, none of them have been able to challenge Bitcoin's market supremacy. The Bitcoin system has been branded as a refuge for organized crime, security breaches, greedy mining, money laundering, and extreme volatility, and unpredictability of future prices with its increasing popularity and public awareness. This chapter aims to provide insights on the use of AI techniques to help researchers and practitioners in the Cryptocurrency domain make fact-based decisions. The chapter offers a thorough overview of the history of fiat currencies, Bitcoin, and other Cryptocurrencies and the challenges associated with them, and the role of AI techniques in resolving those challenges.

Chapter 8 is about deferred tax asset (DTA) which is a tax/accounting concept that refers to an asset that may be used to reduce future tax liabilities of the holder. It usually refers to situations where a company has either overpaid taxes, paid taxes in advance or has carry-over of losses (the latter being the most common situation). DTAs are thus contingent claims, whose underlying assets are the company's future profits. Consequently, the correct approach to value such rights implies necessarily, the use of a contingent claim valuation framework. The purpose of this chapter is exactly to propose a precise and conceptually sound mathematical approach to value DTAs, considering future projections of earnings and rates, alongside the DTA's legal time limit. With this proposed evaluation techniques, valuation of companies will be much more realistic (special emphasis on the banking sector), and smaller. Although there are simpler methods to get a good estimate on DTAs, the method described in this chapter will yield optimum results, though at the cost of a higher complexity.

Chapter 9 refers to Deferred tax asset (DTA) is a tax/accounting concept that refers to an asset that may be used to reduce future tax liabilities of the holder. In a company's balance, it usually refers to situations where it has either overpaid taxes, paid taxes in advance or has carry-over of losses (the latter being the most common situation). In fact, accounting and tax losses may be used to shield future profits from taxation, through tax loss carry-forwards. The purpose of this chapter is exactly to propose a precise and conceptually sound approach to value DTAs. For that purpose, making use of an adapted binomial CRR (Cox, Ross and Rubinstein) algorithm, we derive a precise way to value DTAs. This way, the DTAs are valued in a similar way of the Binomial Options Pricing Model (Cox et al., 1979), and the subjectivity of its evaluation is greatly reduced. We will see that with the proposed evaluation techniques, the DTA's expected value will be much lower than the values normally used in today's practice, and the bank's financial analysis will lead to much more sound and realistic results.

Chapter 10 is related to The Integrated Value Model (IVM) which depicts the interactions of policies, plans, performance measures, priorities, and programs (P5). Modeling these interactions helps analysts understand, communicate, and change P5 in the context of those interactions. The IVM supports efforts in strategic communications and planning, change management, and performance metrics. We describe how to create an Integrated Value Model for an organization, and we describe how to use the model to identify, communicate, create, and increase business value.

Chapter 11 is related with the biggest 2020 scam in by one of the major new private sector banks i.e., Yes bank. It provides the details of the misuse of the power of banks in providing the benefits some specific loan seekers under political party leaders that led the partial breakdown of the banking system in India. the chapter also discussed the global presence of yes bank, reason to begin crisis with NPAS growth, contributors to the NPA, moratorium imposed on yes bank, RBI interventions with draft plan for reconstruction, deteriorating bank's financial position, effect of downfall. On another side of the coin, it shows revival of bank with SBI deal, analysis of banking industry and lessons for future. This chapter gives the weight on the role of RBI and because of the effectiveness actions of RBI for YES bank, Indian banking system is showing strength. The chapter finally also provides importance of the role of independent management, auditor, and other regulators.

Acknowledgment

This book is my first book as solo editor, and I am delighted to complete this during this pandemic era. I congratulate my all chapter authors for their valuable submissions and keeping patience during critical review process. I wish to thank all reviewers as well who spared their precious time for the review process.

I am thankful to my beloved wife Yogita and my sunshine son Devansh for giving me eternal happiness and support during the entire process.

Last but not the least, I am thankful to almighty god for blessing me with wonderful life and showing me right paths in my all ups and downs during the so far journey of life.

Sandeep Kautish
Lord Buddha Education Foundation, Nepal

Chapter 1
Cold Calling as a Strategic Tool to Improve the Recruitment and Selection Processes

Shivani Agarwal

https://orcid.org/0000-0002-3205-552X
KIET School of Management, KIET Group of Institutions, Delhi, India

Priyansh Teotia
KIET School of Management, KIET Group of Institutions, Delhi, India

ABSTRACT

Cold calling has been an essential tool for decades in marketing of goods and services. On the other hand, with time, recruitment and selection has become a hectic and hefty task for organizations. This report tries to highlight the scope and importance of cold calling in recruitment and selection. It also highlights the effectiveness and efficiency of recruitment agencies and their proficiency in finding the best possible candidate. It also tries to find the importance of various factors like company image, remuneration, job position, etc. that shape the attitude of a potential candidate towards a job offer. The chapter also puts focus on the skills of the sales representative that have an important effect in shaping the attitude of a prospect towards the job opening.

DOI: 10.4018/978-1-7998-7716-5.ch001

1. INTRODUCTION

1.1 Cold Calling in Recruitment and Selection

Cold-Calling has been an indispensable part of selling for decades and with the advent of technology and digital media, it too has adapted itself and took up on new roles. But before looking into the role of Cold Calling in process of Recruitment and Selection, we shall first proceed with enlightening ourselves with the terms Cold Calling, Recruitment and Selection.

1.2 Cold Calling

Maney, K. (2003) mentioned that Cold Calling, as we practice it today, was first archived in 1873 by John Patterson, who was the author of the NCR Corporation.

Today, we've got a good range of recent instruments and techniques yet by the day's end, selling continues to be best depicted as a procedure of proactively meeting outsiders, fascinating them with regards to changing part or all of the way within which they maintain their business, at that time persuading them that a sale of your item or administration will create important advantages for them. That hasn't changed.

Now a days, cold calls are very common in marketing environment that use predictive dialers, to make high number of calls everyday. Cold calls are considered not as efficient as other, low noticeable, or more "warm" methods of the primary outreach.

Repetitions can enhance the possibility of a cold call by forming credit with the lead in advance. It can also use social media sites like Twitter or LinkedIn to deliver messages, leave comments and likes, and collect facts that they can reveal during the exchange. Numerous sales tools that exhibit background information about the organization, as well as any lead history before each call, so repetitions can get an understanding and build fluency without added work that can harm their sales productivity.

1.3 Recruitment

Recruitment process may be a process of recognizing the roles vacant places, examining the task requirements, screening, reviewing applications, shortlisting and selecting the correct candidate.

To increase the efficiency of hiring, it's recommended that the HR team of a company follows the five best practices (as shown within the following image). These five practices ensure successful recruitment with none interruptions. additionally, these practices also ensure consistency and compliance within the recruitment process.

Figure 1. Recruitment process

1.4 Selection

Selection is that the process of choosing the correct candidate, who is best fitted for a vacant position in a company. The selection of a right applicant for a vacant position are going to be an asset to the organization, which can be facilitating the organization in achieving its objectives.

Figure 2. Selection

1.5 Steps Involved in Recruitment and Selection

Step # 1. Temporary or Permanent Employee

The first step within the selection and recruitment process is to work out if the work should be filled by employing a short lived or a permanent employee. When an employee suddenly exits from the organization discarding a vacancy to be filled urgently, it's worthwhile in most instances to search out a short lived employee to fill the post to permit for suitable timeframe for formal selection and recruitment of a permanent employee.

In other scenarios, a specific job could also be seasonal in nature and thus, temporary employees would be more suitable for such employment. for instance, retail stores usually increase the quantity of employees during the festival season like Deepawali, Christmas, and Eid, keeping seeable the large rush of shoppers during this point. Many of those employees are temporary and are laid-off after the season gets over.

Step # 2. Perform Job Analysis and Create Job Description

Successful employee selection depends on a transparent understanding of a job's components. employment analysis is employed to spot job tasks and responsibilities. The tip results of job analysis is that the verbal description and specifications.

Step # 3. Determine the Recruitment Strategy

The next step involves reaching bent the intended audience with the data that a vacancy exists for a selected position within the company. the target here is to possess as many candidates as possible for the vacancy in order that the employer gets ample option to find the most effective candidate for the work.

Many times, people come searching for work when there's no vacancy existing within the organization at that time in time. it's a decent idea to form them top off a straightforward form (requiring bare minimum information) so they'll be contacted when there's a relevant opening. Such a database is extremely handy for expanding the applicant pool for employment vacancy within the due course.

Step # 4. Determine the Selection Tools to Be Used and the Sequence Thereof

There are various tools to test the skills, knowledge, and skills of the applicants. as an example, preliminary screening (say by using group discussions), application forms/resumes, written tests, personal interviews, reference checks, letters of recommendations, medical check-up, etc. Some tools are better than the opposite in some respects. Therefore, it's best to use a mix of them in an exceedingly predetermined sequence.

The questions and situations to be employed in the assorted methods deployed-in the choice process have to be finalized beforehand keeping in sight the assorted attributes to be gauged within the applicant. a number of the tools just like the preliminary screening and application forms is also wont to eliminate a proportion of the applicants when the quantity of applicants is extremely large. The sequence of the hurdles (in the shape of selection tools) is mostly kept specified the costlier and time-consuming selection tools are used later within the selection process.

Step # 5. Perform a Pre-Interview Orientation

A pre-interview orientation is very supportive for the likely candidates. This orientation briefs them of the company profile, its activities, and future prospects. It allows the candidates to clear up any doubts about the job and the company by raising questions. It also helps in catching the interest of the potential candidates to apply for the job in the company.

Step # 6. Preliminary Screening

When the number of interviewees for a job is very large, preliminary screening is often performed to eradicate less worthy candidates. The communication skills, listening skills, team skills, and leadership qualities of the candidates are tested through group discussions. Some organizations prefer to conduct objective-type tests to screen out less worthy candidates.

Step # 7. Review Application Forms and Resumes

Well-drafted application forms aid in capturing the academic and employment history of candidates. Similarly, resumes and curriculum vitae (CV) are helpful in this regard. The advantage of a standard application form vis-a-vis resume is that it facilitates easy comparison of the profile of two or more candidates on various parameters—gaps in employment, too short stints with organizations in the past, etc.—evident in the application form provide opportunity to the selection committee to seek clarifications later during the personal interview stage.

Step # 8. Conduct Written Test

Written tests constitute the following step within the selection process. There are various styles of tests to live knowledge, ability, skills, aptitude, attitude, honesty, and personality. These are – power tests (to gauge the knowledge and analytical abilities), speed tests (to measure the power to perform repetitive tasks during a set time frame), open-book-open-web exams (in which the candidates are allowed access to review material and therefore the Internet), etc.

The formats of the tests can even be varied. Naturally, essay questions are relatively time-consuming during evaluations compared to the objective- type tests (multiple choices), however they supply better insights about the candidate's communication skills.

Step # 9. Conduct Personal Interview

Candidates qualifying within the written test are subjected to the non-public interview. Personal interview provides an ideal opportunity to the choice committee to test the personality, knowledge, verbal communication skills, etiquettes, dressing sense, and talent to reply to situations impromptu. Structured interviews require the questions and their sequence to be determined before the interview. A structured format is useful in comparing the performance of two or more candidates.

Step # 10. Perform Reference Checks

It is important to perform reference checks for the candidate, if found worthy during the private interview stage. It provides countless insights about the character, educational and employment history of the applicant. The most points of the people to be contacted for referencing is often sought from the candidate within the appliance form/resume itself. Unless the candidate gives permission to undertake and do so, this employers should not be contacted because it's going to unnecessarily create challenges of various sorts for the candidate. Reference checks is performed through email or by phone calls.

Step # 11. Make the Job Offer

If the reference checks lead to good feedback about the candidate, offer letters sent to the candidate. Otherwise, it's customary to send a proper rejection letter. it's not uncommon that some candidates don't accept the ultimate offer of employment made by a corporation.

If no response is received from the candidate or a negative response in regards to the offer is received, the records of the candidate are put in archives for future action as per company policies. The policies of some organizations prohibit such an applicant from applying again for employment, while other organizations have a lenient and open policy whereby the candidate gets a chance to use again in future.

Step # 12. Medical Examination

A post-offer pre-employment medical (of the candidate and dependent relations) may be a must especially when the corporate must cover the candidate and his dependent family members by medical insurance. the value of such a examination is borne by the employer. Such tests form an integral a part of pre-employment testing.

Step # 13. Induction and Orientation

The new employees are most receptive to alter in their career time, once they are joining a replacement employment. Therefore, formal induction and orientation of the workers help them in understanding the varied facets of the organization.

2. MAKING A SUCCESSFUL COLD CALLING IN RECRUITMENT AND SELECTION

From a recruiter perspective the term Cold Calling generally means making telephone calls to those who aren't expecting to listen to from you a couple of job. The person can typically be a "passive" job seeker who isn't trying to find a replacement job or a contended employee who is happy to figure within the current organisation and isn't searching for employment change. Making these styles of cold calls is one in every of the foremost difficult jobs for a recruiter, and yet one amongst the foremost satisfying after you hit upon the right candidate.

The process of making a successful call for recruitment can be easily summed up with the help of the following heads:

2.1 Prepare for Making the Calls

Think of the call as a pleasant conversation, not an confrontational one. You've got a great job to market, and remember it could be a great prospect for the right person.

- Know all the little details of the job you're marketing and be ready to sell your agency. Ask what's distinctive or USP about the agency or the opportunity that will attract any potential candidate.
- Be clear on the actual obligations and accountabilities and any skills or training required.
- Talk with the signing authority; find out exactly what kind of applicant is perfect for the opening. Get the details.
- If it is difficult to find candidates, find out what has been missing from those offered so far. Ask the manager what he or she is looking for in a candidate resume. Get the specifics.
- Market and sell the opening to the likely candidate.

2.2 Develop a Script

This can be as simple as putting down a few key points to help you recall what to say, or as intricate as writing a minor story to refer to once you get the candidate on the phone. Use it as something to peep at as you take the call.

- Practice, practice, practice the script.
- Divide your candidates/prospects into A and B lists; let the A list include 'preferred candidates' while List B include 'acceptable candidates'; practice on the B list (acceptable candidates) first; the more calls you make the better you'll get. With more practise Sell the opportunity with experience in List A.
- Check the web for data about the current organisation where the individual is employed. Start the call by discussing the prospect's business, not yours.

2.3 Make the Call

- If the call is to a applicant found on a job board or online, you have the perfect introductory. You have a pretext to call them because they were presenting their skills on their resume.
- For referred candidates, don't forget to mention that it was a referral. The candidate will be pleased that someone else felt they were skilled for the position.
- If you tracked the person and they are not interested in the position, politely ask them if they know anyone who would be a great candidate. Ask something like "it sounds like this isn't right for you, who do you know that might be qualified." From this point, the call is no longer cold.
- Smile whenever you are making the call; the smile is felt on the other end of the line. You only have about 20 seconds to catch the other person's attention.

- If you reach a "gatekeeper" make them your friend. They prove to be prized sources of information; they can easily direct you to the right person and help you understand how the company functions.
- Stay focused on the script. Give a brief description of the designation and agency.
- Try to close with something like "What do you think?" Confirm their e-mail address and ask them if you should send over the job announcement for their review. Invite them to apply for the post.
- Give them the opportunity to ask more and more questions regarding the job and in case you are unable to answer them all, send them the details after the call.
- End the call by expressing thanks, ask for their resume with a possibility to keep in touch as well.

2.4 After the Call

- Straightaway send or e-mail information that will be needed by the candidate.
- Track all calls made. Know who you have spoken with and what you have sent to them.
- Stick with it; follow-up on potential candidates and keep calling.
- Record your information and keep files of resumes and your notes for future recruitment openings.

3. OBJECTIVES OF THE STUDY

The objective of the study is to find out the changing role and scope of Cold-Calling in recruitment and selection. Data has been primarily collected with the help of a questionnaire and responses were recorded from people residing in the Delhi NCR region.

Additionally, discussions were held with HR Mangers in various firms and Recruitment Agencies.

The main objectives behind this research are as follows:

1. To analyze Cold Calling as a valuable tool in attracting potential clients for Recruitment process.
2. Measure the comfort level of individuals towards sharing their professional information on a cold-call.

3. Find and Identify the priorities of potential clients that incites them to switch their current job or take up on the new opportunity and make a cold-call successful.

4. RESEARCH DESIGN / METHODOLOGY

The research methodology used in conducting this survey was exploratory research & sample size was 124 customers.

For this purpose, a questionnaire was framed consisting of 8 questions. Additionally, discussions were held with employees working in various companies and recruitment agencies.

The responses of the survey were analyzed and inferences were drawn on the basis of primary result. Demographic profile of respondents is shown in table 1

Table 1. Demographical details

Demographic n=148		No. of Respondents	Percentage (%)
Age	20-25	120	81.1
	25 and beyond	28	18.9
Profession	Student	118	79.7
	Working	30	20.3

5. DATA ANALYSIS

The findings of the data were represented in the form of bar graph and pie charts for easily understanding to the large number of audiences.

In response to the first question i.e. Cold Calling can be a valuable tool in attracting target customers, 67.1% of the respondents replied that yes it can be a valuable tool while only 5.3% of the respondents denied it being a valuable tool. It highlights the role and importance of cold calling in attracting target clients.

The second findings about the question that a cold call before sending an email can be a good way to catch the customer's interest shows that majority of 60.5% respondents accepted that yes it can be good way to catch the customer's interest while 15.8% of the respondents denied.

Next, when asked how likely the respondents were to respond to a cold call regarding a job opening, more than 64% of the respondents were interested in accepting such call, while only a meagre 13.1% respondents denied entertaining such calls.

Figure 3. Cold Calling can be a valuable tool in attracting target clients

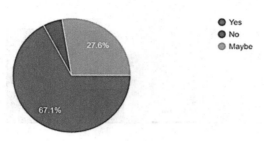

1. Do you think that cold-calling can be a valuable tool in attracting target clients?
76 responses

Figure 4. A cold-call can be a good way to catch customer's interest

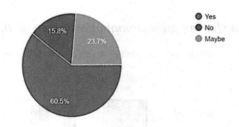

2. Do you think that a cold-call before sending an email can be a good way to catch the customer's interest?
76 responses

Figure 5. Likely responses to a cold-call regarding a job opening

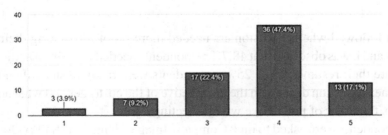

3. As a client, how likely are you to respond to a cold-call regarding a job opening?
76 responses

Next, rating the skills of the caller in attracting target clients, 51.3% of the respondents rated them important and 28.9% respondents rated them of paramount importance.

Figure 6. Rating the importance of the skills of the caller

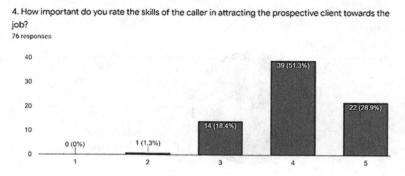

4. How important do you rate the skills of the caller in attracting the prospective client towards the job?
76 responses

While testing the comfort level of respondents in sharing their professional information it was observed that 82.9% of the respondents were fairly comfortable in sharing uch information while 17.1% respondents denied sharing such information.

Figure 7. Comfort level in sharing professional information on the call

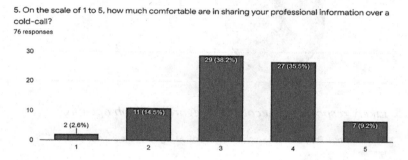

5. On the scale of 1 to 5, how much comfortable are in sharing your professional information over a cold-call?
76 responses

Next followed whether Customers needed more proof for sharing their CVs or resumes and it was observed that 48.7% respondents needed more information before they share their resumes while 25% respondents were ready to share their CVs.

The next question deals with the perspective of the customer and what according to him is the order of preference while selecting a job.

Respondents were asked to rank Company Image, Handsome Salary, Job Profile and Job Location as per their preference and what they believe can be the most important factor while attracting a client for a job.

I**st** **Rank:** For the first rank 37 respondents (i.e. 48% respondents) admitted that 'Company Image' was most important while 22 respondents (i.e. 28%

respondents) answered that 'Handsome Salary' was most important to attract a client.

IInd Rank: The second rank was dominated by 'Handsome Salary' with 32 respondents (i.e. 42% respondents) voting in its favour while 22 respondents (i.e. 28%) favoured 'Job Profile' for the second rank.

IIIrd Rank: Third rank was occupied by 'Job Profile' wherein 34 respondents (i.e. 44% respondents) Voted in its favor, while a total of 25 respondents (i.e. 32% respondents) placed 'Handsome Salary' on this rank.

IVth Rank: The penultimate rank was occupied by 'Job Location' with 35 respondents (i.e. 46% respondents) finding it the least important while attracting a consumer for a job,

Figure 8. Sharing resumes and CVs with the caller

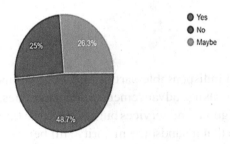

6. Do you need more proof than a call and an email before you share your resume with the caller?
76 responses

Figure 9. Ranking of priorities while looking for job

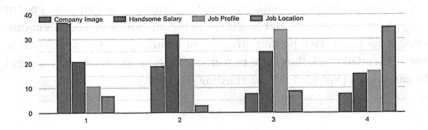

7. Rate the following from 1 to 4 (with no. 1 being the top priority) , in regards to their importance in attracting a client towards the job opening?

Lastly, while asking if respondents believed that Recruitment Agencies have an extended reach to tap the best of prospects; 72.4% answered a yes, thus highlighting the importance and efficiency of Recruitment Agencies. While a mere 10% respondents denied to such expertise on the hands of such Agencies.

Figure 10. Recruitment Agencies can tap the very best of prospects

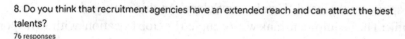

8. Do you think that recruitment agencies have an extended reach and can attract the best talents?

76 responses

6. CONCLUSION

Cold Calling has been an indispensable part of marketing of numeral decades but even today with groundbreaking advancements in technologies, it has secured its rank not only in selling of goods and services but also in marketing human resources.

This report highlights that a handsome majority still believes that Cold Calling is an effective way to target potential clients for Job openings. It further goes to state that Company Image and Renumeration remain the most important factors that attract a candidate towards a job while Job Position and Job Location often take the back seat.

The report also goes to highlight the importance of Art in Marketing, since the skills of the caller remain essential in attracting prospects towards the openings.

Lastly, with Recruitment and Selection being an extensive and strenuous task, recruitment agencies have proven effective in handling such task efficiently; and with their extended reach they have proven their mettle in tapping and sourcing the best fit candidates (Wooden, M., & Harding, D.,1998).

REFERENCES

Maney, K. (2003). *The maverick and his machine: Thomas Watson, Sr. and the making of IBM*. John Wiley & Sons.

Wooden, M., & Harding, D. (1998). Recruitment practices in the private sector: Results from a national survey of employers. *Asia Pacific Journal of Human Resources*, *36*(2), 73–87. doi:10.1177/103841119803600207

Chapter 2
Credit–Market Imperfection and Monetary Policy Within DSGE Models

Salha Ben Salem
iD https://orcid.org/0000-0002-4946-7782
University of Monastir, Tunisia

Nadia Mansour
iD https://orcid.org/0000-0001-7690-7096
University of Sousse, Tunisia & University of Salamanca, Spain

Moez Labidi
University of Monastir, Tunisia

ABSTRACT

This survey presented the various ways that are utilized in the literature to include financial market frictions in dynamic stochastic general equilibrium (DSGE) models. It focuses on the fundamental issue: to what extent the Taylor rules are optimal when the central bank introduces the goal of financial stability. Indeed, the latest financial crisis shows that the vulnerability of the credit cycle is considered the main source for the amplification of a small transitory shock. This conclusion changed the instrument that drives the transmission of monetary policy through the economy and pushed the policymakers to include financial stability as a second objective of the central bank.

DOI: 10.4018/978-1-7998-7716-5.ch002

INTRODUCTION

The great recession reminds us cruelly that credit frictions are a key driver of business cycle variation. Imbalances can construct up during apparently tranquil periods until a trigger leads to great and persistent wealth destructions potentially spilling over to the real economy. While in normal times, the banking (financial) sector can mitigate credit (financial) frictions, in crisis periods the banking (financial) sector's vulnerability aggravates the instability. Adverse feedback loops and liquidity spirals lead to non-linear impacts that can lead to a credit crunch. There has been a large body of empirical literature target to analyze the properties of how to go about modeling the financial crisis in a DSGE framework.

In this chapter, we examine the hypothesis adopted by the DSGE models before the financial crisis and how modelers reacted to the crisis and its aftermath. Inevitably, models must distract from some characteristics of the real economy, raising the issue: which characteristics should we introduce and which characteristics should we eliminate to better model the individuals' behavior? Starting from this question, we survey what the key characteristics of pre-financial crisis models were and why the introduction of these characteristics was justified. We then study how DSGE models extended in reaction to the subprime crisis and how central banks improved the monetary policy rule to better respond to financial instability.

Models discussed in this survey suppose diverse financing restrictions. Depending on the underlying economic friction, financing constraints can arise in different forms. For instance, the financial accelerator model of Bernanke et al (1999) assumes that the returns on capital may be impacted by idiosyncratic shocks and that the posterior performance of this return is private information, which the lenders can observe if they pay a monitoring cost. This cost increases the lending interest rate and decreases the investment project. In contrast, the collateral constraint model of Kiyotaki and Moore (1997) assumes that the borrower cannot borrow as soon as its assets, which uses as collateral, covers at least the entire loan requested. Besides, this model assumes that the entrepreneur never goes bankrupt because the debt is a fraction of its wealth value. Contrary, in the context of the financial accelerator the entrepreneur is faced with the default of the payment since their credit can exceed its net value. However, until here, the payment default of the financial firms was not treated since in both models the bank finances only by the deposit of the households. Also, the impact of bank capital deterioration and the holding effect of toxic assets are excluded in these two models.

After being criticized following the subprime crisis, the DSGE models stand as incomplete models for anticipating the vulnerability of the real economy. The emerging literature on DSGE modeling with financial frictions since the start of the crisis either spells out a banking system or adds financial frictions and/or shocks to establish the intermediation process between entrepreneurs and deposits. As proposed by (Brazdik et al. (2012), Gertler et al. (2016), Karmelavicius and Ramanauskas (2019)) the introduction of a banking system could help to better understand the transmission mechanism of different shocks and analyze if this mechanism is altered by the presence of a banking system. Moreover, including a banking sector permits DSGE models to put in evidence the different interest rates applied by the banks.

This paper focuses on two objectives: First, we aim to review the most important ways of including financial frictions in a DSGE model and to show the effect of these frictions on monetary policy conduct. Second, we target to study the different ways of introducing financial variables into the monetary policy to mitigate the aftermath of the financial crisis.

The rest of the paper is structured as follows: firstly, we will present the famous Pre-crisis DSGE models, which deal with credit frictions on the demand side framework. In the second section, we focus on the weak points of these models especially following the subprime crisis, and in the third section, we look at what has changed in these models. Section four aims to present the transmission mechanism of monetary policy and the different manner of modeling this policy in the DSGE models. Finally, we conclude with a discussion of new instructions for DSGE modeling.

1. PRE-CRISIS DSGE MODELS: CREDIT FRICTIONS ON THE DEMAND SIDE FRAMEWORK

Credit frictions (financial friction) refer to market imperfections that threaten the transmission of credit flows (other liquidity types) between borrowers and lenders, creating a gap between the cost of external and internal funds. The credit frictions caused generally follows the problems of adverse selection, which occurs before the signing of the credit contract, the problem of moral hazard, which realized after the signing of the contract and, the application of a high monitoring cost that allows the bank to distinguish between the low-risk borrowers and the high-risk borrowers[1].

In this section, we will present the most important DSGE models that integrate the friction in the demand loan side, especially the financial accelerator and the collateral constraint models.

1.1 Bernanke et al. Model (1999) and Its Extension: Financial Accelerator Models

The first friction analyzed is the external finance premium form. This friction was examined by the pioneering model of Bernanke and Gertler (1989) and then developed in the general equilibrium framework by Bernanke, Gertler, and Gilchrist (1999) co-called financial accelerator models. Bernanke et al. (1999) tried to analyze the optimal contractual arrangement, between borrowers and lenders in the framework of a problem agency, occurs in debt contracts. Specifically, they assume that the returns on capital may be impacted by idiosyncratic shocks and that the posterior performance of this return is private information, which the lenders can observe if they pay a monitoring cost. In equilibrium, the lending interest rate is composite by the risk-free rate, which reflects the opportunity cost for internal funds, and the external finance premium, which represents the risk that the borrower will not repay its debt.

The fundamental equation of Bernanke et al. model is given as follow:

$$E\left[R_{t+1}^{K}\right] = \left(\frac{N_{t+1}^{j}}{Q_{t}K_{t+1}^{j}} \right) R_{t+1}, S'\left(.\right) < 0 \tag{1}$$

Where R_{t+1}^{K} represents the borrowers' expected returns to capital, S is the external finance premium - depends negatively on the fraction of the firm's capital investment that is funded by the entrepreneur's net worth. N_{t+1}^{j} represents the borrower's net value and Q_{t} is the price of the capital.

The positive relationship between the external finance premium, which is a counter-cyclical variable, and the entrepreneur's net worth, which is a cyclical variable, represents the fundamental mechanism for a financial accelerator model: a negative productivity shock pushes the entrepreneur to request more credit for a given investment. Nonetheless, since the higher leverage signifies a higher exposure for the lenders, therefore, they will apply a higher premium. This higher premium raised the lending cost which generates the drop in investment and the own net worth of a contractor. These second-round impacts amplify the first recession in the economy, and a vicious circle occurs.

The famous financial accelerator mechanism has inspired a vast literature on financial imperfection into the DSGE model.

Christensen and Dib (2008) analyze the effect of the financial accelerator in the amplification and propagation of shocks. Using the maximum likelihood test, they point out that a model with a financial accelerator fits better the US data. They base on Ireland (2003) and Bernanke et al. (1999) models with a closed economy. Distinct from Ireland, they use sticky prices by introduced price-setting behavior based on (Calvo 1983) alternative than quadratic price adjustment costs. Furthermore, unlike, Bernanke et al. (1999) model, they introduce capital adjustment costs and nominal credit contracts. These nominal contracts consider the effect of inflation on the dynamics of the debt, as previously brought forward by Fisher (1933). With this hypothesis, the lender integrates unexpected inflation in the real debt payment. For instance, with unanticipated deflation, the borrower must pay a high-interest rate which negatively affects their net worth generating an increase in the risk premium. This hypothesis appears highly realistic, particularly in the US.

Benedictow and Hammersland (2020) estimate the implementation of a financial sub-model in a structural macro-econometric model for the Norwegian economy, KVARTS, partly inspired by Hammersland and Træe (2014). "KVARTS is expanded by a financial sub-model where aggregate credit and equity prices in Norway are determined simultaneously in a system characterized by a two-directional contemporaneous causal link, designed and estimated with the help of a new procedure for simultaneous structural model design (Hammersland, 2017)".

1.2 Kiyotaki and Moore Model (1997): Collateral Constraint Models

Another standard approach to the accelerator financier mechanism consisted to integrate limit available resources. This approach emphasizes that the borrower cannot borrow as soon as its assets, which uses as collateral, covers at least the entire loan requested. In the event of investment's bankruptcy, the lender recovered, automatically, these assets. Therefore, the nominal value of the collateral completes the amount of the loan that the borrower can get. This is the collateral constraint principle proposed by Kiyotaki and Moore (1997).

Kiyotaki and Moore (1997), henceforth KM, building a theoretical model in which durable assets such as land, serve as collateral to obtain the external resource. KM differentiates two types of agents: a patient agent, (the gatherer) which is a net saver, and an impatient agent (the farmer) which is the net borrower. The impatient agent is an entrepreneur who wishes to obtain the external resources from the gatherer, to finance his investment. The most important hypothesis of this model present in a collateral constraint that limits the amount of credit that the farmer could acquire from the gatherers.

The principal equation, the borrowing constraint equation, gives as follow:

$$b_t \leq mE_t\left[\frac{q_{t+1}h_t\pi_{t+1}}{R_t}\right] \tag{2}$$

This equation assumes that if borrowers do not pay their credit obligations, the lenders can recover the borrowers' assets by paying an equivalence transaction cost $mE_t(q_th_t)$. In this case, the maximum amount b_t that a borrower can borrow is determined by $mE_t\left(\dfrac{q_t h_t}{R_t}\right)$, in the real term. Therefore, this equation shows that the ability of the borrower to request a loan is impacted by the price of collateralized assets.

Since the loan is secure, the model demonstrates how temporary productivity shocks of firms provoke significant fluctuations that propagate and amplify on the whole economy. Consider, for instance, that the firm uses the land (which doesn`t depreciate) to secure his loans as well as of production. The total supply of land is determined. Assumes also, that this firm has a credit constraint and extremely levered due to past borrowing activity. Supposing that in the period t, a few firms suffer a negative shock to the price of land that decreases their net worth. These will be impacts the price of land, affecting also the activity of all constrained firms. This mechanism forces the firm to deeper cuts in their investment and thus, their output for a longer period. As we can see, the source of this persistent cut in output was just a temporary productivity shock, which spread through the next periods via the accelerator financial constraints of the firms. This mechanism will be clarified in the figure below.

Figure 1. Collateral constraint enhancer effect in the event of a negative shock

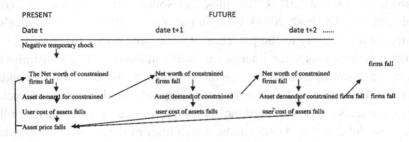

The original model of KM has inspired several researchers to evaluate the quantitative relevance of collateral constraints in the amplification of exogenous shocks. In 2005, Iacoviello integrated the KM mechanism into a pre-crisis neo-Keynesian general equilibrium macroeconomic model, for better adapted to the effective economy.

Iacoviello (2005) added two new hypotheses in the model of KM: housing stock, used as collateral, and nominal credit contract. The first hypothesis suggests that the collateral required by the borrower to obtain credit is no land but, the real estate stock possessed by the entrepreneurs. The second important originality introduced the effect of the price change into the credit contract. This novelty allows measuring the effect of inflation in the credit processes.

The basic framework of the model takes into consideration four types of agents: a patient household (lender), an entrepreneur (borrower), a retailer, and a Central Bank. The patient households and entrepreneurs consume, work, and demand real estate assets. In the steady-state, the patient household is the lender while, the entrepreneur is a borrower. The retailers operate in a monopoly environment, buy intermediate goods and turn it into final goods to sell it to households

Iacoviello shows that a positive demand shock has an amplifying effect through the housing price and the nominal credit contract. It leads to stimulate aggregate demand and therefore, rising consumption and asset prices.

Iacoviello's model rapidly became a benchmark to analyze the accelerator effect played by housing prices in the economic cycle. A particularly interesting extension of this model was investigated by Iacoviello and Neri (2010) in the US house market. Their results confirmed the importance of the collateralized debt mechanism, as it extends the financial accelerator impact and propagates shocks from the real estate market to the US business cycle. Another recently empirical work proposed by (Berger et al 2017) points the consumption reactions to house price variation.

Although the financial accelerator model appears similar to the collateral constraint model[2], there are differences between these two models, mentioned in particular by Brázdik and Marsal (2011), Iliopulos and Sopraseuth (2012), and Christiano, Eichenbaum, and Trabandt 2018). First, in the context of the financial accelerator, credit drying due mainly to the presence of additional costs, the external finance premium, which increased the interest rate while in the collateral constraint model the drying up of credit is caused by the limited availability of wealth. Secondly, the debt ratio in Bernanke and al (1999) model depends on the economic cycle, and therefore, it affects the evolution of the debtor interest rate, whereas in the collateral constraint model this rate is exogenous, which implies the uniqueness between the credit rate and the risk-free rate. Third, the KM model assumes that the entrepreneur never goes bankrupt because the debt is a fraction of its wealth value. Contrary, in the context of the financial accelerator the entrepreneur is faced with the default of the payment since their credit can exceed its net value.

In sum, due to asymmetric information characterized the credit market, the lenders impose collateral which is usually either the financial assets, Kiyotaki and Moore (1997), or a high-interest rate that covers the risk of non-payment Bernanke and Gertler (1989), Bernanke et al 1999, real estate properties Iacoviello (2005), Iacoviello and Neiri (2010). These collaterals have an accelerating effect on the events of negative shocks. The global financial crisis reveals that financial accelerator models are essential but insufficient because the hypothesis adopted by these models does not allow the economist to anticipate and explain the spillover of the financial crisis.

2. THE SUBPRIME CRISIS REVEALS THE WEAK POINTS OF THE DSGE MODEL

Pre-crisis DSGE models have been criticized on three levels: first, at the expectation level, it did not anticipate, correctly, the growing vulnerability of the real activity in the United State economy. Second, at the financial friction-level, they include only the imperfection of borrowers and suppose the perfectly of the banking sector. Third, at the monetary policy level, they assume that the standard monetary policy is the optimal one to ensure financial stability. Here, we show the point of view of some economists about these failures[3].

The precipitate of the financial crisis occurs in the shadow-banking system and the real estate sector (Irani et al., 2018). The speculative behavior of the most indebted shadow banking, borrowed in the short-term to invest the long-term assets, pushed this crisis. This behavior coincided with the rapid and successive rise in real estate prices, especially the housing price, in the United States: the US National real estate Price Index increases by a factor of approximately 2.5 between 1991 and 2006 (Christiano et al, 2018). Furthermore, the wrong anticipations, the subprime market, decrease lending conditions in mortgage markets, and the flexible monetary policy presented as a runway that collapses the rush of the crisis.

The excessive increase in housing prices and the favorable financial condition prompted the shadow banks to largely investing in "mortgage-backed securities". However, in mid-2006, housing prices started to fall, leading to lower asset prices of the shadow-banking sector. This situation presents the starting point on which the financial crisis is possible. The financial crisis did occur and shadow banks had to sell their asset-backed securities at very low prices, creating the global recession.

Against this background, the pre-crisis DSGE model failure to expect the evolution of housing price and then the growing vulnerability of the real activity, in the United State economy. This criticism is right in which the modelers, the regulators, and the policymakers didn't give importance to the friction in the banking sector and especially, in shadow banking. "The common belief was that if a country had deposit insurance, bank runs were a thing of the past. The failure was to allow a small shadow-banking system to metastasize into a massive, poorly-regulated sector that was not protected by deposit insurance or lender-of-last-resort backstops", Christiano et al (2018).

This conclusion leads us to present the second criticism of standard DSGE models, especially that they did not sufficiently discuss the financial frictions' variables.

Indeed, the models treating the borrower-level friction are often based on Modigliani and Miller (1958) theorem with a perfect financial sector. Besides, the assumption of financial market efficiency means that default probabilities and risk premium are ignored in standard DSGE models. Under this assumption, financial institutions can diversify their risk without limit, without constraint and fear of contagion for the rest of the banks, De Walque, Pierrard, and Rouabah (2010).

Indeed, most recessions in the United State and Europe were due, mainly, to the disruption of the real market, such as the debt crisis. Even, the Savings and Loans crisis in the US in 1987 was an interned effect that did not grow into a systematic crisis as the great recession. Likewise, the crush of the stock market in 1987 and the collapse of the technology bubble in 2001 only had marginal impacts on real activity, Christiano et al. (2018). The multiplication of these real crises explains, among other things, the exclusion of an active banking sector by the modelers in the period before the crisis.

We turn now to the third criticism of standard DSGE models, namely that they assume "price stability ensures financial stability". The consensus on the conduct of monetary policy, in the pre-crisis period, concludes that the central bank should limit its actions strictly to price stability and promotes the use of macro-prudential policies to react to financial stability concerns. It considers that aggressive inflation targeting policy is sufficient to guarantee financial stability. It's the so-called "Modified Jackson Hole Consensus", (Smets 2014).

Woodford (2012) comments on this potential issue and argues that there will be no significant conflict between monetary policy and financial stability objectives. He states that there will be tension, but this tension is similar to the conflict between price stability and output gap stabilization. Assenmacher and Gerlach (2010) show that the policy rate should not be used to fight financial imbalances, while (Fahr et al. 2013) investigate the performance of the inflation targeting regime altered by financial stability objective and they conclude that it leads to an improvement in macroeconomic performance. Svensson (2016) supports this idea and calls for monetary policy to target only macroeconomic stability. He argues that macro-prudential policies are effective tools for targeting financial stability in most countries but that monetary policy is not.

Since the financial crisis, support for the "modified Jackson Hole consensus" has reduced (Malliaris, 2020), and there is important literature analyzing the role of monetary policy because of the financial imbalances, Agenor et al. (2013), Badarau and Bopescu (2015), Verona et al. (2017). Most of these researches develop conceptual contexts that had better include a financial variable in the standard Taylor rule[4].

We summarize, the pre-crisis standard DSGE models failed to anticipate the financial crisis because they did not model an active financial firm. However, the imperfections of the financial sector and the holding of toxic assets by banks are considered as major factors in triggering crises such as the Great Depression or the global financial crisis. These crises show that the financial firms are exposed to various risks such as capital reduction, holding of risky assets, drying up of liquidity, financing constraint on the interbank market, and risk of default, which it is the most important of all, especially in countries where the financial market is not too developed. In the next section, we discuss how modelers have included these elements and others.

3. TOWARD POST-CRISIS DSGE MODELS: CREDIT FRICTION ON THE SUPPLY SIDE FRAMEWORKS

As we say, the standards DSGE models analyzed the financial frictions of the firm's side and considered the banking sector as a perfect actor. The target was mainly focused on the friction in the credit market demand. Although, the financial crisis has justified that also the supply credit market is subordinate to imperfections.

Figure 2a and 2b demonstrate the crucial role played by the banking sector in supplying credit to the real business cycle in developed (USA, France, Japan, and Australia) and undeveloped countries (Jordan, Lebanon, Morocco, and Tunisia). Since the financial crisis was principal, caused by the sudden crash of the credit market, then the introduction of leveraged financial institutions into DSGE models became a necessity. This crisis prompted modelers to study the question of how this crush can be formed within a DSGE model and how the central bank reacts to this crush. That is the goal of this section.

Figure 2a. Bank private credit to GDP in a developed country

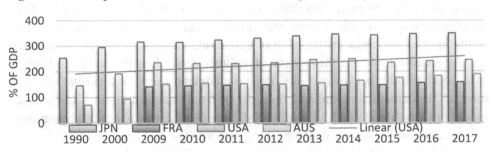

Figure 2b. Bank private credit to GDP for an undeveloped country

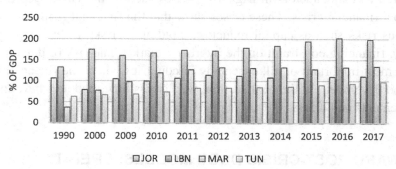

The introduction of a banking system could help to understand several facts in the credit market. It could help to better understand the transmission mechanism of different shocks and analyze if this mechanism is altered by the presence of a banking system. Moreover, including a banking sector permits DSGE models to put in evidence a fundamental feature of the credit market: there are very different interest rates due to the cost of the credit activity and the asymmetric information between agents. This latter pushes banks to pay high monitoring costs every time they provide loans or they adjust the conditions of the contract. The application of different interest rates can be explained also, by the risks that the bank is facing, especially the non-payment risk.

The initiation of the DSGE model with the active bank sector was modeled by Goodfriend and McCallum (2007). Using their model, the authors analyze the role of various interest rate and intermediation activity in monetary policy transmission. Moreover, based on Bernanke et al. (1999) model the authors include the active effect of loan and bank balance sheet channels. Loans are generated by the banking sector, which is constructed similarly as a standard competitive firms' sector. They conclude two inverse effects. First, through the financial accelerator effect, the rise of the interest rate reduces the value of collateral, and thus increases the external finance premium. Second, through the attenuator effect, where the decrease of output associated with higher interest rate drops the demand for bank deposits, which in turn, fall the demand for loans and, thus, the external finance premium. The seminal model of Goodfriend and McCallum (2007) opened the way to several researchers that tried to assess the role of the banking sector in the real economy.

In what follows, we will present some survey on DSGE models that integrate the endogenous bank capital channel and the phenomenon of a bank run and mismatch liquidity

3.1 Endogenous Bank Capital Channel

Gertler and Karadi (2011, 2013) and Cespedes et al. (2017) have merit to present a model where financial intermediaries face endogenously determined balance sheet constraints and prices are rigidity. The financial friction is introduced also in the model through the fact that, after collecting deposits, the banker can distract a fraction of assets collected from the household and declare bankruptcy, if the bank is not adequately profitable. This implies that the ability of a bank to attract deposits and to extend loans to firms is positively related to its current net worth and its expected future earnings. Therefore, the intermediaries' leverage ratio facing an endogenous constraint. This constraint held on bank capacity to offer credit is playing an amplification role similar to the financial accelerator in the Bernanke et al. (1999) model. The model permits also for the analysis of unconventional monetary policy by the central bank, which acts as an intermediary by loaning funds from a depositor and lending them to investors.

By assembling the approaches of Gertler and Karadi (2011) and Bernanke et al. (1999), Rannenberg (2016) constructs a DSGE model with endogenous bank leverage. His model based on two main hypotheses: The first emphasizes the agency problem between banks and entrepreneurs generating the external finance premium of Bernanke et al (1999): When interest rates are small and asset prices increase, the higher net worth of entrepreneurs raising the collateral values softens loaning constraints and permits for excess credit accumulation. This approach endogenous the balance sheet conditions of the entrepreneur.

The second hypothesis suggests the moral hazard problem between banks and deposit supported by Gertler and Karadi (2011). This problem signifies that households will accept to make deposits if the banker default probability is low, that is if the final wealth expected value of the banker, $V_t^b(q)$, is higher than the portion of credit offered to the borrower,

$$\lambda L_t^e(q), [V_t^b(q) > \lambda L_t^e(q)]$$

Contrary to Gertler and Karadi, Rannenberg supposes that banks grant credits to firms by purchasing equity stakes, which gives them effective ownership. The banker channels two types of loans. The first type is "risky inter-period loans", $L_t^e(q)$ to entrepreneurs who use it to purchase the capital stock at the period t + 1. The second type is "risk-free intra-period working capital loans", $L_t^r(q)$, to retailers who use it to pay for the labor and capital services exploited in production processes. The first type of loan due at the period t+1 while the second one is due at the end of period t. Therefore, the moral hazard problem described below only affected inter-period loans. The model supposes no friction in the relationship between banks and retailers. Which meaning that in the "intra-period working capital loans" the equilibrium loan rate similar to the deposit rate.

The notable results of this seminal contribution are: In a world with only a monetary policy and a productivity shock, the model success to match the pro-cyclicality and vulnerability of bank leverage checked in the real data, whereas bank leverage is highly countercyclical and very vulnerable in the model of Gertler and Karadi (2011). Moreover, their model succeeds to show the pro-cyclical effect of the external finance premium and the GDP better than the one found in the financial accelerator model of Bernanke et al. (1999).

3.2 Endogenous Bank Runs and Liquidity Mismatch

Bank runs are the main features of the financial crisis that many emerging and advanced countries have experienced over their history. During a run, depositors precipitate to withdraw their deposits because they anticipate the failure of the bank. The massive withdrawal of deposits will push the bank to fair sell its assets and to accept large losses and even to declare its bankruptcy. The phenomenon can propagate from one bank to another if depositors lose confidence in the whole banking system causing large damage in the financial system and disruption of production. The most common examples of these disruptions are a great depression (1930) and the great moderation (2008) where the run was on investment banks.

The Bank run, caused mainly by liquidity mismatch. Diamond and Dybvig (1983) are the first who model this phenomenon and then it was adopted by several authors, especially after the financial crisis, such as Gertler and Kiyotaki (2015), Gertler et al (2016).

Diamond and Dybvig (1983) have the merit to present a model where the economy could converge to bank run equilibrium through the bank liquidity mismatch, which causes follows the liquidity transformation function inherent in the banking sector. In their model, consumers are subject to consumption needs similar to liquidity shock that arrive randomly and generates a liquidity need. Banks investigate short term illiquid projects by offering deposits contracts to collect deposits and protect consumers against liquidity risks. The Bank is also investing in long term illiquid projects by providing transformation services. This function inherent to financial intermediation makes banks vulnerable to runs. Demand deposits contracts that improve risk-sharing between agents in the economy is correlated with multiple equilibriums, one of them is bank run. If there is a bank run, all depositors panic and withdraw immediately their deposits even those who are not interested in the

Bank's failure. For Diamond and Dybvig (1983) the two principal solutions for this bank run problem are the suspension of convertibility and demand deposit insurance.

Unlike to classic bank run model of Diamond and Dybvig (1983), Gertler et al. (2016) suppose that there are various forms to ensure payment on past short term debt. The economy in this model is populated by three economic agents: households, retail banks, and wholesale banks (Mierau and Mink, 2018). Households consume and save in the form of direct capital detentions and bank deposits. The retail and wholesale banks are identical except for their capacity to manage capital at the margin; wholesale banks support a zero marginal cost, whereas retail banks face a positive cost (but it is less than households' cost). Both forms of the bank can directly access the capital market and can supply funding from households and other banks.

The assumption of bank run introduces in this model when the wholesale bank cannot be capable to reimburse its interbank debts. That is if the leverage of wholesale banks is important (and thus the resale value of capital is low), the interbank borrowing rate is high and the global productivity is low. If the equilibrium reaches such a situation, the liquidity portfolio of wholesale bank is effectively deteriorated and hence, can be absorbed by economic agents or retail bank, which are both not efficient at administering capital, Brunnermeier and Sannikov (2014). The wholesale sector so has to reconstruct itself slowly so that new banks come into the market.

The financial accelerator mechanism is introduced here through the important role represented by the wholesale sector. Leverage worse the impact of the decrease in global productivity on bankers' net worth, generating in a raising of credit spread which tightens the financial constraints. As a result, wholesale sectors sell off credits, which leads to the decline of asset values and, thus bank net worth. The stronger wholesale bank leverage is, the higher this feedback typically is, pushing large-scale liquidations of their assets and decreasing their request for interbank loans. As a consequence of this fire sale, retail bankers rise their asset purchasing and absorb, with privet agent, the capital that the wholesale banks sell in the market. However, as retail banks and private agents are low efficient in intermediation, so the fire sale is pricey. This will increase the cost of bank credit to nonfinancial borrowers and worse the decrease of aggregate output, (Duncan and Nolan 2018).

Gertler et al. (2016) present a new way to develop the classic DSGE framework by incorporating credit intermediation and bank run phenomenon. However, the policy implications of these models are as yet provisional. On the one hand, it remains the case that the major lever of banks in these models does not have their own funds, in real, regulators may adapt to address the soundness of the intermediation sector. On the other hand, the moral hazard problem occurs by the banking support operations are difficult to evaluate. An instance, (Gertler, et al. 2016) suggest the huge costs held the economy if the wholesale banks liquidate their assets, which is particularly very pricey in the event of a bank run.

4. MONETARY POLICY AND DSGE MODELS

4.1 Transmission Channel of Monetary Policy

The target of this section is to understand the instrument that drives the transmission of monetary policy through the economy. Research in this field has suggested a diversity of transmission channels each of which informs a particular category of economic agents' reactions followed by a monetary policy impulse. For more details see, for instance, (Mishkin 1995), (Ehrmann and Worms 2004), (Boivin, Kiley, and Mishkin 2010) and (Miroljub and Milica, 2019).

In a more particular way, the literature deals with two groups of monetary policy transmission channels depending on whether the financial system is considered a veil or not. As suggested by Ehrmann and Worms (2004) Boivin et al. (2010) these two channels can be categorized into neoclassical and non-neoclassical channels. Neoclassical channels transmit the monetary policy impulse assuming efficient financial markets that is the financial system is represented as a perfect agent. Among these channels, we find real and nominal interest rate channels, asset price channels, and exchange rate channels, which are analyzed by the majority of standard DSGE models. In contrast, non-neoclassical channels .put the importance of imperfections on the financial market. These channels work through the firm' balance sheet positions, bank-based channels (the bank lending channel and capital channel), and risk-taking channel. Given this chapter's focus on credit market imperfection, the discussion is especially interesting on the non-neoclassical channel with a brief overview of the neoclassical channel.

As a starting point, fig. 3 highlight the artificial representation of monetary policy transmission. The figure draws the types of monetary policy channels from the left to the real and financial sphere on the right[5]. Initially, from a theoretical and empirical perspective, a monetary policy action provokes variation in the money market interest rate and/or inflation anticipations. On the one hand, the Fisher equation confirms that the inflation anticipations present an important factor in monetary policy transmission, in particular through their impact on real interest rates, Ehrmann, and Worms (2004). On the other hand, most channels show the relevance of controlling a nominal interest rate or the money supply in different ways. Accordingly, the effect of the monetary policy adopted on the money market represents the beginning point of several neoclassical channels, Boivin et al. (2010). In contrast, the evolution of companies' and banks' financial position because of monetary policy actions is primordial for understanding the non-neoclassical channel.

As is stressed in the below figure, the Neoclassical channels support the fact of financial market frictionless so, they associate the variation of money market interest rates and inflation anticipations to aggregate demand factors as well as price and wage stickiness. On the contrary, the non-neoclassical channels introduce an intermediate step to emphasize the effect of financial market imperfection in the monetary policy action and economic stability. As tracing in the figure the balance sheet firm's channel mainly affects the credit demand, while both the bank balance sheet and the risk-taking channels work through credit supply.

Figure 3. Monetary policy transmission in financial friction Market

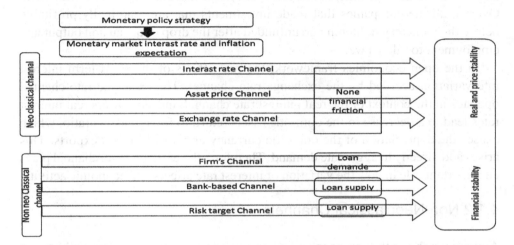

4.1.1 Neoclassical Channels

The real interest rate channel is one of the most knows for monetary policy transmission. With the assumption of prices and wage rigidity, this channel involves the impact of interest rates variation on the capital 'cost and hence on business and household investment spending. In particular, a restrictive monetary policy (a rise in the interest rate) often increases the cost of capital leads to reduce investment spending and aggregate output. Since the relative price between saving and consumption depends on the variation of real interest rate, thus, restrictive monetary policy in the form of higher short-term interest rates will draw future consumption through the intertemporal substitution effects, and thus results in the drop of real economic activity. This channel occurs also with a nominal interest rate at a floor of zero when the money supply grows, the anticipated inflation raises and thereby lowers the real interest rate. This channel is an essential element of the Monetarist framework of why the United States economy didn't suffer in a liquidity trap during the Great Recession and why lower interest rate could obviate a sharp decrease in output during this period, Mishkin (1996)

The investment provides, also, a mechanism in which monetary policy can impact economic activity through asset price channels. Tobin (1969) measures q as the ratio of the stock market value of a firm to the replacement cost of the physical capital that is possessed by that firm. He stressed that an increase in the short-term nominal interest rate makes bonds "more attractive" compared to equities; hence, a restrictive monetary policy leads to a devaluation of equity prices will fall q. With a lower value of q, each firm must issue more new shares of stock to finance any new investment project; in this sense, investment becomes pricier for the firm. Overall, all the companies that made investments that are marginally profitable before the monetary tightening go unfunded after the drop of q, causing output and employment to fall, as well.

In the open economies framework, the real effects of the short-term interest rate variation accrued by the exchange rate channel. The exchange rate channel operates in the context of the real interest rate channel: indeed, lowers real interest rates lead to a decrease in the domestic assets return to foreign assets ratio, which causes the depreciation of the domestic currency and arises the net exports. This arises add directly to aggregate demand. Therefore, the exchange rate channel plays an important role in how the variation of interest rate affects real economic activity.

4.1.2 Non-Neoclassical Channels

As we noted above, the non-neoclassical transmission mechanisms occur with market imperfections. Such channels can deal through imperfections in private markets (such as asymmetric information) or market fragmentation that creates barriers to perfect financial markets performance. In general, these non-neoclassical transmission mechanisms are given the name "credit view" since they involve frictions in credit markets. There are two canonic non-neoclassical channels that we discuss here: the firm's balance-sheet channels (affecting both firms and households) and the bank's balance sheet channel (affecting lending and bank capital).

The firm's balance sheet channel is one of the most known in the framework of the standard DSGE model. In the context of asymmetric information problems, lower net worth means that the agent has less collateral, which increasing the adverse selection problem and then boost risk-taking. As a result, lenders will be more reluctant to supply loans either by reducing the quantity of lent or demanding a higher interest rate. In both cases, external financing will be more expensive than internal financing. The Firm's balance sheet channel arises from this principle.

There are several ways in which the firm's balance sheet channel is affected by monetary policy. The first way is through the asset price: restrictive monetary policy causes a decrease of the asset price value, particularly equity prices, which declines the net worth of firms which worsens the adverse selection and moral hazard problems.

This mechanism lower loans and down aggregate production, Kiyotaki and Moore 1997. Another way that monetary policy can impact firms' balance sheets is through cash flow: a restrictive monetary policy rise lending interest rate, as well as firms' financial charge, thus declining cash flow. However, decreasing cash flow tends to be linked to less collateral. Since this mechanism has further feedback effects over subsequent periods, this amplification and propagation process through balance sheets has been termed 'financial accelerator', Bernanke et al. 1999. Several economists include the impact of monetary policy on the firms' balance sheet channel, in the context of credit frictions, like (Carlstrom, Fuerst, and Paustian 2009), Cúrdia and Woodford (2010), Badarau and Popescu (2015).

Other than firms, this balance sheet channels impact households through real estate prices. Since the real estate serves as a guarantee, so any increase in these goods leads to improve both the quantity and terms of credit available to these households. Similarly, central bank policies can affect the household balance sheet channel through real estate prices: a higher interest rate leads can reduce real estate prices, thereby tightening credit supply conditions and reducing aggregate demand,(Iacoviello and Minetti, 2008).

Next, turn to channels where the banks play a specific role in the transmission process. There are two types of bank-based transmission channels: The bank lending channel and capital channel the main assumption of these two channels is that the banks cannot substitute his deposits with other forms of financial assets.

Let's start with the traditional bank lending channel, where banks have an exceptional role in the financial system because they are appropriate to solve asymmetric information problems in financial markets. Thanks to banks' special role, some borrowers cannot access credit markets except, they borrow from banks. As long as there is no perfect applicability of retail bank deposits with other financial sources. Expansionary monetary policy, which rise bank reserves and bank deposits, increases the loans that will cause investment and consumer spending to grow.

The theory of bank lending channel highlights that monetary policy has a greater impact on smaller firms, which are more dependent on bank loans than it has on large firms, which can provide direct financing through stock and bond markets (and not only through banks). Although this channel was supported by several empirical research, (e.g., Gertler and Gilchrist, 1998, Kashyap and Stein, 1995, Peek and Rosengren, 1995b, 1997), but, it is strongly criticized after. Particularly, at the level of assumption that banks cannot easily accommodate a shortfall in bank deposits by other liquid funding options. Forth more the critics also relate to the balance sheet structure, which can be further disaggregated to recount to other aspects such as bank liquidity, bank assets, or bank capital, Boivin et al. (2010).

In the context of the bank-based channel, we can talk about the bank capital channel which occupies a crucial place, especially, after the financial crisis of

2007. In this channel, the bank balance sheet structure has a significant impact on lending's condition.

In a period of financial stress, the shortage of bank capital can reduce the credit supply: since external financing for banks can be expensive, thus the most cost-effective way for banks to increase their capital to asset ratio is to reduce their asset base by cutting back on lending. This "deleveraging process" means that bank-dependent borrowers are now no longer capable to obtain credit and so they will cut back their spending and aggregate demand will drop, Peek and Rosengren (2010). Furthermore, lower capital to asset ratio increases the bank's financing-cost because it perceives very risky from its depositors, Richelany, and Sette (2016).

The monetary policy can affect bank balance sheets in two ways. First, shallow short-term interest rates tend to grow net interest margins and so lead to increase bank profits which results in an improvement in bank balance sheets over time. Second, expansionary monetary policy can raise asset prices and lead to instant improvements in bank capital. Thus, expansionary monetary policy boosts bank capital, loaning, and hence aggregate demand by permitting bank-dependent borrowers to invest more, Boivin et al. (2010).

Finally, the risk-taking channel has occurred importance since the global financial crisis. This channel shows the impacts of monetary policy on the quality of bank credit and risks taking by agents, (Borio et Zhu 2012). This channel is based usually on expansionary monetary policy to discern the effects of lower long-term interest rates on the bank's behavior. According to this channel, expansionary monetary policy can increase the risk-taking of agents, especially, banks. Much research shows that maintain a lower interest rate in the run-up to the crisis, leads to an asset price boom, stimulating banks to amplify their risk-taking (Borio and Zhu, 2012, Adrian and Shin, 2009, and Taylor, 2009).

The theory offers ambiguous predictions on the links between the real interest rate and bank risk-taking. The neoclassical risk-taking channel shows that a restrictive monetary policy leads to reduce risk-taking. A greater interest rate on safe assets causes a reallocation of toxic assets towards safe securities, thus reducing the riskiness of the overall portfolio. Contrary, the non-neoclassical risk-taking channel anticipates a positive relationship between long term interest rates and bank risk-taking. In these models, the asymmetric information between banks and their borrowers impedes depositors to measure risk at the margin. Overall, the risk-taking channel arises to be a fertile framework for future research.

4.2 Modeling Monetary Policy in DSGE Models

The microfinance arises with two macroeconomic models, RBC (Real Business-Cycle Theory) and DSGE models. RBC-models suppose that prices and wages are entirely flexible and can then optimally adjust each period. The monetary policy has no impact on these models, but their results were exploited as a reference case in some issues. However, the economic works show that monetary policy has real effects if we introduce the nominal rigidities. Suppose, for instance, that prices are fully flexible, companies can usually fix their prices as a function of the mark-up over marginal costs.

Within the DSGE models, there are several manners to model nominal rigidities. Romer (2012) explains seven approaches and shows that these can have quite separate implications for price-adjustment. One of the very popular approaches is the Calvo-price setting. The Calvo model is based on the Poisson process in which the opportunities to change prices depending on the time. Since only a part of the firms can reset their prices each period, there is only a progressive adjustment to nominal shocks which signifies that modification in nominal variables has real effects.

The introduction of nominal rigidities in DSGE models proves the impact of monetary policy on the real economy. This impact arise several questions especially; how the policymaker reacted to the crisis and its aftermath? How the monetary authority should formulate and implement its policy decisions to best foster ultimate policy objectives such as price stability and full employment over time? (Orphanides and Williams 2007)

These questions have permitted the New Neoclassical Synthesis to draw some major hypotheses about the role of the monetary policy. First, monetary policy can have a long-lasting impact on the real economy due to the price adjustment, which rejects the money neutrality hypotheses of the Real business cycle theory. Second, an important improvement in welfare could be gained through the removal of inflation, which should eliminate relative price distortions and transaction costs. Third, a little trade-off between inflation and output is feasible even in the short run. Fourth, this theory was capable to analyze some evidence about best practices in the conduct of monetary policy, particularly, the role of credibility and commitment to simple and transparent rules.

There are various ways to introduce monetary policy rules in a dynamic stochastic general equilibrium model: The rules will depend on the introduced objectives and the data upon which they are estimated. The most known monetary policy rule in the literature is the Taylor-rule, as was estimated by Taylor him in 1993.

In his seminal article (Taylor 1993), Taylor model the behavior of the Fed during the period 1987-1992 in the form of a simple equation associating the nominal interest rate to a very small number of macroeconomic variables, namely inflation and output-gap. The Taylor rule has generally taken the following form:

$$i_t = \overline{i} + \phi_\pi \left(\pi_t - 0.02 \right) + \phi_y \left(y_t - y_{t-1} \right),$$

where π is the current inflation and $\left(y_t - y_t^p\right)$ is the output-gap. Taylor rule implicitly supposes that the FED is targeting an inflation rate of 2% and that the FED react more strongly to the deviation of inflation from the target than the output-gap, $\phi_\pi > \phi_y$. This equation, which, at first, had a normative vocation, has quickly become a benchmark for all theoretical and empirical work analyzing the behavior of Central Banks.

The main goal of policymakers, before the financial crisis, was to stabilize the fundamental macroeconomic variables, which are the inflation and the output gap, through the application of the standard Taylor rule. Nevertheless, when financial intermediation added to the standard DSGE models, interest rate spreads can also affect loan supply through credit market frictions, such as asymmetric information between borrowers and lenders that gives rise to an external finance premium, Bernanke et al (1999) model. To account for these frictions, several variables were added to the standard Taylor rule, especially after the subprime crisis.

The prevailing indicators include the interest rate spreads of Curdia and Woodford (2010), (Gilchrist et Zakrajšek 2011), credit over GDP (Schularick et Taylor 2012) (Drehmann et al. 2010), the credit growth of Agenor et al. (2013) and Badarau and Popescu (2015), assets price and credit growth by (Gambacorta et Signoretti (2013). All these authors support the idea of introducing the financial indicator into the central bank's reaction function to weaken the fluctuation of macroeconomic and financial fundamentals. Drehmann et al. (2010) introduce several other variables and show that the credit to GDP ratio is the best one for forecasting crises. Likewise, Verona, et al (2017) consider several financial indicators such, bond spread, loan spread, total credit and find that the augmented Taylor rule that introduces these indicators is better than the standard one in the financial friction time.

Brazdik et al. (2012) point out that the potential gains occurring from introducing financial frictions in central banks' prediction models can be large. The extension of the models used by central banks to introduce financial frictions helps to improve the fit of these models and our understanding of the historical evolution of economic variablesExtended models also strengthen anticipation capability and thus improve the conduct of monetary policy.

Once the model is specified through its hypothesis, an optimal monetary policy rule can be determined based on welfare effects. These optimal rules are determined in two steps. The first step is that there is a welfare loss function. In the pre-crisis DSGE model, the loss function includes the variance of the output and inflation that the monetary authority desires to minimize. While in the post-crisis DSGE model, the loss function adds the variance of financial variables, to the traditional variable's variance. In the second step, the "optimal" monetary rule is determined by evaluating which coefficients for the indicator minimize the loss. For example,

(Cogley et al. 2011) analyze the optimal monetary policy rules for the Smets and Wouters (2007) and Bernanke et al. (1999) models. They find that the optimal rule, in Bernanke et al model, is a Taylor rule that reacts strongly to inflation with a low-interest rate smoothing and output gap indicator.

Benchimol and Fourçans (2019), aim to determine the optimal Taylor rule, in line with the economic conjuncture of the US economy, using several loss function measures. In their analysis, twelve monetary policy rules were exploited and the optimality of these rules was tested via a general monetary authority loss function. This function includes the variance of the output gap, the variance of the nominal interest rate, and the wage inflation variance. they Bayesian estimation indicates that the various central bank rules, be they the nominal GDP level target or Taylor rule, are more adequate to reach the central bank's objectives whatever the economic conjuncture (growth, crisis, recovery).

CONCLUSION

The literature on financial frictions remains a dynamic and important area of research. There has been a great treat of progress since the financial crisis in understanding the features of both the crisis and its aftermath, as well as in how modeling crises in a DSGE framework (Claus and Krippner, 2019).

In this paper, we have presented various ways, which are utilized in the literature to include financial market frictions into DGSE models. Pre-crisis dynamic models focused primarily on the friction in the demand loan side. In this context, two principal models arise; the Financial accelerator and the collateral constraint models. The financial accelerator literature concentrates on the external finance premium (which decreases the business cycle dynamics) to demonstrate how an inter-temporal shock can quickly be transmitted into a prolonged period of down economic growth. In the context of the collateral constraint models, there isn't an endogenously fixed financial premium but instead, the borrower cannot borrow as soon as its assets, which uses as collateral, covers at least the entire loan requested. In the event of investment's bankruptcy, the lender recovered, automatically, these assets. Therefore, the nominal value of the collateral completes the amount of the loan that the borrower can get.

Also, we have focused on the phenomenon of a bank run and Mismatch liquidity of Gertler et al. (2016) in which during a run, depositors precipitate to withdraw their deposits because they anticipate the bank to fail. The massive withdrawal of deposits will push the bank to fair sell its assets and to accept large losses and even to declare its bankruptcy. The phenomenon can propagate from one bank to another if depositors lose confidence in the whole banking system causing large damage in the financial system and disruption of production. Ultimately, we focus on the fundamental issue; to what extent the Taylor rules are optimal when the central bank introduces the goal of financial stability.

REFERENCES

Adrian, T., & Shin, H. S. (2009). *Money, Liquidity, and Monetary Policy*. Social Science Research Network. SSRN Scholarly Paper.

Assenmacher, K., & Gerlach, S. (2010). Monetary policy and financial imbalances: Facts and fiction. *Economic Policy*, *25*(63), 437–482. doi:10.1111/j.1468-0327.2010.00249.x

Badarau, C., & Popescu, A. (2015). Monetary policy and financial stability: What role for the interest rate? *International Economics and Economic Policy*, *12*(3), 359–374. doi:10.100710368-014-0307-6

Benchimol, J., & Fourçans, A. (2019). *Central Bank Losses and Monetary Policy Rules: A DSGE Investigation*. Social Science Research Network. SSRN Scholarly Paper.

Benedictow, A., & Roger, H. (2020). A ðnancial accelerator in the business sector of a macro-econometric model of a small open economy. *Economic Systems*, *44*(1), 100731. doi:10.1016/j.ecosys.2019.100731

Bernanke, Gertler, & Gilchrist. (1999). The financial accelerator in a quantitative business cycle framework. In Handbook of Macroeconomics. Elsevier.

Bernanke & Gertler. (1989). Agency Costs, Net Worth, and Business Fluctuations. *The American Economic Review, 79*(1), 14-31.

Boivin, J., Kiley, M. T., & Mishkin, F. S. (2010). *How Has the Monetary Transmission Mechanism Evolved Over Time?* Social Science Research Network. SSRN Scholarly Paper. doi:10.3386/w15879

Borio, C., & Zhu, H. (2012). Capital regulation, risk-taking, and monetary policy: A missing link in the transmission mechanism? *Journal of Financial Stability*, *8*(4), 236–251. doi:10.1016/j.jfs.2011.12.003

Brázdik & Marsal. (2011). *Survey of research on financial sector modeling within DSGE models: what central banks can learn from it*. Available at SSRN 2274689.

Brazdik, F., Hlavacek, M., & Maršál, A. (2012). Survey of research on financial sector modeling within DSGE models: What central banks can learn from it. Finance a Uver - *Czech. Journal of Economics and Finance, 62*, 252–277.

Calvo, G. A. (1983). Staggered prices in a utility-maximizing framework. *Journal of Monetary Economics, 12*(3), 383–398. doi:10.1016/0304-3932(83)90060-0

Carlstrom, C. T., Fuerst, T. S., & Paustian, M. (2009). Inflation Persistence, Monetary Policy, and the Great Moderation. *Journal of Money, Credit and Banking, 41*(4), 767–786. doi:10.1111/j.1538-4616.2009.00231.x

Céspedes, L. F., Chang, R., & Velascode, A. (2017). Financial intermediation, real exchange rates, and unconventional policies in an open economy. *Journal of International Economics, 108*(1), 76–86. doi:10.1016/j.jinteco.2016.12.012

Christensen, I., & Dib, A. (2008). The financial accelerator in an Estimated New Keynesian model. *Review of Economic Dynamics, 11*(1), 155–178. doi:10.1016/j.red.2007.04.006

Claus, I., & Krippner, L. (2019). Contemporary Topics in Finance: A Collection of Literature Surveys. Wiley. *Business Economics (Cleveland, Ohio).*

Cúrdia, V., & Woodford, M. (2010). Credit Spreads and Monetary Policy. *Journal of Money, Credit and Banking, 42*(s1), 3–35. doi:10.1111/j.1538-4616.2010.00328.x

De Walque, G., Pierrard, O., & Rouabah, A. (2010). Financial (in)stability, supervision and liquidity injections: A dynamic general equilibrium approach. *Economic Journal (London), 120*(549), 1234–1261. doi:10.1111/j.1468-0297.2010.02383.x

Diamond, D. W., & Dybvig, P. H. (1983). Bank Runs, Deposit Insurance, and Liquidity. *Journal of Political Economy, 91*(3), 401–419. doi:10.1086/261155

Drehmann, M. (2010). Countercyclical Capital Buffers: Exploring Options. *SSRN Electronic Journal.* https://www.ssrn.com/abstract=1648946

Duncan, A., & Nolan, C. (2018). Financial Frictions in Macroeconomic Models. In *Oxford Research Encyclopedia of Economics and Finance.* Oxford University Press. doi:10.1093/acrefore/9780190625979.013.168

Ehrmann, M., & Worms, A. (2004). Bank Networks and Monetary Policy Transmission. *Journal of the European Economic Association, 2*(6), 1148–1171. doi:10.1162/1542476042813904

Fahr, S., Motto, R., Rostagno, M., Smets, F., & Tristani, O. (2013). A monetary policy strategy in good and bad times: Lessons from the recent past. *Economic Policy*, *28*(74), 243–288. doi:10.1111/1468-0327.12008

Gambacorta & Signoretti. (2013). *Should Monetary Policy Lean against the Wind? An Analysis Based on a DSGE Model with Banking*. Bank of Italy, Economic Research, and International Relations Area.

Gertler, M., & Karadi, P. (2011). A Model of Unconventional Monetary Policy. *Journal of Monetary Economics*, *58*(1), 17–34. doi:10.1016/j.jmoneco.2010.10.004

Gertler, M., & Kiyotaki, N. (2015). Banking, Liquidity, and Bank Runs in an Infinite Horizon Economy. *The American Economic Review*, *105*(7), 2011–2043. doi:10.1257/aer.20130665

Gertler, M., Kiyotaki, N., & Prestipino, A. (2016). Wholesale Banking and Bank Runs in Macroeconomic Modeling of Financial Crises. In Handbook of Macroeconomics. Elsevier.

Gilchrist & Zakrajšek. (2011). *Credit Spreads and Business Cycle Fluctuations. National Bureau of Economic Research*. Working Paper.

Goodfriend & McCallum. (2007). *Banking and Interest Rates in Monetary Policy Analysis: A Quantitative Exploration*. National Bureau of Economic Research. Working Paper.

Hammersland, R. (2017). The Financial accelerator and the Real economy: evidence using a data-based procedure of simultaneous structural model design. *Proceedings ITISE 2017*, 1007–1034.

Hammersland, R., & Træe, C. B. (2014). The financial accelerator and the real Economy: A small macro-econometric model for Norway with financial frictions. *Economic Modelling*, *36*, 517–537. doi:10.1016/j.econmod.2013.04.051

Iacoviello, M. (2005). House Prices, Borrowing Constraints, and Monetary Policy in the Business Cycle. *The American Economic Review*, *95*(3), 739–764. doi:10.1257/0002828054201477

Iacoviello, M., & Minetti, R. (2008). The credit channel of monetary policy: Evidence from the housing market. *Journal of Macroeconomics*, *30*(1), 69–96. doi:10.1016/j.jmacro.2006.12.001

Irani, R. M., Iyer, R., & Meisenzahl, R. R. (2018). *The Rise of Shadow Banking: Evidence from Capital Regulation*. Finance and Economics Discussion Series Divisions of Research & Statistics and Monetary Affairs Federal Reserve Board.

Karmelavicius, J., & Ramanauskas, T. (2019). Bank credit and money creation in a DSGE model of a small open economy. *Baltic Journal of Economics, 19*(2), 296–333. doi:10.1080/1406099X.2019.1640958

Kiyotaki, N., & Moore, J. (1997). Credit Cycles. *Journal of Political Economy, 105*(2), 211–248. doi:10.1086/262072

Malliaris, A. G. (2020). *Asset Price Bubbles and Central Bank Policies: The Crash of the 'Jackson Hole Consensus.* Oxford University Press.

Mierau, J. O., & Mink, M. (2018). A Descriptive Model of Banking and Aggregate Demand. *De Economist, 166*(2), 207–237. doi:10.100710645-018-9320-4

Miroljub, L., & Labus, M. (2019). Monetary Transmission Channels in DSGE Models: Decomposition of Impulse Response Functions Approach. *Computational Economics, 53*(1), 27–50. doi:10.100710614-017-9717-1

Mishkin, F. S. (1995). Symposium on the Monetary Transmission Mechanism. *The Journal of Economic Perspectives, 9*(4), 3–10. doi:10.1257/jep.9.4.3

Mishkin, F. S. (1996). *The Channels of Monetary Transmission: Lessons for Monetary Policy.* National Bureau of Economic Research. Working Paper.

Modigliani, F., & Miller, M. H. (1958). The Cost of Capital, Corporation Finance and the Theory of Investment. *The American Economic Review, 48*(3), 261–297.

Orphanides, A., & Williams, J. (2007). Robust monetary policy with imperfect knowledge. *Journal of Monetary Economics, 54*(5), 1406–1435. doi:10.1016/j.jmoneco.2007.06.005

Ranneberg, A. (2016). Bank Leverage Cycles and the External Finance Premium. *Journal of Money, Credit and Banking, 48*(8), 1569–1612. doi:10.1111/jmcb.12359

Schularick, M., & Taylor, A. M. (2012). Credit Booms Gone Bust: Monetary Policy, Leverage Cycles, and Financial Crises, 1870-2008. *The American Economic Review, 102*(2), 1029–1061. doi:10.1257/aer.102.2.1029

Sergi, F. (n.d.). L'histoire (faussement) naïve des modèles. *DSGE,* 42.

Smets, F. (2014). Financial Stability and Monetary Policy: How Closely Interlinked? *International Journal of Central Banking, 10*(2), 263–300.

Smets, F., & Wouters, R. (2007). Shocks and Frictions in US Business Cycles: A Bayesian DSGE Approach. *The American Economic Review, 97*(3), 586–606. doi:10.1257/aer.97.3.586

Stiglitz, J. E. (2017). *Where Modern Macroeconomics Went Wrong*. National Bureau of Economic Research. Working Paper.

Svensson, L. E. O. (2016). *Cost-Benefit Analysis of Leaning Against the Wind*. National Bureau of Economic Research. Working Paper.

Taylor, J. B. (1993). Discretion versus Policy Rules in Practice. *Carnegie-Rochester Conference Series on Public Policy, 39*, 195–214. doi:10.1016/0167-2231(93)90009-L

Tobin, J. (1969). A General Equilibrium Approach To Monetary Theory. *Journal of Money, Credit and Banking, 1*(1), 15–29. doi:10.2307/1991374

Verona, Martins, & Drumond. (2017). Financial Shocks, Financial Stability, and Optimal Taylor Rules. *Journal of Macroeconomics, 54*(PB), 187-207.

Woodford, M. (2012). *Inflation Targeting and Financial Stability*. National Bureau of Economic Research, Inc. NBER Working Paper.

ENDNOTES

[1] As we are concentrated on the way to introduce credit friction into DSGE models, we ignored the definition of friction forms. For a better understanding of these forms, we promote the reader to see Handel et al. (2018), Dong (2019).

[2] Both models highlight the balance sheet channel. Both models analyze friction on the demand credit side and assume then, passive role of the banking sector. Households in these models cannot receive their deposits until the next period, which eliminates bankruptcy bank.

[3] Money neutrality, the unicity of the interest rate, the passive role played by the government, the basic estimation method, are not critical in this chapter. For more literature, on pre-crisis DSGE models see Emmanuel (2010), Modigliani and Miller (1958), Anton Korinek (2015), Sergi (2015), and Stiglitz (2017).

[4] See section 4.2 for more literature on the introduction of financial variables into monetary policy.

[5] Our goal of this paper is not to explain the friction that occurs between monetary policy instruments and operating targets, for example, the Federal Fund rate, but we discuss rather the frictions that happen subsequently as indicated by the arrows. So, the analysis of monetary policy transmission channels onsets after the monetary policy action has touched the Federal Fund rate and inflation anticipations.

Chapter 3
Exploring Shared Work Values and Work Collaboration With a Network Approach:
A Case Study From Italy

Aizhan Tursunbayeva
University of Twente, The Netherlands

Stefano Di Lauro
University of Sannio, Italy

Gilda Antonelli
University of Sannio, Italy

ABSTRACT

A real-life case study presented in this chapter reports on how organizational network analysis approach was used in a medium-sized Italian company with circa 100 employees to examine how the company employees were connected by shared values at work, what these values are, and whether and how their value connectedness impacted the quality of their collaboration. The findings indicate that there was a positive correlation between shared work values and work collaboration, present benchmarks for network parameters, as well as propose macro-categories of work values. To the best of the authors' knowledge, this is the first study to use the network-analysis approach to explore shared values and employee collaboration at work. The chapter should be of substantial interest not only to academic scholars but also to organizational leaders and HR practitioners.

DOI: 10.4018/978-1-7998-7716-5.ch003

INTRODUCTION

Collaboration at work is typically described as an interaction among employees within and across teams, organizations and sectors to achieve a shared goal (Bedwell et al., 2012). Although it helps organizations to be creative and flexible, and thus increase competitive advantage, collaboration often does not come naturally to employees. The culture of competition which prevailed in organizations for many decades is often seen as one likely cause of this phenomenon (Kelly & Schaefer, 2014). Organizations seek to break-up of organizational silos and to increase collaboration among their employees by introducing cutting-edge technologies (e.g. Slack). However, to be effective and sustainable, collaboration needs to be embedded in an organizational culture (Kelly & Schaefer, 2014), which includes, among other factors, values that guide the behavior of members of the organization (The Business Dictionary, 2018). This implies that values can be the key to understanding how people collaborate at work.

Values provide a bonding mechanism between people, set the tone for the environment, and produce a culture that facilitates work toward common goals (Meglino et al., 1989). Previous research has demonstrated that when employees are similar in terms of their values, these values result in congruent interpretations and compatible perceptions regarding tasks and environments (Cannon-Bowers & Salas, 2001). However, there needs to be more work to investigate specifically the association between work values and employee work behavior or work outcomes including, for example, collaboration at work (Mazzocchi, 2008). Indeed, few of the existing studies that have looked at the values employees share, and their work behavior or outcomes, has taken into consideration that in the workplace personnel interact not only with their line managers or direct co-workers but with a range of different people employed by the company (e.g. Kristof-Brown et al., 2005). Especially, considering that these may work in different departments or at diverse geographical locations. This limitation in the current published literature was meant to be addressed in a real-life single case, in which a medium-sized Italian company examined how its employees were connected by shared values at work, what these values were, and whether and how this value-connectedness impacted the quality of their collaboration. To the best of our knowledge this is the first study to use network-analysis approach to explore shared values and employee collaboration at work.

LITERATURE REVIEW

Social Network Perspective

The 'social network perspective' is concerned with the structure and patterning of actual relationships (including informal networks) between different actors, be they individuals, groups, organizations or enterprises (Tichy et al., 1979). It first emerged nearly a century ago, independently, in psychology and in cultural anthropology (Cross et al., 2002). In the last few decades, interest in this perspective has led to a substantial body of research focusing on both intra- and inter-organizational networks (Ahuja, 2000). For example, a quick search for 'social network analysis' keyword in the Scopus international literature database generated more than 12,000 returns. 85% of these were published since 2010. This is not a surprise, as the use of this approach in Human Resource (HR) management research is being actively promoted (Cross et al., 2013). Moreover, this perspective has generated significant interest among practitioners (Tursunbayeva et al., 2018). For instance, 'organizational network analysis' (the term commonly used in organizations for referring to the analysis of intra-organizational networks) has been named as one of the People Analytics crucial areas to pay attention to in 2018 (Deloitte, 2018). Indeed, it is one of the People Analytics approaches organizational leaders would like to learn more about (Green, 2018). This interest has been triggered by recent developments of graph theory that have enabled the visualization of more complex relationships, and consequent developments in the HR technology, as represented by organizational network analysis technology vendors such as Trustshare or Polinode.

Research on inter-organizational networks looks at the relationships between organizations, while research on intra-organizational networks views employees as entities embedded in social networks within organizations (Totterdell et al., 2004). Previous studies on intra-organizational networks of employees and their structures have investigated how employees' feelings depend on the network of people with whom they work, as well as shed light on such organizational outcomes as employees' innovation behavior, influence or performance (e.g. Totterdell et al., 2004). However, current research on intra-organizational networks still has not provided an understanding of how employees are connected with shared work values and how these affect their work collaboration. Thus there is a myriad of studies investigating and promoting the value of collaboration at work, but very few studies that focus on the role that work values have in employees' collaboration at work (RQ1). As a result, organizations are guided more by vision than evidence in their organizational development projects and human resource strategies focused on work values and work collaboration.

Work Values, Their Types, and Employee Behavior/Outcomes

Values have a noticeable place in scholarly literature and are studied at diverse levels. The analysis of values started from the individual level, but since then has expanded to include collective and organizational levels (Fitzgerald & Desjardins, 2004), where they are reported to have an influence on organizational marketing, structure (Kabanoff et al., 1995), identity, and strategy (Bansal, 2003).

Work values can inform modes of conduct, communication and decision-making of employees within an organization (Simmerly, 1987). When employees are similar in terms of their values, those shared values can result in agreeable interpretations and compatible perceptions about tasks and environments (Cannon-Bowers & Salas, 2001). In other words, members' shared values enable well-matched interpretations of the context, which foster high-level performance.

There have been several attempts to explore how employees are connected by work values. For example, back in the 1990s McDonald and Gandz conducted a study involving 45 management consultants and senior managers to understand shared values for a modern organization. In 2012 Bradshaw concluded that for the company to be successful employees' individual values and work values need to be aligned, while Meglino and colleagues (1989) found that an alignment between organizational, departmental, and employee values can have a positive influence on employee satisfaction, commitment, and perception of feeling involved in an organization's decision-making process (Kautish, 2008; Kautish & Thapliyal, 2012). However, the association of work values and employee outcomes is mostly neglected in the published literature (Mazzocchi, 2008). This is a limitation we hoped to address in the present study. Specifically, we aimed to investigate the work values employees share and their relation to employees' work collaboration (RQ1.1&1.2).

Scholars have invested in studying the dimensions of work values reporting that these can vary between two (e.g. Gahan & Abeysekera, 2009) and 15 categories (Warr, 2008). However, despite this scholarly attention to work values, organizational statements about values such as teamwork, a commitment to quality, or ethics do not provide clear guidelines regarding employee conduct (Fitzgerald & Desjardins, 2004). Moreover, little is still known about how work values are created, except where existing work codes are used to create work values (Ueda & Ohzono, 2012). However, this approach to values creation has been identified as not suitable for all job categories, because work codes can vary for jobs, as in the case of the American Nurses Association's Code of Conduct (Dempsey, 2009) or the Protestant Ethic of the employees (Kidron, 1978). Therefore here we applied an intra-organizational network approach to understand the work values employees believe they have and share with others, as well as whether these can be understood in terms of the categories hitherto employed by those who have theorized work values. (RQ1.3). The results of this analysis have the potential to shed light also on whether and how intra-organizational network analysis can be deployed in the process of values creation.

METHODOLOGY

The relationship between shared work values and work collaboration was examined in this study in the following stages. First, we identified employees who share work values (RQ1.1), paying attention also to what these values are (RQ1.3). Secondly, we identified employees collaborating on work-related matters and looked at whether and how employees' shared work values impacted their collaboration (RQ1.2).

A mixed-method case study approach was employed because it "works particularly well for case study research [where]… qualitative data can be quantitized or quantitative data can be qualitized to extract meaning from the data sets that might otherwise be hidden" (Kitchenham, 2010).

Research Setting

The Case Company is a medium-sized Italian product- and service-oriented company with 14 international branches. The Company belongs to a larger family group that is the second largest in Italy in their specific sector. Most of the company staff have the same academic specialization, and/or quantitative scientific background.

The Case Company was selected for several reasons. First, although it had a clearly defined mission and statement, the Company was revisiting its work values. Second, because all three authors collaborated with the Company to some extent, while some of them were directly involved in the values creation process. As such, research findings were triangulated with authors' primary observations (Kitchenham, 2010).

Data Collection and Analysis

Among diverse approaches to the collection of network data, including passive (e.g. surveys) and active (e.g. employee emails or their calendar activity) data sources (Green, 2018), following the tactic adopted by Cross and colleagues (2002), the data for this study derived from a survey questionnaire created in ONASurveys (identified by Cohen and Nair (2017) as a useful tool for social network analysis). The survey questions (see Appendix A) were inspired by the webinars organized by Connected Commons community led by ONA guru Professor Rob Cross (2017).

The survey was circulated to all Company employees (n=100) located both in Italy and in international branches (87% of employees completed the survey). The survey started with generic demographic questions comprising employees' tenure, hierarchical position, and division, and aimed to investigate:

- Employees' work values network, considering also what these values were. In addition to determining diverse work values network parameters (see Appendix B) we calculated also a 'shared value score', which is the number of employees mentioning that they shared work values with each other respondent. No predefined set of values was used, so the respondents could input their own terms in the questionnaire. These were then 'open-coded' (Glaser & Strauss, 1967), and grouped into emerging categories.
- Employees' collaboration on work-related matters was estimated with a created 'work collaboration score'. This was based on how many people any given employee was found to collaborate with, combined with the quality of this collaboration as assessed by the respondents on a scale of 0 to 5. The relationship between work collaboration and shared values was also inspected, specifically regarding whether employees who had common work values were more likely to cooperate at work. Thus each identified work relationship (with a score from 0 to 5) was matched with the appropriate values relationship between the same pair of employees. The model was estimated with R analysis software. The values relations were rescaled from 0 (no relation) to 5 (when both employees believed they shared values), with 2.5 representing a situation in which only one of the pair believed they both shared values. The same analysis was conducted for employees working in the same division as for employees working in different divisions. Furthermore, diverse work network parameters were also calculated.

The Open Graph Viz Platform-Gephi program was used to visualize the relationship data.

RESULTS

Work Values Network (RQ1.1)

595 shared work values relationships emerged from the analysis, with the average shared values score being 5.95 (min=0; max=29; STD=6.27). As such on average respondents believed that they shared one or more reported values with 6 other colleagues. 5 clusters emerged in the values network (Figure 1), indicating groups of employees that tend to share more work values amongst themselves than with employees outside of their clusters. The network diameter is 6, and the average

path length is 2.5. The most central node in the values network is the Company CEO. The other biggest work values influencers came from different divisions and positions, and with the length of time they had worked for the Company varied. However, the majority of employees with the highest values relationships were all located in the Head Office.

Work Collaboration Network (RQ1.2)

723 work relationships were identified in the Company, with an average work collaboration score being 18.835 (min=0; max=128.5; STD=21.5). An average work collaboration is 2.5. As such on average each survey respondent collaborated with and helped improve the performance of 7.5 other employees. 4 clusters emerged in the work network (see Figure 1). The network diameter is 4 with an average path length of 2.2. The most central node is Head of IT. Other work influencers belonged to diverse divisions, had varying hierarchical positions, and their seniority of service varied, although the majority of employees with the highest scores for work relationships were all located in the Head Office. Level of collaboration is 9.4% (of 100% possible). The analysis also demonstrated that 69% of all work collaborations in the Company occurs between individuals from different departments.

Figure 1. Work values and work collaborations networks visualization

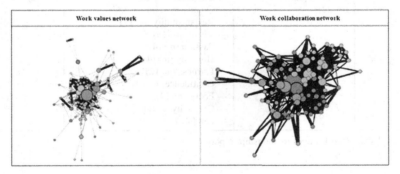

Work Collaboration and Values Relationship (RQ1.1 & RQ1.2)

The correlation between shared values and work collaboration equaled to 0.32. This demonstrates a potential for a positive relationship between these two categories. A further regression analysis helped to produce the following model: Work_relation=2.19+0.2*values_relation. This means that if two employees both believe they share one or more common values the strength of their work relation will be 1 point higher than if the contrary holds (0.2*5). The analysis also demonstrated a positive effect of shared values on work collaboration for employees within the same division and for employees of different divisions.

Types of Values (RQ1.3)

Four primary category groups emerged from an open-coding of values reported by survey respondents (see Table 1).

Table 1. Categories of values that emerged from an open coding

Who We Are?	What Do We Do/Offer?	How Do We Do It?	Who Does It?
– Organization (n=18)*	– Services (n=51)* – Products (n=41)* – Online platform (n=22)*	— Professionalism (n=111)* — Scientific Approach (n=46)* — Competence (n=46)* — Seriousness (n=45)* — Precision (n=43)* — Ethics (n=42)* — Expertise (n=32)* — Innovation (n=29)* — Commitment (n=28)* — Diligence (n=27)* — Reliability (n=26)* — Customer care (n=25)* — Quality (n=20)* — Responsibility (n=17)* — Vision (n=15)* — Passion (n=14)* — Honestly (n=14)* — Fairness (n=12)* — Confidence (n=12)* — Focus (n=12)* — Creativity (n=11)* — Kindness (n=10)*	– Employees (n=42)*

* Number of shared work values relationships reported

DISCUSSION, CONCLUSION, AND FURTHER RESEARCH

The literature on applications of social network analyses is growing (e.g. Cross et al., 2013). However, this study is one of the few theoretically informed attempts of applying network analysis approach to understanding how employees are connected by shared work values, what these values are, and whether and how employees' connectedness by shared values can impact their work collaboration.

Our findings reveal that employees' positions, whether defined in terms of hierarchical status, job tenure, or company division, had no impact on their work collaboration or shared work values, although we did not test this significance statistically. For example, one of the authors of this paper who had worked in the company as a manager for less than a year was identified as an 'influencer' in both the work and values networks. Meanwhile, both networks also included 'influential' junior employees who had worked in the Company for several years. However, although this was outside the scope of our research, similarly to Neeley (2017) we also noted that employees in the Head Office and in Italy in general were more central to both the work values and the work collaboration networks, while employees working in the international branches occupied more peripheral positions. Future research might look into this further by evaluating whether employees' tenure and hierarchical positions jointly influence work collaboration and work values relationships, as well as whether the geographical location of employees has any influence on these networks.

The overall rate of work collaboration in the company is low (i.e. 9.4% out of 100% possible). For instance, evidence coming from other earlier investigations suggests that an ideal work collaboration rate is in the range 25%-35% (Cross et al., 2010). The average path length between employees for work collaboration is 2.2. This demonstrates a relative disconnection among employees, especially taking into account the moderate size of the company workforce (n=100 employees) (Cross et al., 2010). As a result, to get a response to any inquiry, staff need to cross another employee, which might imply that employees often cannot get the information they need in a timely and efficient way. This quantitative finding was fully confirmed by the qualitative observations of the authors.

The rate of interdepartmental work collaboration is 69%. Although this result, regarded as a standalone, seems satisfactory, it is important to note that it was not possible to compare it to those of other organizations, as benchmark values are not available. This is a significant gap, given that fruitful collaboration between different departments or organizations within the same enterprise network is often linked to success in respect of new product development (Cordon-Pozo et al., 2006) and the innovation performance of an organization (Cujipers et al., 2011). Future scholars might want to study the interdepartmental collaboration rates of the best-in-class organizations such as companies from Fortune 500 list or organizations from different industries or countries to produce such benchmark values for varying network parameters. These might help to offer recommendations to other companies.

The positive correlation of shared work values and work collaboration that emerged from our analysis is an encouraging indication for companies looking for approaches to improve their work collaboration, since it may indicate that an enabler such as shared values is a significant factor in promoting work collaboration of employees within and across departments, and that efforts invested in communicating the importance of work values sharing between employees could be rewarding (although it is important to remember that these findings demonstrate only correlation - not causation - between work collaboration and shared work values). However, more generically, the relatively small sample size, and a single case study research design adopted in this study precludes fully confident general conclusions. As such we encourage future scholars to test the generalizability of these findings by seeking to replicate this analysis in other companies with larger samples, and possibly also from different industries. Future scholars might also like to consider control variables which were not taken into consideration in our study, but which could potentially account for the relationships found in our analysis such as employees' position or roles. For example, whether employees with the same position (e.g. from Research and Development team) are more likely to report collaborating and more likely to share values such as scientific approach due to the role they hold. Overall, we suggest lead users of the network analysis approach to actively share their projects and results. For example, an Italian multinational manufacturer and distributor of electricity and gas recently conducted a similar project on creating and promoting organizational values (Stratta, 2017). However, the literature is still silent about this case study covering a large sample of employees located internationally.

The value categories that emerged from our research differ slightly from those produced by other studies, although some actual values reported were similar to those of previous research. For example, ethics and creativity values were reported also by Busacca and colleagues (2010). These findings was not unexpected, as previous research mostly aimed to explore staff work values (Wang et al., 2010), while this study also aimed to group them into emerging macro categories. The analysis also showed that employees shared some categories of work values more than others. Thus, for the highly professional quasi-scholarly staff of the Company, it was vital "how the work is done" (e.g. scientific rigor or professionalism), and what products they developed, rather than "who we are as an organization" as a whole. The latter finding echoes the findings of another recent study carried out in this Company and illustrating low organizational identification of employees with the company on their personal social media accounts (Di Lauro et al., 2018). Additionally, the category 'whom all the work is done for' (i.e. customers) was neglected, although the value of 'customer care' was shared by some employees. This lack of attention to customer-care among employees might be associated with their academic background, and the fact that scholars are often not focused on generating revenue (Welsh et al., 2008), which is the primary objective of companies. Future researchers could test this hypothesis, and investigate whether shared work values and their categories depend on the educational background of employees or the industry in which they work.

Overall, our findings proved to be beneficial in providing the Company with an x-ray on their current work collaboration and shared work values networks. For example, they were used to highlight imperfections in work collaboration between employees of the Head Office and those in the international branches. They also helped the Company to grasp that values are important to their employees. The research results and associated recommendations were presented to the Company management. Recommendations included: (a) revisiting Company values taking into consideration the values proposed by respondents, while incorporating also a value category 'whom the work is done for' to increase the focus of employees on customers in their daily work; (b) involving influencers identified in this study in future organizational change management or organizational development activities; and (c) using the results of this study and industry benchmarks to set intra-organizational work collaboration levels desired by the Company, and introduce appropriate strategies to achieving them.

The findings of this study make a number of contributions to the scholarly field. It is one of the few empirical case studies that investigate employee work collaboration and shared work values with a network perspective derived from academic theorization. Most of the previous publications on this topic were largely descriptive or published by practitioners (Cross et al, 2010), thus not advancing *theoretical* or *methodological* understanding on this topic. The clear macro-categories of values that emerged from our analysis address the current limitation of the existing value types in use, which did not provide clear guidelines for employees' conduct (Fitzgerald & Desjardins, 2004). In consequence, this paper will be of substantial interest not only to academic scholars studying HR, organizational collaboration or behavior, but also to HR practitioners, and consultants helping organizations with organizational development initiatives. This is a *practical* implication of this paper.

To conclude, given the latest technological developments, organizations no longer require special skills to perform complex analysis, or calculate network parameters manually, because social/organizational network analysis tools such as Polinode or Trustshare allow the collection and analysis of network data without scientific or technical training (see Green, 2018 for a review of vendors). We therefore expect research and practice projects involving a network approach to continue blooming. Thus, it is important to highlight that these initiatives need to consider not only legal issues (e.g. recently enforced General Data Protection Regulation), but also questions regarding ethics and employee privacy aspects. This can include obtaining respondents' consent before data is collected or analyzed, especially if passive data collection sources are used, involving legal or compliance colleagues, and communicating to study participants the project goals, data types or methods of analysis to be used, especially if data are to be analyzed down to an individual level.

REFERENCES

Ahuja, G. (2000). The duality of collaboration: Inducements and opportunities in the formation of interfirm linkages. *Strategic Management Journal, 21*(3), 317–343. doi:10.1002/(SICI)1097-0266(200003)21:3<317::AID-SMJ90>3.0.CO;2-B

Bansal, P. (2003). From Issues to Actions: The Importance of Individual Concerns and Organizational Values in Responding to Natural Environmental Issues. *Organization Science, 14*(5), 510–527. doi:10.1287/orsc.14.5.510.16765

Bedwell, W. L., Wildman, J. L., DiazGranados, D., Salazar, M., Kramer, W. S., & Salas, E. (2012). Collaboration at work: An integrative multilevel conceptualization. *Construct Clarity in Human Resource Management Research, 222*(2), 128–145. doi:10.1016/j.hrmr.2011.11.007

Bradshaw, A. (2012). *Putting Value Alignment to Work to Drive Positive Organizational Outcomes*. DeGarmo Group.

Busacca, L. A., Beebe, R. S., & Toman, S. M. (2011). Life and Work Values of Counselor Trainees: A National Survey. *The Career Development Quarterly, 59*(1), 2–18. doi:10.1002/j.2161-0045.2010.tb00126.x

Cannon-Bowers, J. A., & Salas, E. (2001). Reflections on shared cognition. *Journal of Organizational Behavior, 22*(2), 195–202. doi:10.1002/job.82

Cohen, D. G., & Nair, S. (2017). Measuring the Middle: The Use of Social Network Analysis in Middle Management Research. In S. W. Floyd (Ed.), *Middle Management Strategy Process Research*. Edward Elgar Publishing Ltd. doi:10.4337/9781783473250.00024

Cordon-Pozo, E., Garcia-Morales, V. J., & Aragon-Correa, J. A. (2006). Inter-departmental collaboration and new product development success: A study on the collaboration between marketing and R&D in Spanish high-technology firms. *International Journal of Technology Management, 35*(1–4), 52–79. doi:10.1504/IJTM.2006.009229

Cross, R., Borgatti, S. P., & Parker, A. (2002). Making Invisible Work Visible: Using Social Network Analysis to Support Strategic Collaboration. *California Management Review, 44*(2), 25–46. doi:10.2307/41166121

Cross, R., Kase, R., Kilduff, M., & King, Z. (2013). Bridging the Gap between Research and Practice in Organizational Network Analysis: A Conversation between Rob Cross and Martin Kilduff. *Human Resource Management, 52*(4), 627–644. doi:10.1002/hrm.21545

Cross, R. L., Singer, J., Colella, S., Thomas, R. J., & Silverstone, Y. (2010). *The Organizational Network Fieldbook: Best Practices, Techniques and Exercises to Drive Organizational Innovation and Performance*. Jossey-Bass.

Cuijpers, M., Guenter, H., & Hussinger, K. (2011). Costs and Benefits of Inter-Departmental Innovation Collaboratio. *Research Policy*, *40*(4), 565–575. doi:10.1016/j.respol.2010.12.004

Deloitte. (2016). *Organizational Network Analysis Gain insight, drive smart*. Author.

Deloitte Insights. (2018). *2018 Global Human Capital Trends report*. Author.

Dempsey, J. (2009). Nurses values, attitudes and behavior related to falls prevention. *Journal of Clinical Nursing*, *18*(6), 838–848. doi:10.1111/j.1365-2702.2008.02687.x PMID:19239663

Di Lauro, S., Tursunbayeva, A., Antonelli, G., & Martinez, M. (2018). Measuring organizational identity via LinkedIn: The role played by employees' tenure, type of employment contract and age. *Studi Organizzativi*, *2*, 114–129.

Fitzgerald, G. A., & Desjardins, N. M. (2004). Organizational Values and Their Relation to Organizational Performance Outcomes. *Atlantic Journal of Communication*, *12*(3), 121–145. doi:10.120715456889ajc1203_1

Gahan, P., & Abeysekera, L. (2009). What shapes an individual's work values? An integrated model of the relationship between work values, national culture and self-construal. *International Journal of Human Resource Management*, *20*(1), 126–147. doi:10.1080/09585190802528524

Glaser, B. G., & Strauss, A. L. (1967). *The Discovery of Grounded Theory: Strategies for Qualitative Research*. Aldine Pub. Co.

Green, D. (2018). The role of Organisational Network Analysis in People Analytics. *LinkedIn*. https://www.linkedin.com/pulse/role-organisational-network-analysis-people-analytics-david-green/

Kabanoff, B., Waldersee, R., & Cohen, M. (1995). Espoused Values and Organizational Change Themes. *Academy of Management Journal*, *38*(4), 1075–1104.

Kautish, S. (2008). Online Banking: A Paradigm Shift. E-Business. *ICFAI Publication, Hyderabad*, *9*(10), 54–59.

Kautish, S., & Thapliyal, M. P. (2012). Concept of Decision Support Systems in relation with Knowledge Management–Fundamentals, theories, frameworks and practices. *International Journal of Application or Innovation in Engineering & Management*, *1*(2), 9.

Kelly, K., & Schaefer, A. (2014). *Creating a Collaborative Organizational Culture*. UNC Executive Development.

Kidron, A. (1978). Work Values and Organizational Commitment. *Academy of Management Journal*, *21*(2), 239–247. PMID:10308606

Kitchenham, A. (2010). Mixed methods in case study research. In A. J. Mills, G. Durepos, & E. Wiebe (Eds.), *Encyclopedia of case study research* (pp. 562–564). SAGE Publications, Inc.

Kristof-Brown, A. L., Zimmerman, R. D., & Johnson, E. C. (2005). Consequences of individuals' fit at work: A meta-analysis of person–job, person–organization, person–group, and person–supervisor fit. *Personnel Psychology*, *58*(2), 281–342. doi:10.1111/j.1744-6570.2005.00672.x

Mazzocchi, M. (2008). *Statistics for Employee Values*. Sage.

McDonald, P., & Gandz, J. (1991). Identification of values relevant to business research. *Human Resource Management*, *30*(2), 217–236. doi:10.1002/hrm.3930300205

Meglino, B. M., Ravlin, E. C., & Adkins, C. L. (1989). A work values approach to corporate culture: A field test of the value congruence process and its relationship to individual outcomes. *The Journal of Applied Psychology*, *74*(3), 424–432. doi:10.1037/0021-9010.74.3.424

Neeley, T. (2017). How to Successfully Work Across Countries, Languages, and Cultures. *Harvard Business Review*.

Simmerly, R. G. (1987). *Strategic Planning and Leadership in Continuing Education*. Jossey-Bass Publishers.

Stratta, G. (2017). *Lo storytelling come strumento per il cambiamento organizzativo: l'esperienza Enel*. Paper presented at the ASSIOA Winter School, Narratives in Organizational Research, Italy.

The Business Dictionary. (2019). *Organizational culture*. http://www. businessdictionary.com/definition/organizational-culture.html

Tichy, N. L., Tushman, M. L., & Fombrun, C. (1979). Social Network Analysis for Organizations. *Academy of Management Review*, *4*(4), 507–520. doi:10.5465/amr.1979.4498309

Totterdell, P., Wall, P., Holman, D., Diamond, H., & Epitropaki, O. (2004). Affect Networks: A Structural Analysis of the Relationship Between Work Ties and Job-Related Affect. *The Journal of Applied Psychology*, *89*(5), 854–867. doi:10.1037/0021-9010.89.5.854 PMID:15506865

Tursunbayeva, A., Di Lauro, S., & Pagliari, C. (2018). People analytics—A scoping review of conceptual boundaries and value propositions. *International Journal of Information Management*, *43*, 224–247. doi:10.1016/j.ijinfomgt.2018.08.002

Ueda, Y., & Ohzono, Y. (2012). Effect of Work Values on Work Outcomes: Investigating Differences between Job Categories. *International Journal of Business Administration*, *3*(2), ●●●. doi:10.5430/ijba.v3n2p98

Wang, C. Y. P., Chen, M. H., Hyde, B., & Hsieh, L. (2010). Chinese employees' work values and turnover intensions in multinational companies: The mediating effect of pay satisfaction. *Social Behavior and Personality*, *38*(7), 871–894. doi:10.2224bp.2010.38.7.871

Warr, P. (2008). Work values: Some demographic and cultural correlates. *Journal of Occupational and Organizational Psychology*, *81*(4), 751–775. doi:10.1348/096317907X263638

Welsh, R., Glenna, L., Lacy, W., & Biscotti, D. (2008). Close enough but not too far: Assessing the effects of university–industry research relationships and the rise of academic capitalism, *Special Section Knowledge Dynamics out of Balance: Knowledge Biased. Skewed and Unmatched*, *37*(10), 1854–1864.

APPENDIX A

ONA Survey Questions

Work Contribution

- Please indicate the frequency with which you typically receive a useful work-related information from each of the person below (at least twice last week)
- Please indicate the frequency with which you typically receive help with technical work-related problems (at least twice last week) from each of the person below

Shared Work Values

- Please select from the list below 5-10 people who you think share with you corporate values
- Please indicate the corporate values that you think you share with each of the person below

APPENDIX B

Table 2. Parameters analyzed in this study for values and work networks*

Parameters	Description
Node	An individual employee within the Company
Tie/edge	Relationship between *nodes*
Graph	Visualization of the *nodes* and *ties*
Betweenness centrality	The number of the shortest paths in a *graph* that go through a certain *node*
Modularity	The strength of division of a network into clusters
Network diameter	The shortest distance between the two most distant *nodes*
Central node/Influencer	An employee with the highest number of ties, who can share information with and influence the group quickly

*Adopted from Deloitte (2016)

Chapter 4
Entrepreneurial Resilience and Market Turbulence in SMEs:
Perspectives From the COVID-19 Pandemic Context

Rodrigo Marques de Almeida Guerra

https://orcid.org/0000-0003-3900-2663
Federal University of Santa Maria, Brazil

Lídia Maria Begot Bento Cardoso
Federal University of Pará, Brazil

Nathalia Maciel Nogueira
Federal University of Pará, Brazil

Marcelo Pamplona Carneiro
Federal University of Pará, Brazil

ABSTRACT

Entrepreneurial resilience is a recent topic and is widespread in scientific research, especially when associated with periods of instability and crises. This chapter aims to analyze the relationship between the variables open-mindedness (OM), entrepreneurial resilience (ER), market turbulence (MT), and overall performance (OP) in SMEs located in the legal amazon. Data collection coincided with the pandemic of COVID-19, with 384 SME managers participating. The sample was analyzed using structural equation modeling (SEM). The results suggest mediation of the variable ER on the relationship between OM and OP, and moderation of the variable MT on OM and ER. The research's originality is attested by the model's

DOI: 10.4018/978-1-7998-7716-5.ch004

empirical relationships, research context, and adverse scenario provided by the COVID-19 expansion. The practical implications indicate that managers should pay more attention to the variables investigated through the creation of new skills and competencies necessary for entrepreneurial activity in periods of economic crisis and market turbulence.

INTRODUCTION

The war scenario caused by Covid-19 caused serious consequences to the population, organizations and the economy. Social isolation was essential to face the pandemic and mitigate the worsening effects. Despite this, Covid-19 still has implications that put the survival of small and medium-sized enterprises (SMEs) at risk.

The purpose of this article is to analyze the relationship between the variables open-mindedness (OM), entrepreneurial resilience (ER), market turbulence (MT) and overall performance (OP) in SMEs located in the Legal Amazon. For this, two specific objectives will be necessary: to investigate the relationship of the mediating variable ER between the variables OM and OP; and, test the construct MT as a moderating variable on the relationship between OM and ER.

The research environment will involve managers of SMEs installed in the Legal Amazon, a region that comprises all the states of Acre, Amapá, Amazonas, Mato Grosso, Pará, Rondônia, Roraima and Tocantins, and part of Maranhão. This area corresponds to about 60% of the Brazilian territory (IBGE, 2020).

The concept of the Legal Amazon arose in the 1950s with the objective of planning and economically developing a region rich in natural resources, biodiversity and ecosystems, which still includes an extensive area of the Cerrado biome and part of the Mato Grosso wetland (IBGE, 2020). Thus, most of the companies installed in the region depend on extractive and natural resources for survival, it is important to investigate the context of organizations located in this territorial area, especially in times of adversity.

The data collection coincided with the Covid-19 pandemic, being a period considered of limitations of mobility and displacement of the population, caused by social isolation. The natural consequence of quarantine, and, in some cases, lockdown, was a reduction in sales and commercial restrictions for most products / services. The environment of market turbulence and uncertainty was caused, mainly, by doubts about the speed of recovery of companies, generating a current and future scenario of economic crisis.

In addition, the moment requires actions by the government, aiming at the development of public policies that stimulate the generation of employment and income of the population. Entrepreneurship can be the necessary fuel for the permanence and retention of SMEs installed in locations with asymmetric resources and difficult access to finance and credit (Lee, Sameen & Cowling, 2015). Therefore, it is necessary to create specific strategies to identify priority regions (Cavalcante, 2020), taking into account areas with resource imbalances and wide socioeconomic diversity. Within this context, an open-mindedness and entrepreneurial resilience seem to be essential variables for the continuity of SMEs in asymmetric regions, especially in periods of economic stagnation.

THEORETICAL FOUNDATION AND HYPOTHESES

Relationship Between Open-Mindedness, Entrepreneurial Resilience and Performance

Open-mindedness is one of the dimensions of learning orientation, being considered a set of values that influences the way organizations create and use knowledge in favor of learning and business competitiveness (Sinkula, Baker & Noordewier, 1997). Learning organizations are inserted in a changing environment that influences managers' thinking, information processing, the ability to share visions and new mental models, aiming to solve problems over time (Senge, 1992; 2006; Sinkula, 1994).

Open-mindedness is the ability that managers have to review and question current management models, with the purpose of differentiated performance in the long time (Senge, 1992). Therefore, the manager must unlearn old management practices, not letting them influence the current scenario (Senge, 1992; 2006). For this reason, open-mindedness is a capacity that managers have to absorb new ideas (Sinkula, Baker & Noordewier, 1997), especially in times of economic crisis (Herbane, 2013; 2019) and market turbulence (Jaworski & Kohli, 1993).

Thus, the open-mindedness construct is an essential element to rethink organizational strategies (Dukeov et al., 2020), aiming to contemplate new theoretical-empirical relationships, such as: entrepreneurial resilience (Salisu et al., 2020; Santoro, Messeni-Petruzzelli & del Giudice, 2020) And Overall Performance (Jaworski & Kohli, 1993; Powell, 1995; Baker & Sinkula, 1999; Lee & Tsai, 2005).

The concept of entrepreneurial resilience is not yet clear (Duchek, 2018; Branicki, Sullivan-Taylor & Livschitz, 2018) being understood under different contexts (Kautish, 2008; Kautish & Thapliyal, 2012) and areas of knowledge, such as: ecology, psychology, management and economics. (Tabassum et al., 2019; Cellini & Cuccia, 2019). Entrepreneurial resilience is a process that involves different situational factors (external and resource support) and individual factors (personal characteristics and resilience resources). The result is a manager aware of his responsibilities, despite the uncertainties and challenges arising from an environment of setbacks (Duchek, 2018).

Recently, entrepreneurial resilience has been associated with adverse scenarios to business activity, such as: business failure or failures (Corner, Singh & Pavlovich, 2017), decisions in war zones (Bullough, Renko & Myatt, 2014), socio-cultural issues (Rahman & Mendy, 2019), gender differences (Tabassum et al., 2019), entrepreneurial intention (Bullough, Renko & Myatt, 2014; Korber & Mcnaughton, 2018), economic crises (Branicki, Sullivan-Taylor & Livschitz, 2018) and environmental disasters (Busch, 2011).

Resilient is the ability to reinvent models and define new business strategies as circumstances change (Hamel & Välikangas, 2003). Entrepreneurial resilience influences organizational performance, due to operational complexity, predictability, control and market conditions (Awotoye & Singh, 2017). Depending on the factors, the company may develop a double management model that includes periods of stability and turbulence (Dervitsiotis, 2003). For this, it is necessary that the manager has the ability to think new learning models (open-mindedness) (Sinkula, Baker & Noordewier, 1997), and is prone to develop new mental models (Senge, 1992), that contribute to solutions to problems related to the enterprise.

However, organizational managers must exercise caution when defining the business strategy due to the influence on performance (Awotoye & Singh, 2017; Santoro, Messeni-Petruzzelli & del Giudice, 2020), especially in times of turbulence. Open-mindedness is one of the ways for companies to deal with turbulent markets, due to the ability of managers to critically question the organization's operational routines (Calantone, Cavusgil & Zhao, 2002), it can be an element that reinforces entrepreneurial resilience (Santoro, Messeni-Petruzzelli & del Giudice, 2020) in periods of instability.

Therefore, the following hypotheses should be tested:

Hypothesis 1a (H1a): The direct relationship between OM and OP is significant.
Hypothesis 1b (H1b): The direct relationship between OM and ER is significant.
Hypothesis 2 (H2): The direct relationship between ER and OP is significant.

Entrepreneurial Resilience as a Mediating Variable

Resilience is a measure of capacity related to stress, anxiety or depression which can be perceived in different ways (Connor & Davidson, 2003) for being associated with troubled scenarios or drastic changes. Resilience is related to the threat posed and the response time of each individual or organization (Akgün & Keskin, 2014; Duchek, 2018), vary depending on the situation (Blanco et al., 2019; Herbane, 2019).

Entrepreneurial resilience is a capacity that can accelerate the manager's response time in adverse moments. It is common for SMEs (Branicki, Sullivan-Taylor & Livschitz, 2018; Rahman & Mendy, 2019) face turbulent scenarios (Dervitsiotis, 2003), economic, financial and operational crisis (Herbane, 2013; 2019), due to the influence of external variables.

The risk and difficulties scenario requires the entrepreneur to develop new strategies, aiming at the company's survival and maintenance in the market (Rahman & Mendy, 2019). However, organizational readiness is directly associated with the managers' ability to quickly transform obstacles (Korber & Mcnaughton, 2018). Thus, the resilient entrepreneur must have an open-mindedness to face new challenges in the organizational context (Cellini & Cuccia, 2019).

Entrepreneurial resilience is a mediating variable. The indirect effect of resilience was verified from the relationship between entrepreneurial intention and underlying factors, such as: attitudes towards entrepreneurship, social norms and self-efficacy (Pérez-López, González-López & Rodríguez-Ariza, 2016). Salisu et al. (2020), examined the effect of consistency of interest and perseverance of effort on the success of the business career (satisfaction and career performance and financial performance).

Recent research has investigated the mediation of the entrepreneurial resilience variable in the individual context (Ahmad et al., 2019; Salisu et al. 2020). However, little has been done to test the indirect effect from the perspective of the organizational environment, especially in periods of economic instability and market turbulence.

This gap suggests analyzing the following hypothesis:

Hypothesis 4 (H4): The ER variable mediates the relationship between OM and OP.

Market Turbulence (MT) as Moderating Variable

Resilience can be affected in different ways. The existence of regional asymmetries can be accentuated by the unemployment rate, income level, education, geographic location, savings capacity, entrepreneurial profile etc. Other factors may be turbulent conditions (Dervitsiotis, 2003) and the economic crisis (Giannakis & Bruggeman, 2017). The ability of a region to cope with economic shocks can help to understand regional asymmetries related to population and business resilience (Cellini & Cuccia, 2019).

In recent years, resilience has gained prominence in the scientific community. Researchers from around the world began to monitor the determinants of resilience (Giannakis & Bruggeman, 2017) and its impact on organizational performance (Awotoye & Singh, 2017), level of stress, depression and anxiety in the individual (Connor & Davidson, 2003; Lauridsen et al., 2017), a nation's recovery power after periods of economic shocks and influence from different regions (Cellini & Cuccia, 2019).

Market turbulence is a moderating variable (Kohli & Jaworski, 1990; Jaworski & Kohli, 1993) that can influence the relationship between two or more constructs. Market turbulence can be conceptualized as a change in customers' preference in purchasing products or difficulty in dealing with market uncertainties (Santos-Vijande & Álvarez-González, 2007).

Thus, one should test the hypotheses:

Hypothesis 3 (H3): The MT variable moderates the relationship between OM and ER.
Hypothesis 5 (H5): ER mediates the relationship between OM and OP when inserted together in the model containing MT as a moderating variable in the relationship between OM and ER.

Mediation

Mediation is used when a researcher wants to investigate the effect of the indirect variable M (mediator), on the direct relationship between two or more independent variables (X) and a dependent variable (Y). Although mediation is a very recurrent resource in scientific research, statistical tests are rarely adopted that demonstrate the significance of the mediating effect of variable M on the relationship between X and Y, for example (Preacher; Hayes, 2004). Mediation is analyzed by equations 1 and 2, where: M is the mediating variable; Y, dependent variable; X, independent variable; c' is the coefficient of the X to Y ratio; i_1 and i_2 are the intercepts of the regression model; e_M and e_y are the errors of the respective estimated variables; and, a and b are the regression coefficients of the model.

$$M = i_1 + {}_aX + e_M \tag{1}$$

$$Y = i_2 + c\mathbb{¢}X + bM + e_Y \tag{2}$$

Moderation

Moderation occurs when the strength of the relationship between two variables (X and Y) is changed by a third variable (W) (Preacher, Rucker & Hayes, 2007). Thus, for moderation to occur, an independent variable (X) must be associated with a dependent variable (Y) through a moderating variable (W), which starts to influence the intensity or direction of X and Y (Baron & Kenny, 1986). Moderation modifies the initially proposed relationship, which can be measured by metric or non-metric variables (Hair et al., 2009). Moderation is usually assessed using a regression equation (Preacher, Rucker & Hayes, 2007), where: i is the regression intercept; b1 represents *t*he main effect of the variable X in Y; b2 correspond*s* to the effect of the X relationship in W; b3 depicts th*e* effect of the interaction between X and W on Y; ey is the esti$_m$ated error of Y.

$$Y = i + \text{b1}X + \text{b2W} + \text{b3}X\text{W} + eY \tag{3}$$

METHODOLOGY

Research Environment

The research involved SMEs located in the Legal Amazon (or Brazilian). This region represents approximately 60% of the Brazilian territory and covers all the states of Acre, Amapá, Amazonas, Mato Grosso, Pará, Rondônia, Roraima and Tocantins, and part of Maranhão. Despite the extensive geographic area, little has been done to investigate the open mind and entrepreneurial resilience of managers who work in SMEs located in the Brazilian Amazon, especially in periods of market turbulence and economic crisis.

In 2017, the Legal Amazon had approximately 29,643 industrial companies (Portal da Indústria, 2020) installed in a wide geographic territory. However, a large part of this region is composed of humid tropical forest that is difficult to access (Skole & Tucker, 1993), belonging, by law, to indigenous tribes, with areas of environmental preservation, navigable rivers of high caliber and depth, covering an area of difficult access, being distant from the main producing and consuming centers.

The present study involved formal companies established in capitals, metropolitan regions or in municipalities in the interior of the states of the Legal Amazon region. In 2017, on average, small (22.4%) and medium-sized companies (4.9%) represent, respectively, 24.9% and 24.6% of job creation in the Legal Amazon industry (around 300 thousand formal jobs) (Portal da Indústria, 2020).

Data Collect

Due to the breadth of the investigated region, data collection was performed electronically with the help of Google Docs between the months of March and June 2020. This period coincided with that of Covid-19, a scenario considered to be turbulence, economic instability, due to the restrictions that generated a high level of stress, tension and uncertainty among respondents regarding organizational activity.

The survey questionnaire was translated from the English version into Portuguese, and then the reverse translation was performed to ensure that the original meaning of the questions was maintained. The translation was carried out by two professionals with knowledge of the languages. The questionnaire was sent online, however it was necessary to make some phone calls to reinforce the importance of the participation of the managers involved. Initially, three sending waves were carried out. The access link was directed to 953 target companies, of which 396 responded, a return rate of 41.6%. The home office activities contributed to obtaining this percentage.

After analyzing the Mahalanobis distance (D2), 12 sever$_e$ outliers were excluded. In addition, 7 cases of error in filling out the questionnaire were detected (excluded from the survey). Thus, the final valid sample was 384 companies. The research data were analyzed using the statistical software IBM SPSS® and AMOS®, versions for Windows.

Measurement of Variables

The research questionnaire gathered 14 specific questions, measured by the five-point Likert scale (1-strongly disagree and 5-totally agree), adapted from Sinkula, Baker and Noordewier (1997), Santoro, Messeni-Petruzzelli and Del Giudice (2020), Herbane (2013), Jaworski and Kohli (1993) and Powell (1995).

Independent variable: The OM variable is a dimension of the orientation for learning. This scale was created by Sinkula, Baker and Noordewier (1997) and perfected by Baker and Sinkula (1999). Due to the focus of this research, the adapted use of the OM construct was chosen. For the purpose of this research, the adapted scale of Sinkula, Baker and Noordewier (1997), composed of three assertions: OM1: The company's management reflects critically on the shared assumptions we make about our customers; OM2: The company's management realizes that the market must be continually questioned; and, OM3: Company management rarely collectively questions its biases about how managers interpret customer information.

Mediating variable: Previous research (Lauridsen et al., 2017) demonstrate wide use and improvement of the individual resilience scale, mainly involving the Connor and Davidson (2003), known as CD-RISC 10. However, little has been done to develop new items to measure ER from an organizational perspective (Akgün & Keskin, 2014). Five assertions of Herbane (2013) and Santoro, Messeni-Petruzzelli and Del Giudice (2020): ER1: The company's management actively seeks ways to replace losses with customers; ER2: The company's management can grow when it assists me in difficult situations; ER3: The company's management looks for creative ways to change difficult situations; ER4: Regardless of what happens to the company, I believe that I can control my reaction to that; and, ER5: The company's management feels the economic crises caused by recessions or the loss of a large customer.

Dependent variable: The OP variable was used by Jaworski and Kohli (1993), and adapted by Baker and Sinkula (1999) and Lee and Tsai (2005). The original construct has only two items for measurement. Baker and Sinkula (1999) obtained a Cronbach's alpha (α) equal to 0.79. Lee and Tsai (2005) reached an α of 0.879. The use of Structural Equation Modeling (SEM) required the creation of three more variables adapted from Powell (1995), which obtained Cronbach's alpha between 0.78 to 0.90. For the purposes of this research, the following items were used: OP1: The ove*rall performance of the company last year was; OP2:* Regardin*g competition, the company's overall performance in the past year was; OP3:* In the *past three years, the company has shown an increasing financial performance compared to its competitors; OP4:* In the *last three years, the company has shown higher revenue (sales) growth; and,* OP5: In the *past three years, the company has been more profitable than our competitors.*

Moderating variable: The MT variables were adapted Jaworski and Kohli (1993). Despite this, three statements were used to measure the construct, a minimum requirement established by the reviewed literature on SEM (Marôco, 2010). The assertions used in this research were: MT1: There *are many promotion wars in the market; MT2:* Anythin*g that a competitor can offer, other companies will be able to respond promptly; and,* MT3: Price *competition is a registered trademark of the market.*

Control variables: The correlations and significance of the gender, state, size, income and sector control variables were analyzed using ordinal or numerical scales, in relation to the dependent variable OP.

RESULTS AND DISCUSSION

Descriptive Statistics

As for the gender of the participants, the sample was well distributed, with 51.6% for females (n=198) and 48.6% for males (n=186). Regarding the age of the respondents, the highest percentage was for the age group between 36 and 45 years old (33.1%, n=127). As for the participating state, the highest percentages were from Pará (n=125, 32.6%), Amazonas (n=107, 27.9%), Maranhão (n=43, 11.2%) and Mato Grosso (n=31, 8.1%). The survey involved small (n=299, 77.9%) and medium-sized (n=85, 22.1%) companies, members of the industrial sector (n=222, 57.8%) and service (n=162, 42.2%), such as: computer, electronic and optical (n=66, 17.2%), beverages (n=65, 16.9%), petroleum products and biofuels (n=61, 15.9%), extraction of non-metallic minerals (n=42, 10.9%), rubber and plastic (n=40, 10.4%), cellulose and paper (n=39, 10.2%), extraction of metallic minerals (n=28, 7, 3%), construction (n=28, 7.3%) and food (n=15, 3.9%).

Exploratory Factor Analysis (EFA)

EFA was carried out because the constructs analyzed had never been analyzed jointly in previous research. The empirical model was adapted from previous research (Jaworski & Kohli, 1993; Baker & Sinkula, 1999; Santoro, Messeni-Petruzzelli & del Giudice, 2020). EFA was analyzed based on the following indices: Cronbach's alpha, KMO (Kaiser-Meyer-Olkin), Bartlett's sphericity test, ETV (explained total variance), rotated component matrix (Varimax) and commonality.

Cronbach's alpha value was 0.854 (for 14 items); KMO equal to 0.843, with significance p <0.001 for Bartlett's sphericity test; the ETV was 63.98%, consisting of the items OP, OM, MT and ER; and, commonality reached values ≥ 0.5. Similarly, all factorial loads recorded values> 0.6, higher than the required minimum of 0.5 (Marôco, 2010).

Thus, the rates obtained by EFA are satisfactory (Hair et al., 2009), multivariate analysis can be continued.

Pearson's Correlation

Pearson's correlation (r) is associated with the existence (or not) of a relationship between two or more variables, which can vary between -1 to +1, the greater the intensity of the relationship, the closer the index will be to +1 (the reverse is also true) (HAIR et al., 2009). For Cohen (1992), the effect of Pearson's correlation may be small ($0.10 \leq r \leq 0.29$), moderate ($0.30 \leq r \leq 0.49$) or strong ($r \geq 0.5$).

Table 1. Pearson's correlation

Variables	Mean	SD	1	2	3	4	5	6	7	8	9
1. Gender	1.48	.50	1								
2. State	4.61	2.20	.014	1							
3. Size	1.22	.42	.010	.045	1						
4. Income	1.98	.90	-.091	-.051	.273**	1					
5. Sector	1.58	.49	.163**	.069	.062	-.005	1				
6. OM	11.00	2.62	-.018	-.128*	-.014	.037	-.073	1			
7. ER	11.63	2.29	-.063	-.097	-.002	-.049	-.006	.381**	1		
8. OP	18.05	3.93	.111*	-.169**	.070	-.079	-.097	.422**	.369**	1	
9. MT	11.68	2.25	-.015	-.082	-.059	-.110*	-.101*	.319**	.416**	.505**	1

Note: OM = Open-mindedness; ER = Entrepreneurial resilience; OP = Overall performance; MT = Market turbulence; SD = Standard deviation; p <0.01 **; p <0.05 *.
Source: Research data (2020)

The values in bold (Table 1) indicate variables with acceptable levels of significance ($p<0.01$** and $p<0.05$*). Regarding the correlation coefficient (r), it is noticed that the variables MT and OP correlate with a strong effect ($r\geq0.5$). In turn, the variables ER, OP and MT showed a medium effect ($0.3\leq r<0.5$) in relation to their respective variables. The items sector, income, OM, OP and MT indicate a small correlation effect ($r\leq0.29$) when analyzed in relation to the other variables.

Confirmatory Factor Analysis (CFA)

Initially, the normality of the data was verified using the asymmetry ($|sk|<3$) and kurtosis ($|ku|<10$) indices. Through the analysis of the factorial loads (loading>0.5), results of the AVE (Average Variance Extracted) and the CR (Composite Reliability) it was possible to confirm the convergente ($AVE\geq0.5$) and discriminant validity ($0.75\leq CR\leq0.84$; $0.67\leq$ Cronbach's alpha≤0.70). The CFA indicated adequate factorial loads (between 0.55 to 0.93).

The discriminant validity was achieved due to the results of the bold diagonal (Table 2) being superior to those of the respective line and column (Fornell & Larcker, 1981). For that, it was necessary to calculate the values of the square roots of the AVE and compare them to the results of the respective Pearson correlations of the constructs. Thus, the values of the square root of the AVE (diagonal in bold) were higher than those of the respective rows and columns (Fornell & Larcker, 1981).

Table 2. Mean, SD, Cronbach's alpha, AVE, CR and Pearson's correlation

Variables	Mean	SD	Cronbach's alpha	AVE	CR	1	2	3	4
1. OM	11.00	2.62	0.72	0.50	0.75	**0.71**			
2. ER	11.63	2.29	0.67	0.50	0.75	.381**	**0.71**		
3. OP	18.05	3.93	0.82	0.51	0.83	.422**	.369**	**0.71**	
4. MT	11.68	2.25	0.71	0.65	0.84	.319**	.416**	.505**	**0.80**
		Mean	0.73	0.54	0.79				

Note: OM=Open-mindedness; ER=Entrepreneurial resilience; OP=Overall performance; MT=Market turbulence; SD=standard deviation; AVE=Average Variance Extracted; CR=Composite Reliability; **p <0.01.
Source: Research data (2020)

The CFA indicated a good fit of the model ($\chi2 = 173.216$; gl = 65; p-value <0.001; $\chi2 / gl = 2.665$; CFI = 0.938; GFI = 0.941; IFI = 0.939; TLI = 0.914; AGFI = 0.905; and, RMSEA = 0.066) for a sample of 384 valid cases. For this, it was necessary to consult the MI (Modification Indices) of the statistical software AMOS® (Marôco, 2010).

Structural Equation Modeling (SEM)

SEM has been widely used to solve problems involving research in the social sciences. SEM is considered a multivariate data analysis technique (Hair et al., 2009) that brings together concepts of regression, factor analysis and path analysis (Vieira & Ribas, 2011; Hair et al., 2009). SEM has the purpose of evaluating statistical models, through tests of goodness of fit (Vieira & Ribas, 2011). Table 3 indicates good adjustment rates for the hypotheses, which corroborate with the theoretical review (Marôco, 2010).

The academic literature has not yet reached a consensus on SEM indicators (Marôco, 2010). Despite this, the researcher's challenge lies in the holistic interpretation of different adjustment measures (Bagozzi, 2011), since there is no "magic" index (Hair et al., 2009; Bagozzi, 2011). Model estimation was performed by ML (Maximum Likelihood), which requires normal data distribution, and is commonly used in SEM (Hair et al., 2009).

Table 3. Result of the adjustment of the tested models

Indexes	Reference*	H1a (OM→OP)	H1b (OM→ER)	H2 (ER→OP)	H3 (Mod.)	H4 (Med.)	H5 (Mod. and Med.)
$\chi 2$	The smaller the better	37.314	35.112	51.674	46.743	101.111	205.900
gl	The smaller the better	17	8	19	14	41	57
p-value	<0.001	0.003	<0.001	<0.001	<0.001	<0.001	<0.001
$\chi 2$/gl	< 5.0	2.195	4.389	2.720	3.339	2.466	3.612
CFI	≥ 0.9	0.980	0.947	0.966	0.985	0.955	0.951
GFI	≥ 0.9	0.977	0.970	0.968	0.971	0.956	0.926
IFI	≥ 0.9	0.980	0.948	0.966	0.985	0.955	0.951
TLI	≥ 0.9	0.967	0.901	0.950	0.969	0.939	0.933
AGFI	≥ 0.9	0.951	0.922	0.940	0.924	0.929	0.882
RMSEA	≥ 0.05 ≤ 0.08	0.056	0.094	0.067	0.078	0.062	0.083

Note: $\chi 2$=Chi-square; gl=degrees of freedom; p-value=significance; $\chi 2$/gl=Chi-square divided by degrees of freedom; CFI=Comparative Fit Index; GFI=Goodness of Fit Index; IFI=Incremental Fit Index; TLI=Tucker-Lewis Index; AGFI=Adjusted Goodness of Fit Index; RMSEA=Root Mean Square Error of Approximation; Mod.=Moderation; Med.=Mediation; *Reference values obtained based on the theoretical review.

Source: Research data (2020)

Hypothesis Testing

The hypotheses were tested with the help of statistical software IBM SPSS® and AMOS®. The indirect effects took into account the boostrapping by the macro process procedure. Macro process is a statistical tool used to calculate, based on linear regression and path analysis, results of indirect relationships, such as: mediation, moderation and/or moderated-mediation (Hayes, 2015).

Macro process can be applied to simple statistical models, involving only three variables, or to analyze complex relationships, with simultaneous mediators and moderators (Hayes, 2015). Initially, it was necessary to couple it to the IBM SPSS® statistical software. Following, the analysis patterns were defined: selection of the dependent and independent variable(s), choice of the model according to the mediating and/or moderating variable, boostrapping with 5,000 resamples, 95% CI, for a significance level of $p<0.005$, being applied for mediation and moderated together (H5).

The hypotheses H1a, H1b and H2, performed in isolation, were confirmed by the AMOS® software. The H2 hypothesis was confirmed by the strong relationship between ER→OP ($\beta=0.631$, t=6,800, $p<0.001$). Similarly, H1a was also accepted for indicating a strong effect between OM→OP ($\beta=0.529$, t=5.847, $p<0.001$). The H1b hypothesis was supported ($\beta=0.372$, t=4.540, $p<0.001$), although the effect between OM→ER was less intense.

The results of moderation (H3) and mediation (H4) were summarized in Figure 1. Panel A (Figure 1) indicates the result of MT moderation over OM→ER, which reinforces the acceptance of hypothesis H3 ($\beta=-0.09$, t=-3.280, $p<0.001$). Moderation is also confirmed by the macro process, making it possible to accept hypothesis H3 (Index=-0.006, BootSE=0.001, BootLLCI=-0.0085, BootULCI=-0.0030, $p<0.005$). This result is also validated by not changing the signs of the lower and upper limits of boostrapping.

Figure 1. Summary of isolated results from moderation and mediation
Note*: Continuous arrow represents the direct effect; Dashed arrow indicates indirect effect.*
Source: Research data (2020)

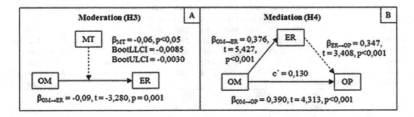

Panel B (Figure 1) suggests mediation of the ER variable on the OM→OP ratio, since the result of the coefficient c´=0.130 is less than the coefficient c ($\beta_{OM→OP}$ = 0.390) and all significant relationships for $p<0.05$. These results indicate mediation by the ER variable, making it possible to confirm hypothesis H4 (c´=0.130). The strength of the mediating variable ER was also confirmed by the macro process (H4: Index=0.093, BootSE=0.023, BootLLCI=0.0494, BootULCI=0.1395, p<0.005). In the case of the analysis of mediation by the macro process, one must consider that the sign of the lower and upper limit of the bootstrapping were positive, which qualifies the result.

Through the analysis of simultaneous mediation and moderation, it is possible to confirm H5 (Index=-0.003, BootSE=0.001, BootLLCI=-0.0052, BootULCI=-0.0007, p<0.005). The results prove RE as a mediating variable and TM with a moderating effect in the same model tested (H5). This finding is important for the administration area due to the complexity of the empirical relationships, the context of adverse research and the market turbulence scenario that demand an open-mindedness, entrepreneurial resilience and overall performance on the part of SME managers.

Analysis of Control Variables

Control variables were analyzed using hierarchical regression (Table 4). For this, three models were developed: **model 1** (only with the control variables); **model 2** (all variables in model 1 plus the OM and ER dimensions); **model 3** (all variables in model 2 plus moderation), using the dependent variable OP. Through the results, it is possible to infer significance (p<0.05) for all control variables, except for the result of the sector variable (model 3) that obtained p<0.1.

Table 4. Result of hierarchical regression

Dependent variable = OP	Model 1				Model 2				Model 3			
Variables	β	t	p	VIF	β	t	p	VIF	β	t	p	VIF
(Constant)		17.212				6.173				7.996	0.000	
Gender	0.136	2.686	0.008	1.057	0.159	3.566	0.000	1.065	0.156	3.743	0.000	1.065
State	-0.170	-3.423	0.001	1.012	-0.105	-2.401	0.017	1.031	-0.106	-2.58	0.010	1.031
Size	0.109	2.116	0.035	1.091	0.107	2.380	0.018	1.092	0.122	2.878	0.004	1.094
Income	-0.122	-2.34	0.020	1.110	-0.119	-2.616	0.009	1.117	-0.087	-2.029	0.043	1.129
Sector	-0.114	-2.278	0.023	1.036	-0.098	-2.224	0.027	1.042	-0.071	-1.708	0.089	1.050
OM					0.317	6.731	0.000	1.192	0.261	5.831	0.000	1.228
ER					0.251	5.33	0.000	1.192	0.151	3.264	0.001	1.306
Moderation (MT*OM→ER)									0.331	7.381	0.000	1.231
R^2		0.082				0.301				0.375		
ΔR^2						0.219				0.089		
F		5.592				58.687				54.479		

Note: β = Beta; S.E. = error; t = t statistic; p = significance; VIF = Variance Inflation Factor; R^2 = coefficient of determination; ΔR^2 = difference between the determination coefficients.

Source: Research data (2020)

Furthermore, it is noticed that, with the addition of the other variables, it is possible to verify an increase in the result of R^2, which suggests intermediate strength of models 2 and 3 ($0.3 < R^2 < 0.5$) (Cohen, 1992). The result of the hierarchical regression (Table 4) confirms the acceptance of hypotheses H1a ($\beta=0.317$, t=6.731, p<0.000), H2 ($\beta=0.251$, t=5.330, p<0.000) and H3 ($\beta=0.331$, t=7.381, p<0.000), being possible according to the variable TM as moderator.

CONCLUSION

The present study achieved the specific objectives of investigating the relationship of the mediating variable ER between the variables OM and OP; and, test the construct MT as a moderating variable on the relationship between OM and ER. The research findings confirm the hypotheses demonstrating the originality of the relationships. The uniqueness of the model is considered an advance for the administration area, as it attests to the mediating effect of ER and moderator of TM. In other words, entrepreneurial resilience is a mediating variable in the relationship between OM and OP; and, MT moderates the relationship on OM and ER.

In general, little has been done to test the double indirect effect through joint mediation and moderation. Vieira (2009) suggests that more research should analyze the indirect effects of mediation and moderation due to the low number of publications and, often, inconsistent results.

This research generates empirical contributions and practical implications for decision-making by managers working in SMEs located in the Legal Amazon. Managers must pay more attention to the variables investigated through the development of skills and competencies necessary to deal with entrepreneurial activity in adverse periods.

Future studies should test the relationships in another context. Scenarios similar to the one investigated are interesting, since they can generate even more robust implications. Analyzing the constructs from a new perspective by SME managers seems to be sensible, especially involving ethnic-racial differences (Cunningham & Mcguire, 2019), gender diversity (Tabassum et al., 2019) and performance of companies managed by ethnic-minorities (Hogan & Huerta, 2019). Asymmetric regions are more prone to unequal relations, especially in emerging countries (Eijdenberg et al., 2019).

The absence of public policies aimed at regions with fragilities can put the survival of SMEs at risk, negatively affecting the generation of employment and income of the population. The scarcity of credit lines for SMEs aggravates the establishment of companies located in areas with unequal competition. Given this scenario, it is necessary for organizational managers to have new mental models and resilience, in order to improve organizational performance. To this end, entrepreneurial education can be an alternative for the development of SME managers with an open mind and entrepreneurial resilience, especially in emerging countries.

ACKNOWLEDGMENT

To researchers from the research group GESCOM/UFPA (Strategy and Competitiveness in Organizations in the Amazon), PIBIC/UFPA scholarship holders and PPGAd/UFPA.

REFERENCES

Ahmad, B., Latif, S., Bilal, A. R., & Hai, M. (2019). The mediating role of career resilience on the relationship between career competency and career success: An empirical investigation. *Asia-Pacific Journal of Business Administration*, *11*(3), 209–231. doi:10.1108/APJBA-04-2019-0079

Akgün, A. E., & Keskin, H. (2014). Organisational resilience capacity and firm product innovativeness and performance. *International Journal of Production Research*, *52*(23), 6918–6937. doi:10.1080/00207543.2014.910624

Awotoye, Y., & Singh, R. (2017). Entrepreneurial Resilience, High Impact Challenges, and Firm Performance. *Journal of Management Policy and Practice*, *18*(2), 28–37.

Bagozzi, R. P. (2011). Measurement and meaning in information systems and organizational research: Methodological and philosophical foundations. *Management Information Systems Quarterly*, *35*(2), 261–292. doi:10.2307/23044044

Baker, W. E., & Sinkula, J. M. (1999). The Synergistic Effect of Market Orientation and Learning Orientation on Organizational Performance. *Journal of the Academy of Marketing Science*, *27*(4), 411–427. doi:10.1177/0092070399274002

Baron, R. M., & Kenny, D. A. (1986). The Moderator-Mediator Variable Distinction in Social Psychological Research: Conceptual, Strategic, and Statistical Considerations. *Journal of Personality and Social Psychology*, *51*(6), 1173–1182. doi:10.1037/0022-3514.51.6.1173 PMID:3806354

Blanco, V., Guisande, M. A., Sánchez, M. T., Otero, P., & Vázquez, F. L. (2019). Spanish validation of the 10-item Connor–Davidson Resilience Scale (CD-RISC 10) with non-professional caregivers. *Aging & Mental Health*, *23*(2), 183–188. doi:10.1080/13607863.2017.1399340 PMID:29116825

Branicki, L. J., Sullivan-Taylor, B., & Livschitz, S. R. (2018). How entrepreneurial resilience generates resilient SMEs. *International Journal of Entrepreneurial Behaviour & Research, 24*(7), 1244–1263. doi:10.1108/IJEBR-11-2016-0396

Bullough, A., Renko, M., & Myatt, T. (2014). Danger zone entrepreneurs: The importance of resilience and self-efficacy for entrepreneurial intentions. *Entrepreneurship Theory and Practice, 38*(3), 473–499. doi:10.1111/etap.12006

Busch, T. (2011). Organizational adaptation to disruptions in the natural environment: The case of climate change. *Scandinavian Journal of Management, 27*(4), 389–404. doi:10.1016/j.scaman.2010.12.010

Calantone, R. J., Cavusgil, S. T., & Zhao, Y. (2002). Learning orientation, firm innovation capability, and firm performance. *International Journal of Research in Marketing, 31*(6), 515–524.

Cavalcante, L. R. (2020). Abrangência geográfica das políticas de desenvolvimento regional no Brasil. *Revista Brasileira de Gestão e Desenvolvimento Regional, 16*(2), 407–420.

Cellini, R., & Cuccia, T. (2019). Do behaviours in cultural markets affect economic resilience? An analysis of Italian regions. *European Planning Studies, 27*(4), 784–801. doi:10.1080/09654313.2019.1568397

Cohen, J. (1992). Statistical power analysis. *Current Directions in Psychological Science, 1*(3), 98–101. doi:10.1111/1467-8721.ep10768783

Connor, K. M., & Davidson, J. R. T. (2003). Development of a new Resilience scale: The Connor-Davidson Resilience scale (CD-RISC). *Depression and Anxiety, 18*(2), 76–82. doi:10.1002/da.10113 PMID:12964174

Corner, P. D., Singh, S., & Pavlovich, K. (2017). Entrepreneurial resilience and venture failure. *International Small Business Journal: Researching Entrepreneurship, 35*(6), 687–708. doi:10.1177/0266242616685604

Cunningham, J., & Mcguire, D. (2019). Business support and training in minority-ethnic, family-run firms: The case of SMEs in Scotland. *Human Resource Development International, 22*(5), 526–552. doi:10.1080/13678868.2019.1608124

Dervitsiotis, K. (2003). The pursuit of sustainable business excellence: Guiding transformation for effective organizational change. *Total Quality Management & Business Excellence, 14*(3), 251–267. doi:10.1080/1478336032000046599

Duchek, S. (2018). Entrepreneurial resilience: A biographical analysis of successful entrepreneurs. *The International Entrepreneurship and Management Journal*, *14*(2), 429–455. doi:10.100711365-017-0467-2

Dukeov, I., Bergman, J. P., Heilmann, P., & Nasledov, A. (2020). Impact of a firm's commitment to learning and open-mindedness on its organizational innovation among Russian manufacturing firms. *Baltic Journal of Management*, *15*(4), 551–569. doi:10.1108/BJM-04-2019-0128

Eijdenberg, E. L., Thompson, N. A., Verduijn, K., & Essers, C. (2019). Entrepreneurial activities in a developing country: An institutional theory perspective. *International Journal of Entrepreneurial Behaviour & Research*, *25*(3), 414–432. doi:10.1108/IJEBR-12-2016-0418

Fornell, C., & Larcker, D. F. (1981). Evaluating Structural Equation Models with Unobservable Variables and Measurement Error. *JMR, Journal of Marketing Research*, *18*(1), 39–50. doi:10.1177/002224378101800104

Giannakis, E., & Bruggeman, A. (2017). Determinants of regional resilience to economic crisis: A European perspective. *European Planning Studies*, *25*(8), 1394–1415. doi:10.1080/09654313.2017.1319464

Hair, J. F., Black, W. C., Babin, B. J., Anderson, R. E., & Tatham, R. L. (2009). *Análise multivariada de dados. 6*. Bookman.

Hamel, G., & Välikangas, L. (2003). En busca de la resiliencia. *Harvard Business Review*, *81*(9), 40–52. PMID:12964393

Hayes, A. F. (2015). An Index and Test of Linear Moderated Mediation. *Multivariate Behavioral Research*, *50*(1), 1–22. doi:10.1080/00273171.2014.962683 PMID:26609740

Herbane, B. (2013). Exploring crisis management in uk small- and medium-sized enterprises. *Journal of Contingencies and Crisis Management*, *21*(2), 82–95. doi:10.1111/1468-5973.12006

Herbane, B. (2019). Rethinking organizational resilience and strategic renewal in SMEs. *Entrepreneurship and Regional Development*, *31*(5–6), 476–495. doi:10.1080/08985626.2018.1541594

Hogan, R., & Huerta, D. (2019). The impact of gender and ethnic diversity on REIT operating performance. *Managerial Finance*, *45*(1), 72–84. doi:10.1108/MF-02-2018-0064

IBGE. (n.d.). *Cidades e Estados*. Disponível em: www.ibge.gov.br

Jaworski, B. J., & Kohli, A. K. (1993). Market Orientation: Antrcendent and Consequances. *Journal of Marketing*, *57*(3), 53–70. doi:10.1177/002224299305700304

Kautish, S. (2008). Online Banking: A Paradigm Shift. E-Business. *ICFAI Publication, Hyderabad*, *9*(10), 54–59.

Kautish, S., & Thapliyal, M. P. (2012). Concept of Decision Support Systems in relation with Knowledge Management–Fundamentals, theories, frameworks and practices. *International Journal of Application or Innovation in Engineering & Management*, *1*(2), 9.

Kohli, A. K., & Jaworski, B. (1990). J. Market orientation: The construct, research propositions, and managerial implications. *Journal of Marketing*, *54*(2), 1–18. doi:10.1177/002224299005400201

Korber, S., & Mcnaughton, R. B. (2018). Resilience and entrepreneurship: A systematic literature review. *International Journal of Entrepreneurial Behaviour & Research*, *24*(7), 1129–1154. doi:10.1108/IJEBR-10-2016-0356

Lauridsen, L. S., Willert, M. V., Eskildsen, A., & Christiansen, D. H. (2017). Cross-cultural adaptation and validation of the Danish 10-item Connor-Davidson Resilience Scale among hospital staff. *Scandinavian Journal of Public Health*, *45*(6), 654–657. doi:10.1177/1403494817721056 PMID:28707513

Lee, N., Sameen, H., & Cowling, M. (2015). Access to finance for innovative SMEs since the financial crisis. *Research Policy*, *44*(2), 370–380. doi:10.1016/j.respol.2014.09.008

Lee, T.-S., & Tsai, H.-J. (2005). The effects of business operation mode on market orientation, learning orientation and innovativeness. *Industrial Management & Data Systems*, *105*(3), 325–348. doi:10.1108/02635570510590147

Marôco, J. (2010). *Análise de Equações Estruturais: Fundamentos teóricos, Software & Aplicações*. ReportNumber.

Pérez-López, M. C., González-López, M. J., & Rodríguez-Ariza, L. (2016). Competencies for entrepreneurship as a career option in a challenging employment environment. *Career Development International*, *21*(3), 214–229. doi:10.1108/CDI-07-2015-0102

Portal da Indústria. (n.d.). *Perfil da indústria nos estados*. Disponível em: www.portaldaindustria.com.br

Powell, T. C. (1995). Total quality management as competitive advantage: A review and empirical study. *Strategic Management Journal, 16*(1), 15–37. doi:10.1002mj.4250160105

Preacher, K. J., & Hayes, A. F. (2004). SPSS and SAS procedures for estimating indirect effects in simple mediation models. *Behavior Research Methods, Instruments, & Computers, 36*(4), 717–731. doi:10.3758/BF03206553 PMID:15641418

Preacher, K. J., Rucker, D. D., & Hayes, A. F. (2007). Addressing moderated mediation hypotheses: Theory, methods, and prescriptions. *Multivariate Behavioral Research, 42*(1), 185–227. doi:10.1080/00273170701341316 PMID:26821081

Rahman, M., & Mendy, J. (2019). Evaluating people-related resilience and non-resilience barriers of SMEs' internationalisation: A developing country perspective. *The International Journal of Organizational Analysis, 27*(2), 225–240. doi:10.1108/IJOA-02-2018-1361

Salisu, I., Hashim, N., Mashi, M. S., & Aliyu, H. G. (2020). Perseverance of effort and consistency of interest for entrepreneurial career success: Does resilience matter? *Journal of Entrepreneurship in Emerging Economies, 12*(2), 279–304. doi:10.1108/JEEE-02-2019-0025

Santoro, G., Messeni-Petruzzelli, A., & Del Giudice, M. (2020). Searching for resilience: The impact of employee-level and entrepreneur-level resilience on firm performance in small family firms. *Small Business Economics*, 1–17. doi:10.100711187-020-00319-x

Santos-Vijande, M. L., & Álvarez-González, L. I. (2007). Innovativeness and organizational innovation in total quality oriented firms: The moderating role of market turbulence. *Technovation, 27*(9), 514–532. doi:10.1016/j.technovation.2007.05.014

Senge, P. (2006). *Peter Senge the Fifth Discipline*. Doubleday Currency.

Senge, P. M. (1992). Mental models. Planning Review, 20(2), 4–44.

Sinkula, J. M., Baker, W. E., & Noordewier, T. (1997). A framework for market-based organizational learning: Linking values, knowledge, and behavior. *Journal of the Academy of Marketing Science, 25*(4), 305–318. doi:10.1177/0092070397254003

Skole, D., & Tucker, C. (1993). Tropical deforestation and habitat fragmentation in the Amazon: Satellite data from 1978 to 1988. *Science, 260*(21), 1905–1910. doi:10.1126cience.260.5116.1905 PMID:17836720

Tabassum, N., Shafique, S., Konstantopoulou, A., & Arslan, A. (2019). Antecedents of women managers' resilience: Conceptual discussion and implications for HRM. *The International Journal of Organizational Analysis*, 27(2), 241–268. doi:10.1108/IJOA-07-2018-1476

Vieira, P. R. (2011). *Análise Multivariada com uso do SPSS*. Ciência Moderna Ltda.

Vieira, V. A. (2009). Moderação, mediação, moderadora-mediadora e efeitos indiretos em modelagem de equações estruturais: uma aplicação no modelo de desconfirmação de expectativas. Revista de Administração - RAUSP, 44(1), 17–33.

Chapter 5
Strategic Analytics Augmented Organization:
Fueling the Business Value and Growth

Samir Yerpude
Symbiosis Centre of Innovation and Research, Symbiosis International University (Deemed), India

ABSTRACT

Business strategy is all the actions and decisions taken by the management to achieve the business goals for sustaining the competitive edge. A successful business strategy determines the longevity of the organization. The strategists analyse the vision, mission, and values to frame and articulate the business strategy. Different tools such a Business Model Canvas, etc. are then used to create the business model. Once the business strategy is created, it is also equally critical to evaluate the same amidst the changing business environment. For the validation of strategies at all levels, data plays a vital role for the management to proceed with fact-based decision making. Informed decisions based on facts reduce the probability of erroneous results assisting the businesses align to the documented strategy. Strategic analytics practice creates the essential understanding about how the quantitative techniques and methods can be deployed using the structured and unstructured data that assists strategic decision making for the organization.

DOI: 10.4018/978-1-7998-7716-5.ch005

INTRODUCTION

For developing a business strategy, the organizations should apparently be clear about what does the organization exist for and what it wants to achieve. The clarity is achieved when the organizations formulate their vision, mission and values. Vision fundamentally covers what the organization wishes to achieve in the future. Horizon is defined by the management for example 5 year or 10 years. Mission covers the core purpose of the organization and how it will benefit mankind while value encompasses the basic principles that will be followed to achieve the stated mission and vision. The strategists analyse the vision, mission and values to frame and articulate the business strategy. Different tools such a Business Model Canvas etc. are then used to create the business model.

Business Model Canvas offers a template to the management to create or even evaluate an existing business model aligned to the business strategy. There are nine segments in the template which include the following:

1. Key Partners:
   a. Who are the key partners/suppliers of the organization
   b. What are the motivations of the partnerships
2. Key Activities:
   a. What are the key activities required for creating the value proposition
   b. What are the important activities in the different segments of the BMC
3. Value Proposition
   a. What is the unique selling proposition offered to the customers
   b. What are the customer needs that are satisfied by the organization
4. Customer Relationship
   a. What type of relationships are desired by the customers from the organization
   b. What are ways to integrate the same in business
5. Customer Segment
   a. Define the customer segments for whom the value needs to be created
   b. Who are the critical customers
6. Key Resources
   a. What are the key resource requirements to meet the value propositions
   b. What are the important resources in the different segments of the BMC
7. Distribution Channel
   a. What are channels through which the organization will reach the customers
   b. Which channels work best and how much do they cost

8. Cost Structure
    a. What are the different costs connected to business
    b. Which are the most expensive key resources / activities
9. Revenue
    a. What are the different revenue streams and their contributions
    b. What are the values for which the customers ready to pay

Figure 1 indicates the Business Model Canvas template.

Figure 1. Business Model Canvas

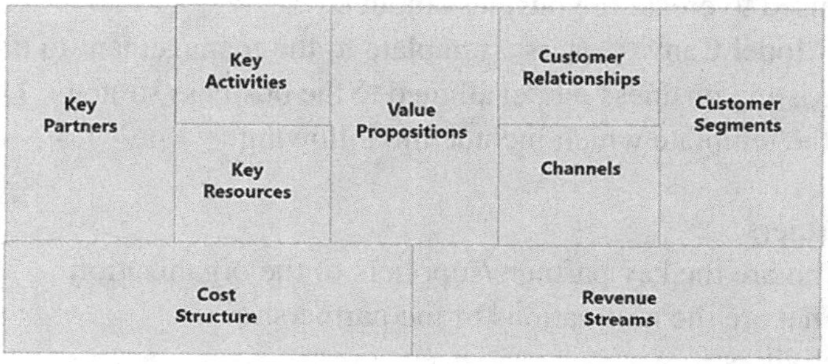

Once the business strategy is created, it is also equally critical to evaluate the same amidst the changing business environment. The evaluation primarily addresses a couple of most important questions. Is the documented strategy successful or failing? Will the strategy help the organization meet the targeted goals? And finally does the business strategy help achieve and align to the vision, mission and values. The strategies generally are created at three levels such as strategic (strategy), tactical (business) & operational (functional). Firms exist to do business and ensure that profits are generated from the same. For the validation of strategies at all levels data plays a vital role for the management to proceed with fact based decision making. Informed decisions based on facts reduce the probability of erroneous results assisting the businesses align to the documented strategy. There is enormous data getting generated today from the social platforms, finance management systems, customer relationship management systems augmented with internal and external sources to the organization. Managers are exposed to continual crisis and turbulence due to the variability in the market scenarios. There are significant trends and causal relationships that are hidden in the data that have to be unearthed. Management integrate the analytics with the strategic management process. The challenge faced by managers is the management of this humongous data and derive the right insights for deciding on the actions to be taken. Organizations have to deploy powerful quantitative techniques and models for executing management by exceptions.

Strategic planning includes the identification of problems in the current business model and further envisaging the emerging problems basis the trends before the competition. Although business have not been able to yet decide on a clear demarcation between the two or what precedes, but it definitely defines the future of the organization. Businesses collate data from all the sources stated earlier i.e. financial management system, customer relationship management and construct complex business models to validate the strategies. There is a simple logic followed in strategic analytics which determines how the qualitative and quantitative data can be used to make strategic decisions. Strategic analytics should not be misunderstood as an additional job for the managers for whom the pre-requisite would be to be a data scientist with skills in quantitative techniques including statistics. Rather the prime activity of the management should be to create teams which are subject matter experts in their domain but able to converse in a common language understood by all. Strategic Analytics practice creates the essential understanding about how the quantitative techniques and methods can be deployed using the structured and unstructured data that assists strategic decision making for the organization. It assists in determining the distinctive strategies in the market that wins customers for the organization. Strategic analytics is sometimes used interchangeably with Business Analytics. While they are related but yet distinct in execution. Business Analytics deals with the usage of statistical techniques with continuous iterations and explorations of past business performance data to execute data driven business and business planning changes.

Strategic Analytics offers different alternatives to solve the business problems and not just an easy or fixed solution. The alternatives offered are entirely different than the traditional ways of using qualitative techniques to solve business problems. Future managers need to develop the skills of interpreting the dashboards and develop insights basis the trends etc. The requirement emerges from the fact that the managers get exposed to problems which are not structured in nature at a strategic or a tactical level. The problems practically get complex with drastic changes in the market scenarios and volatile customer demands. Typically for the organization, there are four fundamental steps when they intend to use analytics. The first step includes data gathering and collation from different and varied sources. Since the data is collated from discrete sources, there could be a fair mix of structured as well as unstructured data. Analysts have to perform tasks on the data in order to transform the same into a form that can be fed for analysis. The second step encompasses the analysis of the data with the help of different techniques and models. We will be discussing these techniques at greater depth is the chapter. The second step offers different alternative and analysis of the data collated. Deriving insights from the analysis with the help of data visualization techniques augmented with predictive analytics to foresee and envisage the future is a part of third step. The final and fourth step is all about converting the insights into actions that are related to all the aspects of management may it be strategic, tactical or operational. The current chapter would encompass the following:

1. Understanding of Business Strategy
2. Data Categories and Sources
3. Different types of Data Analytics
4. Strategy Analytics
5. Case Studies
6. Conclusion

Usage of strategic analytics is not limited to any particular sector or industry but there are case studies which are widespread and created turnaround stories for organizations globally. We shall analyse the same during the study.

Understanding of Business Strategy

The businesses have to develop a strategy by virtue of which the value offered to the customers is more than that of competition in order to survive in the market. Organizations have to look past the traditional processes, modernize them, and use sophisticated systems to ensure that the right data gets captured. Strategies that deliver unique values to the customer create the competitive edge, contributing to the growth of the organization in terms of worth and market presence. Which implies that strategies are created to ensure maximum satisfaction of the customers helping the organization retain them. Differentiation is offered by the strategy which provokes the customer to prefer a particular brand over its competitors. The value derived by the customer is to some extent subjective as different customer appreciate and take different positions for the product and their willingness to pay for the same. Thus we can state here that value has two parts (Özemre & Kabadurmus, 2020):

1. The internal value creation which is a result of the business processes followed to produce the product or service.
2. The external value as perceived by the customer due to which there is a willingness to pay for the product or service.

Having identified and understood the difference in the value, it is equally critical then to segment the customer who have similar perceptions of value. This enables organizations to focus and target the different segments with products matching their tastes. This is a very important activity and termed as "Segmentation". This activity further adds a capability to the organization of comparing the competing products in a particular segment. The process encompasses:

1. Variable identification for Segmentation: This requires a thorough study of the customers in the market wherein variables are to be identified that characterize the customers of a particular value. Customers can be identified as per their requirements of size, or geographic location, styles or culture. Second segment could be basis the complexity of technology and others such as price, design features, performance. Some other variables include occasions of purchase, cultural and social influencers. Two facets particularly looked at include substitution or correlation which decide the strategy for the segments.
2. Mapping of segments in the Markets: Post the first step, the segments in the market can be created and they have to be mapped with the market. Special terms and conveniences are added for each of the customer segments as applicable.
3. Evaluation of the Value adds: The evaluation of the segments is critical at a strategic level as profitability is the most important objective and reported to the stakeholders too. Substitutes and Correlation need careful analysis here. Substitutes are the consumer deployed products in different segments without any modification, while correlation are products or services where the variables or dimensions are strongly related.
4. Identification of segments to compete: The decision is taken basis various facets of business. The dimensions or the output of the decision could be whether the organization would compete only in one segment or multiple segments basis the strategy and analysis performed earlier. Other variables such as business processes similarity, resource sharing, channel partners and economies of scope etc. do play a vital role in this decision.

In the year 1998, Porter documented the two dimensions of value for the customers. These primarily branch out at a cost level or the differentiation offered to the customer. This can be depicted very clearly with the help of Figure 2 (Islami, Mustafa & Latkovikj, 2020; Tanwar, 2013; Porter & Advantage, 1985).

The focus of all the strategies is to contribute in the value generation process for the customers. There are a number of methods and frameworks available for the identification and formulation of processes that contribute towards the customer value generation. There was a mention earlier in the chapter about Business Model Canvas which is a very strong tool for the purpose of identification of activities for value generation. The others include Value Chain framework and Activity System Map. These framework are used by different organizations for the set purpose as it aids the formulation of the specific models for the business processes.

Figure 2. Market Strategies for segments

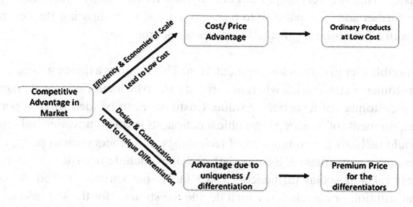

Cost Advantage Strategy: This strategy simply means provisioning of the products for the customer at a lesser price than the competition. It is very important for the organization to closely study each and every cost associated with the activities performed on the product. There is a clear focus of the businesses to try and reduce the cost associated with every activity so that the product can be offered at a lower cost. The drivers of cost are explicitly spelt out so that they can be monitored closely. The process includes the identification of activities that are responsible to generate value. Assignment of each activity with the cost and the resource involved. There could be two approaches adopted here. Either the organization has a better control than the competition on the associated costs or the processes are reengineered and re-configured more efficiently as compared to the competitors. There are a number of cost drivers defined such as:

1. Economies of scale
2. Learning/experience reducing cost
3. Capacity utilization
4. Activity linked interrelations between business &
5. Timing to ensure cost benefits and strategic choices.

Differentiation Strategy: This strategy includes creation of a unique selling proposition in the market which is critical for the organization. The parameters related to customer satisfaction are studied and the processes are aligned to achieve the dimensions that are vital to achieve the same. The differentiation can be created in the product or the marketing strategies which are identifiable to the customers. This approach allows the organizations to price the product at a level that can be higher than the competition. Customer requirements are maintained at the centre of the innovation drive identifying the key activities that deliver them. Customer identification along with understanding of customer behaviour formulates the first step so as to evaluate the products to be offered. Another critical consideration is the cost of creating the differentiation for the customer and generate value for the organization. The balance is maintained by performing some activities at low cost while funds are invested in creating the differentiation for the customer. The differentiation drivers can be listed as strategic choices

1. Strategic choices of Technology, service level, product configurations, quality etc.
2. External linkages of complex products and services
3. Locations that offer uniqueness to customers
4. Customer experience and associated learnings that assist the organization in offering the differentiation to customers
5. External Integrations
6. Economies of scale to produce a product at a scale
7. Understanding how the customer perceives the differentiation in product

Blue Ocean Strategy: Exploring completely new markets or avenues for the products which are completely uncontested by competitors instead of getting into an existing competition is encompassed in this strategy. Usually business tools like business model canvas or a strategy canvas is used to represent this strategy and the parameters or elements incorporated. Tools like strategy canvas facilitate the comparison of competitors on the same plane. This strategy also includes considering completely new segments of customers who do not consider the current products or the competition. There are new market boundary conditions defined to reach the customers who are not approached by the organization until then. The strategy defines new products, new customers, new markets and new value propositions. The associated tools along with the blue ocean strategy form an effective combination with business model canvas forming an exhaustive tool set to determine the strategies.

Data Categories and Sources

Data analytics profoundly covers quite a few different types of data analysis. The improvements in an organization are planned basis the insights generated with the help of information derived from the data collected. Data analytics has a much wider scope than just pointing towards the anomalies but also deriving the alternative solutions to the business problems. The major steps involved in data analytics include the following (Hindle & Vidgen, 2018):

1. The first steps involves identification of the business context and measurable objectives. This helps in validating the data requirements and the levels at which it will be needed. The data is humongous in itself and needs some kind of aggregation which could be done at different levels. For example in case of customers, it could be aggregated by age, demographics, sex, income level etc. to form clusters or segments.

2. Second step is determining the data collection process. The different processes of data collection could be bifurcated into online and offline methods. The online method involves usage of tools such as surveys, questionnaires etc. while offline is carried out by individuals with the help of physical tools and relevant scales.

3. For the organizations to analyse the data that is collected, it is extremely important to organize the data. Different software's are available to perform this task quite efficiently so that the data can be analysed effectively.

4. Data cleansing is the next vital step before analysis. This step ensures the completeness of data and also curbing of the anomalies recorded. Deduplication is carried out with removal of data outliers to maintain the sanctity of data. Also the data is validated for data sanity and corrected wherever required.

5. Post the above steps, there are different techniques that are deployed to analyse the collated data to generate the business insights.

Data collection is an important activity for an organization so that analytics can be performed to build strategic, tactical as well as operational dashboards that offer insights to business. Profoundly the data is an unanalysed, unrelated, unorganized raw entity. Adding the time dimension along with the context and reference transforms it into information. This information augmented with the experience and association with similar findings converts it into knowledge. Applying the knowledge offers wisdom or insights to the managers to take fact based decisions. The data collected is fundamentally of two categories (Yerpude & Singhal, 2017):

1. Qualitative
2. Quantitative

The qualitative data is a non- numeric type of data while quantitative data set is numeric data which can be used in the analytical models. Quantitative data can be measured directly while qualitative data cannot be counted. Both these categories are equally important in deriving meaningful analytics. The different data sources for the quantitative data include structured surveys using liner scales or ratings scale. The other sources include data captured with the help of digital technologies such as Internet of Things etc. This data is extremely important as it is used in determining the strategic directions with the help of analytical models build around the corporate objectives. Other data sources for the organization include the data collated from portals. This data is critical for the organization as it assists in capturing the customer behavioural and attitudinal data. With the help of the click data the organization portal is able to create customer segments for offering personalization. Globalization has influenced customer largely. Customers are constantly looking for personalized services that adds to customer satisfaction. Customer retention is directly proportional to the customer satisfaction derived by the customer. Among the other tools includes survey which aids business collate the customer view point. Surveys could be structured, semi-structured or unstructured. Data collated through surveys is critical as the intent is known to the respondent and feedback is with a context from the customers (Kudyba, 2014).

On the other hand qualitative data is conceptual and descriptive in nature. The data source for qualitative data includes questionnaires, interviews or observations. The collation of data is usually in narrative form. The analysis is conducted using the text mining techniques to draw inferences from this data gathered. Key words are registered and opinions or inferences are drawn. Especially in the social media world today, the social media expressions (SME) play a vital role in conducting sentiment analysis and social listening. A brand with the help of web pages successfully collects the customer emotions and sentiments. There are a significant number of tools that analyse these sentiments and publish meaningful dashboards for the organization. Another technique involves web crawlers that are deployed to gather the text around the brand and action based strategies are created. Tools like personal interviews and focussed group discussion too generate significant amount of textual data. Generally interviews are recorded and techniques such as voice analytics are used to get the relevant insights from the respondents.

While we have analysed the data categories and the major sources, it is critical to understand the usage of this data. A structured approach is followed for conducted the data analytics to convert the collated data into relevant insights that help business in taking fact based decisions to organizational problems. Let's study the different type of data analytics to validate the use of data further.

Different Types of Data Analytics

The contemporary organizations are largely data driven. What it essentially means is that the organization are using analytics extensive as there is huge amount of data which is getting generated in every transaction and through various other sources. Analytics allows the organizations to implement strategies for the different insights that are generated with the help of data analytics and compete effectively. Data analytics gives the competitive edge to the organization in terms of understanding the customer and personalizing the customer needs. Simplest of the forms of data analytics is to use descriptive statistics, but it is limited to the extent of data collated. It does not offer the foresightedness to the organization. In the current era it is essential for the businesses to know the environment much better in terms of future trends, predict customer behaviours and accordingly adjust the business operations. The usage of data analytics allows organizations to operate differently and mitigate the future market risks. While we state the benefits of using data analytics, it is equally important that there is a complete change in the organization strategy to embrace the data and bring about a cultural change to take data driven decisions. It's a major change in the organization culture and requires a strong change management. With data analytics, the data generated and collated becomes one of the key assets for the organization assisting data driven decisions. The data or business analytics essentially consists of three key components:

1. Competencies and capabilities of humans involved
2. Business processes that drive the organization
3. Technology or Information system required to operate.

Necessarily it means that all the three aspects i.e. people, processes and technology are critical and have equal weightage in the business analytics. Business or Strategic analytics fundamentally is an amalgamation of statistics, information systems and management science. It is about acquisition, generation, assimilation and presenting the data in a way that the insights generated can be used in decision making. There are three traditional types of analytics depicted by experts (Williams, 2011; Davenport & Dyché, 2013):

1. Descriptive Analytics: Organization internal as well as external data is collated and statistically processed to represent it in an actionable format. It fundamentally addresses the need to study the past performance of the business in order to assess the current performance. Scientific explorations are carried out on the data to further deep dive into the reasons behind the results. Data mining techniques are deployed with dashboards delivered on the business intelligence layers. These allow cascading from the aggregated data to the details for analysing the results further. Businesses define the key performance indicators to track the defined strategies. For example a metric such as return on investment is used by many industries to track the utilization of the investments made. Descriptive analytics allows the organizations to track the metrics along with reasons for the achieved results.

2. Predictive Analytics: It fundamentally facilitates business to uncover and predict the future trends and events basis the past events and data captured. There is

a significant usage of statistical and mathematical techniques to predict the future for the organizations. Neural networks, decision trees, text analytics, causal or regression analysis, trend analysis or time series forecasting method, are some of the commonly used techniques. Predictive Analytics provides valuable insights to business in terms of the future predictions for gearing up against the eventualities. The forecasting models created over the years have matured with the help of data and learnings from the same. The accuracy of the forecast generated is quite reliable and can be used as a guideline by the organizations. This type of analytics also relies on the machine learning algorithms that help identify the data trends while the volume, variety and velocity of data is continuously increasing.

3. Prescriptive Analytics: This is a very unique capability of analytics which fundamentally assesses the alternatives that are recorded and simulates the best alternative along with the optimization possible. Organizations deploy the prescription analytics in all the domain of business such as finance, operations, sales and marketing as well as logistics. Prescriptive analytics is able to generate answers to business problems or dilemmas prevailing primarily due to the uncertainties. It assists the data driven decisions which are essentially informed decisions. Analytics proves to be the best option as any action taken basis the data reflects further on the data pattern for analysis and corrective actions.

Strategy Analytics (Kunc, 2018)

While we discuss on the analytics, it is important to understand that currently businesses have two types of data. One which is collected traditionally from the different interactions and transactions with the customers and environment. Second type of data is the digital data stream flowing in from different digital sources. The digital data can be structured as well as unstructured and most of it being received without the businesses having much control over it. One of the issues which influences the analytics is the availability of specified data and the time period when it was required. The strategies get impacted with the data and the knowledge (Kautish, 2008, Kautish & Thapliyal, 2012) derived from the same. On the other hand the digital data streams create new business opportunities or new avenues in the existing business to generate revenue. But care needs to be exercised due to the velocity of data changes. Analytics helps in generating the business insights for data driven decision making, while statistics and management science power the generation of insights. Management science specifically plays a significant role in the strategy making and encompasses the following major constructs:

1. Domain expertise: Knowledge with regards to specific fields or domain in particular specific areas is generated by management science. This knowledge assists in developing deeper understanding of the data collected and the probable bearing of the same on the performance of the organization.

2. Strategy recommendation: With the domain knowledge existing as a part of the management science assists in formulating and recommending different strategies. These strategies are very useful for corporates as it links the data collected and the domain knowledge along with the future predictions.

3. Role play: Management science plays multiple roles in the data analytics journey. The different roles enacted are of a strategic advisor or of an analyst. In the strategic advisor role it is critical to understand and translate the requirement from the decision makers. In the analyst role management science enables the validation of values and improve the quality of decisions. It fundamentally eradicates the different types of biases and limitations which get introduced in the process.

4. Democratizing the decisions: Businesses have objectives for the stakeholders which are ethical in nature. Typically in practical scenarios there are situations where the decisions are overpowered. The decisions that are influenced may or may not be in the best interests of the organization. Analysts and scientists practicing management science support the views and suggestions that are overpowered.

It is important to convert the strategic problem into an analytical model. Once the model is created the next stage is to identify the data requirements clearly laying down the underlying assumptions. The structure of the model and the assumptions can be validated. The output of the model imitates the existing and the future performance of the strategic problem. The model is never the only solution but it exists as a part of multiple models which triangulate and publish the results. The organizations are challenged with the model creation when the strategic problems are not defined appropriately or the parameters are not quantifiable.

For such cases business refer to the qualitative methods of analysis. Causal loop analysis, cognitive mapping, scenario analysis, decision trees, analytic hierarchy process etc. are some of the major qualitative methods used in management science. While statistics, probabilistic, Monte Carlo etc. are some major quantitative methods to calculate the one attribute in management science. In case of one attribute calculation there are two broad types: deterministic and stochastic. In case of deterministic methods there is a simple analysis of one attribute with reference to all other parameters considered. For example, profit can be attributed to the efficiency of different processes and units. Stochastic methods go ahead with the postulation that there are no single values but a range of values and the method chosen depends upon the purpose. The method apart from the one parameter determination includes a replication method or method to replicate. These methods assist in comprehending the past behaviour of the model or system along with current and future behaviour basis the models and their interactions. The major quantitative methods used in replication encompass discrete event simulation, system dynamics or agent based simulation. Third method is termed as the optimization method, wherein the objective includes finding the best alternative from the solutions. These models fundamentally contain two components. The first component is the objective function which is nothing but a set of decision variables whose optimal solution needs to be derived. The other component consists of the constraints that limit the values of the decision variables. There are two major types of optimization methods: deterministic and stochastic. Having understood management science, we also need to understand the strategic management as a part of strategic analytics (Rooyen, 2005; Pröllochs & Feuerriegel, 2020).

Strategic Management

Strategic Management is primarily a progressive process in which the strategies are developed with a sequence of suggestions or offers and a variety of processes. Building strategy is an important part of business as they are built for future considering all the uncertainties considering all the risks in the plans. Planning, creation, evaluation are the essential steps of strategy management, but the critical one includes the change management on ground. Implementation of the strategy involves multiple interactions between the people, process and technology. Further implementation of the strategy is mostly unidirectional with internal and external processes aligned to the strategy. To reverse an implemented strategy, it is at times impossible since there are many elements which are modified during the change management that are irreversible. Strategic management is a framework which is conceptual and can be used by the decision makers for creating strategies. Once implemented there is a performance framework created to monitor the success of the strategy over time. The feedback is carefully gathered and put to action by the managers to improve upon the strategy implemented. The problems arising out of a strategy implemented are long term and strategic in nature that require to be addressed. Operational issues, complexity, significant time lag, and irreversible effects are some of the major problems reported (Grover et al., 2018).

Implementation of Strategic analytics includes the pure play integration of management science and strategic management. With strategic analytics implemented, businesses capitalize on the qualitative and quantitative data to take strategic decisions. It definitely does not mean that the managers are expected to be statisticians or quantitative data scientist. In strategic analytics there are no easy answers to the strategic problems but it offers a variety of alternatives and reasonable justifications to select the right alternatives. The aim is to amalgamate the strategic concepts with the analytics tools for enabling managers with the proficiency to solve strategic issues. There are certain prerequisites for an organization before conducting the strategic analytics. It is important to relate the strategic analytics to the performance scorecards and targets which business wishes to achieve. Second important aspect is to validate the data sources along with its consistency and reliability. The analyst need to know the importance of qualitative data and the methods to analyse the same as it is equally important in strategic analytics. Building the causal model and gaining insights at each stage until maturity probably would be the last step before applying strategic analytics for decision making. Understanding of causal methods is significantly critical for the organization as it points towards the change in process improvement tools such as six sigma or lean etc. Once these pre-requisites are met, organizations have to ascertain the structural issues as these are critical in strategy implementation.

- Appropriate delegation of authorities to take decision including cross functional functions.
- The needs of the organization not met by the delegated authorities.
- The culture of the organization needs to be evaluated for the change management that strategic analytics will bring in.

Post these structural issues are addressed the possibility of successful implementation of strategic analytics get higher. Let understand the major steps in the strategic analytics implementation (Levenson, 2015):

1. Analytics to diagnose the competitive advantage: From a couple of decades organizations have realized the advantages of having data and performing analytics. This analytics is typically targeted towards exploring the customer data to offer more than the competitors and gain competitive advantage. Data enabled learning creates an unmatched knowledge within the organization. It helps builds the competitive defence for the different activities to be conducted in the market. Analytics also assists organizations with building of a strategy that creates entry barriers for new entrants in the market. All the activities that create a competitive advantage are in focus. The organization strength and weaknesses are evaluated along with the opportunities and threats prevailing. Next step includes building of the causal model that establishes the different relationships. Post this the relevant stakeholders are aligned to meet the designed objectives of the analysis. The care that needs to be exercised during this activity

is to ensure that while individual function level objectives are discussed, the sight of the strategic objective is not lost.

2. Analytics to analyse the enterprise: Enterprise and the dynamics prevailing have a significant impact on the roll out of a strategy. As discussed in the previous step the causal relationships are formed between the different parameters. These causal relationships are validated at various stages in the enterprise. Management science is required extensively for this validation and analytics to come up with the right alternatives. The different stages could be at an organization level, or a business unit level or possibly at a business process level. During this stage the assessment is carried out to diagnose with the help of analytics whether the organization is falling short in meeting the strategic objectives that were outlined.

3. Analytics to analyse the Human Capital: This is one of the critical steps as the strategies have to be rolled out by the individuals. Human capital is important and needs to be aligned to the strategic objectives of an organization. All the individuals working for an organization are fundamentally working basis the roles assigned to them. The analytics at this stage is advanced which means significant amount of data is analysed at this stage. Most importantly the right questions need to be asked and the right data sets need to be made available to generate the insights. The business and people issues need to be tied together to achieve the common objective. This stage also assesses whether the people who are the decision makers have the right set of insights to look at. Further it also validates the skillset possessed by these individual and its fitness to the role assigned. If not then strategic analytics helps and enables the corrections in the system along with the changes.

Strategic analytics in the contemporary organizations has become a norm where management science and strategic management integrate. The analytics and strategies are dependent on each other while the analytics objectives are dependent on the organizational strategy. Each of the functions in the organizations are supported by the analytics insights cascaded and integrated with all the functions (Vahdati, Nejad, & Shahsiah, 2018).

CASE STUDIES

Contemporary organizations possess significant amount of data from all the functions and transactions. The data has not just grown in volume but also in terms of the variety, veracity, and diversity. The richness in the quality of data has exhibited tremendous growth over the years making it simple for the management science. We discussed about the analytics which consumes the data collated. Most of the large contemporary organizations have implemented digital technologies to gather real time data from the different customer transactions. Technologies such as Internet of Things in conjunction works decently for data collection. Machine Learning algorithms have improved constantly. The physical world has come closer to the virtual world. There are opportunities which are capitalized by the firms during the complete customer journey and basis the strategy outlined consumed in analytics to generate insights for decision making. Different industries track the data differently and align the same to the corporate strategy. Organizations execute descriptive, predictive and prescriptive analytics aligning the management science and strategy management to empower the decision makers with strategic analytics. In this section we shall be deliberating on the use cases of strategic analytics to validate the impact of the same on the organization (Akter et al., 2016; Morabito, 2015).

Use Case #1

Business strategy: Growth and expansion strategy was adopted by Amazon deploying the innovations in Information Technology simultaneously delivering customer experience.

Personalization (Godin, 2018): It can be simply be stated as analytics basis the log captured. Business are keen to monitor and design the business processes for the customers on the portals for a personalized experience. The portal is architected such that every click made by the customer and sections viewed are recorded in a separate database. This data is very useful to capture the behavioural and attitudinal information of the customer. This data is collected, processed and analysed to personalize the product offerings. The personalization encompasses the core product, associated merchandize, allied products and services that add value to the customer. The recommendation engines captures the data and basis the past orders, recommends the other products that the customer can buy (Nelson, 2019). The organization that one can look at is Amazon. The business strategy of growth, customer retention etc. was clearly laid out and linked to the strategic analytics. Management science contributed with the domain knowledge of retail business. The individual customer locations were tracked to map them with the nearest retail outlet to optimize the transportation costs. Amazon further collects the user time spent on pages and helps recommend similar category of products increasing the opportunities of cross sell and up sell. Amazon uses the collected data in different types. With collaborative filtering which is a subset of personalization, they have been able to achieve descent numbers in up sell. With the complete view of the customer such as wallet share, address, products bought etc. Amazon is able to fairly predict what products and customers can be nudged for sales. With strategic analytics deployed using big data following were the benefits derived:

1. Better understanding of the market with descriptive and predictive analytics
2. Increased satisfaction amongst the customers with the personalization offers
3. Improvement in sales revenues
4. Optimization of costs
5. Reduction in lead time
6. Opportunities for cross sell and up sell
7. Alternate revenue streams

In the year 2007, the count of employees working for amazon for about 17 thousand, which by 2020 has risen to 5.7 plus lac employees. The annual net revenue of Amazon in the year 2007 was around \$14.84 Bn USD which saw an exponential growth recording \$386 Bn USD in the year 2020. Amazon with the knowledge of customer demands launched their Amazon prime services. The customer satisfaction can be measured with the growth of Amazon prime customers. On in USA, from 25 million subscribers in 2013, it grew to 119 plus million subscribers at the start of year 2020 (Statista, 2019). These are significant growth numbers that can be contributed to the usage of strategic analytics.

Use Case #2

Business Strategy: Thames water organization formed a strategy which included achieving operational efficiency and highest customer service with reduction in wastages.

Customer service: Usually whenever there is a mention of usage of analytics in business there are few case studies which are commonly discussed. These include customer analytics, power grid analytics, manufacturing analytics, human resource analytics, sales and marketing analytics, health care analytics etc. The use case we are now going to discuss deals with the efficient usage and monitoring of river water. Thames is the largest provider of water in UK and supplied 2600m litres of water per day. This was one of the pioneer analytics projects where the objective was to manage the water supplies as well as monitor the assets remotely. The project involved usage of real time data. As a part of the project the success criteria defined was to assess the efficiency of the system. Customer expectations and experience was maintained at the centre while the strategy formation. Single view of the operating systems was created including all the facilities. The efficiency of the water supplies was improved greatly while the assets were monitored remotely. The data enabled predictive analytics to envisage the failures of any of the equipment's. The real time data further enabled a significant reduction in the lead time of repairs of such critical systems. The fluctuations in demand were predicted and acted upon proactively. The system also took into account the weather parameters and manifested the supply conditions. The effective usage of analytics offered significant benefits to the consumers too. The bill amount for the consumers were the lowest as compared to other systems. The quality of water supplies too improved considerably. This was one of the most unique implementations of analytics that makes this case study noteworthy (Valahu & Devraj, 2014; IBM, 2013).

Use Case #3

Business strategy: Northern Power Grid Holdings Company documented the business strategy of achieving operational efficiency with high customer service levels.

The third case we will discuss represents the usage of strategic analytics in the power supply domain. The area covered by the Northern power grid was around 25 thousand kilometres. The power supply was designed to cater to almost 3.9 million consumers within this area. This domain in particular is affected majorly by the demand volatility. The usage of electricity is difficult to predict. Also the supplies need to be regularized as soon as possible in case of any interruptions due to an unforeseen event. The strategy outlaid was to ensure customer satisfaction by meeting the customer needs and maintaining the quality of suppliers. Strategic analytics works superlative in such cases with the consumption data patterns and predicting the requirements of power supplies. With the implementation of analytics, there was a seamless power supply maintained to such a large community. The demand forecasting techniques deployed utilized the past data and other input parameters such as weather conditions etc. and anticipated the demand. The anomalies in the data were also handled with some exception handling procedures that enabled the company to monitor and maintain the assets. The maintenance schedule was pre-empted by the system to safeguard the infrastructure. Looking at the successful implementation, the same model was then deployed in other power grids to ensure the optimization of resources and improved customer service (Edge Analytics, n.d).

Use Case #4

Business Strategy: Nissan Motors drafted a business strategy of reviving from the financial losses and creating a profitable organization delivering value to its stakeholders.

This case is related to an automobile organization named "Nissan Motors", which was facing financial crisis. As a part of the recovery plan the management of the firm engaged a consulting firm to conduct a detailed study. A revival plan was documented to ensure that the firms returns on a profitable track. Key performance indicators were observed along with deployment of a web portal. The key objective of this portal was to strengthen the financial controlling capability. The long term plan included alignment of the parameters to the international accounting standards. Standard ERP software was deployed so that the entire data gets recorded in the database. The transparency of data improved the operational efficiency significantly creating collaboration within different functions of the organization. The systems were rolled out in phases and deployed across locations to ensure uniformity of business processes. Post the successful implementation, the data was used to generate insights that were linked to the key performance indicators defined at the start of the program. Close monitoring and immediate corrective actions enabled Nissan Motors to revive as a dynamic company within two years recoding exceptional profits and highest earnings in a year. The strategy amalgamated with the data analytics and management science assisted the organization record a turnaround in business. Similar approach was deployed by the organization in the connected vehicle domain with analytics driven insights at the core. These insights enabled Nissan Motors deploy the connected vehicle use cases for its customers simultaneously offering world class customer experience (Cloudera, n.d.; Petty, 2007).

Use Case #5

Business Strategy: Uber business strategy clearly recorded transportation as reliable as running water, everywhere for everyone.

Uber of the world's largest fleet operating with eight million plus customers and one billion trips deployed analytics to deliver customer experience. The solution simply included a mobile application for the rider to choose his location and book his ride. The ride is then made visible to the drivers who are in vicinity to the customer location. Basis the confirmation from the driver, the information is passed on to the customer regarding the driver and vehicle details. The underlying data layer deployed enables leveraging the insights generated for intelligent decision making. This data when combined with the traffic and global positioning system data helps Uber with a unique functionality of dynamic pricing. Other vital insights include face rides, driver behaviour etc. that power the operational efficiency ensuring safety and trust of the customer. There are different algorithms configured in the backend to manage and match the right combinations of riders and drivers. Uber further records and stores the data of each customer and rides over a period of time. This data is successfully used in demand forecasting of vehicle requirements (Dezyre, 2021).

CONCLUSION

It is proven that the problems in an organization are directly proportional to the size of the organization. Due to the size of the organization being larger, the sources of data collection and volume of data is very high that needs to be collated and administered. Focussed initiatives need to be planned which are aligned to the corporate strategy of an organization. The holistic view of the data is necessary to ensure that the decision making is accurate and comprehensive. The use cases depicted above and many other success stories proves that strategic analytics proves to be an important tool for business transformation. It clearly demonstrates the growth in the business simultaneously optimizing on the organizational resources. The returns on investments is significantly high along with value generation and newer streams of revenue getting unearthed. The data driven organizations conduct an in-depth study for the data requirements to conduct the strategic analytics. The data strategy as studied earlier is linked to the organization strategy. The objective is to drive the organizational effectivity and efficiency. The approach required necessarily includes strategy, research, analysis and finally the analytical models that are in line with the corporate strategy. Table 1 depicts the different linkages discussed so far.

The critical questions for the business are identified and validated. Basis this the planning is done for the data analytics and target is to create a system that fundamentally builds value and simultaneously delivers the competitive advantage for the organization in the market. The other benefits that are targeted include cost reductions, saving of resources, time and most prominently deliver the customer satisfaction. Strategic analytics as we discussed is a blend of management science and strategy management along with analytics. The cautions mentioned in the chapter need due attention during the data collection. The data needs to be accurate and comprehensive for the analytics model to deliver the right insights for decision making. The measures of data quality are reliability and validity of the data. As seen in the use cases depicted above with strategic analytics implemented, organization bring about a business transformation. It has become mandatory for the organization who intend to derive maximum value for the organization with the resources possessed. Strategic analytics is vital for organizations as it assists in:

1. Validating and improving the customer experience
2. Raises the efficiency of the business processes
3. Fact based decision making
4. Fraud identification
5. Reduction in manufacturing costs
6. Improved forecasts and reduction in uncertainties
7. Competitive position in the market

Table 1. Use Cases

Use Case #	Organization	Business Strategy	Solution	Results
1	Amazon	Growth and expansion strategy was adopted by Amazon deploying the innovations in Information Technology simultaneously delivering customer experience	Usage of Strategic Analytics to create Personalization delivering highest level of customer experience	-Increase in workforce from 17 thousand to around 5.7 lacs with revenue rising to $ 386 billion USD from $14 billion USD in about 12 years. - Optimization of costs - Reduction in lead time - Creation of new revenue streams
2	Thames Water Organization	Thames water organization formed a strategy which included achieving operational efficiency and highest customer service with reduction in wastages	Deployment of Strategic Analytics, augmented with real time data analytics creating effective monitoring and supply systems delivering customer service	- The efficiency of the water supplies was improved greatly while the assets were monitored remotely. - The data enabled predictive analytics to envisage the failures of any of the equipment's. - The real time data further enabled a significant reduction in the lead time of repairs of such critical systems. - The fluctuations in demand were predicted and acted upon proactively
3	Northern Power Grid Holdings Company	Northern Power Grid Holdings Company documented the business strategy of achieving operational efficiency with high customer service levels	Implementation of Strategic Analytics to create and maintain customer service levels	- Demand forecasting techniques utilized the past data and other input parameters such as weather conditions etc. and anticipated the demand. - Exception handling procedures that enabled the company to monitor and maintain the assets. - The maintenance schedule was pre-empted by the system to safeguard the infrastructure.
4	Nissan Motors	Nissan Motors drafted a business strategy of reviving from the financial losses and creating a profitable organization delivering value to its stakeholders	Data Analytics aligned to the revival strategy deployed to monitor the Key Performance Indicators along with exception handling	Nissan Motors recovered as a dynamic company within two years recoding exceptional profits and highest earnings in a year
5	Uber	Uber business strategy clearly recorded transportation as reliable as running water, everywhere for everyone	Data analytics based platform aligned to the business strategy	- Perfect matching of rider and driver - Tracking of Driver Behaviour -Demand forecasting of vehicle requirements - World's largest fleet operator

8. Generates profit for the organization.

With the above benefits there are some implicit concerns that the organization needs to be aware of, such as:

1. Complete knowledge of the domain data
2. Availability of experts
3. Costs associated with the newer technologies
4. Needs extensive data
5. Choice of the alternatives depends upon the individual taking decision.

Thus as demonstrated strategic analytics is very beneficial for the organization, provided the implementation is done correctly. The insights generated also should be available in correlation with the business domain knowledge. Care must be exercised during the data collection of maintaining a similar time period for all the parameters contributing to the model calculations. This eradicates the error in calculations and the results are much more relatable.

REFERENCES

Akter, S., Wamba, S. F., Gunasekaran, A., Dubey, R., & Childe, S. J. (2016). How to improve firm performance using big data analytics capability and business strategy alignment? *International Journal of Production Economics*, *182*, 113–131. doi:10.1016/j.ijpe.2016.08.018

Cloudera. (n.d.). *Nissan | Customer Success | Cloudera*. Retrieved 28 January 2021, from https://www.cloudera.com/about/customers/nissan.html

Davenport, T. H., & Dyché, J. (2013). Big data in big companies. *International Institute for Analytics*, *3*, 1–31.

Dezyre. (2021). *How Uber uses data science to reinvent transportation?* Retrieved 28 February 2021, from https://www.dezyre.com/article/how-uber-uses-data-science-to-reinvent-transportation/290

Edge Analytics. (n.d.). *Edge Analytics Northern Powergrid: Utility Planning | Edge Analytics*. Retrieved 18 March 2020, from https://edgeanalytics.co.uk/northern-powergrid/

Godin, M. (2018). *3 Unbelievable Amazon Success Stories*. Retrieved 3 January 2021, from https://crazylister.com/blog/amazing-amazon-success-stories/

Grover, V., Chiang, R. H., Liang, T. P., & Zhang, D. (2018). Creating strategic business value from big data analytics: A research framework. *Journal of Management Information Systems*, *35*(2), 388–423. doi:10.1080/07421222.2018.1451951

Hindle, G. A., & Vidgen, R. (2018). Developing a business analytics methodology: A case study in the foodbank sector. *European Journal of Operational Research*, *268*(3), 836–851. doi:10.1016/j.ejor.2017.06.031

IBM. (2013). *IBM helps transform Thames Water using Big Data Analytics in preparation for future growth.* Retrieved 9 January 2021, from https://newsroom.ibm.com/2013-05-16-IBM-helps-transform-Thames-Water-using-Big-Data-Analytics-in-preparation-for-future-growth

Islami, X., Mustafa, N., & Latkovikj, M. T. (2020). Linking Porter's generic strategies to firm performance. *Future Business Journal*, *6*(1), 1–15. doi:10.118643093-020-0009-1

Kautish, S. (2008). Online Banking: A Paradigm Shift. E-Business. *ICFAI Publication, Hyderabad*, *9*(10), 54–59.

Kautish, S., & Thapliyal, M. P. (2012). Concept of Decision Support Systems in relation with Knowledge Management–Fundamentals, theories, frameworks and practices. *International Journal of Application or Innovation in Engineering & Management*, *1*(2), 9.

Kudyba, S. (2014). *Big data, mining, and analytics: components of strategic decision making.* CRC Press. doi:10.1201/b16666

Kunc, M. (2018). *Strategic analytics: integrating management science and strategy.* John Wiley & Sons. doi:10.1002/9781119519638

Levenson, A. (2015). *Strategic analytics: Advancing strategy execution and organizational effectiveness.* Berrett-Koehler Publishers.

Morabito, V. (2015). Big data and analytics for competitive advantage. In *Big Data and Analytics* (pp. 3–22). Springer. doi:10.1007/978-3-319-10665-6_1

Nelson, P. (2019). *Six Big Data Use Cases for Modern Business | Accenture.* Retrieved 11 January 2021, from https://www.accenture.com/us-en/blogs/search-and-content-analytics-blog/big-data-use-cases-business

Özemre, M., & Kabadurmus, O. (2020). A big data analytics based methodology for strategic decision making. *Journal of Enterprise Information Management*.

Petty, R. (2007). *Nissan: Success Story of a Dramatic Turnaround.* Retrieved 16 January 2021, from https://www.capgemini.com/fr-fr/ressources/nissan-success-story-of-a-dramatic-turnaround/

Porter, M. E., & Advantage, C. (1985). Creating and sustaining superior performance. *Competitive Advantage, 167,* 167-206.

Pröllochs, N., & Feuerriegel, S. (2020). Business analytics for strategic management: Identifying and assessing corporate challenges via topic modeling. *Information & Management, 57*(1), 103070. doi:10.1016/j.im.2018.05.003

Statista. (2019). *U.S. Amazon Prime subscribers 2019 | Statista.* Retrieved 13 February 2021, from https://www.statista.com/statistics/546894/number-of-amazon-prime-paying-members/

Tanwar, R. (2013). Porter's generic competitive strategies. *Journal of Business and Management, 15*(1), 11–17.

Vahdati, H., Nejad, S. H., & Shahsiah, N. (2018). Generic Competitive Strategies toward Achieving Sustainable and Dynamic Competitive Advantage. *Revista Espacios, 39*(13).

Valahu, A., & Devraj, J. (2014). *Accenture to Help Thames Water Prove the Benefits of Smart Monitoring Capabilities.* Retrieved 5 February 2021, from https://newsroom.accenture.com/industries/utilities/accenture-to-help-thames-water-prove-the-benefits-of-smart-monitoring-capabilities.htm

Van Rooyen, M. (2005). *A strategic analytics methodology* (Doctoral dissertation).

Williams, G. (2011). Descriptive and predictive analytics. In *Data Mining with Rattle and R* (pp. 171–177). Springer. doi:10.1007/978-1-4419-9890-3_8

Yerpude, S., & Singhal, T. K. (2017). Internet of Things and its impact on Business Analytics. *Indian Journal of Science and Technology, 10*(5), 1–6. doi:10.17485/ijst/2017/v10i5/109348

Chapter 6
A Study on the Use of Business Intelligence Tools for Strategic Financial Analysis

Guneet Kaur
University of Stirling Innovation Park Ltd, UK

ABSTRACT

The research work is focused on examining the role of business intelligence (BI) tools in strategic financial analysis. The effective utilization of data is essential in order to survive in today's competitive business environment. Traditionally, data analysis was performed manually by using a spreadsheet. However, due to big data proliferation at an unprecedented pace, it becomes difficult for the financial services industry to manage large datasets. Therefore, to address this issue, both academia and industry practitioners have come forward to meet the needs of a growing business with the help of BI tools. In this context, this chapter aims to assist the BI researchers and practitioners in the financial services industry to make fact-based decisions by using popular BI tools like Power BI, Tableau, and SAS analytics. Consequently, the chapter provides a detailed review of the applications of these BI tools in strategic financial analysis and to enhance overall corporate performance.

1. INTRODUCTION

The rise of data generation and exponential growth of technology radically change the way industries and individual businesses work. By its very nature, the financial services industry is considered to be one of the most data-intensive industries, representing a unique opportunity to store, analyze and exploit data usefully. For

DOI: 10.4018/978-1-7998-7716-5.ch006

instance, vast quantities of customer data are being generated by the banks, such as point-of-sale transactions, customer profile data collected for know your customer (KYC), deposits, and withdrawals at automatic teller machines (ATMs), and online payments (Kautish, 2008). Still, they are not very good at using these rich data sets because of their silo and product-oriented nature. Data numbers have historically been crunched, and decisions have been taken based on inferences derived from measured trends and risks. However, hundreds of millions of financial transactions occur every day and the massive volumes of data present ever-new problems for the financial sector (Hasan et al., 2020). Therefore, companies require more efficient tools like business intelligence (BI) software (than conventional strategic management tools and ratio analysis) that can help shape the business strategy for tomorrow and facilitate real-time decision-making (IşıK et al., 2011). As computers have usurped the manual data analysis functionality, the need for more sophisticated data visualization and analytics capabilities has increased over time.

Financial services firms can now focus on emerging data-driven market opportunities by collecting and exploiting large volumes of data with business intelligence software. Business intelligence is characterized by Khan & Quadri (2014) as the process of taking large quantities of data, analyzing that data, and providing a high-level collection of reports that condense the nature of that information into the basis of business behavior, allowing management to make fundamental business decisions on a daily basis. Moreover, financial business intelligence is a term used to define strategies to collect, process, and analyze financial data from databases in real-time and make informed business decisions with the assistance of advanced business intelligence tools (Rasmussen et al., 2002). The use of BI in the financial services industry provides various benefits as listed below-

1. Forecasting potential future financial scenarios.
2. Shaping business strategy through reliable, factual insights rather than intuition.
3. Gaining in-depth knowledge of key trends and take steps to maximize organizational success.
4. Helping in reduction of costs, raise profitability and improves the value of the business.
5. Understanding customers' needs based on consumer profiles, purchasing history, expectations, and demographics.
6. Finding and targeting the most profitable clients.

This chapter is organized into various sections- section 2 discusses the importance of strategic financial analysis. Various issues related to conventional strategic management tools have been discussed in section 3. Section 4 discusses the role of BI in strategic financial decision-making. Section 5 provides a detailed review of BI applications and tools for the financial services industry. Section 6 throws light on the key research gaps addressed by the researcher. Section 7 discusses the study's limitations, followed by section 8 that provides direction for future work. Finally, the chapter is concluded in section 9.

2. IMPORTANCE OF STRATEGIC FINANCIAL ANALYSIS

Strategic financial analysis is used to identify the method of controlling a company's finances to achieve its strategic objectives (Liu, 2010). It is a management strategy that uses various techniques and financial instruments to formulate a strategic plan. Strategic financial analysis ensures that the selected strategy is applied (Liu, 2010). Multiple features of strategic financial analysis include the following (Helfert & Helfert, 2001):

1. It focuses on the management of long-term assets, taking a strategic viewpoint into account.
2. It is a continually evolving method to adapt and revise strategies to meet the company's financial targets.
3. It can, as well, be versatile and organized.
4. It involves a multidimensional and imaginative approach to solve business problems.
5. It encourages the company's profitability, prosperity, and presence over the long term and strives to optimize shareholders' wealth.
6. It helps formulate appropriate strategies and oversee action plans to be compliant with business goals.
7. Using empirical financial methods with quantitative and qualitative reasoning, it analyzes factual details.
8. It allows financial managers to make decisions about investing in and funding assets.

Hence, strategic financial analysis is intended to define potential methods capable of optimizing the company's market value. It also ensures that the company successfully implements the strategy to achieve the required short-term and long-term objectives and maximize shareholder value (Krylov, 2015). The strategic financial analysis controls the organization's financial resources to achieve business objectives.

3. ISSUES WITH CONVENTIONAL STRATEGIC MANAGEMENT TOOLS

The standard strategic management tools used to conduct an internal and external analysis of a company are SWOT (Strengths, Weaknesses, Opportunities, Threats) analysis, Porter's five forces model, and PEST (Political, Economic, Socio-cultural, Technological) analysis (Berisha Qehaja et al., 2017). The SWOT analysis identifies organizational strengths, weaknesses, opportunities, and threats, which is the critical component of strategic planning (Kearns, 1992). Though it helps the organization understand its strategic competitive position, SWOT can be a shallow and even deceptive exercise (Kearns, 1992). SWOT analysis produces a one-dimensional model that categorizes each problem attribute's power, weakness, potential, or hazard. As a consequence, it seems like each attribute has only one effect on the issue being studied.

Nevertheless, one element may be both strength and a weakness. For instance, a high inventory turnover ratio indicates both strength (i.e., strong sales) and weakness (i.e., insufficient inventory) (Rao & Rao, 2009). Therefore, tools like SWOT analysis can misguide companies while making crucial business decisions. Porter's Five Forces is a straightforward yet effective instrument for understanding the competitiveness of a company's market environment and recognizing the possible viability of the strategy (Grundy, 2006). However, this framework is qualitative in nature and cannot be used to evaluate a company's financial position. Additionally, this model is static and takes no account of time, according to Thyrlby (1998). Therefore, defining markets with higher competitive dynamics is even more challenging because they can shift very rapidly.

PEST analysis is used to gauge external factors that could influence a company's profitability (Ho, 2014). As this tool considers only external factors, internal factors impacting a company's financial position are ignored. For instance, the factors like cost and capital structure of a company, liquidity, and solvency position of a company are ignored. It demands the continuous development of new models and tools to aid management with strategic decision-making.

4. ROLE OF BUSINESS INTELLIGENCE (BI) IN STRATEGIC FINANCIAL DECISION MAKING

4.1 Different Viewpoints on Business Intelligence

Global & Kim (1986) defined BI as a management theory and instrument, which helps companies manage and optimize business information to make successful decisions. The objective of the BI systems is to capture data and information to make informed decisions faster than business events. BI was used as an analysis tool, offering automated decision-making on revenue, market trends, consumer demand, product preference, etc. (Farrokhi & Pokoradi, 2012). Moreover, business intelligence is described by the Data Warehousing Institute (a provider of data warehouse and BI industry education and training) as the technologies, procedures, and resources necessary to turn data into information, which can further be transformed into knowledge, and knowledge into plans that leads to profitable business actions (Farrokhi & Pokoradi, 2012). Business intelligence is characterized by Stackowiak et al. (2007) as the process of taking large quantities of data, analyzing that data, and providing a high-level collection of reports, allowing management to make fundamental business decisions on a daily basis. However, Zeng et al. (2006) described BI as the method of collecting, processing, and disseminating information to reduce uncertainty in making strategic business decisions. Strategic decisions are related to the execution and assessment of the purpose, vision, goals, and objectives of the organization with a medium to long-term effect on the organization, as opposed to tactical decisions related to regular business activities (Schmidt & Wilhelm, 2000). Furthermore, Evelson et al. (2007) define BI as a collection of procedures and technologies that convert raw, meaningless data into useful and actionable information. During every day operating processes, it utilizes a large amount of data gathered and converts the data into meaningful information to prevent its ignorance in terms of its performance.

Therefore, BI mainly performs two crucial functions: firstly, the compilation, interpretation, and dissemination of information and, secondly, to facilitate the strategic decision-making process. Furthermore, various processes that assist financial decision-makers in improving corporate performance include the following-

1. **Statistical analysis:** Taking the findings from descriptive analytics and exploring the data further by using statistics such as how and why a particular pattern occurred (Nybakk, 2018).
2. **Querying:** Asking detailed questions about the data by pulling the responses from the datasets (Gartner, 2021).
3. **Benchmarking and performance metrics:** Comparing current performance data to historical data using personalized dashboards to monitor performance against objectives (Gartner, 2021).
4. **Data preparation:** Compilation of various data sources, identification of dimensions and measurements, and data analysis preparation (Gartner, 2021).
5. **Descriptive analytics:** To determine the root cause of a problem based on preliminary data analysis (Schmidt & Wilhelm, 2000).
6. **Data mining:** To discover patterns in massive datasets using statistics, databases, and machine learning (Powel, 2017).

7. **Data visualization:** Turning data interpretation into visual representations to consume data more quickly, such as graphs, maps, and histograms (Gartner, 2021).

8. **Visual analysis:** Expressing data in the form of visual storytelling to help readers understand the complex data in an easy way (Gartner, 2021).

9. **Reporting:** Sharing the study of data with stakeholders to draw conclusions and make decisions (Foley & Guillemette, 2010).

4.2 BI Capabilities

Business intelligence (BI) platforms enable businesses to create BI applications by offering three types of capabilities such as analysis (e.g., OLAP, i.e., online analytical processing), delivery of information (e.g., dashboards and reports); and integration of data (e.g., data warehouse) (Gartner, 2021). These elements are explained as follows:

1. **Analysis:** It refers to how business users can slice and determine their way through data using advanced tools that allow dimensions such as hierarchies or time to be navigated (Marius et al., 2009). An OLAP offer summarized multidimensional views of business data and is used to optimize the enterprise's modeling, reporting, research, and planning processes (Abelló & Romero, 2009).

2. **Delivery of information:** It refers to storytelling through dashboards and reports. A business intelligence dashboard is a tool for information management used to control metrics, key performance indicators (KPIs), and other main data points that are important to a department, an organization, or a particular process (Rivard & Cogswell, 2004). Dashboards simplify complicated data sets using data visualizations to provide users with knowledge of current performance and take necessary action (Rocha et al., 2017). Similarly, BI reporting extracts relevant insights from the data gathered through various sources and suggestions, and comments on business trends, empowering decision-makers to act (Rivard & Cogswell, 2004).

3. **Integration of data:** By integrating data from multiple heterogeneous sources that support structured and ad hoc queries, analytical reporting, and decision making, a data warehouse is constructed (Ranjan, 2009). The data sources can be historical data, relational databases, operational databases, external data (e.g., from the Internet). Furthermore, data sources can contain structured information (such as spreadsheets or tables) or unstructured information (such as plaintext, images, and other multimedia data).

4.3 BI and Corporate Performance Management (CPM)

According to Gartner (2021), BI services are concerned with the design, development, and implementation of enterprise processes and the integration, support, and management of applications and systems related to BI technologies. These include enterprise and technology applications, analytics needs, and infrastructure for data warehousing (Gartner, 2021). In addition to it, BI solutions include analytics and CPM. In a complex business climate, the CPM is a BI tool that can help companies overcome the challenge of making strategic business decisions. To achieve organizational efficiency, these systems combine management practices (e.g., planning, analysis, and management) and information technology (IT) (Richards et al., 2019). CPM takes a systematic approach to the execution and monitoring of organizational strategy. It combines the business processes, business methodologies, and business systems (Sharma & Djiaw, 2011). Business processes refer to the procedures that match the right resources and information to strategic priorities (Sharma & Djiaw, 2011). Business methodologies include frameworks like balanced scorecards used within strategic planning (Sharma & Djiaw, 2011). Business systems refer to the technology solutions that incorporate business processes and business methodologies into a single system (Isik et al., 2016).

Additionally, based on the Resource-Based Theory (RBT), it is evident that that technology influences business processes that affect organizational performance in turn (Olszak, 2016). The RBT's basis is that a company's resources have capabilities that allow it to succeed in the marketplace (Olszak, 2016). Moreover, Lucas & Goh (2009) provided that poor information processes and analysis, especially concerning corporate planning played a significant role in the failure of Kodak (a former Fortune 500 business). Therefore, the Integrative Model implies that technology is an internal resource that must be supported by complementary assets (e.g., such as workplace practices) to facilitate business processes that contribute to organizational success (Richards et al., 2019). Hence, corporate management activities may be regarded as strategic processes supported by the BI system based on this model (Richards et al., 2019).

4.4 BI and Strategic Financial Analysis

The banking and finance industry is being transformed by technology. Due to the proliferation of mobile devices and apps and the power of the internet, today's financial institutions face changing consumer expectations, cut-throat competition, and the need for strict control and risk management in a highly competitive business environment (Isik et al., 2011). In this scenario, analytics may help businesses estimate which aspects of their products or services are more likely to succeed, regardless of global economic conditions. Companies must evaluate their source of income by using data when the danger of a recession arises. It will help organizations reduce risk, drive profitability, create competitive advantage, and make informed business decisions (Schick et al., 2012). These goals can be of vital importance in crisis times when both businesses and consumers become more cost-conscious, and practical usage of resources can become a question of survival (Antoniadis et al., 2015). Therefore, organizations need analytical tools than reliable financial statements and reports in today's highly competitive business climate. They need forward-looking, predictive insights than overreliance on SWOT Analysis and PEST analysis (i.e., conventional strategic management tools) that can help shape the business strategy for tomorrow and facilitate real-time everyday decision-making.

Moreover, the future of financial planning, reporting, and analysis (FP&A) is becoming more complex as smart technologies proliferate and begin to change the way companies work. In order to be more streamlined, efficient, and adaptive to this changing environment, finance leaders must now re-engineer and transform their financial operations. Farrokhi & Pokoradi (2012) provided that business intelligence tools offer reporting, visualizations, predictive analytics, and other features to help finance leaders see facts clearly and make better business decisions.

The formula for developing a strategy for business intelligence solutions includes data, people, technology, and enterprise objections and strategic vision (TCS, 2014) as explained below:

1. **Data:** The degree of centralization required within the BI architecture should be taken into consideration. Data should be sourced from internal and external sources, from all functions, and supporting information should meet business needs.
2. **People:** The end-users who build and ingest knowledge are employees. A degree of autonomy and access to the BI specifications must be provided to them (TCS, 2014). The effectiveness of a BI system depends on how well end-users embrace the solution, which can be enhanced by ensuring that enough training and support are given.
3. **Technology:** The interfaces and components need to be seamless and incorporated within the BI device architecture (TCS, 2014). In order to make efficient decisions at the right time, the systems should have the necessary analytical capabilities.
4. **Enterprise:** Before developing and implementing a BI system, organizations need to identify a BI system target. Proper due diligence ensures compliance with the pre-defined goal during the formulation of specifications. The budget allocation must rely on a cost-benefit analysis of the possible market advantages

that are likely to arise from a robust BI-supported collaborative decision-making process (TCS, 2014).

In the following section, a detailed study has been outlined that discusses business intelligence applications in the financial services industry based on the previous works carried out by various researchers and industry practitioners.

5. BI APPLICATIONS AND TOOLS FOR THE FINANCIAL SERVICES INDUSTRY

Financial services include international finance, banking (mortgage banks, savings, and lending firms, credit unions, and commercial banks), and securities exchanges (investment banks, brokerages) (Muhammad et al., 2014). Various BI applications and tools for the financial services industry will be discussed in the sections below.

5.1 Risk Management

Risk management can be defined as detecting, reviewing, and either embracing or reducing uncertainty in the investment decision-making process. Risk management is about handling risks linked to threats (Froot et al., 1993). Risk management is about the management of threat-related uncertainties. In the financial services industry, one of the critical financial risks is related to credit risk. Therefore, banking institutions need to rely more on fact-based actionable knowledge, gathered from ever-increasing data assets, in a rapidly evolving and unpredictable financial environment to decrease risk wherever possible (Muhammad et al., 2014). BI is commonly used in the banking industry to estimate the efficiency of its clients for risk management. Lack of information about potential customers may prove to be a significant risk when expanding credit lines to existing customers, offering credit cards to new customers, and authorizing loans.

Furthermore, following the global financial crisis of 2008, the banking sector is facing increased requirements related to risk management (Nybakk, 2018). Because of the Basel Capital Requirements, banks must do credit modeling and scoring, and they face different challenges related to this requirement (Nybakk, 2018). The credit analyst, who produces scoring models, also needs IT support. It is a timely job to gather data for different modeling and reporting purposes, ensuring that the data is at the risk of being obsolete by the time the analyst reports on it (Nybakk, 2018). Therefore, real-time BI tools like SAS® credit scoring can be required to address these challenges and help money-lending institutions to track and assess customers' credit risk scores (Yap et al., 2011). Yap et al. (2011) built credit scoring models using SAS® credit scoring tool called SAS (Statistical Analysis System) Enterprise Miner 5.3 and achieved an accuracy of 71.2% and 71.9% for decision tree and logistic regression models, respectively.

Nybakk (2018) noted various benefits of SAS credit scoring as listed below-

1. **The credit analyst:** SAS® Credit Scoring for Banking brings versatility to the credit analyst's working duties. Through a user-friendly graphical interface, modeling data is readily accessible, and the analyst can quickly build segmented models to achieve improved accuracy. Furthermore, the ability to exchange variables and models with other analysts offers greater insight into the bank's underlying data and credit models.

2. **Customers:** Improved consumer goods are supported by precise credit models, split into segments for better prediction. For specific clients, the reason their loan is approved could be an improvement in model accuracy.

3. **The IT department:** There will be less labor-intensive credit scoring-related data management. From repeatedly designing in-house data processing models to tracking clients' behaviors, the IT department's job duties will be decreased.

4. **The Bank:** The solution offers back-testing and model validation reports consistent with Basel II. Small banks may maintain an analytics platform traditionally reserved for large companies with SAS Credit Scoring for Banking. The capacity to check the precision of the model and its strengths and limitations decreases the risk of the model. With lower model risk, the increased visibility into credit models allows for better business strategies.

Rao & Kumar (2011) provided that such BI tools are efficient in evaluating bank performance by using historical data in order to make decisions about the future.

5.2 Fraud Detection

Fraud-related losses and damages are suffered by the financial services sector involving financial transactions. For instance, the fines levied for money laundering and penalty violations have exceeded a whopping $28 billion since 2008 (Scott & McGoldrick, 2018). Tier one banks also spend around $1 billion annually on activities involving financial fraud. The laws on financial crime are subject to constant development, and new ones are being enforced, requiring additional measures to be taken by financial institutions to stay in compliance (Scott & McGoldrick, 2018). Additionally, a transition to the digital space has opened new avenues for delivering financial services and opening new opportunities for fraudsters. Therefore, a proactive approach is needed to expose risk and ensure compliance by using robust and intuitive analytics to explore all the organization's financial data. BI tools like

SAS financial crime analytics help finance professionals flag suspicious behavior until it is too late, detect fraud, and warn their stakeholders. Copeland et al. (2012) applied a business intelligence system to review Medicaid claim transactions to identify fraud and provide guidance to decision-makers tasked with utilizing the best available funds. This realistic implementation of BI gives a government agency the ability to simultaneously minimize personnel and boost operational quality (Copeland et al., 2012).

Kaur (2019) developed a BI outlier system to predict and manage fraud in financial payment services. The researcher deployed an XGBoost (Extreme Gradient Boosting) classifier model that provided 96.46% accuracy, i.e., the model could classify fraudulent and genuine transactions effectively (Kaur, 2019). Other tools like SAS Financial Crimes Suite provide a shared framework for analytics and module-based solutions that offer adequate protection against financial crime losses by increasing the efficiency and effectiveness of identifying and preventing fraud (SAS, 2014). By automating decisions, SAS uses predictive alert analytics to significantly reduce false positives to identify the most significant threats more accurately before beginning an investigation (SAS, 2014). With a system that integrates anti-fraud and anti-money laundering processes and can simultaneously run multiple scenarios and risk factors, anti-money laundering analysts (AML) can monitor more transactions and risks in less time. Moreover, by using the suite's dashboard reporting capabilities, analysts, investigators, and managers can concentrate on and continually monitor key performance indicators in their particular areas of interest (SAS, 2014).

5.3 Forecasting Trends Based on Data Visualization

Power BI & Tableau are both immersive business intelligence software for data visualization. Data visualization brings data to life, making the insights contained inside the numbers the master storyteller for organizations. Data visualizations let users quickly and efficiently gain valuable market insight through live dashboards, interactive reports, maps, graphs, and other visual representations (Diamond & Mattia, 2017). Although beautiful rich graphics can be excellent tools to express ideas, data visualization's ultimate advantage is its ability to drive better decision-making. According to Jain (2017), the insights generated by visualizations can further be used to forecast or predict future sales, expenses, budgeting, profits, etc. Therefore, data visualization helps in strategic decision making in the following ways:

1. **See the bigger picture:** There is a simple picture of performance hidden in the transaction, contact, process, and behavioral data found in the organizations' structures. Data visualization helps organizations understand the broader context and the higher-level situation within it. As a result, once businesses

start looking at numbers on their own, trends will be noticed, and patterns that they may not be able to see will be recognized (Diamond & Mattia, 2017).

2.   **Address pain points:** It allows organizations to recognize insights that lead to better decision making, preparation, tactics, and behavior by adding visual clarity to the story hidden inside their data. It answers various questions such as the major pain points, how an organization works, what needs to be altered, and where it should concentrate its resources? (Diamond & Mattia, 2017). More efficient operations and decisions are informed by the capacity to understand the importance of an organization's results.

5.3.1 Tableau for Data Visualization

As forecasting is the act of analyzing and mining data in order to predict what will happen in the future, financial managers can forecast future financial performance based on the current parameters, which can be typically accomplished by using a BI application like Tableau, Power BI, etc. (Ali et al., 2016). Tableau forecasting utilizes a method known as exponential smoothing (Akhtar et al., 2020). In measures that can be continued, forecast algorithms try to find a regular pattern. There are multiple exponential smoothing models. Tableau selects seven to eight best models, and then the one with the highest quality is selected as the final forecast model (Akhtar et al., 2020). Although Tableau public is available free of charge, one has to buy a desktop version license (Ali et al., 2016).

5.3.2 Power BI for Data Visualization

Power BI is a Microsoft cloud-based business analytics service that allows everyone to visualize and analyze data with more incredible speed and effectiveness (Vijayakumar, 2017). It is a versatile and robust tool for linking and exploring a wide range of knowledge. The ease of use of Power BI comes from the fact that it has an interface for drag and drop. This role allows tasks such as sorting, comparing, and evaluating to be done very quickly. With several outlets, including Excel, Structured Query Language (SQL) Server, and cloud-based data repositories, Power BI is also compatible, making it an excellent option for data scientists, financial analysts, business analysts, and business intelligence experts (Aspin, 2014).

Power BI consists of different components that can be used solely and are available separately on the market, such as Power BI Desktop, Power BI Mobile apps, Power BI Embedded, Power BI service, Power BI gateway, Power BI report server, and Power BI visuals marketplace (Powell, 2017). Organizations can choose a specific component based on their needs. Power BI helps in the quick consolidation of data sets from large to enormous data sets in financial organizations. The application provides a feature called "what-if parameters" for data projections that produce interactive data projections and are highly efficient for comparison (Becker & Gould, 2019). It is a critical tool for making critical financial decisions about profitability, business expenses, and budgeting. The solution comes from data analysis expressions (DAX) calculations using the DAX language from Microsoft (Becker & Gould, 2019). DAX is a library containing functions and operators to construct expressions and formulas in Power BI and SQL Server Analysis Services (Jain, 2017). Furthermore, the unique data projection systems provided by Power BI can be used for financial forecasts, and many significant decisions can ultimately be taken from such financial projections. Hence, it is an integral part of every enterprise's data processing systems (Becker & Gould, 2019).

Diamond & Mattia (2017) concluded that BI tools like Tableau and Power BI are imperative for strategic business decisions.

5.4 Cost Management

Cost management can be regarded as a collection of methods and strategies for managing and enhancing the processes and operation of an organization, its goods, and services to achieve cost efficiency by gathering, analyzing, assessing, and reporting cost information to assist managers in decision-making for predicting budgeting, and tracking costs (Hanid et al., 2011). Furthermore, Hanid et al. (2011) identified various issues with conventional cost management methods such as failure to forecast, inadequate support for inter-organizational cost control, and failure to recognize opportunities for change. This gap can be filled by using BI tools like Power BI. Becker & Gould (2019) suggested that the Power BI cost management dashboard can be useful for finance and accounting professionals to manage inventory at the organization. This involves activities such as monitoring the cost fluctuations in product supplies or cash flows regularly (Powell, 2017). Organizations can gain useful insights such as turnover ratio, stock inventory levels, and inventory costs. Thus, companies can formulate more effective intervention strategies with this data-driven transparency to optimize strategic planning, reduce costs, and enhance financial efficiency (Powell, 2017).

5.5 Customer Acquisition and Retention

Decreasing product differentiation, intense competition, and comparable prices are the firms' critical issues offering financial services. In order to re-engineer their processes, financial services firms have been utilizing customer relationship management (CRM) solutions to acquire and retain customers. CRM solutions are used to manage relationships with their customers (Pokharel, 2011). Best customers can be identified and targeted based on recency, frequency, and monetary criteria (RFM) (Chen et al., 2009). Effective strategies can be made based on customers' purchasing patterns, average purchase amount, and frequent purchases. Due to the data-intensive nature of the financial services industry, implementation of CRM solution is highly challenging and will require huge investments. This challenge can be addressed by using CRM with BI tools like Tableau to monitor the flow of customer behaviour (Nair, 2005). Therefore, banks and other financial institutions can make profitable investments based on customers' behavior, segment customers based on profitability, and understand customer attrition rates to develop solutions to retain them and acquire new customers (Nair, 2005). Based on these insights, organizations can predict future sales and revenues.

5.6 Financial Modeling

A financial model is built in spreadsheet software like MS Excel to predict an organization's financial results in the future (Lukić, 2017). Usually, the forecast is based on the organization's future expectations, past performance, and preparation of an income statement, balance sheet, and cash flow statement (Lukić, 2017). The output of a financial model is used for making decisions about making acquisitions, capital allocation, raising capital, budgeting, and forecasting. However, an Excel model's efficiency can be improved by using BI tools like SAS (Guerard et al., 2019). SAS helps create more comprehensive budgets, enhance consolidation capacity, and incorporate detailed drivers of expense, sales, and profitability. SAS can assist in a wide variety of activities in the finance sector, including streamlined planning, budgeting, and financial reporting, as well as crucial process automation (Guerard et al., 2019). SAS helps organizations to explore various scenarios and facilitate better production of forecasts. The platform enables finance professionals to conduct consolidations on-demand to close books more rapidly.

5.7 Financial Reporting

The performance quality in financial reporting tasks requires an understanding of quality, speed, flexibility, numerous data sources, and reporting activity automation (Homocianu & Airinei, 2014). Though financial reporting can be effectively done using software like Microsoft Excel, Tableau provides outstanding financial reporting services. Using Tableau, financial reporting, such as balance sheets, P&L reports, and cash flow statements, becomes interactive, dynamic, and automated (O'Brien & Stone, 2020). The financial professionals can use the insights generated from Tableau to fuel business strategy. Similarly, Microsoft Power BI financial reporting can help companies develop a comprehensive collection of financial statements from a trial balance, including profit and loss statement, balance sheet, and cash flow statement, and completely automate the month-end reporting process (Powell, 2017).

5.8 Cash Flow Management

Cash flow is the most crucial element of financial reporting. Traditionally, using Excel-based manual data processing, a cash flow statement is compiled. This strategy, however, is resource-intensive and time-consuming. It can also lead to data accuracy problems and standardization of reports. BI and analytics software helps businesses automate the analysis of cash flow and provide the tools they need to consolidate information, simplify planning and forecasting of cash flow, and speed up decision-making. For effective management of cash inflows and outflows, BI software helps in the following ways-

1. **Data Management:** The most time-consuming aspect of spreadsheet cash flow analysis is data aggregation from various sources. Organizations can analyze the data in real-time by using BI software that interacts with the CRM solution. The insights and up-to-date reports generated by the cash flow analysis can be used for fast, informed decision-making (Rivard & Cogswell, 2004).

2. **Intelligent Forecasting:** Financial projections provide a straightforward roadmap to achieving your business objectives and help organizations prepare for capital allocation and budgeting. Cash forecasts can be generated automatically with BI software (Guerard et al., 2019). Financial managers will remain updated at all times with this skill, with advanced notice of cash shortages or surpluses. This enables a business to respond rapidly to growth opportunities or to scale back as needed.

3. **Inventory Planning:** There are some hidden costs associated with inventory. It ties up cash in goods, and excess inventory can work against the cash flow. Organizations can find a reasonable balance between demand and supply with BI software and deliberate about inventory spending (Becker & Gould, 2019).

4. **Project Management:** Big projects can have an immense effect on cash flow. For cash flow planning and strategic development, financial managers need to control what comes in and what comes out. BI software can enhance financial managers' ability to analyze the necessary resources, expenses, and payment terms to achieve overall project efficacy (Kerzner, 2017).

6. KEY RESEARCH TOPICS IDENTIFIED BY THE RESEARCHER

The study mentioned above on the applications of business intelligence tools in the financial services industry indicates that BI software can solve various issues related to the strategic financial analysis, including manual handling of repetitive tasks, handling large data sets, planning, reporting, and interpreting financial information. The review of BI's role in strategic financial analysis revealed that such tools successfully help in financial management and shape the business strategy through reliable, factual insights. Following are some of the glimpses of using BI tools in financial analysis tasks-

1. Technology is an essential internal resource that contributes to organizational success (if combined with complementary assets such as workplace practices).
2. BI tools help money-lending institutions track and assess customers' credit risk scores and manage credit risk effectively.
3. BI tools help finance professionals flag suspicious behavior of the customers, detect fraud, and warn their stakeholders to take necessary action.
4. BI tools like SAS analytics, Tableau, and Power BI are imperative for strategic business decisions.
5. Data visualizations let users quickly and efficiently gain valuable market insight through live dashboards, interactive reports, maps, graphs, and other visual representations.
6. Companies can formulate more effective intervention strategies with this data-driven transparency to optimize strategic planning, reduce costs, and enhance financial efficiency.
7. Integration of CRM with BI tools like Tableau can help monitor the flow of customer behavior, and strategies can be developed to retain existing customers and acquire new ones.
8. BI tools enhance the capabilities of an excel model by helping organizations with streamlined planning, budgeting, and financial reporting.
9. Microsoft Power BI financial reporting can help companies generate a comprehensive collection of financial statements from a trial balance, including profit and loss statement, balance sheet, and cash flow statement, and completely automate the month-end reporting process.
10. Businesses can automate the analysis of cash flow with the help of BI tools. As a result, the decision-making process takes less time.

7. LIMITATIONS OF STUDY

The study has effectively captured the banks and other financial institutions' issues due to the data-intensive nature of the financial services industry. Various BI applications in the strategic financial analysis have been sufficiently discussed from both academic and industry perspectives. The use of three software, i.e., Power BI, SAS analytics, and Tableau, have been covered in this study. However, the study did not cover other BI tools like Qlik view, Rapid Miner, Pentaho, Datapine, and Zoho analytics. The comparison with other BI tools would have provided a comprehensive view of BI's role in strategic financial analysis. Moreover, the study has not covered any issues concerning the resistance to adoption of BI in the financial services industry, which, if covered, would have provided solutions to such problems. Another limitation is that the study has not covered the comparative analysis of Power BI, SAS analytics, and Tableau to reveal which tool is the best one to be utilized for strategic financial analysis purposes.

8. FUTURE WORK

The use of BI effectively addresses the problems associated with strategic financial analysis arising from the rise of data generation and exponential technology growth. Additionally, BI's applications in strategic financial analysis and real-life examples of suitable software have been provided to assist financial managers with strategic decision making and enhance the overall corporate performance. However, few areas remain unattended in this study. These include:

1. **Comparative analysis of BI tools:** Comparative study of Power BI, SAS analytics, and Tableau to recommend the best tool to be utilized for strategic financial analysis purposes. The comparative analysis is essential to provide a broad view of the application of BI tools in a particular area in the financial services industry.
2. **Discussion on technologies:** The technologies behind the BI tools discussed in this study can be researched upon and explained in future work to help beginners in the business intelligence field understand how the BI tools execute intelligence.
3. **Discussion on qualitative data analysis:** The current research work is mostly concerned with analyzing quantitative data, and the importance of qualitative data has been neglected. The importance of qualitative data for strategic financial analysis and how such data is processed, explored, and interpreted

by the BI tools can be discussed in future work. Such an analysis is essential to enhance the credibility of BI tools.

9. CONCLUSION

With an ever-increasing influx of raw data, companies have almost unlimited potential. If companies can collect even a fraction of the data available and then mine it for relevant information, they can have an advantage over other rivals that are less data-minded. Due to big data proliferation at an unprecedented rate, many businesses find it challenging to manage the sheer amount of available data. One of such companies in the financial services, due to its data-intensive nature, faces issues while handling large data sets. Therefore, the financial services industry needs efficient tools like business intelligence (BI) tools to locate, collect, analyze, interpret, and document data. Business intelligence incorporates data mining, business analytics, data visualization, data infrastructure, and best workplace practices to help companies make more data-driven decisions. The research works done in the past have revealed that BI tools can be used in the strategic financial analysis to assist financial decision-makers in terms of credit risk management, fraud detection, forecasting trends, customer acquisition and retention, cost management, financial modeling, financial reporting, and cash flow management. At the end of the chapter, the present study's research gap has been discussed, followed by the future work. Such gaps will serve as the motivation to conduct a more rigorous analysis of the BI tools and their strategic financial analysis application.

REFERENCES

Abelló, A., & Romero, O. (2009). Online Analytical Processing. Encyclopedia of Database Systems, 20, 2731-2735.

Akhtar, N., Perwej, A., & Perwej, Y. (2020). Data analytics and visualization using Tableau utilitarian for COVID-19 (Coronavirus). *Global Journal of Engineering and Technology Advances, 3*(2), 28-50.

Ali, S. M., Gupta, N., Nayak, G. K., & Lenka, R. K. (2016, December). Big data visualization: Tools and challenges. In *2016 2nd International Conference on Contemporary Computing and Informatics (IC3I)* (pp. 656-660). IEEE.

Antoniadis, I., Tsiakiris, T., & Tsopogloy, S. (2015). Business Intelligence during times of crisis: Adoption and usage of ERP systems by SMEs. *Procedia: Social and Behavioral Sciences, 175*(1), 299–307. doi:10.1016/j.sbspro.2015.01.1204

Becker, L. T., & Gould, E. M. (2019). Microsoft Power BI: Extending excel to manipulate, analyze, and visualize diverse data. *Serials Review, 45*(3), 184–188. doi:10.1080/00987913.2019.1644891

Berisha Qehaja, A., Kutllovci, E., & Shiroka Pula, J. (2017). Strategic management tools and techniques: A comparative analysis of empirical studies. *Croatian Economic Survey, 19*(1), 67–99. doi:10.15179/ces.19.1.3

Chen, Y. L., Kuo, M. H., Wu, S. Y., & Tang, K. (2009). Discovering recency, frequency, and monetary (RFM) sequential patterns from customers' purchasing data. *Electronic Commerce Research and Applications, 8*(5), 241–251. doi:10.1016/j.elerap.2009.03.002

Copeland, L., Edberg, D., Panorska, A. K., & Wendel, J. (2012). Applying business intelligence concepts to Medicaid claim fraud detection. *Journal of Information Systems Applied Research, 5*(1), 1–14.

Diamond, M., & Mattia, A. (2017). Data visualization: An exploratory study into the software tools used by businesses. *Journal of Instructional Pedagogies, 18.*

Evelson, B., McNabb, K., Karel, R., & Barnett, J. (2007). It's time to reinvent your BI strategy. *Intelligent Enterprise.*

Farrokhi, V., & Pokoradi, L. (2012). The necessities for building a model to evaluate Business Intelligence projects-Literature Review. *The International Journal of Computer Science & Engineering Survey, 3*(2), 1–10. doi:10.5121/ijcses.2012.3201

Foley, É., & Guillemette, M. G. (2010). What is business intelligence? *International Journal of Business Intelligence Research, 1*(4), 1–28. doi:10.4018/jbir.2010100101

Froot, K. A., Scharfstein, D. S., & Stein, J. C. (1993). Risk management: Coordinating corporate investment and financing policies. *The Journal of Finance, 48*(5), 1629–1658. doi:10.1111/j.1540-6261.1993.tb05123.x

Gartner. (2021). *Definition of Business Intelligence (BI) Services - Gartner Information Technology Glossary.* Retrieved 19 February 2021, from https://www.gartner.com/en/information-technology/glossary/business-intelligence-bi-services

Gartner. (2021). *Gartner Glossary.* Retrieved 19 February 2021, from https://www.gartner.com/en/information-technology/glossary/bi-platforms

Gbosbal, S., & Kim, S. K. (1986). Building effective intelligence systems for competitive advantage. *Sloan Management Review, 28*(1), 49.

Grundy, T. (2006). Rethinking and reinventing Michael Porter's five forces model. *Strategic Change, 15*(5), 213–229. doi:10.1002/jsc.764

Guerard, J., Wang, Z., & Xu, G. (2019). *Portfolio and Investment Analysis with SAS: Financial Modeling Techniques for Optimization*. SAS Institute.

Hanid, M., Siriwardena, M., & Koskela, L. (2011, September). What are the significant issues in cost management? In *RICS Construction and Property Conference* (p. 738). Academic Press.

Hasan, M. M., Popp, J., & Oláh, J. (2020). Current landscape and influence of big data on finance. *Journal of Big Data, 7*(1), 1–17. doi:10.118640537-020-00291-z

Helfert, E. A., & Helfert, E. A. (2001). *Financial analysis: tools and techniques: a guide for managers*. McGraw-Hill.

Ho, J. K. K. (2014). Formulation of a Systemic PEST analysis for strategic analysis. *European Academic Research, 2*(5), 6478–6492.

Homocianu, D., & Airinei, D. (2014). Business Intelligence facilities with applications in audit and financial reporting. *Financial Audit*.

Işı, K. (2013). Business intelligence success: The roles of BI capabilities and decision environments. *Information & Management, 50*(1), 13–23. doi:10.1016/j.im.2012.12.001

Isik, O., Jones, M. C., & Sidorova, A. (2011). Business intelligence (BI) success and the role of BI capabilities. *Intelligent Systems in Accounting, Finance & Management, 18*(4), 161–176. doi:10.1002/isaf.329

Jain, A. (2017). Big Data for Supply Chain Management: An Insight to the Analytical Aspects of Tableau & Power BI. *International Journal of Scientific Research, 6*(10), 1–5.

Kaur, G. (2019). *Development of Business Intelligence Outlier and financial crime analytics system for predicting and managing fraud in financial payment services*. Available at: http://www.cs.stir.ac.uk/courses/ITNP097/PastProjects/exemplars/Guneet_Kaur.pdf

Kautish, S. (2008). Online Banking: A Paradigm Shift. *E-Business, 9*(10), 54–59.

Kearns, K. P. (1992). From comparative advantage to damage control: Clarifying strategic issues using SWOT analysis. *Nonprofit Management & Leadership*, *3*(1), 3–22. doi:10.1002/nml.4130030103

Kerzner, H. (2017). *Project management metrics, KPIs, and dashboards: a guide to measuring and monitoring project performance*. John Wiley & Sons. doi:10.1002/9781119427599

Khan, R. A., & Quadri, S. M. K. (2014). Business intelligence: An integrated approach. *International Journal of Management and Innovation*, *6*(2), 21.

Krylov, S. (2015). Applied strategic financial analysis within strategic management of organization finance. *European Journal of Business and Management*, *7*(15), 1–16.

Liu, Z. (2010). Strategic financial management in small and medium-sized enterprises. *International Journal of Business and Management*, *5*(2), 132. doi:10.5539/ijbm.v5n2p132

Lucas, H. C. Jr, & Goh, J. M. (2009). Disruptive technology: How Kodak missed the digital photography revolution. *The Journal of Strategic Information Systems*, *18*(1), 46–55. doi:10.1016/j.jsis.2009.01.002

Lukić, Z. (2017). The art of company financial modelling. *Croatian Operational Research Review*, *8*(2), 409–427. doi:10.17535/crorr.2017.0026

Marius, G., Aref, M., & Bilal, H. (2009). Real time online analytical processing for business intelligence. *UPB Scientific Bulletin, Series C. Electrical Engineering*, *71*(3), 79–88.

Muhammad, G., Ibrahim, J., Bhatti, Z., & Waqas, A. (2014). Business intelligence as a knowledge management tool in providing financial consultancy services. *American Journal of Information Systems*, *2*(2), 26–32.

Nair, V. R. (2015). Customer Acquisition and Retention Strategies in Financial Services. *Journal of Indian Management*, *1*(1), 21–25.

Nazier, M. M., Khedr, A., & Haggag, M. (2013). Business Intelligence and its role to enhance Corporate Performance Management. *International Journal of Management & Information Technology*, *3*(3), 8–15. doi:10.24297/ijmit.v3i3.1745

Nybakk, E. (2018). *SAS® Credit Scoring for Banking – An Integrated Solution from Data Capture to Insight*. Capgemini. Retrieved from https://www.sas.com/content/dam/SAS/support/en/sas-global-forum-proceedings/2018/2751-2018.pdf

O'Brien, A. D., & Stone, D. N. (2020). Yes, You Can Import, Analyze, and Create Dashboards and Storyboards in Tableau! The GBI Case. *Journal of Emerging Technologies in Accounting, 17*(1), 21–31. doi:10.2308/jeta-52760

Olszak, C. M. (2016). Toward better understanding and use of Business Intelligence in organizations. *Information Systems Management, 33*(2), 105–123. doi:10.1080/10580530.2016.1155946

Pokharel, B. (2011). Customer relationship management: Related theories, challenges and application in banking sector. *Banking Journal, 1*(1), 19–28. doi:10.3126/bj.v1i1.5140

Powell, B. (2018). *Mastering Microsoft Power BI: expert techniques for effective data analytics and business intelligence*. Packt Publishing Ltd.

Ranjan, J. (2009). Business intelligence: Concepts, components, techniques and benefits. *Journal of Theoretical and Applied Information Technology, 9*(1), 60–70.

Rao, G. K., & Kumar, R. (2011). Framework to integrate business intelligence and knowledge management in the banking industry. *Review of Business and Technology Research, 4*(1), 1–14.

Rao, M. C., & Rao, K. P. (2009). Inventory turnover ratio as a supply chain performance measure. *Serbian Journal of Management, 4*(1), 41–50.

Rasmussen, N. H., Goldy, P. S., & Solli, P. O. (2002). *Financial business intelligence: trends, technology, software selection, and implementation*. John Wiley & Sons.

Richards, G., Yeoh, W., Chong, A. Y. L., & Popovič, A. (2019). Business intelligence effectiveness and corporate performance management: An empirical analysis. *Journal of Computer Information Systems, 59*(2), 188–196. doi:10.1080/08874417.2017.1334244

Rivard, K., & Cogswell, D. (2004). Are you drowning in BI reports? Using analytical dashboards to cut through the clutter. *Information & Management, 14*(4), 26.

Rocha, S., Bernardino, J., Pedrosa, I., & Ferreira, I. (2017, April). Dashboards and indicators for a BI healthcare system. In *World Conference on Information Systems and Technologies* (pp. 81-90). Springer. 10.1007/978-3-319-56535-4_8

SAS. (2014). *SAS® Financial Crimes Suite*. Retrieved from https://www.sas.com/content/dam/SAS/en_us/doc/productbrief/sas-financial-crimes-suite-106022.pdf

Schick, A., Frolick, M., & Ariyachandra, T. (2012). Competing with BI and analytics at monster worldwide. *International Journal of Business Intelligence Research*, *3*(3), 29–41. doi:10.4018/jbir.2012070103

Schmidt, G., & Wilhelm, W. E. (2000). Strategic, tactical and operational decisions in multi-national logistics networks: A review and discussion of modelling issues. *International Journal of Production Research*, *38*(7), 1501–1523. doi:10.1080/002075400188690

Scott, B., & McGoldrick, M. (2018). Financial intelligence and financial investigation: Opportunities and challenges. *Journal of Policing. Intelligence and Counter-Terrorism*, *13*(3), 301–315. doi:10.1080/18335330.2018.1482563

Sharma, R. S., & Djiaw, V. (2011). Realising the strategic impact of business intelligence tools. *Vine*, *41*(2), 113–131. doi:10.1108/03055721111134772

Stackowiak, R., Rayman, J., & Greenwald, R. (2007). *Oracle data warehousing & business intelligence SO*. John Wiley & Sons.

TCS. (2014). *Business Intelligence in Finance & Accounting: Foundation for an Agile Enterprise*. Tata Consultancy Services. Retrieved from https://www.iqpc.com/media/1000431/50415.pdf

Thurlby, B. (1998). Competitive forces are also subject to change. *Management Decision*, *36*(1), 19–24. doi:10.1108/00251749810199202

Yap, B. W., Ong, S. H., & Husain, N. H. M. (2011). Using data mining to improve assessment of creditworthiness via credit scoring models. *Expert Systems with Applications*, *38*(10), 13274–13283. doi:10.1016/j.eswa.2011.04.147

Zeng, L., Xu, L., Shi, Z., Wang, M., & Wu, W. (2006, October). Techniques, process, and enterprise solutions of business intelligence. In *2006 IEEE International Conference on Systems, Man and Cybernetics* (Vol. 6, pp. 4722-4726). IEEE. 10.1109/ICSMC.2006.385050

Chapter 7
Implementing AI Techniques to Address the Challenges Surrounding Cryptocurrencies

Guneet Kaur
University of Stirling Innovation Park Ltd, UK

ABSTRACT

The research work is focused on examining the role of artificial intelligence (AI) in addressing challenges associated with cryptocurrencies like Bitcoin, Ethereum, etc. The popularity of Bitcoin has sparked the emergence of new alternative cryptocurrencies, commonly referred to as 'altcoins'. Simultaneously with its growing popularity and public awareness, the Bitcoin system has been branded as a haven for security breaches, selfish mining, money laundering, extreme volatility, and unpredictability of future prices. To address these challenges, stakeholders accepting cryptocurrencies must apply AI techniques to process and analyze large amounts of cryptocurrency data. In this context, this chapter discusses the recent research work to assist the researchers and practitioners in the cryptocurrency domain to make fact-based decisions by using AI techniques. Consequently, the chapter provides a detailed review of the background on fiat currencies, cryptocurrencies, challenges associated with cryptocurrencies, and the role of AI techniques in addressing those challenges.

DOI: 10.4018/978-1-7998-7716-5.ch007

1. INTRODUCTION

The global financial market experienced rapid growth from the 20th century to the early 21st century. As financial systems are the circulatory system of world economies, they are constantly transforming, evolving, and adapting to certain economic and technological requirements, providing an atmosphere for the efficient functioning of financial relations and commodity-money (Mikhaylov, 2020). Since its inception, money has been changing its form, but it still serves the same basic functions as a store of value, a medium of exchange, and a unit of account. As a consequence, money is now one of the most powerful social and financial instruments. It is impossible to imagine a world without cash or noncash in daily life. While it is impossible to say that noncash money is replacing cash, their turnover is faster than cash. This is due to the ease of use of electronic payment systems and the current state of technological advancement, which allows for contactless transactions at the terminal and online transactions over the Internet (Beck, 2018). Since they reflect a modern understanding of the type of money and the security of transactions, digital currencies have the ability to develop existing payment systems and financial institutions (Seetharaman et al., 2017). For example, since 2019, one of the world's financial leaders, the United States, has been conducting research and taking steps to integrate Cryptocurrencies into its internal payment system (Mikhaylov, 2020). The US Congress passed the 'Crypto-Currency Act of 2020' for consideration at the end of 2019 (Mikhaylov, 2020).

Since the inception of the Cryptocurrency craze in 2009, many investors have flocked to Cryptocurrencies in the hopes of finding the hippest way to 'get rich fast' (Baum, 2018). As a result, numerous Cryptocurrencies have been created since 2009, with over 4000 in existence as of 2021 (Statista, 2021). Many crypto-investors have profited handsomely from their investments in Cryptocurrencies and reaped the advantages of having money in a decentralized exchange. This nascent Cryptocurrency industry, however, has a dark side. Fraudsters and con men have grown with the times, discovering new ways to defraud unsuspecting crypto-investors every day, as they have for decades. This new wave of fraudsters has invented new ways to coordinate pump, dump schemes, build fictitious initial coin offerings, commit Ponzi schemes, pull exit schemes, and formulate many other schemes to steal investors' Cryptocurrencies. According to a recent survey conducted by Bitcoin.com News, Cryptocurrency investors lose an average of $9.1 million every day to Cryptocurrency fraud (Baum, 2018). Furthermore, since any government legislation does not yet govern Cryptocurrencies, it is difficult to pursue redress for losses incurred by fraud (Jung et al., 2019).

With millions of transactions being conducted via various exchange services and a large number of Cryptocurrencies being used as financial assets, Cryptocurrencies are vulnerable to trading problems and difficulties similar to those seen in the financial domain. Therefore, a clear need arises to apply data mining techniques to process and analyze huge volumes of Crytopcurrencies' data. Artificial intelligence (AI) techniques can analyze and discover trends in the vast amount of data, making trading and mining easier and more stable (Diadiushkin et al., 2019). Due to the privacy and security risks that Cryptocurrencies face, discovering trends in money-laundering transactions and other fraudulent transactions and trading schemes will help reduce the crimes involving Cryptocurrencies (Sabry et al., 2020). Other applications include volatility forecasting, price and trend forecasting, cyber security, privacy of the users. Therefore, AI approaches can help solve these challenges for Cryptocurrencies, which are beyond human ability to analyze and evaluate (Sabry et al., 2020). In this context, this chapter is focused on the following exploratory questions:

1. What are the problems in the Cryptocurrency domain that needs to be addressed analytically?
2. Which artificial intelligence techniques can be used to address the challenges in the field of Cryptocurrencies?
3. What are some potential research gaps and areas of improvement that should be explored further?

The remainder of this chapter is structured in the following manner. The background on fiat currencies, Bitcoin, and other Cryptocurrencies are covered in Section 2. Section 3 portrays key challenges associated with Cryptocurrencies and reviews artificial intelligence (AI) and machine learning (ML) techniques that address these issues. Section 4 summarizes key research contributions and section 5 discusses potential study discrepancies and areas for improvement, and the chapter is concluded in Section 6.

2. BACKGROUND

2.1 History of Fiat Currencies

The world's most popular currencies have been convertible into fixed quantities of gold or other precious metals since the 19th and 20th centuries (Yermack, 2015). Many currencies have been minted directly from gold or silver species for thousands of years before that. This direct correlation between money and gold instilled public faith in a currency's worth. Nonetheless, between the 1920s and the 1970s, most countries abandoned the gold standard, partially due to the stresses of funding two

World Wars, but more likely as a result of global gold demand struggling to keep pace with economic development (Yermack, 2015). Almost every major economy has released paper fiat currency (e.g., USD, EURO, Yen, GBP, Renimbi) since then (Bhalla, 2011).

Although the Japanese Yen grew in popularity as a foreign currency during the 1980s, the USD has remained a global currency for decades (Seetharaman et al., 2017). In international finance, both the Chinese Renminbi and the Euro have recently questioned the USD. Moreover, the dollar's share of the reserve currency is declining, even though the global Reserve Currency is rising (Seetharaman et al., 2017). However, due to valuation issues, neither the Yuan nor the Euro can compete effectively with the US dollar. The Chinese Yuan is considered undervalued, while the Euro is considered overvalued (Seetharaman et al., 2017). While the Renminbi will become a viable option at some stage in the future, the dollar will remain the dominant currency for the foreseeable future. The Euro was the closest competitor, but after the financial crisis, the accumulation of EURO currency reserves has decreased. Similarly, Yuan lacks the most significant criterion (i.e., convertibility) for being a global currency. As a result, no currency, including the US dollar, is immune to global economic challenges. However, as long as there is no viable substitute, the US dollar will remain the world's reserve currency of preference. Moshirian (2007) discovered that there would be a global currency that will eliminate these weaknesses of fiat currencies and gold-based money in the future.

2.2 The Birth of Bitcoin

Satoshi Nakamoto developed the Bitcoin protocol in 2009 to allow non-trusting individuals to transact. Since 2009, Bitcoin has been a massive success as a financial commodity, and there are now about 18 million Bitcoins (BTCs) being traded and exchanged. However, from an economic perspective, Bitcoin does not resemble other conventional properties (Klein et al., 2018). From a technical perspective, Bitcoin depends on a peer-to-peer network that allows users to share money using economic rewards rather than trusted authorities. The network is built on Blockchain technology, which is a decentralized public ledger that keeps track of all transactions in an immutable manner using novel concepts, including Nakamoto consensus and proof of work (PoW). To validate transactions, all nodes in the network sync this Blockchain. Miners compete to solve a cryptographic puzzle and then apply transactions to the Blockchain in blocks.

2.1 Process of Mining New Bitcoins

The process of verifying crypto transactions and adding them to the decentralized ledger is known as Cryptocurrency mining. Various steps are performed to mine Cryptocurrencies. Figure1 presents the steps involved in the mining of Bitcoin. According to Liu et al. (2017), to sign a transaction between the sender's and receiver's Bitcoin addresses, Bitcoin uses the elliptic curve digital signature algorithm (ECDSA). Bitcoin addresses are 26-35 alphanumeric character identifiers created by hashing the sender's or receiver's public keys (Sabry et al, 2020). These addresses gave Bitcoin transactions the appearance of anonymity. Nonetheless, they are only pseudo-anonymous. The Blockchain needs proof-of-work (PoW) to protect the distributed ledger from tampering. This is accomplished by solving a difficult-to-solve but simple-to-verify computationally intensive cryptographic problem. The nodes compete to find a nonce that produces a block hash with a predetermined number of leading zeros (Vranken, 2017). In addition to transaction fees from senders, the winner node adds a block of transactions to the network and receives a block reward set by the Bitcoin protocol. The block reward was set at 50 BTC initially, and it is halved when every 210,000 blocks are added to the chain. This process of halving occurs roughly every four years (Meynkhard, 2019). Currently, the block reward is 6.25 BTC. This whole process is called Bitcoin mining. The PoW problem's complexity was relatively simple in the early days of Bitcoin, and Bitcoin mining was achieved with a personal computer with a decent central processing unit (CPU). However, nowadays, higher hash rates are needed to solve the crypto-puzzle as the complexity increases. Therefore, miners start creating alternative Cryptocurrencies to address these challenges.

Figure 1. Steps involved in the mining of Bitcoin.

2.3 The Rise of Other Cryptocurrencies

Namecoin was the first altcoin to improve the domain name system's speed (DNS), decentralization, privacy, and stability (Sabry et al., 2020). Other Cryptocurrencies include Litecoin, Monero, Ripple, Zcash, Ethereum, Dash, and BCH. These

Cryptocurrencies (altcoins) outperform Bitcoin in terms of price, anonymity, or other features. A stablecoin is also a Cryptocurrency with an underlying mechanism for price stability, such as the use of fiat currencies or government bonds as collateral. The Libra project is the most well-known the most publicized stablecoin initiative (Sandner et al., 2020). Libra was announced in June 2019 by the Libra Association. There are currently 27 companies in the Libra consortium, including Facebook's subsidy Novi, Spotify, and Uber (Sandner et al., 2020). However, Bitcoin dominates the industry, accounting for more than 70% of all transactions (Sabry et al., 2020).

2.3 The Inherent Risks of Cryptocurrencies

The risks associated with Cryptocurrencies are explained in the below section and presented in figure 2.

2.3.1 Anonymity, Security Breaches and Financial Crime

Even though all transactions are registered on the Blockchain and accessible to everyone, Bitcoin users maintain their privacy by identifying themselves solely via public keys and signing transactions with corresponding private keys. Taking advantage of the anonymity, criminals easily exploited the site's popularity to defraud other users by setting up numerous scams Sabry et al., 2020). According to an empirical study of Bitcoin-based scams, at least $11 million was stolen from 13,000 victims in 2015 (Vasek & Moore, 2015). It is virtually impossible to undo a fraudulent transaction due to the Blockchain's immutability and users' privacy (Sabry et al., 2020). Many scams are based on offline precedents such as Ponzi schemes, a 150-year-old hoax that imitates a high-return investment programme that can only be cashed out if enough new customers pay the benefit with their investment (Jung et al., 2019). As a result, early investors profit off newer investors' backs, who end up with nothing (Jung et al., 2019). Furthermore, U.S. authorities shuttered the Silk Road marketplace, an Internet platform for the sale of illegal drugs, after arresting its operator in San Francisco in October 2013 (Yermack, 2015). With the rise in Bitcoin's value, exchanges have become targets for hackers; Mt. Gox announced three denials of service attacks in April 2013, each of which resulted in a dramatic reduction in trading volume on different dates (Yermack, 2015). Also, Mt. Gox crashed on 25th February 2014, leaving many Bitcoin investors stranded (Trautman, 2014). Mt. Gox lost nearly 70,000 Bitcoins in a long-running fraud estimated at $400 million during that time (Trautman, 2014). Liebau & Schueffel (2019) provided another means of scams called initial coin offerings (ICOs). An ICO is an unregulated method of raising funds that Cryptocurrency companies commonly use to replace other financial institutions' limited funding methods. According to a study by Bloomberg, over 80% of ICO funding went to scams (Phan et al., 2019). According to a 2017 estimate, scams received $1.34 billion, accounting for 11% of the overall funding of $11.9 billion (Phan et al., 2019).

Due to the lack of mature legislation in the Cryptocurrency industry, Cryptocurrencies have become a tool of financial crime. These scams are damaging the credibility of the entire Cryptocurrency ecosystem. To overcome this problem, several countries have recently imposed know-your-customer (KYC) and anti-money laundering (AML) policies on Crypto exchanges and are introducing Central Bank-regulated digital currencies. Central banks have increased their efforts to issue their own digital currencies, known as CBDCs, in response to developments surrounding stablecoins and the Libra project's announcement (Sander et al., 2020).

2.3.2 Selfish Mining

According to Eyal & Sirer (2014), miners can earn money even though they only have 25% of the computing power. This is referred to as 'selfish mining attacks.' The idea is that instead of broadcasting the discovered blocks to the network after mining them, the "selfish miners" keep them private in the hopes of eventually forking the chain. While the honest nodes continue to mine on the public chain, greedy miners continue to mine new blocks and hold them for themselves. When the private chain's length surpasses that of the public chain, the private chain becomes the new trusted chain. This incentivizes honest nodes to become selfish miners, resulting in larger selfish mining pools. Moreover, Cryptocurrency 'mining' is energy-intensive, requiring complex computer calculations to validate transactions. According to Cambridge University researchers, it uses about 121.36 terawatt-hours (TWh) each year and is unlikely to decrease unless the currency's value falls (Criddle, 2021). Furthermore, without constant price increases, the rising energy requirements to produce a single Cryptocurrency would almost certainly lead to a cliff of negative net social benefits. For example, Goodkind et al. (2020) demonstrated a case (for Bitcoin) in which the 'cryptodamages' to human health and climate change approximately equal each $1 of coin value generated in December 2018. Understanding the negative environmental externalities of Cryptocurrency mining progresses, but it is still a work in progress.

2.3.3 Extreme Volatility

Baur & Hoang (2021) provided that Bitcoin's volatility is severe. The line chart in figure 3 presents the volatility of Bitcoin. Because of Bitcoin's volatile existence, external events have the biggest effect on its price volatility. Investors respond to these events in one of two ways: positively or negatively, resulting in panic selling or purchasing (Cermak, 2017). Prices fluctuate significantly not only over longer time horizons but also regularly. According to Harvey (2014), Bitcoin's volatility is eight times higher than that of stocks. Corbet et al. (2018) and Smales (2019) have reported similar findings (2019). Consequently, it cannot be considered a valuable unit of account because merchants that accept Bitcoin are required either to use an intermediary or automatically convert Bitcoin to a fiat currency after the exchange has cleared (Yermack, 2015). Due to its extreme volatility and confusion on whether Bitcoin would maintain its value in the absence of any intrinsic value, Bitcoin is not suitable as a store of value (Cermak, 2017).

Figure 2. Risks associated with Cryptocurrencies

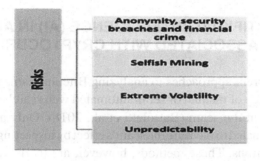

Figure 3. Severe Volatility of Bitcoin.

2.3.4 Unpredictability

In reality, Bitcoin is a database management system (Andolfatto & Spewak, 2019). If database management systems are designed to meet a specific constituency's needs, they can have a fundamental value to fall back upon (Cheah & Fry, 2015). A risk-neutral rational agent usually pays the fundamental price of a financial asset, which is determined by discounting projected future cash flows from the asset (Chaim & Laurini, 2019). Since potential cash flows are not observed, determining Bitcoin's fundamental price is difficult. It is because Bitcoin provides users with a money storage and transfer system with two main features, including permissionless access; the decentralized way of managing databases. According to the first property, no one can stop a user from sending any amount of Bitcoin from one account to another. The protocol's second property indicates that it is not reliant on a delegated authority's presence to control accounts and pass funds. Therefore, fundamental demand for Bitcoin stems from the fact that at least some people value these features, which sets a non-zero lower bound on Bitcoin's price. According to economic theory, an unbacked asset's price dynamics would be extremely volatile and potentially unpredictable (Andolfatto & Spewak, 2019).

3. ROLE OF ARTIFICIAL INTELLIGENCE (AI) IN ADDRESSING CHALLENGES ASSOCIATED WITH CRYPTOCURRENCIES

The majority of current approaches to analyzing Bitcoin scams necessitate a time-consuming initial step of manual or semi-automated web searches to obtain Bitcoin addresses involved in the scam (Bartoletti et al., 2018). Only after this stage, the analysis can be automated to measure the scam's effect by inspecting the corresponding Blockchain transactions. These methods, however, are ineffective when the scam addresses are not publicly accessible, such as when they are communicated privately to registered users or only available on the deep web or dark web. In these situations, tools that automatically scan the Bitcoin Blockchain for suspicious activity and recognize the addresses linked to fraudulent activities will be useful. Similarly, the rapidly expanding Cryptocurrency market poses the challenge of evaluating the vast volume of trades and transactions for various Cryptocurrencies on various exchanges. Therefore, AI techniques have become almost important for automatically extracting meaningful patterns for fraud detection, considering the ever-increasing amounts of data to be handled (i.e., millions of distinct addresses and 300 million transactions). Artificial intelligence techniques are classified into evolutionary-based techniques, machine learning techniques, and knowledge-based techniques (Kautish and Thapliyal, 2012). Such techniques can be beneficial for several stakeholders in the Cryptocurrency ecosystem, as explained below.

1. Regulatory Institutions: These institutions can use artificial intelligence techniques to learn from data about potential financial frauds and risks.
2. Security Analysts: Security experts can use these techniques to examine and assess the security and privacy of Cryptocurrencies and identify potential threats to prevent them in the future.

3.   Traders: For trading decisions and high returns for the investors, automated traders can evaluate and learn from Cryptocurrencies' market prices to make informed decisions. This helps decide when to purchase, hold, or sell a stock based on various indicators that change over time.

4.   Miners: Miners can use AI techniques to boost their profits while also conserving electricity for environmental reasons.

Moreover, banking already implements AI techniques for fraud detection (Kautish, 2008), conversational banking, risk evaluation, and credit underwriting. Additionally, voice assistants and financial chatbots that mimic live employees in the financial sector deepen customer relationships and provide personalized insights and suggestions are examples of AI software systems. Furthermore, AI is widely used in intelligent trading systems to forecast stock market and currency price movements. The aforementioned issues are also present when trading Cryptocurrencies on the financial market. Just like financial services, artificial intelligence reduces the risk of human error in Cryptocurrencies. Fraud detection, volatility prediction, price and trend prediction, privacy and security are various challenges that can be resolved by using AI techniques to obtain insights and indicators about various Cryptocurrencies. The role of AI techniques in addressing these challenges is discussed in the section below.

3.1 Fraud Detection

The usage and credibility of Bitcoin and other Cryptocurrencies in aiding illegal activities is a major source of concern, as it has an impact on Cryptocurrency security and confidence. Cryptocurrencies are known to attract cyber criminals due to their pseudo-anonymity and willingness to function independently of government and bank regulations. Ponzi schemes, hacking, buying illicit narcotics, digital fraud, phishing, pump-and-dump schemes, and money laundering in the black market are just some of the scams and criminal activities that can occur in Cryptocurrencies (Kaur, 2019). In this context, fraud detection is focused on detecting anomalies and suspicious behavior using the historical data of transactions and Bitcoin prices (Monamo et al., 2016).

Monamo et al. (2016) used trimmed k-means and k-means clustering based on the transactions graph's features in a semi-supervised way to identify fraudulent behavior in the Bitcoin transactions network due to a lack of labeled events or examples for different fraud activities. Both algorithms were able to produce the best clustering results. The trimmed algorithm was able to detect 5 of the 30 well-known anomalies, such as the Linode Hack, Mt Gox, and 50 BTC thefts (Monamo et al., 2016). They were able to identify two more frauds using k-d trees. The authors used supervised classification models to explain the relationship between the labels and predictor variables based on outliers' clustering labels.

On the other hand, Bartoletti et al. (2016) created a dataset of real-world Ponzi schemes by reviewing Bitcoin Blockchain transactions for scams to detect Ponzi schemes automatically. Through a manual search on bitcointalk.org and Reddit, they were able to find a list of 32 Ponzi schemes advertised as high-yield investment programmes (HYIPs) or casino games (Bartoletti et al., 2016). They used Bayes Network, RIPPER, and Random Forest classifiers in their detection model's induction stage, which reflect three different learning strategies. The **Bayes network** is a probabilistic model that depicts the conditional dependency relationship among a collection of variables as a directed acyclic graph (the features and the target class, in the context of classification problems). **RIPPER** is a propositional rule learner that extracts classification rules directly from training data using a sequential covering logic. This method is especially well suited for dealing with imbalanced classification tasks, such as fraud detection, since the algorithm is structured to offer the least frequent class higher priority. **Random Forest** is an ensemble approach that uses multiple decision trees constructed from random variants of the same data to solve a problem. Random Forest is a computationally powerful learner that has demonstrated to be 'best in class' in many domains, including fraud detection (Bhattacharyya et al., 2011). Random forest was the best classifier, correctly classifying 31 of the 32 Ponzi schemes.

For binary classification of HYIP and non-HYIP addresses, Toyoda et al. (2019) used random forest (RF), gradient boosting classier (XGBoost), artificial neural network (ANN), support vector machines (SVM), and k-NN. Based on seven features that characterize transactions, random forest generated the best performance.

3.2 Price and Trend Prediction

Traders and Domain observers must conduct Bitcoin/Cryptocurrency analytics and forecast Cryptocurrency prices in order to trade Cryptocurrencies. Many factors influence the price of Bitcoin, including demand, supply, and investor interest. Sabry et al. (2020) categorize these factors into four types such as Cryptocurrency market factors, Blockchain factors, online factors, and other market factors. Cryptocurrency market factors include the history of BTC prices, market capitalization, market spread, trade volume, and price momentum. Blockchain factors include Blockchain size, hash rate, BTC volume, cost per transaction, and the number of unique BTC addresses. Online factors include Twitter sentiment, forum articles on bitcoinntalk. org, Twitter Volume, and Wikipedia views. Other market factors include Crude oil price, gold and silver price, NASDAQ, S&P 500 Index, Dow Jones, and exchange prices between USD and EUR.

Before deciding which algorithm/model should be used to predict Bitcoin prices, the first step is to collect time-series data. Therefore, price prediction becomes a time-series prediction task when various variables' historical data is used. To predict the closing price based on a collection of indicators, it can be modelled as a *regression* problem. By encoding the Cryptocurrency price time series output variable in terms of rise and fall, it can also be modelled as a *classification* problem to predict whether there will be a rise/fall or no change in the price a co

3.1.1 Techniques for Prediction

In order to forecast and analyze Bitcoin prices, a variety of statistical techniques and models can be employed. Georgoula et al. (2015) used multiple linear regressions to model the relationship between Bitcoin Cryptocurrency price and certain predictor variables, including economic and financial variables. Furthermore, public interest in Bitcoin was measured using Google Trends, Twitter feeds, and Wikipedia views relevant to Bitcoin. They discovered that the tweet volume, rather than the tweets' sentiment, is a good predictor of Bitcoin price (Abraham et al., 2018). The predictability of the most liquid twelve Cryptocurrencies (Monero, Ripple, Bitcoin Cash, EOS, Ethereum, Ethereum Classic, Bitcoin, Iota Litecoin, OmiseGO, Dash, and Zcash) is examined on a regular and minute-by-minute basis using machine learning classification algorithms by Akyildirim et al. (2021). The algorithms include SVM, logistic regression, ANN, and random forests. The analysis was done using historical price data and technical indicators as model features. They discovered that the average classification accuracy of four algorithms was consistently above 50% for all Cryptocurrencies and timescales, indicating some predictability of price patterns in the Cryptocurrency markets. However, in terms of predictive accuracy, support vector machines provide the highest and most reliable performance.

Senthuran & Halgamuge (2019) used deep learning techniques to forecast Ethereum and Bitcoin prices in Australian dollars (AUD). Ji et al. (2019) performed a comparison of various deep learning models including, deep neural network (DNN), long-short term memory (LSTM), and ANN for Bitcoin price prediction. The LSTM algorithm aids in the development of a hybrid model that combines sentiment analysis techniques with a predictive machine learning model (Kinderis et al., 2018). They provided that LSTM-based prediction models outperformed other techniques for Bitcoin price regression. Nonetheless, DNN-based models outperformed other techniques for price change classification. They also demonstrated that classification models outperformed regression models in terms of trading profitability (Ji et al., 2019).

Sin & Wang (2017) used an Artificial Neural Network ensemble method called genetic algorithm based selective neural network (GASEN) to investigate the relationship between Bitcoin features and the next day shift in the price of Bitcoin, using a Multi-Layered Perceptron as the base model for each of the neural networks in the ensemble. They demonstrated that GASEN was capable of performing well in the classification task, with accuracy ranging from 58 to 63%. The ensemble achieved a positive result in making a profit of close to 85% using a simple trading strategy (Sin & Wang, 2017). Jang & Lee (2017) used a Bayesian neural network (BNN) and a support vector regression (SVR) to regularize weights of input variables to a neural network to account for Bitcoin's high price volatility. Blockchain and macroeconomic variables and international fiat currency exchange rates were among the input variables. The authors concluded that the SVM model was ineffective for the prediction task.

3.3 Volatility Prediction

The degree of variance in a trading price series over time is known as volatility. It denotes the degree of uncertainty or risk associated with the magnitude of changes in currency value. Bitcoin and other Cryptocurrencies are known for their erratic behavior. Cryptocurrency volatility is largely due to their decentralized existence, making their prices uncontrollable by any entity or government. Chu et al. (2017) suggested the time-series statistical model called generalized autoregressive conditional heteroskedasticity (GARCH) to model volatility. However, Peng et al. (2018) merged the standard GARCH model with SVR, capable of robustly covering multi-variate and complex financial sequence characteristics. It was used to assess alternative risky investments and direct investment decisions by predicting the volatility of three fiat currencies (Euro, British Pound, and Japanese Yen) and three Cryptocurrencies (Bitcoin, Ethereum, and Dash). They offered clear evidence that SVR models outperform conventional GARCH models significantly. Guo et al. (2018) used the incremental learning and rolling method to evaluate a temporal mixture model for output prediction to forecast Bitcoin price volatility. They compared their model to various statistical models (e.g., GARCH, structural time series model) and machine learning baseline models (e.g., Random Forest, Gradient Boosting). However, their temporal mixture model proved to be more reliable, robust, and adaptable to time-varying data.

3.4 Cryptocurrency Mining

The mining method has the drawback of using a lot of energy, which is used by mining pools to participate in PoW computations. Just one miner succeeds in adding a block of transactions, leaving other mining pools with significant energy costs. This drawback jeopardizes the Cryptocurrency's decentralization and makes it vulnerable to monopolization, particularly as the block reward diminishes over time due to

Bitcoin's block reward halving. To model and evaluate a selfish mining strategy in Ethereum, Feng & Niu (2019) proposed a Markov model. They reviewed the PoW mining method as a series of Bernoulli trails searching for a nonce in order to create a new block independently. They discovered that in Ethereum, the computing power threshold that makes selfish mining profitable is lower than in Bitcoin mining. They proposed creating new reward functions that would enable miners to maximize their profits while maintaining a more stable and honest strategy. To address environmental concerns associated with Cryptocurrency mining, computer scientists and ethicists collaborate to create artificial intelligence applications that can make ethical decisions in complicated real-world scenarios (Gladden, 2015). In some of these models, AI-based systems collect and analyze data from their surroundings and make decisions based on a pre-programmed collection of ethical principles. An AI may discover new ethical principles and form its own 'conscience' through communicating with the outside world (Gladden, 2015).

Carlsten et al. (2016) recommended game-theoretic analysis to demonstrate the value of block reward in mining to keep the Blockchain safe, as the transaction fee model could promote selfish mining. Sabry et al. (2020) provided that mining pools can use AI techniques to select which Cryptocurrency to mine and which mining pool to enter based on historical data to reduce energy usage and increase benefit. A study by Wang et al. (2019) uses reinforcement learning (RL), which is a machine learning technique, to develop the optimal Bitcoin-like Blockchain mining strategy. The RL learning system has the advantage of being able to achieve an optimal (or near-optimal) strategy without understanding the specifics of the Blockchain network model. The authors concluded that RL mining can learn the optimal policy for various situations adaptively (Wang et al., 2019). As a result, RL mining can be more stable in a dynamic setting where parameter values change over time.

3.5 Anonymity and Security

Criminals prefer anonymity to conceal their identity when trading illegally for drugs or engaging in money laundering transactions. However, since anonymity is based on pseudonyms for addresses, it is less reliable than it is thought to be. Nagata et al. (2018) used statistics from transaction history and transaction frequency to deanonymize a series of Bitcoin addresses to eliminate this flaw. The results show that the Jaccard distance between subsets of output addresses identified 80.5% of addresses. The number of transactions per address does not affect the average recall or precision score. Conversely, Ermilov et al. (2017) proposed using activity trends and publicly accessible knowledge from off-chain sources, some addresses can be grouped by their ownership. The study's findings indicate that a suggested solution for Bitcoin address clustering is feasible. Users may use it to prevent vulnerable

Bitcoin usage trends, and investigators can use it to do a more sophisticated de-anonymizing analysis. Jourdan et al. (2019) presented a complete probabilistic model of the Bitcoin Blockchain, laying the groundwork for future AI applications based on Bitcoin transactions. They developed a completely observed graphical model of a Bitcoin block based on a collection of conditional dependencies caused by the Bitcoin protocol at the block level. They then expanded the model to include hidden entity attributes like the related logical agent's functional type and derived asymptotic limits on the privacy properties implied by this model. The results show that the model is capable of accurately capturing the actions of most entity types.

Despite the security and privacy features of Blockchain-based Cryptocurrencies, the Cryptocurrency environment remains vulnerable to several security threats, including mining process attacks, attacks on the distributed network, and double spending attacks, according to Sabry et al. (2020). A new model for detecting anomalies in Bitcoin electronic transactions was introduced by Sayadi et al. (2019). The model incorporates two machine learning algorithms: the One-Class Support Vector Machines (OCSVM) algorithm for detecting outliers and the KMeans algorithm for grouping outliers with related types of anomalies. The first algorithm successfully detected 16 anomalies composed of three types of attacks: six double-spending attacks, six denial-of-service (DDOS) attacks, and four attacks with 51% vulnerability (Sayadi et al., 2019). The authors were able to cluster the anomalies observed in the first stage into three clusters using Kmeans in the second stage, with a better clustering result of 0.951. Similarly, Baqer et al. (2016) noted a clustering-based approach to detect spam transactions, which resulted in a Bitcoin DoS attack. On the other hand, Li et al. (2020) used numerical simulations to investigate the effect of the mining pools' strength, the ratio of power to be infiltrated, and the betrayed rate of dispatched miners on the nash equillibrium of the mining process.

Therefore, both supervised machine learning models and simulation models are effective in detecting attacks against Cryptocurrencies in the Blockchain environment.

4. KEY RESEARCH CONTRIBUTIONS BY THE RESEARCHER

The above study provided that technology advancements have influenced the development of Cryptocurrencies by allowing for new ways to store Blockchains, protect the network, mine new coins, and analyze massive amounts of trade volume and Blockchain transactions that are beyond human capabilities. The chapter presented state-of-the-art research that addresses Cryptocurrencies' challenges by using AI techniques. The study revealed that the key problems faced by Cryptocurrencies include the risk of financial fraud, security breaches, extreme volatility prediction, selfish mining, the anonymity of transactions, and unpredictability of digital currencies' prices and returns. The study highlighted that various AI techniques can effectively address these challenges to benefit the miners, traders, regulators, and security analysts. The common techniques used to address a particular challenge are outlined below.

1. Fraud detection: It includes various AI techniques such as trimmed k-means and k-means clustering, Ripper, the Bayes Network, random forest (RF), gradient boosting classier (XGBoost), artificial neural network (ANN), and support vector machines (SVM), and k-NN.
2. Price and trend prediction: It includes statistical models (such as multiple regression, logistic regression), ANN, random forest, SVM, LSTN, DNN, GASEN, and SVR.
3. Volatility prediction: For volatility prediction, various techniques such as GARCH models, SVR, structural time series model, Random Forest, Gradient Boosting were identified.
4. Cryptocurrency mining: Markov model, game-theoretic analysis, and reinforcement learning techniques were commonly used in the literature to model and evaluate a selfish mining strategy.
5. Anonymity and security: It includes clustering and probabilistic models to conduct a de-anonymizing analysis. Moreover, a combination of OCSVM and KMeans, and numerical simulations can be used to detect outliers and prevent double-spending and cyber-attacks.

5. DISCUSSION AND FUTURE WORK

Although the research effectively captured the challenges associated with Cryptocurrencies and AI's role in addressing them effectively, the number of AI study studies covering Bitcoin is substantially higher than those addressing other Cryptocurrencies. Therefore, this can be explored in future research. Further limitations and recommended future work for each challenge are discussed below.

1. Fraud Detection: Another issue is related to a lack of credible datasets due to which fraud detection research has been hampered. Other forms of scams, such as pump-and-dump schemes and fake ICOs, have not been investigated thoroughly, which can be explored in future studies.
2. Price and trend prediction: In terms of price prediction, studies primarily focused on Bitcoin prices in USD and relied on tweets and historical data for forecasting. In future research, an analysis of methodologies for valuing Bitcoin can be covered for a more comprehensive analysis.

3. Volatility prediction: The existing research focused mainly on the GARCH models to predict Bitcoin's volatility. No volatility prediction analysis used text analysis to quantify consumer acceptance and interest in the Cryptocurrency sector, which can be explored in future studies.

4. Cryptocurrency mining: In existing research, Game-theoretic methods were the most successful in simulating the mining strategy. The data regarding total computing power and electricity consumption by miners is not available. The mining research work reviewed for solving the PoW puzzle is still in its early stages and needs further investigation.

5. Anonymity and security: The existing research is mainly focused on the deanonymization of Bitcoin. Therefore, deanonymization research focused on Cryptocurrencies (other than Bitcoin) needs to be investigated in future studies. Furthermore, AI's role in detecting suspicious activities has not been explored thoroughly due to a lack of publicly available datasets. Therefore, the use of synthetic datasets to interpret the efficiency of AI in enhancing network security can be investigated in future studies.

6. CONCLUSION

This chapter organizes and navigates through the overwhelming amount of study that uses AI techniques to address Cryptocurrencies' challenges. It was discovered that Cryptocurrencies are susceptible to trading problems and difficulties similar to those seen in the financial domain due to millions of transactions being performed daily and a large number of Cryptocurrencies being used as financial assets. Consequently, there is a clear need for stakeholders (accepting Cryptocurrencies) to apply AI techniques to process and analyze large amounts of Cryptocurrency data to make fact-based decisions. The research identified five key challenges faced by miners, investors, regulators, and traders in the Cryptocurrency domain. Financial fraud, security breaches, intense volatility, selfish mining, transactions' privacy, and the unpredictability of digital currency prices and returns are among the challenges. For each challenge, several research works focused on applying AI techniques to address these issues were compared. As the researcher did not cite all of the research papers in this area, potential research gaps and future research directions were provided. Researchers, students, and practitioners interested in applying AI and machine learning techniques in Cryptocurrencies would benefit significantly from this chapter. It gives them an extensive overview of a multidisciplinary area concerning traditional finance, decentralized finance, Cryptocurrencies, behavioral finance, AI, ML, and Blockchain and how current research work can be improved in the future.

REFERENCES

Abraham, J., Higdon, D., Nelson, J., & Ibarra, J. (2018). Cryptocurrency price prediction using tweet volumes and sentiment analysis. *SMU Data Science Review*, *1*(3), 1.

Akyildirim, E., Goncu, A., & Sensoy, A. (2021). Prediction of cryptocurrency returns using machine learning. *Annals of Operations Research*, *297*(1), 3–36. doi:10.100710479-020-03575-y

Andolfatto, D., & Spewak, A. (2019). Whither the price of bitcoin? *Economic Synopses*, (1), 1–2.

Baqer, K., Huang, D. Y., McCoy, D., & Weaver, N. 2016, February. Stressing out: Bitcoin "stress testing". In *International Conference on Financial Cryptography and Data Security* (pp. 3-18). Springer.

Bartoletti, M., Pes, B., & Serusi, S. (2018, June). Data mining for detecting bitcoin ponzi schemes. In *2018 Crypto Valley Conference on Blockchain Technology (CVCBT)* (pp. 75-84). IEEE. 10.1109/CVCBT.2018.00014

Baum, S. C. (2018). Cryptocurrency Fraud: A Look Into The Frontier of Fraud (University Honors Program). Georgia Southern University.

Baur, D. G., & Hoang, L. T. (2021). A crypto safe haven against Bitcoin. *Finance Research Letters*, *38*, 101431. doi:10.1016/j.frl.2020.101431

Beck, R. (2018). Beyond bitcoin: The rise of blockchain world. *Computer*, *51*(2), 54–58. doi:10.1109/MC.2018.1451660

Bhalla, S. S. (2011). Euro and the Yuan: Different peas in the same pod. *Comparative Economic Studies*, *53*(3), 355–381. doi:10.1057/ces.2011.20

Bhattacharyya, S., Jha, S., Tharakunnel, K., & Westland, J. C. (2011). Data mining for credit card fraud: A comparative study. *Decision Support Systems*, *50*(3), 602–613. doi:10.1016/j.dss.2010.08.008

Carlsten, M., Kalodner, H., Weinberg, S. M., & Narayanan, A. (2016, October). On the instability of bitcoin without the block reward. In *Proceedings of the 2016 ACM SIGSAC Conference on Computer and Communications Security* (pp. 154-167). 10.1145/2976749.2978408

Cermak, V. (2017). Can bitcoin become a viable alternative to fiat currencies? An empirical analysis of bitcoin's volatility based on a GARCH model. *An Empirical Analysis of Bitcoin's Volatility Based on a GARCH Model.*

Chaim, P., & Laurini, M. P. (2019). Is Bitcoin a bubble? *Physica A, 517,* 222–232. doi:10.1016/j.physa.2018.11.031

Cheah, E. T., & Fry, J. (2015). Speculative bubbles in Bitcoin markets? An empirical investigation into the fundamental value of Bitcoin. *Economics Letters, 130,* 32–36. doi:10.1016/j.econlet.2015.02.029

Chu, J., Chan, S., Nadarajah, S., & Osterrieder, J. (2017). GARCH modelling of cryptocurrencies. *Journal of Risk and Financial Management, 10*(4), 17. doi:10.3390/jrfm10040017

Corbet, S., Lucey, B., Peat, M., & Vigne, S. (2018). Bitcoin futures—What use are they? *Economics Letters, 172,* 23–27. doi:10.1016/j.econlet.2018.07.031

Criddle, C. (2021). *Bitcoin consumes 'more electricity than Argentina'.* Retrieved 1 May 2021, from https://www.bbc.co.uk/news/technology-56012952

Diadiushkin, A., Sandkuhl, K., & Maiatin, A. (2019). Fraud Detection in Payments Transactions: Overview of Existing Approaches and Usage for Instant Payments. *Complex Systems Informatics and Modeling Quarterly,* (20), 72–88. doi:10.7250/csimq.2019-20.04

Ermilov, D., Panov, M., & Yanovich, Y. (2017, December). Automatic bitcoin address clustering. In *2017 16th IEEE International Conference on Machine Learning and Applications (ICMLA)* (pp. 461-466). IEEE. 10.1109/ICMLA.2017.0-118

Eyal, I., & Sirer, E. G. (2014, March). Majority is not enough: Bitcoin mining is vulnerable. In *International conference on financial cryptography and data security* (pp. 436-454). Springer. 10.1007/978-3-662-45472-5_28

Feng, C., & Niu, J. (2019, July). Selfish mining in ethereum. In *2019 IEEE 39th International Conference on Distributed Computing Systems (ICDCS)* (pp. 1306-1316). IEEE. 10.1109/ICDCS.2019.00131

GeorgoulaI.PournarakisD.BilanakosC.SotiropoulosD.GiaglisG. M. (2015). Using time-series and sentiment analysis to detect the determinants of bitcoin prices. *Available at* SSRN 2607167. doi:10.2139srn.2607167

Gladden, M. E. (2015). Cryptocurrency with a conscience: Using artificial intelligence to develop money that advances human ethical values. *Annales. Etyka w życiu gospodarczym, 18*(4).

Goodkind, A. L., Jones, B. A., & Berrens, R. P. (2020). Cryptodamages: Monetary value estimates of the air pollution and human health impacts of cryptocurrency mining. *Energy Research & Social Science, 59*(1), 101281. doi:10.1016/j. erss.2019.101281

Guo, T., Bifet, A., & Antulov-Fantulin, N. (2018, November). Bitcoin volatility forecasting with a glimpse into buy and sell orders. In 2018 IEEE international conference on data mining (ICDM) (pp. 989-994). IEEE. doi:10.1109/ ICDM.2018.00123

HarveyC. R. (2014). Bitcoin myths and facts. Available at SSRN 2479670.

Jang, H., & Lee, J. (2017). An empirical study on modeling and prediction of bitcoin prices with bayesian neural networks based on blockchain information. *IEEE Access: Practical Innovations, Open Solutions, 6*, 5427–5437. doi:10.1109/ ACCESS.2017.2779181

Ji, S., Kim, J., & Im, H. (2019). A comparative study of bitcoin price prediction using deep learning. *Mathematics, 7*(10), 898. doi:10.3390/math7100898

Jourdan, M., Blandin, S., Wynter, L., & Deshpande, P. (2019). A probabilistic model of the bitcoin blockchain. In *Proceedings of the IEEE/CVF Conference on Computer Vision and Pattern Recognition Workshops* (pp. 1-11). 10.1109/CVPRW.2019.00337

Jung, E., Le Tilly, M., Gehani, A., & Ge, Y. (2019, July). Data mining-based ethereum fraud detection. In *2019 IEEE International Conference on Blockchain (Blockchain)* (pp. 266-273). IEEE. 10.1109/Blockchain.2019.00042

Kaur, G. (2019). *Development of Business Intelligence Outlier and financial crime analytics system for predicting and managing fraud in financial payment services.* Available at: http://www.cs.stir.ac.uk/courses/ITNP097/PastProjects/exemplars/ Guneet_Kaur.pdf

Kautish, S. (2008). Online Banking: A Paradigm Shift. E-Business. *ICFAI Publication, Hyderabad, 9*(10), 54–59.

Kautish, S., & Thapliyal, M. P. (2012). Concept of Decision Support Systems in relation with Knowledge Management–Fundamentals, theories, frameworks and practices. *International Journal of Application or Innovation in Engineering & Management, 1*(2), 9.

Kinderis, M., Bezbradica, M., & Crane, M. (2018). *Bitcoin currency fluctuation.* Academic Press.

Klein, T., Thu, H. P., & Walther, T. (2018). Bitcoin is not the New Gold–A comparison of volatility, correlation, and portfolio performance. *International Review of Financial Analysis*, *59*, 105–116. doi:10.1016/j.irfa.2018.07.010

Li, W., Cao, M., Wang, Y., Tang, C., & Lin, F. (2020). Mining pool game model and Nash equilibrium analysis for PoW-based blockchain networks. *IEEE Access: Practical Innovations, Open Solutions*, *8*, 101049–101060. doi:10.1109/ACCESS.2020.2997996

Liebau, D., & Schueffel, P. (2019). Cryptocurrencies & initial coin offerings: Are they scams?-an empirical study. *The Journal of The British Blockchain Association*, *2*(1), 7749. doi:10.31585/jbba-2-1-(5)2019

Liu, Y., Li, R., Liu, X., Wang, J., Zhang, L., Tang, C., & Kang, H. (2017, October). An efficient method to enhance Bitcoin wallet security. In *2017 11th IEEE International Conference on Anti-counterfeiting, Security, and Identification (ASID)* (pp. 26-29). IEEE. 10.1109/ICASID.2017.8285737

Meynkhard, A. (2019). Fair market value of bitcoin: Halving effect. *Investment Management and Financial Innovations*, *16*(4), 72–85. doi:10.21511/imfi.16(4).2019.07

Mikhaylov, A. (2020). Cryptocurrency Market Analysis from the Open Innovation Perspective. *Journal of Open Innovation*, *6*(4), 197. doi:10.3390/joitmc6040197

Monamo, P. M., Marivate, V., & Twala, B. (2016, December). A multifaceted approach to Bitcoin fraud detection: Global and local outliers. In *2016 15th IEEE International Conference on Machine Learning and Applications (ICMLA)* (pp. 188-194). IEEE.

Moshirian, F. (2007). Global financial services and a global single currency. *Journal of Banking & Finance*, *31*(1), 3–9. doi:10.1016/j.jbankfin.2006.07.001

Peng, Y., Albuquerque, P. H. M., de Sá, J. M. C., Padula, A. J. A., & Montenegro, M. R. (2018). The best of two worlds: Forecasting high frequency volatility for cryptocurrencies and traditional currencies with Support Vector Regression. *Expert Systems with Applications*, *97*, 177–192. doi:10.1016/j.eswa.2017.12.004

Phan, L., Li, S., & Mentzer, K. (2019). Blockchain technology and the current discussion on fraud. *Computer Information Systems Journal Articles*.

Sabry, F., Labda, W., Erbad, A., & Malluhi, Q. (2020). Cryptocurrencies and Artificial Intelligence: Challenges and Opportunities. *IEEE Access: Practical Innovations, Open Solutions*, *8*, 175840–175858. doi:10.1109/ACCESS.2020.3025211

Sandner, P. G., Gross, J., Schulden, P., & Grale, L. (2020). The Digital Programmable Euro, Libra and CBDC: Implications for European Banks. *Libra and CBDC: Implications for European Banks.*

Sayadi, S., Rejeb, S. B., & Choukair, Z. 2019, June. Anomaly detection model over blockchain electronic transactions. In 2019 15th International Wireless Communications & Mobile Computing Conference (IWCMC) (pp. 895-900). IEEE.

Seetharaman, A., Saravanan, A. S., Patwa, N., & Mehta, J. (2017). Impact of Bitcoin as a world currency. *Accounting and Finance Research*, 6(2), 230–246. doi:10.5430/afr.v6n2p230

Senthuran, G., & Halgamuge, M. N. (2019). Prediction of Cryptocurrency Market Price Using Deep Learning and Blockchain Information. *Essentials of Blockchain Technology*, 349.

Sin, E., & Wang, L. (2017, July). Bitcoin price prediction using ensembles of neural networks. In *2017 13th International conference on natural computation, fuzzy systems and knowledge discovery (ICNC-FSKD)* (pp. 666-671). IEEE. 10.1109/FSKD.2017.8393351

Smales, L. A. (2019). Bitcoin as a safe haven: Is it even worth considering? *Finance Research Letters*, 30, 385–393. doi:10.1016/j.frl.2018.11.002

Statista. (2021). *Number of crypto coins 2013-2021 | Statista.* Retrieved 22 March 2021, from https://www.statista.com/statistics/863917/number-crypto-coins-tokens/#:~:text=How%20many%20cryptocurrencies%20are%20there,of%20digital%20coins%20in%202013

Toyoda, K., Mathiopoulos, P. T., & Ohtsuki, T. (2019). A novel methodology for hyip operators' bitcoin addresses identification. *IEEE Access: Practical Innovations, Open Solutions*, 7, 74835–74848. doi:10.1109/ACCESS.2019.2921087

Trautman, L. J. (2014). Virtual currencies; Bitcoin & what now after Liberty Reserve, Silk Road, and Mt. Gox? *Richmond Journal of Law and Technology*, 20(4), 1–11.

Vasek, M., & Moore, T. (2015, January). There's no free lunch, even using Bitcoin: Tracking the popularity and profits of virtual currency scams. In *International conference on financial cryptography and data security* (pp. 44-61). Springer. 10.1007/978-3-662-47854-7_4

Vranken, H. (2017). Sustainability of bitcoin and blockchains. *Current Opinion in Environmental Sustainability*, 28, 1–9. doi:10.1016/j.cosust.2017.04.011

Wang, T., Liew, S. C., & Zhang, S. (2019). *When blockchain meets AI: Optimal mining strategy achieved by machine learning.* arXiv preprint arXiv:1911.12942.

Yermack, D. (2015). Is Bitcoin a real currency? An economic appraisal. In *Handbook of digital currency* (pp. 31–43). Academic Press. doi:10.1016/B978-0-12-802117-0.00002-3

Chapter 8
Valuation of Deferred Tax Assets Using a Closed Form Solution

Joao Carlos Silva
ISCTE, University Institute of Lisbon, Portugal

Nuno Souto
(iD) https://orcid.org/0000-0003-3823-4470
ISCTE, University Institute of Lisbon, Portugal

José Pereira
ISEG, Universidade de Lisboa, Portugal

ABSTRACT

Deferred tax asset (DTA) is a tax/accounting concept that refers to an asset that may be used to reduce future tax liabilities of the holder. It usually refers to situations where a company has either overpaid taxes, paid taxes in advance, or has carry-over of losses (the latter being the most common situation). DTAs are thus contingent claims, whose underlying assets are the company's future profits. Consequently, the correct approach to value such rights implies the use of a contingent claim valuation framework. The purpose of this chapter is to propose a precise and conceptually sound mathematical approach to value DTAs, considering future projections of earnings and rates, alongside the DTA's legal time limit. The authors show that with the proposed evaluation techniques, the DTA's expected value will be much lower than the values normally used in today's practice, and the company's financial analysis will lead to much more sound and realistic results.

DOI: 10.4018/978-1-7998-7716-5.ch008

I - INTRODUCTION - THE DEFERRAL OF TAXES

There have been many attempts to reach a conformity about the way income tax is treated, that is, to uniformize tax rates and regulations across international entities, but the complexity of this topic has raised some issues and critics; Hanlon, et al (2005) and Atwood, et al (2010) stated that earnings persistence and the association between current earnings and future cash flows are lower when the level of required book-tax conformity is higher. The potential benefits would include lower compliance costs for reporting income and the potential lowering of incentives to mislead the IRS (Internal Revenue Service) and capital markets (basically deterring entities from engaging into tax shelters and schemes).

The tax return of a company is based on its accounting financial statements. To provide comparable information, financial statements are prepared according to the International Financial Reporting Standards (IFRS), issued by the International Accounting Standards Board (IASB). The IASB was formed in 2001 to replace the International Accounting Standards Committee that issued International Accounting Standards (IAS). Since the previously issued IASs remain effective, we have that the main body of standards that are used worldwide by several countries are comprised of IFRSs and IASs. The companies' income, depicted by the IFRSs and IASs (refereed to simply by the Generally Accepted Accounting Principles GAAP) are their accounting profits, but these may be (and are) different from the taxable profit, since the taxable profit is calculated as a function of the tax law inherent to each country. The number of factors that lead to differences between tax and accounting returns is huge and varies from country to country. One of those factors is of relevance to the present work – the deferral of taxes.

Remove DTAs From the Balance Sheet?

Laux (2013) conducted a study to analyse the relationship between the information content of financial statements and the net deferred taxes account. Naturally, as we evaluate deferred taxes, we may find both deferred tax assets and deferred tax liabilities; the difference will result in net deferred taxes (we will henceforth refer to these net deferred taxes simply as deferred tax assets, or DTAs). The main conclusion was that the exclusion of DTAs from the results helped access the main differences from the different company's performance. This is highly related to the cost/benefit of disclosing information on DTAs since that the cost of acquiring and utilizing this information seems to nullify the benefits. Also, on the same topic, Burgstahler, et al (2002), concluded that in some occasions, managers tend to manipulate the net deferred tax asset account to increase earnings and avoid losses. This possible manipulation (Kautish, 2008; Kautish & Thapliyal, 2012) is also something that should be kept in mind when evaluating balance sheets where such accounts are present.

The problem of accounting DTAs on a present value basis is that under the actual rules adopted by FASB (Financial Accounting Standards Board), the deferred tax accounts are, in many cases, unlikely to reverse in the foreseeable future, since companies seem to be able to defer taxes indefinitely (Ron Colley et al, 2007). These authors address this statement in the study "Deferred Taxes in the Context of the Unit Problem" where they remove the deferred tax assets from the balance sheets. The authors state that income taxation is an aggregate phenomenon and that an aggregate approach is required, making use of the flow-through accounting method. The main argument states that, if we see taxation as a transaction between the private/ public sectors and the governmental authority, then this method would result in an equality of the tax provision and the cash outflow for a certain period, therefore eliminating deferred tax assets and liabilities. The idea of removing deferred taxes from the balance sheet has been supported by other authors like Chaney (1989) and Ketz (2010), that argue that deferred tax accounting is too complex, too expensive and too inconsistent with the US GAAP.

Valuation and Accounting of DTAs

The valuation and accounting of DTAs is the topic that must be discussed and clarified. The most important thing to notice is that deferred tax assets add value to the balance sheet since they represent the net present value of the future tax benefits (it is important to note that classical accounting relations only hold when the DTA value is indeed adjusted to its net present value (Eli Amir et al, 1997)). To determine the best way to account for deferred taxes, Amir and his peers conducted some research where they introduced net deferred taxes as a completely distinct category of assets, using the market value of equity per share as the dependent value. Amir and his team found that the valuation coefficient on deferred tax liabilities from depreciation and amortization was close to zero; also, deferred taxes from restructuring charges had valuation coefficients larger than other deferred tax components. They also concluded that the net realizable value of deferred taxes from losses and credits carried forward were negatively correlated with stock prices. In the end they concluded that even though these types of assets are very different in nature from the rest of the assets in the balance sheet, they should nonetheless be accounted for (with some subjective adjustments) in a way like any other asset or liability.

DTAs and European Options

DTAs may be hard to value, since they are time-limited and may never be used at all. Their value is contingent on the future earnings of the company, and they can be used to shield these future profits from taxation – IAS 12 states that "a DTA should be recognised for all deductible temporary differences, to the extent that it is probable that taxable profit will be available against which the deductible temporary difference can be utilised". Since corporate income taxation works on an annual basis, the shielding opportunities occur once a year. This is equivalent to saying that we are faced with a compound European option (or an annual Bermuda option) that might be exercised until the last year in which the law will permit shielding, or until the DTAs value has been completely depleted by its use. Consistent with this line of thinking, there is an ongoing debate regarding the appropriateness of including DTA in the banks' regulatory capital calculation, since by doing so we are assuming its "full" worth; something that is clearly misleading.

Focus on Bank's DTAs

On the special case of the banking sector, banks are required to maintain certain levels of regulatory capital to provide a buffer against potential future losses (Kim & Santomero, 1998), (Ryan 2007), (Baesens & van Gestel, 2009). In many countries (Kara 2016), banks can count a portion (or all) of their DTAs towards regulatory capital requirements (since the adoption of SFAS[1] No. 109 in 1992 – specifically the establishment of valuation allowances).

Under normal circumstances, a bank's DTAs usually originates in the carry-over of losses (though it can also arise from overpaying some taxes). The corresponding rights are registered in the balance sheet as assets, although in Amir and Sougiannis (1999) it also argued that DTA may have implications for the perception of the firm as a going concern (dubbed as the information effect), since if the DTA arose from past operating losses, future losses would be likely to incur; this means that future liabilities could be more than likely, and thus such "assets" should be regarded with great suspicion).

Throughout the recent financial crisis (2008-2013), major media outlets routinely drew attention to the banks' DTA positions, classifying them as tenuous contributions towards regulatory capital. In Reilly (2009), it was noted that tier 1 capital ratios contained "fluff" – mentioning DTA as the primary culprit, calling in an "airy asset". The Basel Committee on Banking Supervision specifically targeted the removal of DTAs as a potential method for improving the ability of regulatory capital to protect banks from losses[2]. At the same time, the banking industry has pushed for the opposite; namely a greater inclusion of DTA in the regulatory capital calculation, to "ease" the amount of (real) regulatory capital.

Gallemore (2011) investigated the credit risk associated with the deferred tax asset component of bank regulatory capital. He hypothesized that banks that have a larger proportion of regulatory capital composed of deferred tax assets were more likely to fail. He employed a hazard model to test a sample of commercial banks and found that the proportion of regulatory capital composed of deferred tax assets was positively associated with the risk of bank failure during the recent financial crisis. Gallemore (2011) attributed his findings to the fact that the benefits of deferred tax assets couldn't be realized unless banks generated positive taxable income in the future.

High DTAs = Low Creditworthiness

The relationship of DTAs with the creditworthiness of a company has already deserved some work from academic community. The effects of book-tax differences on a firm's credit risk were analysed in Crabtree & Maher (2009), Ayers et al (2010), Edwards (2011) and Gallemore (2011); all agreeing that great amounts of deferred taxes were associated with higher risks and lower earnings quality, resulting in a decline of creditworthiness. Additionally, studies of the impact of DTAs on credit ratings led to the conclusion that deferred tax positions are substantial for many firms (between 5% and 10% of all assets according to Poterba et al (2011).

How to Value?

It is thus clear that the DTAs must be correctly valued, and that simply adding them to a bank's or company's balance sheet in full as an asset might contribute to obfuscate the institution's true financial condition – even a situation in which the DTA is fully used before its expiration date, we still must account for the cost of capital. Moodys (2015) reported DTAs were considered "a low-quality form of assets, and thus a low-quality source of capital", and consequently, Moody's decided to "limit the contribution of DTAs in its calculations of company's tangible common equity (TCE)". As analysed in De Vries (2018), several DTA valuation methods can be used, but they are essentially very subjective, and basically result in a valuation allowance, for which there is no consistent accepted method to calculate – this chapter aims to resolve such shortcomings, by solving for the expected value of the DTA, in the sense of calculating exactly which amounts are expected to be discounted as tax payments, and when.

II - DTA MATHEMATICAL MODEL

Let us consider a DTA with official book value D_{max} and a lifespan of T (in years). The effective (realistic) value of such DTA is contingent on future profits and shall always be (equal or) lower than D_{max}. The effective value of the considered DTA, D, can be represented as:

$$D = \sum_{t=1}^{T} \frac{R_t^+ - R_{t+1}^+}{\prod_{j=1}^{t}(1+\tau_j)}, \tag{1}$$

where τ_j is the interest yield in year j, R_t is the remaining book value DTA in the beginning of year t defined as

$$R_t = D_{max} - \sum_{i=1}^{t-1} u_i^+, \tag{2}$$

u_i is the profit in year i multiplied by taxes (basically, it is the tax payment that is discounted from the DTA) and $(\bullet)^+$ denotes the operation $x^+=\max\{x,0\}$. Both the yearly profits and yields are assumed to be independently distributed random variables (RVs). Then, the following the objective will be to find the expected value of D which can be expressed as:

$$\bar{D} = \sum_{t=1}^{T} E\left[1 \middle/ \prod_{j=1}^{t}(1+\tau_j)\right]\left(E\left[R_t^+\right] - E\left[R_{t+1}^+\right]\right). \tag{3}$$

Computing $\bar{D}$ basically requires finding expressions for the expected value of the interest yield weight $E\left[1 \middle/ \prod_{j=1}^{t}(1+\tau_j)\right]$ and for the expected value of the positive part of the remaining DTA in the beginning of each year t, $E\left[R_t^+\right]$.

Expected Value of the Interest Yield Weight

In order to compute the expected value $E\left[1 \middle/ \prod_{j=1}^{t}(1+\tau_j)\right]$, we first write it as

$$\mathrm{E}\left[1 \Big/ \prod_{j=1}^{t}\left(1+\tau_j\right)\right] = \int\limits_{-\infty}^{+\infty} \cdots \int\limits_{-\infty}^{+\infty} \frac{1}{\prod\limits_{j=1}^{t}\left(1+\tau_j\right)} p_{\tau_1}\left(\tau_1\right) \cdots p_{\tau_t}\left(\tau_t\right) d\tau_1 \ldots d\tau_t \tag{4}$$

where $p_{\tau_j}\left(\tau_j\right)$ is the probability density function (PDF) of the interest yield in year j. We will consider that all the τ_j are independently distributed and follow the same PDF but with different means $\bar{\tau}_j$ and standard deviations σ_{τ_j}.

According to the Cox-Ingersoll-Ross (CIR) model (Cox et al. 1985), the interest yield would follow a non-central chi-squared distribution, but in this chapter, due to the reduced time spans of the DTAs and ability to limit the estimated variability of the interest yield, we will assume an uniform distribution for the interest yield in order to provide mathematical tractability (and obtain a closed form solution). So being, we have:

$$p_{\tau_j}\left(\tau_j\right) = \begin{cases} \dfrac{1}{2\sqrt{3}\sigma_{\tau_j}}, \tau_j \in \left[\bar{\tau}_j - \sqrt{3}\sigma_{\tau_j}, \bar{\tau}_j + \sqrt{3}\sigma_{\tau_j}\right] \\ 0, \text{otherwise} \end{cases} \tag{5}$$

It is now easy to show that

$$\int\limits_{-\infty}^{+\infty} \frac{1}{\left(1+\tau_j\right)} p_{\tau_j}\left(\tau_j\right) d\tau_j = \frac{1}{2\sqrt{3}\sigma_{\tau_j}} \log\left(\frac{1+\bar{\tau}_j + \sqrt{3}\sigma_{\tau_j}}{1+\bar{\tau}_j - \sqrt{3}\sigma_{\tau_j}}\right) \tag{6}$$

which results in

$$\mathrm{E}\left[1 \Big/ \prod_{j=1}^{t}\left(1+\tau_j\right)\right] = \prod_{j=1}^{t} \frac{1}{2\sqrt{3}\sigma_{\tau_j}} \log\left(\frac{1+\bar{\tau}_j + \sqrt{3}\sigma_{\tau_j}}{1+\bar{\tau}_j - \sqrt{3}\sigma_{\tau_j}}\right). \tag{7}$$

a) Expected Value of Remaining DTA

According to (3), the computation of $\bar{D}$ also requires the evaluation of the expected value of the positive part of the remaining DTA in the beginning of each year t, i.e.,

$\mathrm{E}\left[R_t^+\right]$. In order to obtain an expression for $\mathrm{E}\left[R_t^+\right]$, we start with the derivation of the PDF of R_t. First we rewrite (2) as

$$R_t = D_{\max} - U_t,\tag{8}$$

where U_t is the sum of all profits multiplied by taxes up until the year t-1, which is defined as:

$$U_t = \sum_{i=1}^{t-1} u_i^+,\tag{9}$$

comprising a sum of independent, rectified, RVs u_i^+. If each non rectified RV u_i is described by a PDF $p_{u_i}\left(u_i\right)$, then u_i^+ follows the associated rectified PDF which is given by:

$$p_{u_i^+}\left(u_i^+\right) = \left(1 - p_i\right)\delta\left(u_i^+\right) + p_{u_i}\left(u_i^+\right)H\left(u_i^+\right)\tag{10}$$

where $\delta(x)$ is the Dirac delta function, H(x) is the unit step function

$$H\left(x\right) = \begin{cases} 0, x \le 0 \\ 1, x > 0 \end{cases}\tag{11}$$

and p_i is the probability of having positive profit, i.e.,

$$p_i = \int_0^{+\infty} p_{u_i}\left(u_i\right)du_i\tag{12}$$

Note that when the second term in (10) is normalized by p_i, it represents the truncated PDF associated with $p_{u_i}\left(u_i\right)$ which can be written as

$$p_{u_i|u_i>0}\left(u_i\right) = p_{u_i}\left(u_i\right)H\left(u_i\right)\big/p_i.\tag{13}$$

Knowing that the PDF of a sum of independent RVs can be found using the convolution of the individual PDFs (Hogg et al 2004), we can write the PDF of U_t as:

$$p_{U_t}(U_t) = \left(p_{u_1^+} * \ldots * p_{u_{t-1}^+}\right)(U_t)$$
$$= \sum_{k_1=0}^{1} \cdots \sum_{k_{t-1}=0}^{1} p_1^{k_1} \cdots p_t^{k_{t-1}} (1-p_1)^{1-k_1} \cdots (1-p_t)^{1-k_{t-1}} \, \mathrm{C}_{\{k_i\}_{i=1}^{t-1}}(U_t) \tag{14}$$

where $*$ denotes the convolution operation which, for two functions $f(x)$ and $g(x)$ is defined as

$$(f * g)(x) = \int_{-\infty}^{+\infty} f(\nu) g(x - \nu) d\nu . \tag{15}$$

Therefore, in (14) $\mathrm{C}_{\{k\}_{i=1}^{t-1}}(U_t)$ corresponds to the $(t-1)$-fold convolution

$$\mathrm{C}_{\{k_i\}_{i=1}^{t-1}}(U_t) = \left[\left((1-k_1)\delta + k_1 p_{u_1|u_1>0}\right) * \ldots * \left((1-k_{t-1})\delta + k_{t-1} p_{u_{t-1}|u_{t-1}>0}\right) \right](U_t). \tag{16}$$

The second form in (14) makes it explicit all the possible outcomes in terms of years with positive profit and with loss during the timeframe in use. Combining (8) with (14) we can express the PDF of R_t as

$$p_{R_t}(R_t) = \sum_{k_1=0}^{1} \cdots \sum_{k_{t-1}=0}^{1} p_1^{k_1} \cdots p_t^{k_{t-1}} (1-p_1)^{1-k_1} \cdots (1-p_t)^{1-k_{t-1}} \, \mathrm{C}_{\{k_i\}_{i=1}^{t-1}}(D_{\max} - R_t) \tag{17}$$

which allows us to compute $\mathrm{E}\left[R_t^+\right]$ using

$$\mathrm{E}\left[R_t^+\right] = \int_{-\infty}^{+\infty} \max\{R_t, 0\} \, p_{R_t}(R_t) \, dR_t$$
$$= \sum_{k_1=0}^{1} \cdots \sum_{k_{t-1}=0}^{1} p_1^{k_1} \cdots p_t^{k_{t-1}} (1-p_1)^{1-k_1} \cdots (1-p_t)^{1-k_{t-1}} I_{\{k_i\}_{i=1}^{t-1}}(D_{\max}) \tag{18}$$

where we defined the following auxiliary coefficient required for the summation terms

$$I_{\{k_i\}_{i=1}^{t-1}}(D_{\max}) = \int_{0}^{+\infty} R_t \, \mathrm{C}_{\{k_i\}_{i=1}^{t-1}}(D_{\max} - R_t) \, dR_t . \tag{19}$$

In order to evaluate the integral in (19) we will consider four different cases in terms of number of years with positive profit (i.e. #$\{i: k_i \, ^! 0\}$, where # denotes the cardinality of the set): no years with profit, one year with profit, two years with profit and three or more years with profit. A uniform distribution with mean $\bar{u}_i$ and standard deviation σ_{u_i} will be assumed for each yearly profit, u_i, with the PDF expressed as

$$
p_{u_i}\left(u_i\right) = \begin{cases} \dfrac{1}{b_i - a_i}, u_i \in \left[a_i, b_i\right] \\ 0, \text{otherwise} \end{cases},
\tag{20}
$$

where

$$
a_i = \bar{u}_i - \sqrt{3}\sigma_{u_i}
\tag{21}
$$

and

$$
b_i = \bar{u}_i + \sqrt{3}\sigma_{u_i}.
\tag{22}
$$

For this PDF the probability of having positive profit, (12), is simply

$$
p_i = \frac{b_i - a_i^{\,+}}{b_i - a_i}
\tag{23}
$$

b1) Case of No Years With Positive Profit

The sequence without positive profit years ($\#\left\{i : k_i \neq 0\right\} = \varnothing$) results in a trivial convolution of Dirac delta functions in (16) which is also a Dirac delta function. Therefore (19) results simply in

$$
I_{\{k_i\}_{i=1}^{t-1}}\left(D_{\max}\right) = D_{\max}.
\tag{24}
$$

b2) Case of Only One Year, i, With Positive Profit

The convolution in (16) is also trivial to compute for the sequences with only one year with positive profit ($\#\{i: k_i^10\}=1$) as it consists in the convolution of Dirac delta functions with a single truncated (and normalized) PDF obtained from (20), resulting in

$$C_{\{k_i\}_{i=1}^{t-1}}\left(D_{\max} - R_t\right) = p_{u_i|u_i>0}\left(D_{\max} - R_t\right). \tag{25}$$

Inserting (25) into (19) then gives

$$I_{\{k_i\}_{i=1}^{t-1}}\left(D_{\max}\right) = \frac{1}{2\left(b_i - a_i^+\right)}\left\{\left[\left(D_{\max} - a_i^+\right)^+\right]^2 - \left[\left(D_{\max} - b_i\right)^+\right]^2\right\}. \tag{26}$$

b3) Case of Two Years, i and j, With Positive Profit

For the sequences with only two positive profit years ($\#\{i: k_i^10\}=2$), indexed by i and j, (16) simplifies to a convolution of two truncated (and normalized) PDFs obtained from (20), whose resulting expression can be written as

$$
\begin{aligned}
&C_{\{k_i\}_{i=1}^{t-1}}\left(D_{\max} - R_t\right) \\
&= \frac{1}{l_i l_j}
\begin{cases}
D_{\max} - R_t - a_i^+ - a_j^+, & D_{\max} - a_i^+ - a_j^+ - \min\{l_i, l_j\} \le R_t < D_{\max} - a_i^+ - a_j^+ \\
\min\{l_i, l_j\}, & D_{\max} - a_i^+ - a_j^+ - \max\{l_i, l_j\} \le R_t < D_{\max} - a_i^+ - a_j^+ - \min\{l_i, l_j\} \\
R_t - D_{\max} + b_i + b_j, & D_{\max} - b_i - b_j \le R_t < D_{\max} - a_i^+ - a_j^+ - \max\{l_i, l_j\} \\
0, & \text{otherwise}
\end{cases}
\end{aligned}
\tag{27}
$$

where

$$l_i = b_i - a_i^+. \tag{28}$$

After inserting (27) into (19) and performing the integral we obtain

$$I_{\{k_i\}_{i=1}^{t-1}}\left(D_{\max}\right) = \frac{1}{l_i l_j}\left[\left.\left[\frac{1}{3}R_t^3 + \frac{\left(b_i + b_j - D_{\max}\right)}{2}R_t^2\right]\right|_{\left(D_{\max} - b_i - b_j\right)^+}^{\left(D_{\max} - a_i^+ - a_j^+ - \max\{l_i,l_j\}\right)^+}\right.$$

$$+ \left.\left(\frac{\min\{l_i,l_j\}}{2}R_t^2\right)\right|_{\left(D_{\max} - a_i^+ - a_j^+ - \max\{l_i,l_j\}\right)^+}^{\left(D_{\max} - a_i^+ - a_j^+ - \min\{l_i,l_j\}\right)^+} + \left.\left(-\frac{1}{3}R_t^3 + \frac{\left(D_{\max} - a_i^+ - a_j^+\right)}{2}R_t^2\right)\right|_{\left(D_{\max} - a_i^+ - a_j^+ - \min\{l_i,l_j\}\right)^+}^{\left(D_{\max} - a_i^+ - a_j^+\right)^+}\right]$$

(29)

where we adopt the notation $\left.\left(f\left(x\right)\right)\right|_c^d = f\left(d\right) - f\left(c\right)$.

b4) Case of three or more years with positive profit:

For all the sequences with three or more years with profit ($\#\{i: k_i^1 0\}^3 3$), instead of trying to compute all subsequent convolutions we can apply the Central Limit Theorem (CLT) and approximate the sum of the nonzero u_i^+ as a Gaussian distribution with mean $\sum_{i=1}^{t-1} k_i \overline{u_i^+}$ and squared standard deviation $\sum_{i=1}^{t-1} k_i \sigma_{u_i^+}^2$ where

$$\sigma_{u_i^+}^2 = \frac{\left(b_i - a_i^+\right)^2}{12}$$

(30)

and

$$\overline{u_i^+} = \frac{a_i^+ + b_i}{2}.$$

(31)

In this case we can write

$$C_{\{k_i\}_{i=1}^{t-1}}\left(D_{\max} - R_t\right) = \frac{1}{\sqrt{2\pi\sigma'^2}} e^{-\frac{\left(R_t - \mu'\right)^2}{2\sigma'^2}}$$

(32)

where

$$\sigma'^2 = \sum_{i=1}^{t-1} k_i \sigma_{u_i^+}^2$$

(33)

and

$$\mu' = D_{max} - \sum_{i=1}^{t-1} k_i \overline{u_i^+}$$

(34)

Performing the integration in (19) then results in

$$I_{\{k_i\}_{i=1}^{t-1}}(D_{max}) = \frac{\sigma'}{\sqrt{2\pi}} e^{-\frac{\mu'^2}{2\sigma'^2}} + \frac{1}{2}\mu' erfc\left(-\frac{\mu'}{\sqrt{2\pi}\sigma'}\right)$$

(35)

where $erfc(x)$ is the complementary error function defined as

$$erfc(x) = \frac{2}{\sqrt{\pi}} \int_x^{+\infty} e^{-v^2} dv$$

(36)

Case of Independent and Identically Distributed Profits

If we assume that the RVs u_i are not only independent but also identically distributed with mean $\overline{u}$, standard deviation σu and PDF $pu_i u)$, then most of the previous expressions can be simplified. In this case (18) becomes

$$E\left[R_t^+\right] = \sum_{k=0}^{t-1} \binom{t-1}{k} p^k (1-p)^{t-1-k} I_k(D_{max})$$

(37)

where $\binom{t-1}{k}$ denotes number of combinations of t-1 elements taken k at a time,

$$p = \int_0^{+\infty} p_u(u) du ,$$

$$I_k(D_{max}) = \int_0^{+\infty} R_t C_k(D_{max} - R_t) dR_t ,$$

(38)

$C_k(U_t)$ is simply the k-fold convolution of the truncated PDF $p_{u|u>0}(u)$ with itself and p is the probability of having positive profit which, for uniformly distributed RVs (23), simplifies to

163

$$p = \frac{b - a^+}{b - a} \,. \tag{39}$$

Repeating the explicit computation of (38) for the four different cases in terms of years with positive profit we obtain:

$$I_0(D_{max}) = D_{max} \tag{40}$$

for the sequences of no years with positive profit,

$$I_1\left(D_{max}\right) = \frac{1}{2\left(b - a^+\right)} \left\{ \left[\left(D_{max} - a^+\right)^+\right]^2 - \left[\left(D_{max} - b\right)^+\right]^2 \right\}, \tag{41}$$

for the sequences with only one year with positive profit,

$$I_2\left(D_{max}\right) = \frac{1}{\left(b - a^+\right)^2} \left[\frac{2}{3}\left(\left(D_{max} - b - a^+\right)^+\right)^3 - \frac{\left(D_{max} - 2b\right)}{2}\left(\left(D_{max} - b - a^+\right)^+\right)^2 \right.$$
$$- \frac{1}{3}\left(\left(D_{max} - 2b\right)^+\right)^3 - \frac{1}{3}\left(\left(D_{max} - 2a^+\right)^+\right)^3 + \frac{\left(D_{max} - 2b\right)\left(\left(D_{max} - 2b\right)^+\right)^2}{2}$$
$$\left. + \frac{\left(D_{max} - 2a^+\right)\left(\left(D_{max} - 2a^+\right)^+\right)^2}{2} - \frac{\left(D_{max} - 2a^+\right)}{2}\left(\left(D_{max} - b - a^+\right)^+\right)^2 \right] \tag{42}$$

for the sequences with two years with positive profit and (approximately)

$$I_{k \geq 3}\left(D_{max}\right) = \frac{\sigma'}{\sqrt{2\pi}} e^{-\frac{\mu'^2}{2\sigma'^2}} + \frac{1}{2}\mu' erfc\left(-\frac{\mu'}{\sqrt{2\pi}\sigma'}\right) \tag{43}$$

for all the remaining sequences (three or more years with positive profit). In (43), we use $\sigma'^2 = k\sigma_{u^+}^2$ and $\mu' = D_{max} - k\overline{u^+}$.

III - PUTTING THE MATHEMATICAL MODEL TO USE

In order to clarify the use of the presented expressions we describe a simple example of the computation of the expected value of a DTA with a lifespan of $T=3$ years, considering independent and identically distributed uniform RVs for the profits. In this case, according to (3), the intended value is computed using

$$\bar{D} = \sum_{t=1}^{3} \mathrm{E}\left[1 \middle/ \prod_{j=1}^{t}(1+\tau_j) \right]\left(\mathrm{E}\left[R_t^+\right] - \mathrm{E}\left[R_{t+1}^+\right] \right). \tag{44}$$

where the terms inside the summation are

$$\mathrm{E}\left[R_1^+\right] = D_{\max}, \tag{45}$$

(obtained from (37) and (40)),

$$\mathrm{E}\left[R_2^+\right] = \left(\frac{a^+ - a}{b - a}\right) D_{\max} + \frac{1}{2(b-a)}\left\{ \left[\left(D_{\max} - a^+\right)^+\right]^2 - \left[\left(D_{\max} - b\right)^+\right]^2 \right\}, \tag{46}$$

(obtained from (37), (40) and (41)),

$$\mathrm{E}\left[R_3^+\right] = \left(\frac{a^+ - a}{b - a}\right)^2 D_{\max} + \frac{\left(a^+ - a\right)}{(b-a)^2}\left\{ \left[\left(D_{\max} - a^+\right)^+\right]^2 - \left[\left(D_{\max} - b\right)^+\right]^2 \right\} + \left(\frac{b - a^+}{b - a}\right)^2 I_2\left(D_{\max}\right)$$
$$\tag{47}$$

(obtained from (37), (40), (41) and (42)), and

$$\mathrm{E}\left[R_4^+\right] = \left(\frac{a^+ - a}{b - a}\right)^3 D_{\max} + \frac{3\left(a^+ - a\right)^2}{2(b-a)^3}\left\{ \left[\left(D_{\max} - a^+\right)^+\right]^2 - \left[\left(D_{\max} - b\right)^+\right]^2 \right\}$$
$$+ 3\frac{\left(b - a^+\right)^2\left(a^+ - a\right)}{(b-a)^3} I_2\left(D_{\max}\right) + \left(\frac{b - a^+}{b - a}\right)^3 \left(\begin{array}{c} \sqrt{\dfrac{3}{2\pi}}\sigma_{u^+} e^{-\frac{\left(D_{\max} - 3\overline{u^+}\right)^2}{6\sigma_{u^+}^2}} \\ + \dfrac{1}{2}\left(D_{\max} - 3\overline{u^+}\right) erfc\left(-\dfrac{D_{\max} - 3\overline{u^+}}{\sqrt{6\pi}\sigma_{u^+}} \right) \end{array} \right)$$
$$\tag{48}$$

(obtained from (37), (40), (41), (42) and (43)).

Therefore, the expected value for the DTA is given as:

$$\bar{D} = \sum_{t=1}^{3} E\left[1 \Big/ \prod_{j=1}^{t}\left(1+\tau_j\right)\right]\left(E\left[R_t^+\right]-E\left[R_{t+1}^+\right]\right)$$

$$= \sum_{t=1}^{3}\left[\prod_{j=1}^{t}\frac{1}{2\sqrt{3}\sigma_{\tau_j}}\log\left(\frac{1+\bar{\tau}_j+\sqrt{3}\sigma_{\tau_j}}{1+\bar{\tau}_j-\sqrt{3}\sigma_{\tau_j}}\right)\right]\left(E\left[R_t^+\right]-E\left[R_{t+1}^+\right]\right)$$

$$= \frac{1}{2\sqrt{3}\sigma_{\tau_1}}\log\left(\frac{1+\bar{\tau}_1+\sqrt{3}\sigma_{\tau_1}}{1+\bar{\tau}_1-\sqrt{3}\sigma_{\tau_1}}\right)\left(E\left[R_1^+\right]-E\left[R_2^+\right]\right)$$

$$+\prod_{j=1}^{2}\left[\frac{1}{2\sqrt{3}\sigma_{\tau_j}}\log\left(\frac{1+\bar{\tau}_j+\sqrt{3}\sigma_{\tau_j}}{1+\bar{\tau}_j-\sqrt{3}\sigma_{\tau_j}}\right)\right]\left(E\left[R_2^+\right]-E\left[R_3^+\right]\right)$$

$$+\prod_{j=1}^{3}\left[\frac{1}{2\sqrt{3}\sigma_{\tau_j}}\log\left(\frac{1+\bar{\tau}_j+\sqrt{3}\sigma_{\tau_j}}{1+\bar{\tau}_j-\sqrt{3}\sigma_{\tau_j}}\right)\right]\left(E\left[R_3^+\right]-E\left[R_4^+\right]\right)$$

IV - SIMULATION RESULTS

Monte Carlo simulations were run for 10.000 loops, and the DTA's lifespan was assumed to be 10 years, with book value D_{max} =100 (adimensional). Both the yearly interest yield and each year's mean expected profit multiplied by the tax, u_i, assumed a uniform distribution (Note that u_i =10 is equivalent to a profit of 50 and tax rate of 20%, for instance). In Figure 1 we compare the simulated values to the analytical values obtained by the deduced formulas, to find that they coincide. This test was actually executed for all figures and it was observed that the analytical values always matched the simulated values almost to perfection, proving that the CLT based approximation adopted for 3 or more years with positive profit proved to be very accurate. The curves of Figure 1 represent the cumulated DTA usage (to the present value) at the end of each year[3]; whereas the curves of Figure 2 portray the yearly DTA consumption under the same conditions.

Figure 3 and Figure 4 present the same simulations present in Figure 1 and Figure 2, but now with only the simulated results. The variable $\bar{u}_i$ was made to increase from 20 (adimensional) with increments of 5 units each year; all having a fixed standard deviation σ_{u_i} of 10. From Figure 3 notice that the initial DTA value is a

Figure 1. Expected cumulated DTA; increasing mean profits – analytical vs simulated results

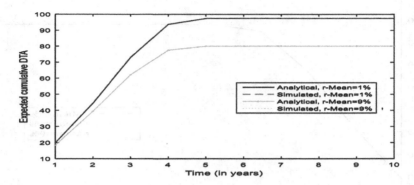

Figure 2. Expected yearly DTA consumption; increasing mean profits – analytical vs simulated results

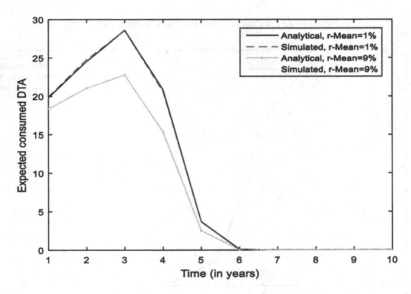

bit less than 20 (due to the discount factor), climbing up to almost 100 (if there was no discount factor, the cumulated DTA would reach 100). As expected, the higher yield will output the lowest DTA value. Looking at Figure 4, we can see that by year 6 the DTA was all used up, which means that it only took 5 years for these DTA to be fully used, each with different present values due to the different yields.

Figure 3. Expected cumulated DTA; increasing mean profits

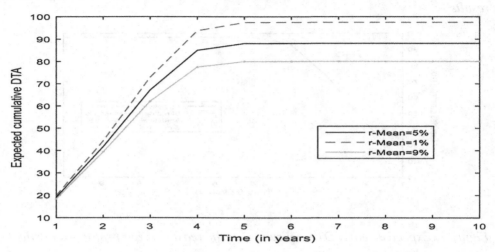

Figure 4. Expected yearly DTA consumption; increasing mean profits

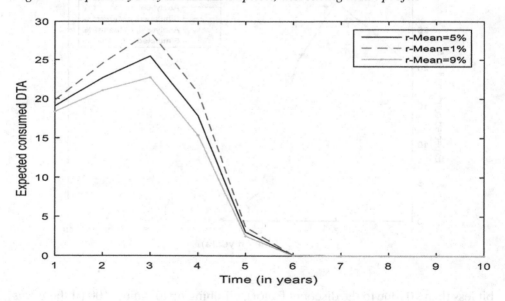

In Figure 5 and Figure 6 we have a similar situation as before, but now with the standard deviation σ_{u_i} starting at 10 and increasing 4 units each year. With this increasing deviation, note that the expected use of the totality of the DTA is deferred to the seventh year (previously it was the fifth year).

Figure 5. Expected cumulated DTA; increasing mean profits and profit deviation

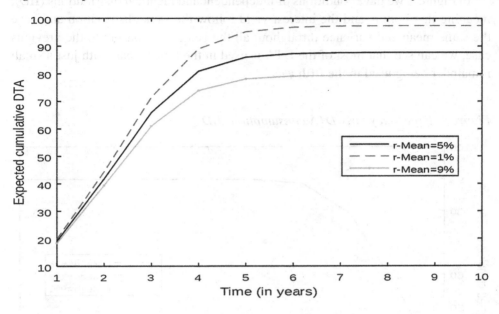

Figure 6. Expected yearly DTA consumption; increasing mean profits and profit deviation

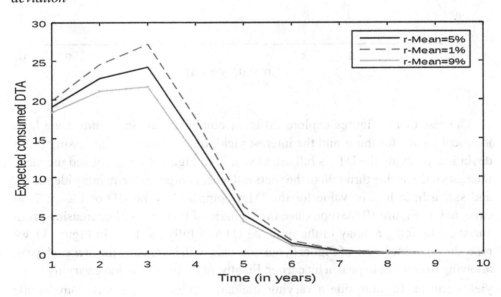

In Figure 7 we have conditions of independent and identical distributions (IID), meaning that both u_i and the interest yield follow the same distribution and have the same mean and variance throughout all the years. Comparing to the previous case, we can see that most of the DTA is used in the fourth year, with just a small remainder being used in the fifth year.

Figure 7. Expected yearly DTA consumption; IID

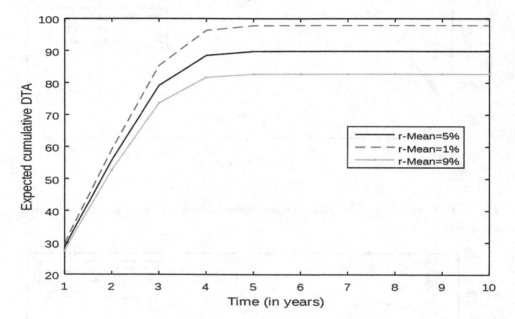

The rest of the figures explore different combinations. In Figure 8 we have identical means for the u_i and the interest yield, but also have an increasing profit deviation, delaying the DTA's full use to year 7. In Figure 9 we simulated the mean interest yield varying throughout the years (all other component remaining identical), and saw a little loss of value for the DTA compared to the IID of Figure 7, as expected. In Figure 10 we reproduce the scenario of Figure 9 with increasing profit variance, noticing a delay in the time the DTA is fully used up. In Figure 11 we reproduced the scenario of Figure 9, but now also with increasing mean u_i each year, allowing the curves to peak a bit earlier. Finally, in Figure 12 we have varying mean yields and profit alongside a varying standard deviation σ_{u_i}, with some subtle differences from the two previous cases.

Figure 8. Expected yearly DTA consumption; increasing profit deviation

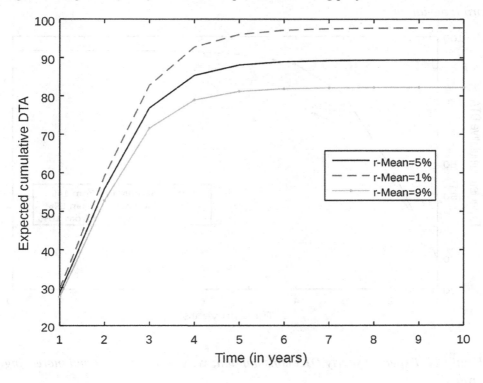

Figure 9. Expected yearly DTA consumption; varying mean yield

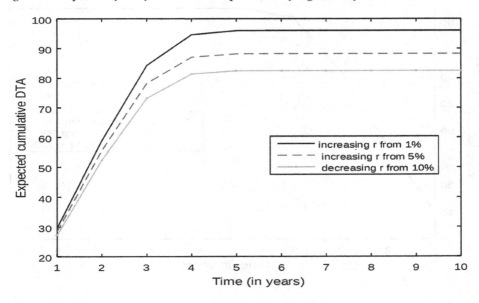

Figure 10. Expected yearly DTA consumption; varying mean yield and increasing profit deviation

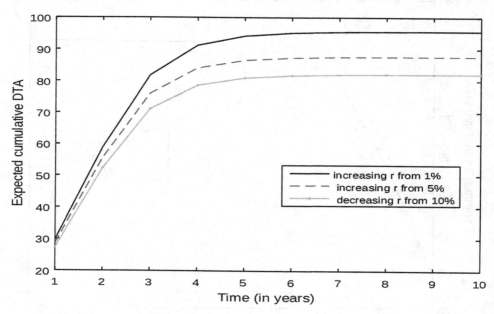

Figure 11. Expected yearly DTA consumption; varying mean yield and increasing profits

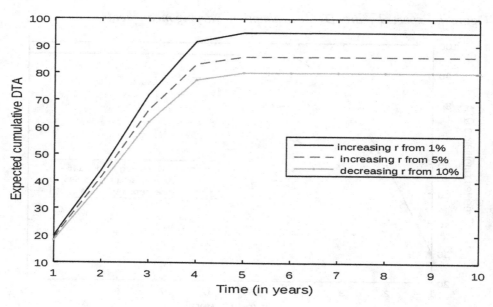

Figure 12. Expected yearly DTA consumption; varying mean yield and increasing mean profit and profit deviation

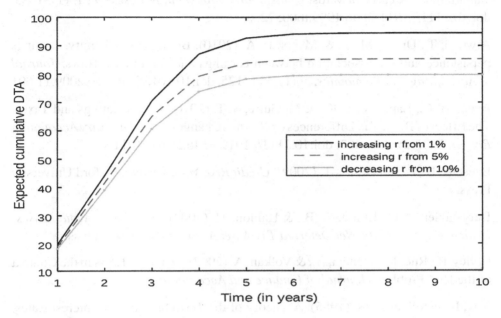

V - CONCLUSION

In this work we valued Deferred Tax Assets (DTAs) according to future projected profits, which is the only correct way that they should be valued. Using this valuation technique, the DTA's value on the balance sheet would always be smaller than its nominal value used nowadays and reflect its realistic value, providing all stakeholders with the company's real asset worth, henceforth preventing future (unavoidable) disappointments. Via the projection of future profits and yields using a uniform distribution with associated standard deviations, we account for the most likely scenarios and reach precise deterministic values for the DTAs, allowing the company and its shareholders to possess all necessary information to correctly estimate the company's financial stance and allow for a realistic strategy for the future.

REFERENCES

Amir, E., Kirschenheiter, M., & Willard, K. (1997). The Valuation of Deferred Taxes. *Contemporary Accounting Research, 14*(4), 597–622. doi:10.1111/j.1911-3846.1997. tb00543.x

Amir, E., & Sougiannis, T. (1999, Spring). Analysts'' interpretation and investors'' valuation of tax carryforwards. *Contemporary Accounting Research, 16*(1), 1–33. doi:10.1111/j.1911-3846.1999.tb00572.x

Atwood, T., Drake, M. S., & Myers, L. A. (2010). Book-tax conformity, earnings persistence and the association between earnings and future cash flows. *Journal of Accounting and Economics, 50*(1), 111–125. doi:10.1016/j.jacceco.2009.11.001

Ayers, B. C., Laplante, S. K., & McGuire, S. T. (2010). Credit Ratings and Taxes: The Effect of Book-Tax Differences on Ratings Changes. *Contemporary Accounting Research, 27*(2), 359–402. doi:10.1111/j.1911-3846.2010.01011.x

Baesens, B., & van Gestel, T. (2009). *Credit Risk Management.* Oxford University Press.

Burgstahler, D. C., Elliott, W. B., & Hanlon, M. (2002). *How Firms Avoid Losses: Evidence of Use of the Net Deferred Tax Asset Account.* Academic Press.

Colley, R., Rue, J., Valencia, A., & Volkan, A. (2007). Deferred Taxes in the Context of the Unit Problem. *Journal of Finance and Accountancy.*

Cox, Ingersoll, & Ross. (1985). A Theory of the Term Structure of Interest Rates. *Econometrica, 53*(2), 385–407. doi:10.2307/1911242

Crabtree, A., & Maher, J. J. (2009). The Influence of Differences in Taxable Income and Book Income on the Bond Credit Market. *The Journal of the American Taxation Association, 31*(1), 75–99. doi:10.2308/jata.2009.31.1.75

De Vries, T. (2018). *Market Consistent Valuation of Deferred Taxes* (MSc thesis). Technical University Delft.

Edwards, A. (2011). *Does the Deferred Tax Asset Valuation Allowance Signal Firm Creditworthiness? Working chapter.* University of Toronto.

Gallemore, J. (2011). *Deferred Tax Assets and Bank Regulatory Capital: Working chapter.* University of North Carolina.

Hanlon, M., & Shevlin, T. (2005). *Bank-Tax Conformity for Corporate Income: An Introduction to the Issues.* Academic Press.

Hogg, R. V. (2004). Introduction to mathematical statistics (6th ed.). Upper Saddle River, NJ: Prentice Hall.

Kara, G. I. (2016). *Bank Capital Regulations around the World: What Explains the Differences?* Finance and Economics Discussion Series 2016-057. Washington, DC: Board of Governors of the Federal Reserve System. doi:10.17016/feds.2016.057

Kautish, S. (2008). Online Banking: A Paradigm Shift. E-Business. *ICFAI Publication, Hyderabad, 9*(10), 54–59.

Kautish, S., & Thapliyal, M. P. (2012). Concept of Decision Support Systems in relation with Knowledge Management–Fundamentals, theories, frameworks and practices. *International Journal of Application or Innovation in Engineering & Management, 1*(2), 9.

Kim, D., & Santomero, A. M. (1988). Risk in banking and capital regulation. *The Journal of Finance, 43*(December), 1219–1233. doi:10.1111/j.1540-6261.1988. tb03966.x

Laux, R. C. (2013). *The Association between Deferred Tax Assets and Liabilities and Future Tax Payments. SSRN*. Electronic Journal.

Moodys Research Report. (2015). https://www.moodys.com/research/Moodys-Reliance-on-global-banks-deferred-tax-assets-poses-potential--PR_340219

Poterba, J. M., Rao, N. S., & Seidman, J. K. (2011). Deferred tax positions and incentives for corporate behavior around corporate tax changes. *National Tax Journal, 64*(1), 27–57. doi:10.17310/ntj.2011.1.02

Reilly, D. (2009, Jan. 28). Citi, BofA Show Investors Can't Bank on Capital. *Bloomberg*, p. 1.

Ryan, S. (2007). *Financial Instruments and Institutions: Accounting and Disclosure Rules* (2nd ed.). John Wilen & Sons.

Sansing, R. C., & Guenther, D. A. (n.d.). *The Valuation Relevance of Reversing Deferred Tax Liabilities*. Academic Press.

ENDNOTES

[1]   Statement of Financial Accounting Standards.

[2]   Consultative document of December 2009, entitled "Strengthening the resilience of the banking sector."

[3]   Note that only the annual results are simulated, and thus the results could be represented only by points; lines joining the points were chosen in order to improve the readability of the results.

Chapter 9
Simple Valuation of Compounded Deferred Tax Assets Using a Binomial Algorithm

Joao Carlos Silva
ISCTE, University Institute of Lisbon, Portugal

Nuno Souto
ⓘ https://orcid.org/0000-0003-3823-4470
ISCTE, University Institute of Lisbon, Portugal

José Pereira
ISEG, Universidade de Lisboa, Portugal

ABSTRACT

Deferred tax asset (DTA) is a tax/accounting concept that refers to an asset that may be used to reduce future tax liabilities of the holder. In a company's balance, it usually refers to situations where it has either overpaid taxes, paid taxes in advance, or has carry-over of losses (the latter being the most common situation). In fact, accounting and tax losses may be used to shield future profits from taxation, through tax loss carry-forwards. The purpose of this chapter is to propose a precise and conceptually sound approach to value DTAs. For that purpose, making use of an adapted binomial CRR (Cox, Ross, and Rubinstein) algorithm, the authors derive a precise way to value DTAs. This way, the DTAs are valued in a similar way of the binomial options pricing model, and the subjectivity of its evaluation is greatly reduced. The authors show that with the proposed evaluation techniques, the DTA's expected value will be much lower than the values normally used in today's practice, and the bank's financial analysis will lead to much more sound and realistic results.

DOI: 10.4018/978-1-7998-7716-5.ch009

INTRODUCTION

The tax return of a company is based on its accounting financial statements. To provide comparable information, financial statements are prepared according to the International Financial Reporting Standards (IFRS), issued by the International Accounting Standards Board (IASB). The IASB was formed in 2001 to replace the International Accounting Standards Committee that issued International Accounting Standards (IAS). Since the previously issued IASs remain effective, we have that the main body of standards that are used worldwide by several countries are comprised of IFRSs and IASs. The companies' income, depicted by the IFRSs and IASs (refereed to simply by the Generally Accepted Accounting Principles GAAP) are their accounting profits, but these may be (and are) different than the taxable profit, since the taxable profit is calculated as a function of the tax law inherent to each country. The number of factors that lead to differences between tax and accounting returns is huge and varies from country to country. One of those factors is of relevance to the present work – the deferral of taxes.

The relationship of DTAs with the creditworthiness of a company as already deserved some work from academic community. The effects of book-tax differences on a firm's credit risk were analysed in (Crabtree & Maher 2009), (Ayers et al. 2010), (Edwards 2011) and (Gallemore 2011); all agreeing that great amounts of deferred taxes were associated with higher risks and lower earnings quality, resulting in a decline of creditworthiness. Additionally, studies of the impact of DTAs on credit ratings led to the conclusion that deferred tax positions are substantial for many firms (between 5% and 10% of all assets according to (Poterba et al 2011)).

Under normal circumstances, a company's DTAs usually originate in the carry-over of losses (though it can also arise from overpaying some taxes). The corresponding rights are registered in the balance sheet as assets, although in (Amir and Sougiannis 1999) it also argued that DTA may have implications for the perception of the firm as a going concern (dubbed as the information effect), since if the DTA arose from past operating losses, future losses would be likely to incur; this means that future liabilities could be more than likely, and thus such "assets" should be regarded with great suspicion).

These assets may be hard to value, since they are time-limited and may never be used at all. Their value is contingent on the future earnings of the company, and they can be used to shield these future profits from taxation – IAS 12 states that "a DTA should be recognised for all deductible temporary differences, to the extent that it is probable that taxable profit will be available against which the deductible temporary difference can be utilised". Since corporate income taxation works on an annual basis, the shielding opportunities occur once a year. This is equivalent to saying that we are faced with a compound European option (or an annual Bermuda option) that might be exercised until the last year in which the law will permit shielding, or until the DTAs value has been completely depleted by its use. Consistent with this line of thinking, there is an ongoing debate regarding the appropriateness of including DTA in the banks' regulatory capital calculation, since by doing so we are assuming its "full" worth; something that is clearly misleading.

Another aspect that must be taken into consideration is that a company can have several DTAs, each with different expiry dates; in this situation it will naturally use the DTA's with the nearest expiry date first. Thus being, the probability of a certain DTA being used is dictated by all DTAs with shorter expiration dates being used or expired, and that the company generates enough profit to cover the DTA. Such scenario may seem hard to quantify at first, but as we will show, it is rather simple via the use of a binomial algorithm.

FOCUS ON THE BANKING SECTOR

On the special case of the banking sector, banks are required to maintain certain levels of regulatory capital to provide a buffer against potential future losses (Kim and Santomero 1998),(Ryan 2007), (Baesens and van Gestel 2009). In many countries (Kara 2016), banks are allowed to count a portion (or all) of their DTAs towards regulatory capital requirements (since the adoption of SFAS[1] No. 109 in 1992 – specifically the establishment of valuation allowances). Throughout the recent financial crisis (2008-2013), major media outlets routinely drew attention to the banks' DTA positions, classifying them as tenuous contributions towards regulatory capital. In (Reilly 2009), it was noted that tier 1 capital ratios contained "fluff" – mentioning DTA as the primary culprit, calling in an "airy asset". The Basel Committee on Banking Supervision specifically targeted the removal of DTAs as a potential method for improving the ability of regulatory capital to protect banks from losses[2]. At the same time, the banking industry has pushed for the opposite; namely a greater inclusion of DTA in the regulatory capital calculation, in an attempt to "ease" the amount of (real) regulatory capital. Gallemore (2011) investigates the credit risk associated with the deferred tax asset component of bank regulatory capital. He hypothesizes that banks that have a larger proportion of regulatory capital composed of deferred tax assets will be more likely to fail. He employs a hazard model to test a sample of commercial banks and finds that the proportion of regulatory capital composed of deferred tax assets is positively associated with the risk of bank failure during the recent financial crisis. Gallemore (2011) attributes his findings to the fact that the benefits of deferred tax assets cannot be realized unless banks generate positive taxable income in the future.

It is thus clear that these DTAs must be correctly valued, and that simply adding them to the balance sheet in full as an asset might contribute to obfuscate the company's true financial condition – even a situation in which the DTA is fully used before its expiration date, we still must account for the cost of capital. In (Moodys 2015), DTAs were considered "a low-quality form of assets, and thus a low-quality source of capital", and consequently, Moody's decided to "limit the contribution of DTAs in its calculations of banks' tangible common equity (TCE)". As analysed in De Vries (2018), several DTA valuation methods can be used, but they are essentially very subjective, and basically result in a valuation allowance, for which there is no consistent accepted method to calculate – this chapter aims to resolve such shortcomings.

Valuation Techniques

In this chapter we will explore two different valuation techniques based on the CRR binomial algorithm; one that resumes itself to the use of an approximated closed formula (with a binomial tree in the background, as a theoretical basis), and another that effectively uses a binomial tree. The CRR binomial algorithm was chosen due to being the main method used to value options. DTAs are somewhat similar to options with same base differences; and thus this chapter simply tweaks the CRR binomial algorithm to account for the main differences, and to allow for a more precise estimate of the DTA's value, such as is currently done for stock options.

Both methods comprise a standard set of steps, explained ahead, which basically provides the framework to use the expected future earnings and current DTAs with their associated expiry date.

Valuation of the DTAs must be performed by following some steps. Initially, a vector must be constructed containing the company's net losses, ordered by the years that each loss is eligible to be used as a DTA. Assuming that N is the maximum number of years that can be accounted for, we have a vector with N positions, where position 1 contains the company's previous losses whose corresponding DTA can only be accounted for in the following year; position 2 contains the company's losses whose corresponding DTA can only be accounted for in the next 2 years, and so on until N. Considering such a framework, we constructed a vector P_Losses{1:N}, compiling all of the company's negative results eligible for consideration in our deferred tax assets' calculations. Note that the vector P_Losses{1:N}, when multiplied by the tax rate (that we assume constant over the years), would yield a vector of DTA{1:N}, ordered by expiration dates; however, for ease of calculations, we will work with the P_Losses{1:N} vector and only multiply by the tax rate at the end of our calculations.

After this first step, we must estimate the company's performance over the next N years. There are many ways to achieve this, however, for the moment, let us focus on the company's projected result for the next year (assumed positive), and on the estimated annual volatility σ of the business, so that we can build up a binomial tree with up and down movements (such as performed in the Binomial CRR options pricing model). If we will only consider yearly time frames, we have $\Delta t = 1$, and thus the up (u^+) and down (d^-) movements are given as (from (CRR 1979), with the condition that the variance of the log of the profit is $\sigma 2$):

$$u^+ = e^{\sigma\sqrt{\Delta t}} = e^{\sigma} \text{ and } d^- = e^{-\sigma\sqrt{\Delta t}} = e^{-\sigma} . \text{ Note that } u^+ = \frac{1}{d^-} .$$

Consequently, from an initial estimate of profits P_1, that is given with a certainty of I_1 ($0 < I_1 \leq 1$), we can project several scenarios with the upward and downward movements of the binomial tree. At first we will only assume projected positive profits throughout the upcoming years, but later we will also allow for a more realistic scenario with negative cash flows.

Method 1A – Simple Mean Value and Positive Profits

In this method, we are only interested on the binomial tree's mean values at each step for valuation, in order to obtain an easy and simple estimate. Looking at the binomial tree, we can infer that the mean values (accounting for the combinations of the inner values; $\binom{n}{k}$) for each year are given by (after some manipulation)

$$P_1 \times \left(\frac{1 + \left(u^+\right)^2}{2u^+} \right)^{t-1} \quad \text{(note that this mean increases every year, since } \frac{u^+ + d^-}{2} > 1\text{)}.$$

We can therefore create a vector with the mean projections of future profits multiplied by the risk neutral probability[3] (this method will only yield positive numbers, since the initial number is assumed positive, and all others are found by applying positive multipliers; other methods that could yield negative numbers must convert the negative numbers into zeros and calculate the resultant mean values with these zeros instead, as will be done in method 2 further along) for the next N years as F_-

$$\text{Profits}\{1{:}N\} = (P1, P1 \times \left(\frac{1 + \left(u^+\right)^2}{2u^+} \right), ..., P_1 \times \left(\frac{1 + \left(u^+\right)^2}{2u^+} \right)^{N-1}).$$

Figure 1. Binomial projection of profits

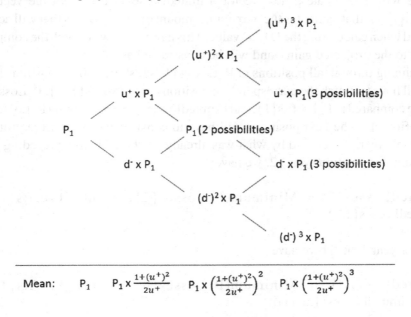

$$\text{Mean:} \quad P_1 \quad P_1 \times \frac{1+(u^+)^2}{2u^+} \quad P_1 \times \left(\frac{1+(u^+)^2}{2u^+}\right)^2 \quad P_1 \times \left(\frac{1+(u^+)^2}{2u^+}\right)^3$$

With the two vectors of previous losses and future profits; P_Losses{1:N} and F_Profits{1:N}, we can now apply the valuation method for the deferred tax assets. Note that, basically, what is at stake here is to "spread" the accumulated losses over the projected earnings of the company for the following years.

Figure 2. Spreading the carry-over of losses through the following years

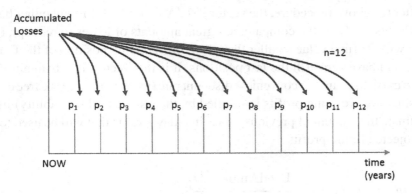

We will now create a new vector, LimitedLosses{1:N}, from the vector P_Losses{1:N}, that estimates the maximum amount of losses/DTAs that will actually be used when calculating the DTAs' value. This new vector will match the company's losses to the projected gains, and will be constructed as follows:

Running through all positions of P_Losses{1:N}, starting from position 1 to N, we will have to match the corresponding positions to F_Profits{1:N}. P_Losses{1} will be compared to F_Profits{1}, and LimitedLosses{1}=Minimum(P_Losses{1}; F_Profits{1}). The next positions will have to consider the sum of the profits up until their year, discounted by what was already attributed by the preceding years. So being, for position (year) 2, we have:

LimitedLosses{2}= Minimum(P_Losses{2}; Sum(F_Profits{1,2})-LimitedLosses{1})).

And for year 1<n≤N we have

LimitedLosses{n}= Minimum(P_Losses{n}; Sum(F_Profits{1,n})-Sum(LimitedLosses{1,n-1}))).

Next we will create a final vector, that will only accommodate the projected profits used to offset to losses, out of the projected mean profits. This vector is easy to build, and basically is similar to the vector F_Profits{1:N}, but with a slight modification; the vector's sum must equal the sum of vector LimitedLosses{1:N} by means of zeroing and reducing the final positions of the vector F_Profits. This operation can be done iteratively, and the base code for calculating each position is given in the Appendix.

After the above procedure, the vector UsedAmount {1:N} might either be equal to F_Profits{1:N} (if the company has great amounts of losses to recoup), or be a vector with its final value smaller than the corresponding position of the F_Profits vector, and have zeros fill the last positions. It is this vector, UsedAmount {1:N}, that we must discount at a convenient discount rate (we will use the risk-free discount rate, since we are using profits multiplied by the risk-neutral probability) in order to estimate the amount of previous losses in today's value that will be used to cover the projected future profits.

$$Recoup\_amount = \sum_{i=1}^{N} \frac{\text{UsedAmount}\{i\}}{(1 + r_f)^i}$$

In the special case of UsedAmount {1:N}=F_Profits{1:N}, we have simply to calculate an annuity, and as such

$$Recoup\_amount = \frac{P_1}{r_f - g}\left[1 - \left(\frac{1+g}{1+r_f}\right)^N\right]$$

With

$$g = \left(\frac{1+u^2}{2u}\right) - 1$$

The final result, the effective value of the DTA (Deferred Tax Assets) is obtained by multiplying the obtained amount at today's value by the tax level T[4] and the probability attributed to P_1, namely I_1. The deferred tax asset for this scenario would thus be

$$Value\_DTA_1 = Recoup\_amount \times T \times I_1$$

If $I_1 \neq 1$, then we would run all S scenarios to cover all probabilities (sum of all "I"s=1) and

$$Value\_DTA = \sum_{i=1}^{S} Value\_DTA_i$$

As a final note, we can calculate the maximum and minimum amount of deferred tax assets by filling the F_Profits vector with the maximum/ minimum projected profit instead of the mean profit (in the special case of UsedAmount {1:N}=F_Profits{1:N}, this would mean a g=u-1 or g=d-1 respectively).

Examples for Method 1A

Taking as an example a situation where the company tax is 20%, the discount rate rf is 5%, the profit projection for the upcoming year is 50.000€ and σ=0,8 (we will assume this value unless stated otherwise[5]), as seen in Table 1.

With the above conditions in mind, we have to arrange our previous losses vector by years left to expiry. In our case (Table 2), we have that losses of 40.000€ have a recoup expiration date of 1 year, losses of 120.000€ have a recoup expiration date of 2 years and so on.

Table 1. Initial conditions

Tax	20%
Discount Rate	5%
Profit projection for 1st year	50.000€
sigma	0,8

Table 2. Losses, Projected Profits and Valuation of DTA, example 1 (in €), method 1A

Years Left to discount	0	1	2	3	4	5
Losses		40000	120000	50000	100000	30000
Mean Projected Profits		50000	66871,747	89436,61	119615,7	159978,2
Limited Losses		40000	76871,747	50000	100000	30000
Used Amount		50000	66871,747	89436,61	90563,39	0
Wrongfully used DTA	68000,00					
Realistic DTA	52007,83					

The mean projected profits vector is easily built, having in mind the initial projected profit and the its volatility, σ. Having these two vectors, we proceed to calculate the limited losses vector, which is basically a projection of how much of our losses are we really expecting to be covered from the DTA. For previous losses whose corresponding DTA has an expiration date of 1 year from now, we have that the future profits will probably fully cover the losses, and thus account the whole value of 40.000€. For year 2, we have losses of 120.000€, and projected profits of only 66.871,75€. From this, we can already infer that the company will lose the right to use part of these losses as DTA. The effective value it will use will be 10.000€ of losses with expiry date of 2 years that will effectively be used in year 1 (to cover the 10.000€ difference between the 40.000€ losses and 50.000€ profits), added to the 66.871,75€ of profits in year 2. Thus, the total loss from year 2 that will effectively be used is 66.871,75€+10.000€ = 76.871,75€ - the rest will be forfeited. For years 3 to 5, the losses will always be less that the profits, and thus full usage is projected.

The Used Amount vector is the most important vector of all. Basically, it tells us what part of the profits we can effectively deduce from having losses carry-over. In year 1, we have it to be 50.000€ (used by the 40.000€ loss with expiration of 1 year, and 10.000€ with expiration of 2 years). In year two, we will discount the full profits of 66.871,75€ with losses ending in the second year. In the third year, the 89.436,61€ will be covered by losses of 50.000€ ending in year 3, and 39.436,61€ of losses ending in year 4. The remaining losses (year 4 and year 5) amount to

90.563,39€, and this amount will all be used in year 4. Year 5 will have no benefit whatsoever from DTA.

With the Used Amount vector constructed, estimating the final amount is easy; simply discount all values of the used amount vector to present day values and multiply it by the Tax rate. This will yield our final value of DTA's worth – 52.007,83€ in this case. Note that current practices value the DTAs simply as the sum of all previous losses multiplied by the tax rate, which in this case would yield 20% x 340.000€=68.000€ (it is always higher than the calculated values, since it assumes that all DTAs are going to be used, without being discounted by any rate at all!).

If we opted for a σ=0,2, then the values would be those summarized in Table 3 (example 2). From the table we can see that, due to the lower projected profits, we wouldn't be able to use the full amount of DTAs, yielding a lower Limited Losses vector, and thus a lower Used Amount vector – although the wrongfully used DTA in the balance sheet is still the same 68.000€, note that the realistic DTA drops to 41.198,11€.

Another example could be the following, with σ=0,8, a different set of DTAs and expiry dates (Table 4, example 3):

Table 3. Losses, Projected Profits and Valuation of DTA, example 2 (in €), method 1A

Years Left to discount	0	1	2	3	4	5
Losses		40000	120000	50000	100000	30000
Mean Projected Profits		50000	51003,338	52026,81	53070,82	54135,78
Limited Losses		40000	61003,338	50000	55097,63	30000
Used Amount		50000	51003,338	52026,81	53070,82	30000
Wrongfully used DTA	68000,00					
Realistic DTA	41198,11					

Table 4. Losses, Projected Profits and Valuation of DTA, example 3 (in €), method 1A

Years Left to discount	0	1	2	3	4	5
Losses		0	120000	0	100000	300000
Mean Projected Profits		50000	66871,75	89436,61	119615,7	159978,2
Limited Losses		0	116871,7	0	100000	269030,4
Used Amount		50000	66871,75	89436,61	119615,7	159978,2
Wrongfully used DTA	104000					
Realistic DTA	81857,51					

In this third example, we keep the same profit projections as in the first, but now the previous losses vector is different; it has some zero value positions, and some high values, especially for the loss whose corresponding DTA has an expiry date of 5 years from now. Note how the limited losses is constructed, with losses whose corresponding DTA have an expiry date of 2 years covering both the first and second year (forfeiting the rest) and notice how the losses whose corresponding DTA have expiry dates of 4 and 5 years cover the whole of the amounts of years 3 to 5. Thus being, all of the projected profits are covered, and effectively the used amount is equal to the profits vector, amounting to a value of 81.857,51€. The wrongfully used value of DTAs, obtained by summing all the previous losses and multiplying by the tax level would equal 104.000€!

In this case, the final recoup amount is thus calculated by discounting all of the used amount (or profits vector[6]), which in this special case is an annuity

$$Recoup\_amount = \frac{P_1}{r_f - g}\left[1 - \left(\frac{1+g}{1+r_f}\right)^N\right]$$

The example above considers that we are sure of yielding a profit of 50.000€ in one year's time – this may not always be the case - If we say that there is a 80% chance of the company yielding a profit of 50.000€ in one year's time with a sigma of 0.8, and 20% chance of yielding losses, we can multiply our final amount by 80% - this is what is done in valuation allowance, but by calculating the used amounts and discounting them correctly, we have a much better estimation. We can also study several scenarios and give a probability value to each, and make a final calculation based on the relative weights of each result.

Method 1B – Simple Mean Value With Possibility of Future Losses (Negative Profits)

In method 1A we assumed only outcomes involving positive profits; that was done merely for simplicity sake. In this method we adjust the model to accommodate for the likelihood of sustaining negative profits (if the company has deferred tax assets to use its because it has incurred in losses before, being therefore likely it will incur on losses again). The consideration of this framework compels us to drift from the multiplicative factors used in the CRR, and use them only to set the initial deviations from the initial projected profit. These deviations will remain fixed for the whole of the tree, allowing for negative profits (the CRR model is built for stock prices that never go below 0) – of course that, for what the DTA is concerned, the negative profits should be converted to 0. Considering $u=P_1 \times (u^+-1)$ and $d=P_1 \times (1-d^-)$. and looking at the binomial tree, we can infer that the mean values (accounting for the combinations of the inner values; $\binom{n}{k}$) for each year are given by $P_1 + (t-1)\left(\dfrac{u-d}{2}\right)$, as long as the whole tree boasts positive values. If the lower portion of the tree crosses the zero threshold, then the mean profit value for consideration should be higher, since the negative values should be considered as zeros for calculating the mean – from this we can state that the mean values without any correction (assuming all values are positive, even if they aren't) will be equal or smaller than when we correct for the negative values (and thus have a lower bound on the DTA valuation, as we will see later).

Figure 3. Binomial projection of profits

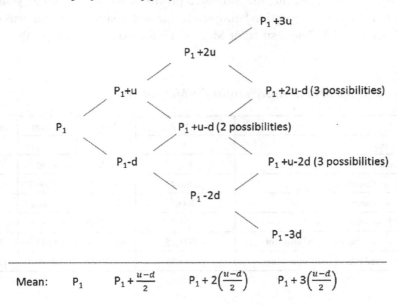

We can therefore create a vector with the mean projections of future profits for the next N years as

$$F\_Profits\{1:N\}=\left(P_1, \ P_1+\left(\frac{u-d}{2}\right), ..., P_1 + (N-1)\left(\frac{u-d}{2}\right)\right), \text{ if } P_1-(N-1)3d>0,$$

else the mean profits vector must be adjusted for the negative profit projections (using zeros instead of the negative numbers), yielding higher values – it is this correction that effectively increases the complexity of this method when compared to method 1A.

Examples for Method 1B (With Possibility of Future Losses)

Taking the same initial conditions as those presented in Table 1 and the same losses of example 1, we have first to adjust the mean projected profits' vector. In fact, since future losses are admissible, we have to adjust the mean of future profits to treat the negative profits as zeros. To do this, we must check the lowest values of the binomial tree in each iteration and adjust the mean of the iteration at hand if necessary. Starting with 50.000 for the first year (mean=50.000 in this case), we will now analyse the following years, from 2 to 5, in Table 5.

From Table 5, we see that the estimated profits of the 3rd. 4th and 5th year had to be adjusted. After this operation being made, the rest is similar to what was done in Table 2, method 1A. The results for Method 1B are now shown in Table 6.

Table 5. Adjustment of negative profits for Method 1B

	2° Year	3° Year	4° Year	5° Year
# of elements	2	4	8	16
Smallest element	P-d	P-2d	P-3d	P-4d
Value of smallest element	22466,45	-5067,1	-32600,7	-60134,2
2° Smallest element	P+u	P-d+u	P-2d+u	P-3d+u
Value of 2° smallest element	111277	83743,49	56209,94	28676,39
Mean Projected Profits w/o adjustment	66871,75	83743,49	100615,2	117487
Mean Projected Profits with adjustment	66871,75	85010,27	104690,3	121245,4

Table 6. Example 1 using method 1B

Years Left to discount	0	1	2	3	4	5
Losses		40000	120000	50000	100000	30000
Mean Projected Profits		50000	66871,75	85010,27	104690,3	121245,4
Limited Losses		40000	76871,75	50000	100000	30000
Used Amount		50000	66871,75	85010,27	94989,73	0
Wrongfully used DTA	68000,00					
Realistic DTA	51971,41					

Looking at the results of Table 6, we see that the DTA value is similar to that of Table 2, though a bit smaller as expected, due to the possibility of negative profits. In Table 7 we reproduced example 3 (of Table 4), now using method 1B, which also yields a smaller DTA value overall.

Table 7. Example 2 using method 1B

Years Left to discount	0	1	2	3	4	5
Losses		0	120000	0	100000	300000
Mean Projected Profits		50000	66871,75	85010,27	104690,3	121245,4
Limited Losses		0	116871,75	0,00	100000	210946
Used Amount		50000	66871,75	85010,27	104690,3	121245,4
Wrongfully used DTA	104000,00					
Realistic DTA	72567,34					

A fourth example can use a total arbitrary Projected Profits Vector (equal for both methods 1A and 1B). In this case, the whole vector is given as input, and the DTA value is calculated accordingly (Table 8).

Table 8. Losses, Arbitrary Projected Profits and Valuation of DTA, example 4 (in €)

Years Left to discount	0	1	2	3	4	5
Losses		0	120000	0	100000	300000
Mean Projected Profits		20000	0	110000	0	0
Limited Losses		0	20000	0	100000	10000
Used Amount		20000	0	110000	0	0
Wrongfully used DTA	104000,00					
Realistic DTA	22813,95					

Once again, notice the dynamics of the limited losses vector and the final used amount vector (which in this case is the same as the mean projected profits, meaning that the previous losses were able to cover the entire profits). This deterministic algorithm is indeed effective and simple to use, although we can't always predict the profits with absolute certainty – notice that now the final value was 22.813,95€, while the wrongfully used value of DTAs is, as in the previous example, equal to 104.000€.

Method 2A - Binomial Tree Alternative With Positive Profits

In this second method, we base our reasoning on a binomial tree of possible outcomes for profits, each with a representing probably. Assuming a binomial state change, the profit will either rise or fall by u^+ or $d^-=1/u^+$ respectively, with probability P_u or P_d. The probability of changing state is calculated by the risk neutral approach (as in the CRR Binomial model), meaning that the previous' year profit will either rise or fall (by the u^+ factor), and being risk neutral, the values of rising or falling multiplied by the respective probabilities and adjusted by the risk-free rate of interest will yield the previous year's profit. Thus, we have that the probability of the profit rising is given by

$$P_u = \frac{\left(1+r_f\right) - \dfrac{1}{u^+}}{u^+ - \dfrac{1}{u^+}}$$

And the probability of the profit falling is $P_d=1-P_u$.
The state tree will be something like Figure 4.

Figure 4. Binomial tree for DTA calculation

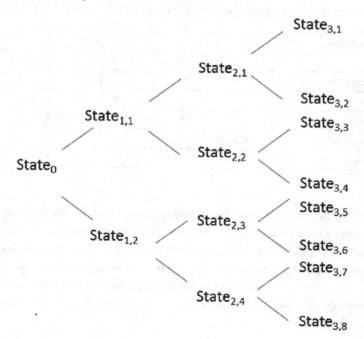

Take notice that the tree is not recombinant; i.e., there is no merging between paths, contrary to the CRR binomial tree of Methods 1A and 1B, since the states will be different in some of its variables. Each state is defined by its estimated profit, the state's current DTA value by accounting all DTA tax shielding up to the current state (from left to right), the state's probability of being reached and the available previous losses vector to the state (ordered by expiration dates of the corresponding DTAs, as explained earlier).

Figure 5. Components of each state in the binomial tree

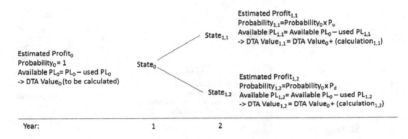

For each state, the DFA value is calculated as follows:

DTA Value = Previous DTA value (if any) + Calculation for current state

The calculation for current state is determined by the expected profit for the current state and the Available PL that comes from the previous state. The Available PL contains only the leftover PL from the previous state whose DTAs have an expiry date that is equal or greater than the year for the current state. If the sum of the available PL is equal or over the projected profit, then only the PL part that covers the projected profit will be used (starting with the PL whose DTAs have lowest expiry dates), and the rest will be transferred to the next states. If the sum of the PL is under the projected profit, all of the PL will be used for the DTA calculation, and the transferred PL to subsequent states will be 0 (basically we are using the intermediate vectors Limited Losses and Used Amount as in method 1). As in the previous method, the values are then multiplied by the tax rate and added to the DTA value.

In order to exemplify the whole procedure, consider the initial conditions for the next 3 years depicted in Table 9, where the initial PL vector states that 130.000€ in losses expires in year 1, 70.000€ in year 2 and 80.000€ in year 3:

We have the values for each state shown in Figure 6.

Table 9. Initial conditions used to illustrate the binomial method

Tax	20%
Discount Rate	5%
Profit projection for 1st year	100.000€
sigma	0,8
Previous Losses Vector	(130.000; 70.000; 80.000)€

Figure 6. Example with state evolution in the binomial tree

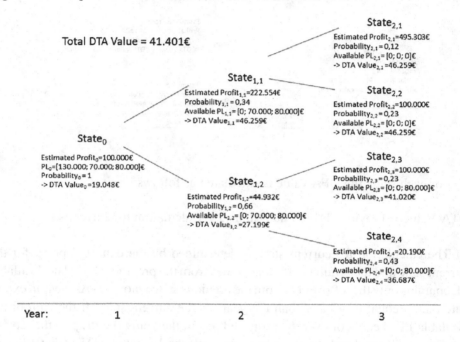

The total DTA value is obtained by the sum-product of all DTA values of the states in year 3, multiplied by their respective probabilities, yielding 41.401€. Notice that this method will yield a smaller value than method 1A, since method 1A assumes that all states have the same probability and calculates a higher mean value for the estimated profits (notice that this method yields a smaller probability of the profits rising (34%) than that of the profits falling (66%)). Using method 1A, the total DTA figure would yield 46.118€ (depicted in Table 10), while the value that is inscribed in the balance sheet is 56.000€; clearly significantly more than the values calculated by both methods (35,3% and 21,4% for the realistic values of 41.401€ (Method 2A) and 46.118€ (Method 1A), respectively).

Table 10. Paralellism of same conditions using method 1A (in €)

Years Left to discount	0	1	2	3
Losses		130000	70000	80000
Mean Projected Profits		100000,00	133743,49	178873,22
Limited Losses		100000	70000	80000
Used Amount		100000,00	133743,49	16256,51
Wrongfully used DTA	56000,00			
Realistic DTA	46118,07			

Method 2B - Binomial Tree Alternative With Possibility of Future Losses (Negative Profits)

In this variant, we once again allow for negative profits (which must be converted to zeros afterwards, since we won't be able to use the DTAs in those situations). So being, the only change to method 2A is the estimated profit in each branch, from year 3 onwards. As already performed in method 1B, the profits will either rise or fall by the amount u or d, and thus we can reproduce Figure 6 in Figure 7 with this new methodology.

Figure 7. Example allowing for negative profits, Method 2B

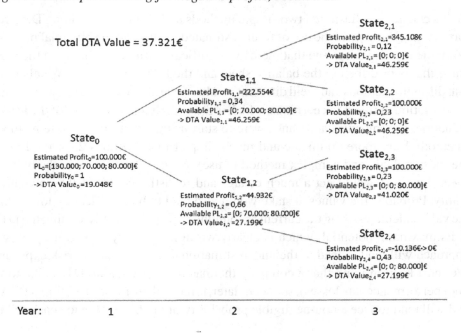

Looking at Figure 7, we can see that indeed state$_{2,4}$ would have a negative profit (-10.136€), and as such was corrected to zero. The DTA value, calculated by multiplying each DTA from year 3 with its corresponding probability (37.321€ from Figure 7) was lower than using method 2A, as expected. Both values are close, and both methods could be employed. If we were to use method 1B (mean projected profit for year 3 calculated as the mean of profits of the third year in Figure 7, yielding 136.277€ in year 3), results would be the same as in Table 10, since the DTAs wouldn't be able to cover the profits in full. These results are shown in Table 11.

Table 11. Paralellism of same conditions using method 1B (in €)

Years Left to discount	0	1	2	3
Losses		130000	70000	80000
Mean Projected Profits		100000	133743	136277
Limited Losses		100000	70000	80000
Used Amount		100000	133743	16257
Wrongfully used DTA	56000,00			
Realistic DTA	46118,07			

CONCLUSION

In this chapter we illustrated two simple methods and variants for valuing Deferred Tax Assets (DTAs), via the use of future estimated results and the binomial method. From the results we can see that there are significant differences between the asset value that is inscribed in the balance sheet and the DTA's real value. We also saw that different methods can yield different results, since all methods are contingent on the evolution of future tax earnings, which is the underlying asset used for the DTA's valuation. If companies and banks were to start using either one of these methods (methods 1 are more optimistic and much simpler than methods 2; method 2B is the most realistic and complex method to use) to value their DTAs in the balance sheet, investors would get a much clearer and realistic picture of the company's equity. Probably, the values at stake would also tend to be significantly lower than the value calculates using the current accounting approach (usually valuing the DTA at its maximum potential, which is clearly wrong). Naturally, this over optimistic approach will tend to lead to the underestimation of the company's risk exposure. We must keep in mind that a company that has been originating DTAs due to its poor performance (tax losses), sooner or later, is most likely to face additional DTAs, and will tend to face a non-negligible probability of not being able to "cash-in" its

DTAs, rendering them worthless – it is essential that DTA valuation methods use realistic earnings projections, and that these are understood (and approved) by the majority of the shareholders.

REFERENCES

Amir, E., & Sougiannis, T. (1999, Spring). Analysts" interpretation and investors" valuation of tax carryforwards. *Contemporary Accounting Research*, *16*(1), 1–33. doi:10.1111/j.1911-3846.1999.tb00572.x

Ayers, B. C., Laplante, S. K., & McGuire, S. T. (2010). Credit Ratings and Taxes: The Effect of Book-Tax Differences on Ratings Changes. *Contemporary Accounting Research*, *27*(2), 359–402. doi:10.1111/j.1911-3846.2010.01011.x

Baesens, B., & van Gestel, T. (2009). *Credit Risk Management*. Oxford University Press.

Cox, J. C., Ross, S. A., & Rubinstein, M. (1979). Option pricing: A simplified approach. *Journal of Financial Economics*, *7*(3), 229–263. doi:10.1016/0304-405X(79)90015-1

Crabtree, A., & Maher, J. J. (2009). The Influence of Differences in Taxable Income and Book Income on the Bond Credit Market. *The Journal of the American Taxation Association*, *31*(1), 75–99. doi:10.2308/jata.2009.31.1.75

De Vries, T. (2018). *Market Consistent Valuation of Deferred Taxes* (MSc thesis). Technical University Delft.

Edwards, A. (2011). *Does the Deferred Tax Asset Valuation Allowance Signal Firm Creditworthiness? Working chapter*. University of Toronto.

Gallemore, J. (2011). *Deferred Tax Assets and Bank Regulatory Capital: Working chapter*. University of North Carolina.

Kara. (2016). *Bank Capital Regulations around the World: What Explains the Differences?* Finance and Economics Discussion Series 2016-057. Washington, DC: Board of Governors of the Federal Reserve System, doi:10.17016/feds.2016.057

Kim, D., & Santomero, A. M. (1988). Risk in banking and capital regulation. *The Journal of Finance*, *43*(December), 1219–1233. doi:10.1111/j.1540-6261.1988.tb03966.x

Poterba, J. M., Rao, N. S., & Seidman, J. K. (2011). Deferred tax positions and incentives for corporate behavior around corporate tax changes. *National Tax Journal*, *64*(1), 27–57. doi:10.17310/ntj.2011.1.02

Reilly, D. (2009, Jan. 28). Citi, BofA Show Investors Can't Bank on Capital. *Bloomberg*, p. 1.

Ryan, S. (2007). *Financial Instruments and Institutions: Accounting and Disclosure Rules* (2nd ed.). John Wilen & Sons.

ENDNOTES

[1] Statement of Financial Accounting Standards.

[2] Consultative document of December 2009, entitled "Strengthening the resilience of the banking sector."

[3] All profits mentioned in this chapter are assumed to be multiplied by the risk-neutral probability, so that they can be discounted using the risk-free rate.

[4] The tax level is also a stochastic variable and could be treated as one; though for simplicity we will assume it as a constant in this chapter.

[5] We used a very high σ due to the forthcoming examples, were we will portray possible negative profit projections.

[6] Again, remember that the profit vector is adjusted by the risk-neutral probability.

APPENDIX

Below is the code for filling out the UsedAmount vector:

```
Total_Losses=Sum(LimitedLosses);
UsedAmount=Zeros{1:N};
Intermediate_sum=0;
For i=1 to N
        Intermediate_sum= Intermediate_sum+Profits{i};
        If Intermediate_sum< Total_Losses
UsedAmount {i}= Profits{i};
Else
        UsedAmount {i}= Profits{i} - (Intermediate_sum -
Total_Losses)
Exit For (leaving the remaining positions of UsedAmount as
zeros, if any)
End
End
```

Chapter 10
The Integrated Value Model (IVM):
A Relational Data Model of Business Value

Basil J. White
Independent Researcher, USA

Beth Archibald Martin
Maryland Institute College of Art, USA

Ryan J. Wold
Civic Studio, USA

ABSTRACT

The integrated value model (IVM) empowers analysis of the interdependent aspects of policies, plans, performance measures, priorities, and programs (P5). As organizations are holistic systems of processes and performance, knowing how P5 adds value becomes critical to success and achievement of internal goals and responses to external demands. Modeling these artifacts and mapping them to policies and practices allows analysts to measure the alignment to initiatives. The IVM supports efforts in strategic communications, change management, strategic planning, and decision support. Elements of P5 have explicit hierarchical and relational connections, but modeling the connections and developing logical inferences is an uncommon strategic business practice. This chapter describes how to use those goals to create a logical model for a public sector organization and how to use this model to identify, describe, and align business value. Further, this chapter demonstrates the model's capabilities and suggests future applications.

DOI: 10.4018/978-1-7998-7716-5.ch010

INTRODUCTION

In February 2007, *The Washington Post* reported on patient overcrowding and poor treatment at the Walter Reed Army Medical Center, a healthcare facility for military service veterans in Washington, DC (Priest & Hull, 2007). In the United States, military and civilian government agencies divide the responsibility for veterans care, and such an effort requires thoughtful coordination. The coverage in the press had shown this to be severely lacking. To resolve these problems, the United States Departments of Defense and Veterans Affairs formed an interagency oversight committee called the Wounded, Ill, and Injured Senior Oversight Committee (SOC).

The committee drafted a plan to bolster collaboration, and tasked an analyst to review it for conflicts and overlaps with other strategic plans. The analyst (White) reviewed the committee's plan in the context of all the organizations' related source documents, including the related civilian and military strategic plans and policies. The analyst's report, or "crosswalk", revealed that with one adjustment, all of the SOC's objectives could be subsumed by another, longer-established joint committee, the VA-DoD Joint Executive Committee. Thus, the prototype of the Integrated Value Model (IVM) was born; the authors will explain in more detail how the model is populated and supports complex modern organizations. Based on this analysis, the VA and DoD agreed to close the SOC and migrate its work to the JEC. This new, expanded JEC was able to perform its existing mission of collaborating and sharing resources as well as direct the care and benefits coordination efforts of the SOC.

IVM Sources, Components and Value Relationships

Modern organizations produce, and are products of, numerous policies, plans, performance measures, priorities, and programs (P5), and the interactions between these affect the efficiency and effectiveness of the overall P5 of the organization. Such source documents guide organizational operations; too often, however, these documents are created and tracked by different teams across an organization who are unaware of how these documents influence each other or how they mutually contribute to a common outcome. When an organization has inventoried its planning documents, such as its annual goals, organizational directives, and budgets, the organization can begin to understand the links between those documents and encode the sources and the components of the sources.

The IVM depicts the P5 interactions that drive modern organizations as a neural network of "nodes" consisting of individual P5 elements. These are connected by "synapses" where one P5 element helps another P5 element achieve its end state. This model helps organizations identify the subnetwork of P5 elements that affect or are affected by a single P5 element, and make changes to that subnetwork holistically to increase synergy and minimize conflicts within that subnetwork.

The IVM is made up of metadata about the P5; this data is structured into a network diagram that shows connections across sources. It allows organizations to use their P5, as well as mission and vision statements, to achieve internal goals and respond to external demands.

The IVM depicts an organization's source documents as a network, shown in Figure 1, where program initiatives are connected to each other via pairs of document components from different sources. These sources and components depend on each other and enable each other to achieve their end states. An Enabling Source document references an Enabling Component that, if delivered, contributes in some measurable way to a Dependent Component within a Dependent Source. If a P5 component (e.g., an objective within a plan), as it moves closer to its end state, is likely to move one or more other P5 elements toward their end states in some measurable way, one may say that this element enables the other elements, which in turn depend on the Enabling Component.

- "Enabling Source" is a document that has goals, objectives, directives or measures.
- "Enabling Component" is a goal, objective, directive or measure in an Enabling Source.
- "Dependent Component" is a goal, objective, directive or measure that moves closer to its end state if its Enabling Component is delivered.
- "Dependent Source" is the document that contains the Dependent Component.

Figure 1. Relationship diagram of IVM pairs showing an Enabling Source, such as a plan or agenda, which has one or more components (e.g., plan objectives or agenda items) that, if delivered, are likely to move a component of a different plan, policy, or agenda toward its intended end state. Values are paired with relationships defined from left to right.

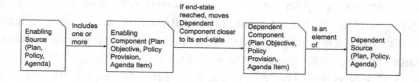

When represented in an information network, strategies include direction of action and effort across nodes within a map (O'Brien & Dyson, 2007, p. 8; Rodrigues,

2017). The IVM is a logical, relational model that depicts P5 as nodes connected in left-to-right pairs, where one node achieving its end state helps the other node achieve its end state. Figure 4 illustrates the Enabling-to-Dependent nodes as they are value-paired in Figure 1.

By depicting P5 as nodes connected by the influence they exert over the end-states of other nodes, the IVM provides two primary insights about the P5 network of an enterprise. The first shows how nodes and subnetworks of P5 align to further other P5 nodes and subnetworks, such as an inventory of all P5 in the organization that directly or indirectly supports a leadership priority. The second depicts the P5 of an organization in the context, syntax and semantics of a set of P5 outside the organization. Collaboration and teamwork are essential elements of relationship management, but these competencies need context to function effectively (Eichorn, 2005, p. 170). When an IVM is used to map P5 inside an organization, such as a guidance memorandum, to P5 of other, external organizations, such as the agenda of an external advocacy group, it can be used to communicate how the first organization advances the P5 of the second organization, using that other organization's language, content and structure. In this regard, IVM can help analysts design more efficient and effective value sequences within the P5 network.

In one instance, as shown in Figure 2 and Figure 3, an external stakeholder uses the term "Women's Health Program" to describe one of the elements in their P5; their counterpart organization uses the phrase "Extension of Certain MWR [Morale, Welfare, and Recreation] Privileges to Certain Veterans and Their Caregivers", which includes certain women's health initiatives pertinent to the stakeholder's P5, among other targeted programs. The IVM can help the organization reframe or communicate its activities and goals in the context of the activities and goals of an external organization, essentially making it easier to communicate the value of the enterprise's P5 using the semantics and syntax of the P5 of a stakeholder. As the authors describe later in this chapter, such reframing helps the organization not only improve internal communication but also with external stakeholders.

The Challenge of Modeling Policies, Plans, and Performance Measures

US Federal laws governing Executive Branch planning and performance metrics, such as the Government Performance and Results Act of 1993, require US Federal Agencies to map their performance metrics to specific objectives in their strategic plans. Those requirements provide an initial framework of metrics and objectives to which other P5 can be added to the model.

Figure 2. A partial dataset displaying Integrated Value Model (IVM) data: Delivering the components of an Enabling Source document (the JEC [Joint Executive Council] Guidance Memo) enables the delivery of components of another planning document (the Veterans Service Organization [VSO] Independent Budget). In the top line of the table, the women's health program depends on, among other initiatives, the extension of certain MWR privileges. If this Enabling Component helps achieve its corresponding Dependent component, it has a positive effect on the external stakeholder's 2021 agenda.

Enabling Source	Enabling Component	Dependent Component	Dependent Source
JEC Guidance Memo FY2019-2020	Extension of Certain MWR Privileges to Certain Veterans and Their Caregivers	Women's Health Program	VSO 2021 Independent Budget
JEC Guidance Memo FY2019-2020	Federal Electronic Health Record Modernization Program Office	Women's Health Program	VSO 2021 Independent Budget
JEC Guidance Memo FY2019-2020	Hire Transitioning SMs into VHA to key clinical and administrative leadership positions	Expand research on emerging conditions prevalent among newer veterans	VSO 2021 Independent Budget
JEC Guidance Memo FY2019-2020	Hire Transitioning SMs into VHA to key clinical and administrative leadership positions	Veterans peer support specialist at each medical center	VSO 2021 Independent Budget
JEC Guidance Memo FY2019-2020	Hire Transitioning SMs into VHA to key clinical and administrative leadership positions	Women's Health Program	VSO 2021 Independent Budget
JEC Guidance Memo FY2019-2020	Joint Plan to Modernize External Digital Authentication	Women's Health Program	VSO 2021 Independent Budget

For example, the Foundations for Evidence-Based Policymaking Act of 2018 established processes for US federal agencies to modernize how they gather and apply evidence to inform policy decisions. Modeling P5 metrics, strategic objectives, and performance measures can enable organizations to improve policy by, for instance, making better use of evidence by highlighting how policies enable and depend on metrics, objectives and other policies.

Organizations, in an effort to improve their own efficiency and effectiveness, make decisions, set policies or incentives, and establish programs that are, as a whole, too complicated for its stakeholders to understand (Business Architecture Guild, 2018). Because modern organizations are incredibly complex, the authors strongly recommend that analysts in these organizations invest time and effort to stay up to date on best practices and new resources and tools. In doing so, they can raise the situational awareness needed throughout the planning, execution, and assessment phases of initiatives.

Figure 3. The same dataset is represented as a network diagram

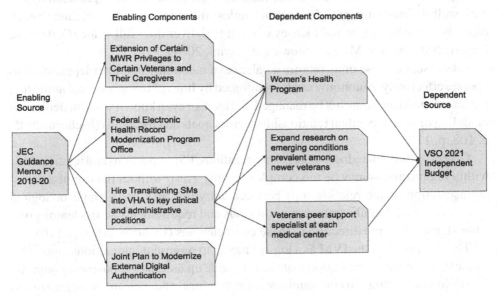

The multiplicative growth in goals and measures experienced in many of today's organizations creates exponential complexity in communicating and coordinating those goals and measures (Eichorn, 2005, p. 61). As we've discussed, these goals and measures interact and impact each other, but this interaction may not be immediately clear to the individuals working within the organization. As such, opportunities for positive change may fail to materialize (Rizardi, 2020). This challenge is not new—indeed, organizations use policies, plans, programs, priorities, and performance measures (P5) to help direct resources to where they add the most value and to raise awareness of the impact of change. But to create useful performance measures, it is critical that organizations understand the factors that influence these measures and understand how to interpret the value that can be derived from the measures. Creating useful performance measures requires organizations to understand the factors that influence the measure and to interpret the values of those measures (O'Brien & Dyson, 2007, p. 89). One way to identify this "meaning" is to include these measures in a logical model and connect those measures to goals and plans in the model, so the connections to the measure define its meaning. As organizations become more complex, it becomes less effective to rely on "ad-hoc" understandings of P5, and the value of a simplified model such as the IVM increases.

McCunn (1998) and O'Brien & Dyson (2007, pp. 290-291) found that 70% of performance measurement initiatives fail, not because of a flaw in the measurement processes, but due to a failure on the part of the organization to understand and define the context and content of the measures. Even though an organization may have well-defined strategies and metrics, unless they are defined in relation to each other, both the strategies and metrics will fail to deliver their full value (O'Brien & Dyson, 2007, p. 308; Melnyk, Stewart, & Swink 2004).

Likewise, business units require a balance of autonomy and interdependence to operate effectively. Autonomy can be reinforced by lines of organizational authority, but interdependence may not be managed, defined, or even known without deliberate modeling of interdependent relationships across goals and measures (Eichorn, 2005, p. 108, p. 170).

Given the interrelatedness of large organizations, P5 connections and relationships within organizations may be too complex to fully grasp without the use of a visual representation of the relationships between activities as a node graph or logical model. A model that illustrates common goals and requirements across teams gives context, meaning and direction to these competencies (Eichorn, 2005, p. 170).

The authors offer the IVM as a logical model to represent interactions among P5 elements within an organization that seeks to scale up its strategic business planning. The IVM is an attempt to communicate, effect change, and measure an organization as a network of P5 elements connected by how they help each other achieve their end states. As discussed, the IVM depicts an organization's P5 model as a node or network graph, with edges or "synapses" that show which P5 nodes help each other deliver their intended end state. This visual artifact can enable individuals and teams within an organization to develop solutions while also taking into account the network of other P5 that are affected by a given solution, in a deliberate, holistic manner. Providing solutions mindful of their contextual effects and coordination costs on the environment affected by the solution may make for more effective, lasting change.

There are dependencies and relationships among interactions that encourage one particular order over another for reasons of dependency, economy, or frequency (White, 2005, p. 16). Strategic decisions have complex implications, creating a need to clearly depict both short and long-term implications (O'Brien & Dyson, 2007, p. 13). The IVM models the relationship between these P5 elements and their impact in the context of an organization. Logical relationships among P5 elements can be established based on the hierarchical and causal nature of these relationships. Similar to a Wardley map (Wardley, 2015), the IVM represents P5 relationships as a directed graph, seen in Figure 4 below, modeled using the software Flourish Studio.

The most common way for organizations to map internal roles and hierarchies is through an organizational chart. Using relational models like the IVM to map and communicate P5, however, is not a common organizational activity, but it can provide a novel adage to this exercise. A concept map derived from the relational network, such as the one in Figure 5, illustrates the functional (as-is) relationships versus the organization chart which may reveal new insights. Analyzing the variances will help an organization understand the hierarchical versus functional relationships, which can increase situational awareness and insight into the overlap of goals and objectives in the business strategy.

Figure 4. This IVM diagram is a network representation of strategic documents from internal and external stakeholders of the U.S. Department of Veterans Affairs; the darker nodes and arrows depict the subnetwork where "VA Secretary Four Priorities for VA" is an Enabling Source that adds value to other Dependent Sources, and/or a Dependent Source that receives value from other Enabling Sources.
Source: Flourish Studio

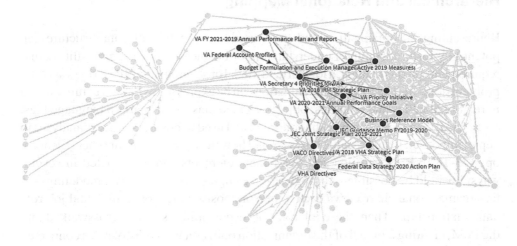

Figure 5. A concept map depicting the relational network of measures, goals, and objectives.

The lack of situational awareness among individual members of an organization can diminish the overall capacity to understand, change, and measure P5. Organizations manage change by adding, editing and deleting P5. With an understanding of the effects of P5 changes on its subnetwork, organizations should be more capable of communicating and managing the overall effect of a change. Changing a P5 element without an adequate understanding of how it interacts with other P5 within its subnetwork may increase the risk of unintended interactions and suboptimal results. In the following sections, the authors will discuss how the IVM can enable organizations to map internal relationships and support decision-making.

Hierarchical and Relational Mapping

Representing an organization and its operations as a logical data structure can potentially foster a common understanding of business elements, capabilities, and requirements. In this context, a logical data model or schema should describe a specific problem domain. The P5 of an organization can be expressed as data structures stored in relational tables and columns, object-oriented classes, or markup language tags.

Logical data models can be diagrammed and used in business process analyses to depict important features of the business and how they relate to one another (Eichorn, pp. 173-189). Relationships across business elements can be depicted in several ways; it would be possible—through reverse engineering of the data modeling—to tie organizational chart views back to person, position, responsibility, and job role data relationships. Then, these job roles or responsibilities can be crosswalked into the IVM, creating a model of the organization both as a hierarchy of roles connected to subnetworks of policies, plans and operations (Everest, 1976).

P5 relationships can be mapped using a relational data model, and often can be mapped using a hierarchical model (White, 1996). Other than a hierarchical organizational chart, mapping P5 of entire organizations using either model is not reported as a common activity.

Business Analytics

Today's complex business environment increases the need for new decision-support processes. The IVM process can help capture decision-support information to change business operations and value dependencies across those operations. Models that depict inter-organizational value relationships support reorganization decisions and develop shared value relationships across teams (Kotter, 2012, p. 56).

As mentioned, organizations develop visions, strategies, plans and budgets that, if realized, add value to each other. But often, these value relationships are not a result of deliberate design. This represents a lost opportunity to integrate value, which may be caused by the different skill sets, and therefore different organizations, needed to develop these forms of guidance (Kotter, 2012, p. 71). The IVM model can close this gap by making it explicit how guidance documents and their stakeholders add and receive value to each other, so employees, customers, stockholders, suppliers, and communities can better understand this value and their role in relation to it. This model emerged from the need to integrate leadership guidance (vision and strategy) and management guidance (plans and performance metrics), to show both the inspirational "why" and directive "how" these individual pieces of guidance relate to each other (Kotter, 2012, p. 80).

By representing an organization as a network of P5, it serves as a reference tool for policy and planning, which can provide a reusable dataset for analysis and reduce duplicative analysis efforts. The logical process model aids impact analysis through its ability to measure change, reduce the cost of change, and increase the organization's responsiveness to evolving circumstances. Further, the IVM answers several logical questions about the enterprise:

- For a single element, what are all the value relationships that affect or are affected by it?
- How can an organization reverse-engineer a new element to create new relationships within the organization?
- If an element loses value or capability, what related elements could become weaker or face a new threat?
- If an element gains value or capability, what related elements could become stronger or face a new opportunity?
- How can the organization measure, identify, and increase the net value of entire systems connected to an element?

These questions guide the content and design of logical representations of P5 relationships where organizations' goals and rules intersect and interact with each other. Many organizations, however, lack a holistic understanding of the impact of various goals and rules, much less the second- or third-order effect of a goal or rule across multiple connections. Depicting goals and rules as a network in the logic model reveals the interactions between them. This can help organizations understand and communicate second- or third-order effects throughout the network.

Similarly, individuals may also lack awareness of how their role affects and is affected by their colleagues and the wider organization. Managers who take the time to explain to employees which goals and rules they affect as part of the network reap the benefit of being able to visualize the direct and indirect effects of their role. This networked understanding of a role can also help define the role of leaders within the organization, showing what elements they "own" and how they affect or are affected by other elements.

IVM Resource Costs

The IVM is an accounting report or chart of accounts; for an organization's IVM to succeed, the organization needs to adopt data modeling as an accepted means of resource management, where the value stream map itself is seen as having value. If the model can become part of another organization's value stream, this would be evidence of adoption and value flow. Friction or push-back may be encountered initially, as there are upfront resource costs when establishing and populating the data model, but long-term maintenance is low-cost and low-effort by our estimates.

For example, the initial outlay to develop the baseline IVM for the US Department of Veterans Affairs, an organization with 412,000 employees and a budget of US$243b as of 2021, took seven months at a rate of 20 hours per week. Ongoing quality improvement, such as integrating inputs from other subject matter experts, improves the reliability of the model. In addition, roughly four hours per week is needed to maintain data currency with new sources and mappings.

Benefits and Purposes of the IVM

The objective of the IVM is to add value to organizational capabilities and activities by providing a common operating picture of the measures, goals, values, and missions of the organization. It provides a check and balance to ensure strategy is aligned with execution, increases strategic knowledge based on logical inferences about P5 relationships, and improves awareness of the sum total of P5 across functional lines that can increase transparency and improve understanding of P5. By integrating and unifying diverse sources of existing P5, the IVM supports solutions that facilitate adjustments across disparate plans and priorities to create systemic change.

The IVM is designed to support a data-driven culture—and its data governance—as policy and planning relationships inform policy and planning decisions. It improves the quality of decisions made, because decision-makers are better able to assess the impact of those decisions. Furthermore, organizations are better able to innovate because they have a more holistic understanding of the effects of innovation. The IVM can identify common risks and objectives in both the internal organization as well as related external organizations that are connected by shared risks and goals as identified by external stakeholders. These risks and goals can be identified by analyzing the source documents and seeing where relationships can be established.

This can be very important when circumstances require a rapid response, or when an agile response could provide a marked advantage. For example, a fictional health service organization (HSO) receives an unanticipated requirement which necessitates costly acquisition of goods and services; as a result, the HSO must respond quickly to the new purchase and report on these mandated goods and services that lie outside the scope of its budget.

Fortunately, the HSO maintains an IVM report, which it uses to analyze the P5 in the context of how the HSO delivers on regulations, initiatives, and organization goals. In just a few hours, the HSO can respond with a logical rationale, showing how it supported existing initiatives and justified the purchase of the required goods and services. In receiving such a request to purchase unanticipated goods or services, the HSO determined whether and how to justify such an expense by viewing a detailed list of P5 it supports and is supported by in this multi-order view of effects on the rest of the network. By extension, the IVM helps to identify the effects of new and proposed mandates and other impacts on P5 and identifies offices or parties responsible for those mandates. Further, these mappings yield a data model that supports communication and change management activities.

Improved Organizational Compliance With Mandates

Recognising the added value of the IVM, several US Cabinet agencies have now fully integrated the model or are running pilots. These agencies use it to map performance measures to objectives in their strategic plans, to identify partners for collaboration, to guide inventory policies related to developing new programs, and to align policies, plans, and programs to the priorities of external stakeholders.

The relative popularity of the IVM model in these agencies can be partly explained by the Government Performance and Results Act of 1993, which requires US Cabinet agencies to publish a five-year strategic plan of goals and objectives, an annual performance plan on the metrics planned for reporting delivery on the strategic goals and objectives, and an annual performance report of the scores of the performance metrics. These agencies are mandated to keep metrics of their work, and the IVM helps provide context for those metrics and their effect on the network, thus allowing them to understand how they are connected and modify those connections effectively if the situation warrants. Further, the Foundations for Evidence-Based Policymaking Act of 2018 requires US federal government agencies to develop a plan ("learning agenda") to identify and track what data they will use and collect to show evidence in support of their policy-making efforts. The IVM can support this mandate by helping agencies improve efforts toward creating a learning organization (Kautish, 2008; Kautish & Thapliyal, 2012) by identifying the measures they might use and statutes that might pose a challenge.

Improved Communication Within the Organization and With External Stakeholders

Mapping an organization's source documents—such as a strategic plan—against external documents—such as the President's Management Agenda—is a way to communicate its value to external stakeholders. Once internal sources have been mapped to an external source, the stakeholder of that external source can understand how one specific P5 element helps the elements of the external source achieve their end states. It helps if the external stakeholder's source document serves both as a Dependent Component to a document, and as an Enabling Component to a different document. The authors do not advise mapping an external document to another external document, as it is unlikely that the organization will exert enough influence to affect relationships between external organizations.

Respond to Data Calls More Rapidly

A "data call" is an event that requires information-gathering from multiple sources within an enterprise, such as gathering all of the P5 related to a sensitive issue. For example, a data call requires a spreadsheet table selected, or filtered, to one Dependent Source or one Dependent Component. The analysis outlines all the Enabling Sources and Enabling Components that affect that one Dependent Source or Dependent Component.

The IVM enables fast, detailed reporting on P5 components related to an external question or issue using the data access affordances of a relational database. At the US Department of Veterans Affairs, these inventories informed responses to US Congress questions for the record and supported revisions to strategic plans and initiatives to improve their relationships to priorities, regulations and goals.

Holistic Change Management

If an organization maps laws to P5, it can show the effect of those laws on sets of policies and programs, and identify which laws to petition for change based on their direct and indirect effect on policies and programs. A team responsible for a particular initiative can use the IVM to clearly distill the relevant laws and policies that relate to that initiative, making it easier for them to adjust the initiative, adjust policy, or suggest change as appropriate.

How to Develop an IVM

Thus far, we have discussed the value complex organizations can derive from mapping their P5 in an IVM model. In the following, the authors will explain how to put it into practice.

To create an IVM, organizations should first identify the two enabling or originating documents that have the most strategic influence on the organization. These are usually policy documents, and might include strategic plans, external agendas, key initiatives, or performance measures. In the private sector, these documents might include reports to stakeholders or internal "black box" documents that are not released publicly. While helpful, it is not imperative that the first few documents selected are indeed the *most* influential—the most important goal is to provide a starting point for the value pairing analysis that will be strengthened through subsequent revisions. The authors suggest selecting source documents which describe the P5 relationships, such as explicitly relating performance measures and objectives to goals and plans.

Some of the relationships analysts intend to map might already be defined within these documents. For example, US Cabinet agencies report their performance measures mapped to specific strategic plan objectives in their Annual Performance Plan and Report.

Once two documents have been selected, the organization must then assess the level of detail in the documents, and decide on an appropriate level of granularity for the components that will be derived from them, for instance on the document-level, subsection-level or paragraph-level. If the scope of the components is too large, they will encompass too many other components to provide a useful basis for analysis. With inadequate scope, the components may not map to anything.

To facilitate the process of deciding on an adequate scope, it is helpful to consider goal hierarchies, which represent problem-solving plans designed for a system (White, 1996, p. 223). An organization can determine a useful level of hierarchy based on a document's table of contents, usually revealing the "parent-child" hierarchy of the content and representing the author's definition of how much granularity is appropriate to define meaningful distinctions within the content. Figure 6 depicts that hierarchy. This level of parent-child detail might represent the right size for each of the components, but often the body of the document uses additional levels of hierarchy not identified in the table of contents.

After an appropriate level of detail has been decided upon, identify the general hierarchical relationship between the two documents. Ask: "Which document, if delivered, is more likely to deliver a subset of the other document?" The document that delivers a subset of value to the other document is the subordinate, "Enabling" Source, and it delivers value to the other, superordinate, "Dependent" Source.

Figure 6. A hierarchical network of plans, goals, objectives, and measures. Such relationships within organizations can be characterized as hierarchical, or as causal relationships within hierarchical and relational data models

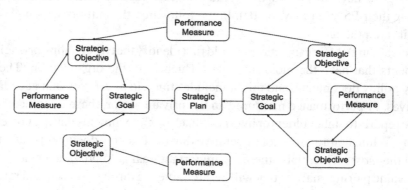

Once the hierarchical relationships between the two documents have been identified, analysts should read the first component of both documents. For example, as depicted in Figure 6, the first component of the strategic plan is the first of two strategic goals; the first component of a strategic goal is one of two strategic objectives; the first component of a strategic objective may be one or more performance measures. Each of these components should be considered in context of its relative partner in the value pairing. Ask: "If the first component of the Enabling Source document is delivered, would that move the first component of the Dependent Source document in any measurable way?"

If so, this relationship becomes a row in a table of Enabling and Dependent sources and components. Then, that same Enabling Component is compared to the second component of the Dependent Source, until the first component in the Enabling Source is compared to every component in the Dependent Source. Next, the second component in the Enabling Source is compared to every component in the Dependent Source, and so on until all the potential pairs of Enabling Components to Dependent Components have been reviewed. This method expedites early understanding of the full scope of the Dependent Source, which in the author's experience is more helpful in performing the mappings than reviewing all of the Enabling Source components first. If there are components that are not connected to other components, the orphan components should not be discarded as future connections may be established. The absence of connections, nevertheless, does merit review and discussion within the organization to consider whether this is indicative of a lack of alignment with other strategic goals. Once you have mapped all the components, the end result is a basic IVM model. You can strengthen this model by increasing the number of source documents considered, as appropriate depending on the context of your organization.

Some Considerations

Data modeling and data visualization are common practices and help to convey the complexity of the information that analysts and service designers create and manage. If managed well, the IVM's utility increases with its complexity. Such modeling is necessary for change management. The IVM can help assimilate and make sense of new or changing requirements. Once the crosswalk demonstrates its value and adoption increases past the tipping point, organizations become more willing to build logical models of their P5 data.

Another consideration is deciding which sources and components represent the most value to the organization. In each organization, the source documents and their related components vary, so standards may not be easily obtainable in the private sector due to the "black box" nature of some close-hold internal sources. In addition, every few weeks, one or two new source documents may become available and must be reviewed and evaluated for mapping. Keeping report artifacts current, however, is also a challenge, thus the crosswalk adds value by providing easy access to current data. The short-term cost of small, infrequent updates more than pays for itself in the value of the situational awareness that having a map provides.

In addition to the value added as outlined above, a number of new and innovative uses of the IVM model have emerged in recent years. Some of the most notable include innovations in acquisitions and legislative proposals, and software tools to support data modeling and change management, which we will briefly discuss below.

Acquisitions Innovation

One exciting avenue for future applications of the IVM model is in the planning of acquisitions. By selecting performance measures, goals, and priorities for an acquisition proposal, procurement professionals who develop or design proposals can incorporate these into the initial concept definition phase of acquisition planning. Likewise, organizations can compare different proposals or offers based on their capacity to support the organization's respective performance measures, goals, and priorities.

Legislative Proposals

The possibility of using an IVM database to assist in legislative proposals is another area of exploration. An IVM database could depict all of the national-level policy directives against their responsible offices and US Code regulations, so if an office wants to revise a policy, they can recruit the office responsible for that policy as a stakeholder, and include the laws related to that policy to propose legislative changes to accommodate the policy revision. Conversely, if an office wants to change a law, they can recruit the offices responsible for the policies that cite that law, collaborate on a legislative proposal, and cite the policies to be revised as part of that proposal.

Software Tools to Support Data Modeling and Change Management

Lastly, modern software development practices, namely extreme programming ("What is extreme programming?", 2019), provide new opportunities to traditional organizational change management practitioners. Extreme programming (XP) asserts the desired behavior from a system by writing automated tests to determine if the system is behaving accordingly; XP strives to keep the cost of change low by making small, atomic improvements to a system so that any given change can stand alone.

Continuous integration ("Continuous integration," 2021) accomplishes this through a practice and a set of tools that include running the tests and, only if the tests are successful, deploying the change in an automated fashion.

The IVM is an encoding of existing organizational systems. The challenge, then, is that these organizational systems typically transcend—are not captured in existing organizational software—as data.

Strategic plans and performance measures exist, but are they integrated coherently? Can the organization's value stream be readily visualized and understood and managed as a "pipeline" that allows for easy consistent updating? Are real-life operations modeled virtually for the purposes of enabling continuous integration of learnings from inside or outside the organization? What is the organization's ability to assimilate information? What is the organization's ability to process that information into behavior change that results in service improvement?

Thinking about operations as continuously integrated systems can be fruitful when practiced while informed by an IVM model. Any given change in a complex model, however, poses the risk of unintended change. Being explicit about the intended P5 behaviors and goals is both necessary and valuable when developing automated test mechanisms. Organizationally, this is similar to ensuring certain service level agreements.

FUTURE RESEARCH AND APPLICATIONS

Future research on the IVM could include how to leverage artificial intelligence (AI) systems to discover trends in the interactions of P5. AI systems could potentially infer which P5 relates to a source document and recommend ways to relate that document to the IVM, so documents that are not P5 could still have explicit relationships in the model.

Likewise, crowdsourced-based policy systems like Regulations.gov could support holistic revisions and discussions of systemic changes to P5.

Sometimes, the most useful discoveries when analyzing information networks relate to the data or nodes that are not explicitly connected in the dataset. Researchers could determine how to reverse-engineer P5 artifacts to discover relationships, create new relationships between previously unconnected groups within the organization, and analyze the pros and cons of these new connections.

US federal agencies are heavily regulated, and as such, analysts must maintain awareness of ever-changing, detailed guidance at different levels of hierarchy. In the private sector, however, analysts mainly attempt to focus on tangible shareholder value but may wish to investigate hypothetical performance increases to obtain more data on the barriers, constraints, and benefits when utilizing the IVM. The authors acknowledge that for these reasons the IVM may be best suited for the public sector, as it begins with, and assumes the constraints of, government agendas, strategic plans, and performance metrics. The IVM's utility increases as the complexity grows; it assimilates and helps make sense of new or changing requirements if managed well. Further expansion of the IVM's utility through a case study, for example, could show how a private sector organization strategically aligns itself to an external organization and its service offerings, acquisition, or competitive analysis.

CONCLUSION

The IVM is a network model and analytical framework of P5, depicted as a network of connections across P5 source components. It allows organizations to leverage P5 relationships, realign P5 to changing goals and priorities, and improve the efficiency and effectiveness of P5 to deliver on those goals and priorities. Understanding how P5 adds value can add critical insight into the mechanics of how and why an organization succeeds (White & Martin, 2020a, 2020b). These P5 elements provide the nodes to build an integrated network of processes and performance (Eichorn, 2005; Bowen & Hallowell, 2002).

The IVM models common organizational artifacts, and illustrates how organizational policies and practices align or fail to align. The IVM can quantitatively measure the alignment of different initiatives within an organization. The IVM supports efforts in strategic communications, change management, strategic planning, and decision support. Elements of P5 often have explicit hierarchical and relational connections to each other, but modeling these connections, and developing logical inferences from them, is not a common strategic business practice.

As all organizations have goals (White & Martin, 2020b), this chapter describes how to identify how those goals relate as elements of a network model of value, and how to use this model to identify, describe, and align that value. This chapter demonstrates the P5 model's capabilities, and suggests future applications of the model, including how to integrate the model into policy and regulatory change and its use in acquisition proposals based on performance measures.

ACKNOWLEDGMENT

The authors would like to acknowledge the help of all the people involved in this project and, more specifically, to the readers and reviewers who took part in the review process. Without their support, this work would not have been realized. The authors would like to thank Anders Brønd Christensen, Andrew Maier, Ryan Walker, and the many anonymous reviewers who kindly provided their feedback.

The IVM and communication about the IVM are products of subjective analysis, and should not be interpreted as an official position of the U.S. Department of Veterans Affairs.

REFERENCES

Bowen, D. E., & Hallowell, R. (2002). Suppose we took service seriously? An introduction to the special issue. *The Academy of Management Executive, 16*(4), 69–72. doi:10.5465/ame.2002.8951329

Business Architecture Guild. (2018). *The business architecture quick guide: A brief guide for gamechangers*. Meghan-Kiffer Press.

Continuous Integration. (2021, March 3). Retrieved from /https://www.agilealliance. org/glossary/continuous-integration/

Eichorn, F. L. (2005). *Who owns the data? Using internal customer relationship management to improve business and IT integration*. Tate Publishing.

Everest, G. C. (1976). *Basic data structure models explained with a common example. Reprinted from Computing Systems 1976. In Proceedings Fifth Texas Conference on Computing Systems. Austin, TX*: IEEE Computer Society Publications Office. https://www.researchgate.net/profile/Gordon_Everest/publication/291448084_ BASIC_DATA_STRUCTURE_MODELS_EXPLAINED_WITH_A_COMMON_ EXAMPLE/links/57affb4b08ae95f9d8f1ddc4/BASIC-DATA-STRUCTURE- MODELS-EXPLAINED-WITH-A-COMMON-EXAMPLE.pdf

Flourish Studio [Computer software]. (2020). Retrieved from https://public.flourish.studio/visualisation/4581015

Foundations for Evidence-Based Policymaking Act of. 2018, H.R. 4174, 115th Cong. (2017). https://www.congress.gov/bill/115th-congress/house-bill/4174

Government Performance and Results Act, S. 20, 103rd Cong. (1993). https://www.congress.gov/bill/103rd-congress/senate-bill/20

Kautish, S. (2008). Online Banking: A Paradigm Shift. E-Business. *ICFAI Publication, Hyderabad, 9*(10), 54–59.

Kautish, S., & Thapliyal, M. P. (2012). Concept of Decision Support Systems in relation with Knowledge Management–Fundamentals, theories, frameworks and practices. *International Journal of Application or Innovation in Engineering & Management, 1*(2), 9.

Kotter, J. P. (2012). *Leading change*. Harvard Business Review Press.

McCunn, P. (1998). The balanced scorecard...the eleventh commandment. *Management Accounting, 76*(11), 34–36.

Melnyk, S. A., Stewart, D. M., & Swink, M. (2004). Metrics and performance measurement in operations management: Dealing with the metrics maze. *Journal of Operations Management, 22*(3), 209–217. doi:10.1016/j.jom.2004.01.004

O'Brien, F. A., & Dyson, R. G. (2007). *Supporting strategy: Frameworks, methods and models*. John Wiley & Sons.

Priest, D., & Hull, A. (2007, February 18). Soldiers face neglect, frustration at Army's top medical facility. *Washington Post*. https://www.washingtonpost.com/archive/politics/2007/02/18/soldiers-face-neglect-frustration-at-armys-top-medical-facility/c0c4b3e4-fb22-4df6-9ac9-c602d41c5bda/

Rizardi, B. (2020, December 8). Solving complex problems in the public sector. *Apolitical*. https://apolitical.co/en/solution_article/solving-complex-problems-in-the-public-sector

Rodrigues, T. C., Montibeller, G., Oliveira, M. D., & Costa, C. A. B. (2017). Modelling multicriteria value interactions with reasoning maps. *European Journal of Operational Research, 258*(3), 1054–1071. doi:10.1016/j.ejor.2016.09.047

Wardley, S. (2015, February 2). An introduction to Wardley (value chain) mapping. *Bits or Pieces?* https://blog.gardeviance.org/2015/02/an-introduction-to-wardley-value-chain.html

What is extreme programming (XP)? (2019, September 24). Retrieved from https://www.agilealliance.org/glossary/xp/

White, B. (1996). Developing products and their rhetoric from a single hierarchical model. *STC Proceedings, Theory and Research*, 223-224.

White, B. (2005, April/May). Using a hierarchical process design. *Capital Letter, 45*(1), 7-16.

White, B., & Martin, B. (2020a, June 30). How to connect the dots between work and the organization's mission. *Apolitical*. https://apolitical.co/en/solution_article/how-to-connect-dots-between-work-and-organisations-mission

White, B., & Martin, B. (2020b, December 11). Not meeting your goals? Use a value network. *Apolitical*. https://apolitical.co/en/solution_article/not-meeting-your-goals-use-a-value-network

ADDITIONAL READING

General Services Administration. (2020, December 27). Federal Acquisition Regulation, Part 7. https://www.acquisition.gov/far/part-7

Government Accountability Office. (2005). Managing for results: Enhancing agency use of performance information for management decision making. https://www.gao.gov/products/GAO-05-927

Government Accountability Office. (2008). Government performance: Lessons learned for the next administration on using performance information to improve results. https://www.gao.gov/products/GAO-08-1026T

Government Performance and Results Act (GPRA) Modernization Act. H.R. 2142, 111th Cong. (2010). https://www.congress.gov/bill/111th-congress/house-bill/2142

Graça, P., & Camarinha-Matos, L. M. (2017). Performance indicators for collaborative business ecosystems—Literature review and trends. *Technological Forecasting and Social Change, 116*, 237–255. doi:10.1016/j.techfore.2016.10.012

Grover, V., Chiang, R. H., Liang, T. P., & Zhang, D. (2018). Creating strategic business value from big data analytics: A research framework. *Journal of Management Information Systems, 35*(2), 388–423. doi:10.1080/07421222.2018.1451951

John, C. H. S., Balakrishnan, N. R., & Fiet, J. O. (2002). Corporate strategy and wealth creation: An application of neural network analysis. In *Neural networks in business: Techniques and applications* (pp. 124–139). IGI Global. doi:10.4018/978-1-930708-31-0.ch008

Laney, D., De Simoni, G., Greenwald, R., Howson, C., Jain, A., Logan, V., & Duncan, A. (2018). *100 data and analytics predictions through 2022.* Gartner. https://www.gartner.com/en/documents/3875982/100-data-and-analytics-predictions-through-2022

Office of Management and Budget. (2013, December 26). OMB Circular A-131. https://obamawhitehouse.archives.gov/sites/default/files/omb/assets/OMB/circulars/a131/a131-122013.pdf

Office of Management and Budget. (2020). OMB Circular A-11. https://www.whitehouse.gov/wp-content/uploads/2018/06/a11_web_toc.pdf

Rahman, N., & De Feis, G. (2009). Strategic decision-making: Models and methods in the face of complexity and time pressure. *Journal of General Management, 35*(2), 43–59. doi:10.1177/030630700903500204

Senge, P. (1990). *The fifth discipline: The art and practice of the learning organization.* Doubleday.

Sharma, R., Mithas, S., & Kankanhalli, A. (2014). Transforming decision-making processes: A research agenda for understanding the impact of business analytics on organisations. https://core.ac.uk/download/pdf/206714720.pdf

KEY TERMS AND DEFINITIONS

Component: The analysis focuses on answering: How do the individual objectives in these *source documents* support the achievement of individual objectives in other source documents? Each individual objective is a component.

Crosswalk: The analyst who reviewed the oversight committee's plan studied that plan, or *source document*, in context with the other strategic plans (source documents). This overarching analysis is a crosswalk; the act of crosswalking *source documents* and their *components* can also be called *mapping*.

Dependent Component: A single goal, objective, directive, or measure that moves closer to its end state if its Enabling Component is delivered.

Dependent Source: A document with at least one component (sub-unit) that progresses closer to its end state if a component of an Enabling Source document reaches its own end state.

Enabling Component: A single goal, objective, directive, or measure in an Enabling Source.

Enabling Source: A source document with at least one component (sub-unit) that helps a Dependent Source document progress to its end state by virtue of the enabling document's reaching its end state.

Mapping: The action to identify value pairs, or chains of relationships, between an Enabling and a Dependent source component.

Neural Network: A group of nodes where each represents the relationship of component sources (in a row) in a *crosswalk* which have been depicted as a three-dimensional visualization. Each source has *component* constellations showing added value to components of other *sources*. See also *value network*.

P5: Policies, plans, programs, priorities, and performance measures.

Source (Enabling, Dependent): A policy, plan, report, etc. that comprises objectives, goals, initiatives, measures, and other elemental parts (components) that, together, represent value to the enterprise.

Value: The technical, economic, service, and social benefits an organization receives.

Value Flow: How value from one P5 element flows into another P5 element as input, either by directly moving the receiving element closer to its end state, or indirectly through a path of value through multiple P5 elements.

Value Network: Where sources in a *neural network* (derived from a *crosswalk*) have *component* constellations of neurons that add value to components of other *sources*.

Chapter 11
Business Value Analysis at Yes Bank:
A Strategic Lesson

Vineet Chouhan
Sir Padampat Singhania Universit, Udaipur, India

Pranav Saraswat
MIT World Peace University, Pune, India

ABSTRACT

This case is related with the biggest 2020 scam by one of the major new private sector banks (i.e., YES bank). The case is related with the misuse of the power of banks in providing the benefits to one person, due to the power and influence granted by the political party leaders that influence providing unlimited loans to one person and further the acts of the bank officials that led to the partial breakdown of the banking system in India. Further, the case deals with the major accused and the shell company's creator as DHFL. The present analysis put lights on the future lessons to be learnt by various sectors in order to prevent heavy losses and loss of customer faith (being the most vital component). It starts by giving a background of the crisis that led the RBI to come into picture. It also shows the effectiveness of the actions of RBI for YES bank. At last, it points out the importance of independent management and the roles of auditors and other regulators in dealing with this crisis.

DOI: 10.4018/978-1-7998-7716-5.ch011

INTRODUCTION

YES Bank is a high quality, customer and service-oriented bank. Since 2004, it has grown into a "full-service commercial bank" offering a full range of technology-based digital products, services, and offerings for businesses, MSMEs and individuals. It was the 4th largest bank of India with 18000 employees throughout the country and having customers like Flipkart, PhonePe, BharatPe, Swiggy, Red bus; in fact, 35% of UPI Transactions of the country relied through this bank. YES bank, India, is the outcome of its promoter Mr. Rana Kapoor's professional entrepreneurship and his extremely competent managing team's efforts to create a high-quality, customer-centric, service-oriented bank serving India's "Sunrise Sector." It is the RBI's only "Greenfield Bank license" granted in the last two decades, and it is backed by some of the world's most prestigious investors. It has gradually built a Corporate, Retail, and SME Banking franchise, with a diverse product portfolio that includes Financial Markets, Investment Banking, Corporate Finance, Branch Banking, Company, and Transaction Banking (figure 6).

GLOBAL PRESENCE

YES bank is a high quality, customer, and service-oriented bank. Since 2004, it has grown into a "full-service commercial bank" offering a full range of technology-based digital products, services, and offerings for businesses, MSMEs and individuals. The bank operates its investment banking, commercial banking and brokerage activities through YES Securities and its investment fund activities through YES Asset Management (India) Limited, two fully acquired subsidiaries of the Bank. It's headquartered in Mumbai and is represented across India in all 28 states and 9 Union territories in India, including an IBU in GIFT City and a representative office in Abu Dhabi. In past 4 years it has shown 11.6 percent growth in balance sheet, stabling the net interest margin at 2.8 Percent, 5.9 percent growth I the deposits globally with CASA ratio of 30.2 Percent (YES bank, 2020) (Table 5.).

YES BANK CRISIS BEGINS

In 2004, Rana Kapoor and Ashok Kapoor established YES bank. After 2008, Rana Kapoor, the then serving head of YES Bank, had a behaviour of aggressively giving bank loans on a high interest rate to companies which were stressed. Companies like Cafe Coffee Day, DHFL, and Anil Ambani Reliance were unable to pay its loans even though RBI had scrutinized the bank since 2017. There was a repeated lending of loans to high-risk companies, which finally led to increasing NPA.

In April 2019, the bank posted its forecast quarterly loss and in November 2019, Rana Kapoor sold all of his stock for a total of 142 crores. Sensex fell and its stock fell after the rumours of YES bank being sold to SBI. After all these incidents, the shares of the bank fell drastically and there was a Panic in the people who were the bank's customers. The bank's saga has taken all the attraction to equip the professionalism, probity, and good corporate governance in the banking sector. Even pertinently, the bank could not keep up with its responsibilities. The Board did not work independently of its promoters. Further, the bait for higher interest led to creation of snowball effect (Chouhan et.al., 2021b; Saraswat, 2021; Dadhich et.al., 2019).

How Did the NPAs of Yes Bank Rise?

In the recent year YES Bank has given loan to many companies/organisations to which other banks have shied away from, these company include

- Reliance Group – A loan of 2892 crore was given which took its tally to 12800 crores. Currently this group is unable to meet its own financial functionality and thus has become an NPA (Wadhwa et.al., 2020).
- Jet Airways- 550 crore loan was given out and now its total debt to bank is 1100 crore (Wadhwa et.al., 2020).
- Café Coffee Day – This company and it promoters are said to have loan of at least 1 billion dollars with YES Bank being its biggest lender with an exposure of at least 1500 crore, while all other banks and financial institution have started to pull out, bank had stayed and given out more loans to the company which is unable to pay even the interest of the loaned amount (Ramchandani & Jethwani, 2021; Wadhwa et.al., 2020;).
- Cox and Kings- Currently the company owes 3642 crores to YES bank (Wadhwa et.al., 2020).

All the company above were not given loans by any other banks but Yes Bank gave them huge loans with an even higher interest rate which these were unable to pay (figure 7 & 8). There are other companies than the mentioned above to which YES bank has given loan and which have failed to return it to them. This has led to increase in NPA and thus causing a financial stress to the Bank. (figure 11 Loans issued by Yes Bank) (Ramchandani & Jethwani, 2021; Wadhwa et.al., 2020; Maina et.al., 2020; Chouhan et.al.,. 2020b; Kautish & Thapliyal 2013).

YES bank resorted to window dressing as it under reported its bad loans or NPAs by more than Rs. 3,000 crores (difference between actual bad loans and reported bad loans) in financial year 2019 (Wadhwa et.al., 2020) (figure 7). Hence it can be said that YES bank resorted to window dressing as it didn't show its actuals NPAs in order to reflect its financial position as healthy (figure 1, 2, and table 5) (while in reality it wasn't so) (Ramchandani & Jethwani, 2021) and wanted to please everyone (especially investors) with its financial statements (Khan et.al., 2014; Kautish, 2013; Chouhan et.al., 2020c).

Moratorium Imposed on Yes Bank

Moratorium was also imposed on the bank by RBI in order to save it from being crashed because if it does then there are serious consequences like freezing of money, RBI's interest rate is affected, etc. So, in order to save Yes bank from the crash, they imposed a moratorium and placed a limit of INR 50,000 on withdrawals per person so that bank does not lose a lot of money due to customers' lack of faith in the bank (figure 3) (Deb, 2021; Sarkar, 2020). General practice is that when banks are about to collapse people withdraw their deposits and the bank has less and less funds which means they have lesser resources to manage. To prevent this, a moratorium is placed so that bank does not lose a lot of money in a split second (Deb, 2021; Devi et.al,2021; Sarkar, 2020).

Now to protect the bank, RBI suggested that Yes bank should not use a government bailout and should resort to private investors who might infuse money into the bank by buying its shares, but that plan failed.

RBI Interventions

The actions of RBI had sufficiently managed to keep the company a going concern till the date. The actions and the recoup plan by the RBI in order to prevent YES bank have given lessons to not only the financial sectors but other sectors as well. It has led to enhancing the function of Board of Directors and the internal auditors in keeping management accountable and tightening the cooperate governance, respectively (Deb, 2021).

YES bank's NPA started increasing. In 2017, RBI noticed it and thereafter it started monitoring the bank strictly. It was noticed that YES bank was hiding its real NPA: A difference of ₹ 3,000 crores was seen by RBI in actual figure while fake data given by the bank it leads RBI to take action and in September 2018, it ordered to remove Rana Kapoor from the head position.

The RBI placed a 30-day suspension, providing a cap of withdrawal @ ₹50,000 per month, on YES Bank, superseding the private-sector lender's board's control under Section 45 of the Banking Regulation Act, 1949. Prashant Kumar (SBI's CFO and Deputy Managing Director) was appointed as the company's administrator. As a result, Yes Bank's shares fell nearly 85% in intraday trade, reaching a new low of ₹5.55 from ₹230/- a year earlier. On March 14, 2020, the Cabinet approved a reconstruction plan proposed by the RBI. Certain banks and investors led by SBI pledged to invest ₹12,000 crores in YES bank as part of the reconstruction programme (Deb, 2021; Pandey et.al., 20190) (figure 9).

RBI was not expected to interfere and impose a lock-in of bank's share as the investors were trapped in a dilemma as they can't pull out their funds from YBL shares till March 2023 and the foreign investors (FII) pulled out their money from its shares due to this lock-in confusion. All of the RBI's decisions have not only weakened SEBI's regulatory authority, but also harmed investor confidence. (Singh & Pathak, 2020)

After analyzing these problems RBI has decided to take care of four things-

- RBI identified the person who gave this loan without proper checks and balances and reappoint someone else (RBI guide) on his position.
- RBI gave statement to depositors like do not worry, we are here to take this case and tell people that you cannot withdraw whole money now, it would put some limit which is called 'cap'.
- RBI with other agencies like E.D will take legal action against those businessmen who had not return the money to bank and these are called defaulters.
- As loan has not return so RBI somehow find a method through which fresh money can be injected into this bank so that life of this bank can be safe and who deposit their money can get their money back.

RBI Draft Plan for Reconstruction

In light of the crisis faced by Yes Bank, when the plan to attract private investment failed, The Reserve Bank of India proposed a reconstruction plan which aimed change the genus or identity of the bank to prevent its collapse (current shareholding pattern- Table 4.). The scheme proposed multiple changes that could equip Yes bank to deal with the change in circumstances.

- The first fundamental change included altering of the authorized capital of the bank. It is the maximum amount of share capital that the entity is authorised to issue.
- The authorised capital was raised from Rs. 800 crores to Rs. 5000 crores. This essentially gave Yes bank the license to collect more than 6 times the

previous threshold amount in order to fill its coffers. From the total amount of Rs. 5000 crores, Rs. 4800 crores can be raised as equity. The higher room for fluctuating dividends in exchange for a decided capital of Rs.2 per share, gives Yes Bank sufficient breathing space.

- Furthermore, any investor bank has been mandated to agree that after subsequent infused It shall hold 49% shareholding with a price of at least Rs. 10 per share. The division of the price per share stood at Rupees 2 face value and Rs. 8 premiums.
- This was complemented by the fact that the investor bank is under a 3 year lockdown period which restricted its divesting rights to just 74% of its total share ownership.
- The State Bank of India played a very important role in the reconstruction of Yes bank. It bought 49% stake in Yes Bank for Rs. 7250 crore, while HDFC and ICICI invested Rs. 1000 and 600 crores each.
- The plan involved issuance of new shares where SBI would hold 45% shares with the aforementioned terms and conditions while HDFC and ICICI would hold around 6% and 4% respectively.
- SBI cannot reduce its holdings less than 25% for the lockdown period of three years. Which increased to 75% for minor investors.
- The main reason for setting these limits was to incline the interest of private investors to buy the shares from initial investors which eventually will result in increase in share price.
- This plan of reconstruction of bank involve issuing new shares in which ICICI and HDFC bank invested Rs 600 crores and 1000 crores respectively having 6% share each.
- Additional tier 1 (AT1) bondholders will get 10.5% of equity shares having value of Rs 1700 crores.

As a result, the Capital requirement has kept increasing and in accordance with that, authorised capital which was initially 800 crores raised to 5000 crores than to 6000 crores till 2021. To counter the moratorium lifted by the RBI, public sector banks deposits in bulk, an amount of 30,000 crores to stabilise the bank.

Accusation

A business organization can survive for a long time by harmonizing profitability and liquidity. Institutions are disorganized due to insufficient liquidity despite sufficient earnings if the bank is a living example. As of March 31, 2019, there were 2,64,41,18,95,000 Rs. Operating profit for the 2018-2019 period was 81,39,40 million Rs. This year's net interest income was 98 billion, 9 crore, 3 lakh, 10,000 rupees. A dividend of Rs 6 billion, Rs 22 million, Rs 40 thousand, Rs 89 thousand was distributed to shareholders in 2018-19. An increase of 206.78% in 2019 and 334% in advances compared to 2020, although the cost-benefit ratio has only increased 4.1% in 5 years (figure 8). In 2018, the bank received 8 awards for its outstanding performance in various fields. Despite these encouraging financial results, Yes Bank can no longer refund its account holders today. The bank has banned withdrawals of more than INR 50,000.

Investors and account holders do business by looking at the bank's balance sheet. Who would not want to plan when they look at such an attractive balance? Even after such a strong financial situation, the collapse of Yes bank raises questions about the entire accounting system (Ramakrishnan, 2020). The CA Institute of apex accounting institute is also suspected. The question is how it happened. Has the bank used creative accounting to create a brand image in its market? The banks was creating a virtual business. This is till secret and RBI is trying to find its answer. Although the bank makes a profit of around 81 billion, Rs 39 million. But 48% (39,03,34,83000 INR) is earned interest. It is the income that has not been received, but the income is accepted as part of it, because the bank acquired in 2018-2019. Therefore, the bank to which the loan was granted had to pay interest on the loan. But he paid only on March 31. On the basis of the accounting concept, the bank has recognized it in results. Which are appropriate from the accounting point of view, but have triggered a liquidity crisis (The Hindu, 2020).

The company's co-founder Rana Kapoor is believed to play a key role in the loans. Rana Kapoor attempted to create a functional brand image of the bank through creative accounting. For example, the level of accumulation looked good in the annual report and paid dividends continuously (The Indian Express, 2020). The faith of the shareholders remains. It shows good benefits when the situation was really bad. Rana Kapoor also loaned money under the political will to certain person (Economic times, 2020). A loan was also granted to one of the BJP legislators in Mumbai. Who has not paid the loan?

Rana Kapoor not only built his credibility in wealthy corporate houses, but also gained the trust of the current government by calling himself a watchdog of nationalism (Nair, 2020). Rana Kapoor also proposed the Prime Minister's Jumla of 5 realities. Even when the Prime Minister announced the demonstration on August 11, 2016, Rana Kapoor congratulated the Prime Minister as a coup. In this way, he gradually approached power. The bank has made loans to companies that are already in debt. Celebrities include Cox & Cuckoos, Café Coffee Day and Dewan Housing Pvt. Ltd., Jet Airways, Ayanal Ambani companies and ILFS.

Response of Yes Bank

In his speech, Mr. Prasun said that Anil Ambani had obtained a loan from some of the country's famous banks, from SBI 1965 crore, from Union bank Rs. 1556 crore, ICICI Bank 1375 crore, AXIS Bank 783 crore Rs., Del Bank of Baroda 847 crore Rs. From the United Bank of India Rs. 582 crore, GNP Rs. 682 crore, OBC Bank 546 crore, Bank of India 503 crore, UCO Bank 468 crore, Corporation Bank Rs 319 million and Panjab and Sindh Bank Rs 376 million INR. He has been detained so often that his financial situation is not good. If the government is not strictly against the security of the authorities, the banking sector cannot collapse like the cards on the card. These are the companies whose founders are very close to the ruling party. This suspicion arises here when the companies were in debt and when they wrote the prayer for their fall themselves, the loan was granted, there was no recommendation from the ruling party, or when corruption was at its peak. Due to the delay in the payment of the loans and interests of these companies, Yes bank experienced a liquidity crisis. How these companies pay their debts, on the one hand, the economic downturn in the market, on the other hand, these companies are in debt, although the bank has significant advantages but cannot make cash payments to account holders. The liquidity crisis worsened so much that there was no money available for daily operations.

The bank's global cash flow table shows that the operating cash flow from operations was 2,46,61,16,64,000 INR negative (Cash flow in INR in business from India shown in Table 3.). Understanding this negative view of long-term financing sources violates the letter's basic rules. In doing so, the bank raised 3,30,39,32 thousand and £ 24,000 from financial activities in 2018-19 to keep operating activities attractive. Attempts have also been made to endanger LIC, a strong public sector company. When, Yes Bank's proven share market share was £ 500. LIC then had to buy 9% of the shares. Today the stock is worth around £ 15. In this way, the FTA suffered large losses. In general, LIC cannot buy more than 9% of the shares of a company. Rana Kapoor has created over 20 fictitious (fuzzy) companies. This person is believed to have previously invested in the market by transferring the bribe he received to these companies. The market value of these companies is currently estimated at Rs 5,000. The bank's income statement and economic activity do not reflect events that affect liquidity. These annual financial statements also do not indicate where significant bank funds were used during the year. Therefore, investors and account holders should consider the details of this institution's cash flow before investing. In this way, with 21 lakh account holders and 18,238 employees, the bank had kept the history of declining cash details secret, but regulators ignored it. The bank also misled people in the country by helping regulators.

Enigma (Deteriorating Financial Position)

Yes Bank's financial position has steadily declined in recent years as it is unable to raise capital to address potential credit losses and the resulting downgrades, leading investors to take advantage of the covenants and withdraw deposits. The bank has recorded insufficient profit and loss in the last four quarters (balance sheet in INR in business from India shown in Table 2.). The Reserve Bank said it was in constant contact with the bank's management to find ways to strengthen its balance sheet and liquidity. Bank management has informed the reserve bank that it has had conversations with various investors and that these may lead success. However, on the other hand the investors have not offered to use the money the bank needed to survive and grow. The bank faced a regular outflow of cash. This means that customer deposits have been deducted from the bank. In reality, deposits are a bank's prime source of earning. At the end of September 2019, the bank's deposit portfolio stood at Rs 2.09 billion. (balance sheet in INR in business from India shown in Table 1.) (Saraswat and Banga, 2012; Saraswat, 2012; Chouhan et.al., 2020a).

Furthermore, the bank's NPAs were not as concerning as those of some of the country's other banks. However, what rendered it more vulnerable to bankruptcy was its failure to genuinely recognise its NPAs on three separate occasions, the most recent of which was in November 2019, when the RBI pulled it up for under-reporting NPAs and failing to properly provide for those bad loans. The bank performed badly on the provision coverage ratio, which effectively maps a bank's capacity to cope with NPAs. (Business today, 2020; Chouhan et.al., 2021a; Kautish, 2008; Chouhan, 2016).

Effect of Downfall

As a result of the downfall, first, the fifty thousand cap on the withdrawal limit imposed by the RBI, which has created a situation of helplessness and panic among its customers. In Lucknow, the panicked customers had gathered at a Yes Bank Branch. People there were completely clueless regarding the decision of the Government, especially because such a decision has been imposed immediately preceding Holi, thereby creating further chaos. As for the Stock Markets, the decline in the shares of Yes Bank by almost 85%, which is largely due to the expectation that the bank which was valued at almost ten thousand crores may in reality be sold for less than 500 crores. The shares might be sold at 1 or 2 rupees per share as opposed to 35-36 rupees per share that it was ruling at. Even though the market is responding to these concerns, it is unlikely that the impact of this crisis would spread to other big lenders.

YES BANK – SBI DEAL

After the Reserve Bank of India put a Moratorium of 30 days on Yes Bank in March 2020, finance minister Nirmala Sitharaman announced that the SBI will buy a 49% stake in bank. But Chairman Rajnish Kumar clarified that there will be no merger between the banks.

After the merger was announced, the onus was on India's largest bank, SBI, to save Yes bank from the crisis. Since share price of bank has gone significantly down the scope of further long-term investments depends on multiple factors. SBI is acquiring some stakes in yes bank and hence there are high chances that the investors will invest more in the bank. There are great chances that the bank will bounce back as the SBI investment will boost the investment and will also pump confidence in the account holders.

Main Reasons That Lead the Bank for This Collapse

- **Deteriorating financial Position**- Over the last few years "Yes Bank" has undergone a steady decline in its financial position due to its inability to raise capital and address potential loan losses and as a part of the downgrades, holders invoked bond covenants and withdrew deposits. Over the past few years, the bank has suffered from setbacks and insufficient income.
- **Governance challenges and legislative restructuring**- In recent years, the bank has faced serious governance issues and policies, which has resulted in the bank's gradual decline. Rana Kapoor, the co-promoter, was ordered to resign by the RBI. Despite continued bad results, the RBI did not implement a timely corrective action system. Several questions have been raised by the Central Bank in recent years, including a significant disparity between the Bank's published financial results and the RBI's findings. In 2018-19, the bank registered Rs 3,277 crore in Non-Performing Assets. As a result, the RBI sent R Gandhi, a former Deputy Governor, to the Bank of the Bank. In 2018-19, the bank registered Rs 3,277 crore in Non-Performing Assets.
- **False Assurance**- The Reserve Bank of India was in regular contact with the Yes Bank management to identify ways to improve the bank's balance sheet and liquidity status. Yes, bank management said that the reserve bank was in talks with several investors and that it was likely to be profitable. However, there was no concrete plan from investors to position the type of capital that the Bank needed to sustain and prosper.
- **Role of Investigating Agencies**- There was a direct relationship between these agencies and Yes Bank after what they did when IL&LS and DHFL unfolded.

- **Bad loans-** According to the central bank's asset quality reports in 2017 and 2018, Yes Bank, a private sector bank, ran into difficulty, resulting in a dramatic rise in its distressed loans ratio, and it has struggled to collect the capital needed to remain above regulatory thresholds as it fights high levels of bad loans. It was dealing with several exposed government lapses, which necessitated a total shift of management. Money deposits by consumers is the lifeblood of every banking business. The bank was seeing a significant outflow of liquidity because of consumer deposits being withdrawn. Customers were removing their investments, resulting in a decline in assets.
- **Non-serious investors-** According to the RBI, the investors did not hold any discussions with senior RBI officials, indicating that the investors are not serious enough to inject money into the bank.

Analysis of Banking Industry

In the present paper the author threw some light on the current banking system of India and how a bank could be revived from NPA with the example of YES Bank and the analysis of the same is as follows: -

- Banks like YES Bank had fallen due to the exorbitant losses which had taken birth due to non-payment of loans by the big companies to which loans were approved and granted by these Bank. In short, higher rate of bad loans is the reason due to which various Public and Private banks had failed. Also, the common people believe that private banks are the one that always fails and government banks are untouchable but in reality, the government banks are much more prone to failure because they are poorly managed. But the government stealthily puts money in the government banks on regular basis, therefore they do not come into limelight.
- It is not advisable to put all your eggs in one basket therefore people should divide their money or savings in 3 or 4 different banks which have lower level of bad loans.
- Private Banks are more efficient in comparison to Public Sector banks. There is a need that the government should take steps to make Public Sector banks more efficient by enhancing their customer services, promoting competition between these banks, instead of infusing funds into the bank at regular intervals Government should also invest their capital in enhancing the skills of the work force of these banks.
- At last, it is the common people who had to bear the brunt of inefficient policies and decisions of banks. To avoid this problem people should be more aware about the transparency which exists in our banking system in

the context of Gross NPA percent and there is a need to include financial education in our education system, not only for commerce students but for the students of every field.

The End Game

The problem starts in the yes bank with the executing agency filed a money laundering case against the founder and former managing director of Yes Bank Ltd, Rana Kapoor. ED is currently seeking loans related to loans made to DHFL (Dewan Housing Finance Ltd) at its home in Worli, Mumbai," said an ED official. This happened after the Reserve Bank of India put the moratorium on the private lender on Thursday night and suspended the bank's board of directors for 30 days. The RBI has limited the monthly payment limit to £ 50,000 (the Indian Express, 2020). The moratorium came after the Rana Kapoor-sponsored bank failed to raise capital to address potential credit losses and after the bank's finances deteriorated. The government said Friday that it had asked RBI to provide a detailed assessment report on the alleged financial irregularities that had contributed to the deterioration of the bank's situation. The ED PMLA case touching Kapoor is a continuation of its investigation in contradiction of DHFL, which found a diversion of funds of £ 12.733 billion to 80 suspected fraud establishments using bogus 1 lakh mortgagors. These transactions date back to 2015. "In some cases, we found that the diverted funds from the DHFL came from Yes Bank. The investigation is to determine the nature of these loans and the irregularity in the granting of these loans," Officially, the ED said. The ED is also supposed to give a notice to Kapoor. The announcement stops investigators from ordering citizens to flee the region. The ED accused DHFL's Kapil and Dheeraj Wadhawan of buying shares in five companies: Faith Realtors, Marvel Township, Abe Realty, Poseidon Realty, and Random Realtors, which then merged with Sunblink. Sunblink's books will have contained the unpaid debts from these five firms, which totalled about £ 2.186 billion in July 2019, to fund the diversion of purchased DHFL loans. As a workaround, the RBI proposed that State Bank of India acquire 49 percent of the bank and retain at least 26 percent over the next three years, and that the so-called Additional Tier 1 (or AT1) capital earned by Yes Bank be fully written off. This ensures that someone who borrowed money to Yes Bank under the AT1 group of bonds will lose their whole investment (The Indian Express, 2020).

The major issue is that how the banks are providing loans under the influence of the political leaders, and how a person is given huge loans by all different public and private sector banks, why the financial position of the bank was not clear to the investor and how the bank cheated with reporting of less NPA's and creating

Provision Coverage vs other banks? How the future of the investors and customers will be assured in such a circle of power and influence?

CONCLUSION

Banks play a crucial role in every economy. Banks and financial institutions must be strong in order for the economy to thrive. They are the guardians of the public funds. Any depositor's lack of faith in a bank is bound to erode the depositor's confidence in the bank as a safe haven for his savings. Since the average person does not grasp the nuances of finance, this can have disastrous consequences. He simply needs his money to be safe in the bank; as a result, the bank and the RBI must instil that trust in him. With banks showing signs of poor financial health, immediate action is needed to develop a roadmap for long-term reforms. The sooner these changes are enforced, the more quickly the economy will recover.

The history of Yes Bank has been very enriching, a private bank founded by two people in 2004, emerging as one of the top five private in the country over the past decade, riding on both foreign and domestic investments. But in a short span of just 17 months, the shares of Yes Bank took a drastic fall, from its lifetime high of Rs 404 in August 2018 to a low of Rs 16.60 in March 2020.

The reason for the failure of Yes Bank were many such as deterioration of financial position due to bad loans and withdrawal of deposits, inability to raise further capital and governance issues which can be looked like strategic issues that needs to be addressed in future. Further after deterioration of bank's position, RBI took a strategic decision for the and charge and appointed an administrator and put a moratorium period of 30 days to prevent the failure of the bank. RBI appointed SBI's CFO as the administrator, who showed interested in making an investment in Yes bank. This is probably the first time that this type of strategic decision is taken by state owned lender that came forward to bail out a new generation bank. RBI and SBI's aim to rescue Yes bank to prevent the loss of trust of depositors in financial system. This Yes bank case is a lesson to the regulatory bodies and urge to bring the needy reforms and improve their strategy for reduction of this types of false transaction as soon as possible, because it is never too late. But if it is delayed it will make it will take no time for another incident to happen.

Another strategic decision of RBI is to give the board of management of the Bank sufficient time to come up with a plan to prevent its failure, when the bank was unable to do so, RBI acted strategically and brought SBI into the picture as an investor. RBI reconstructed the board and named Prashant Kumar, former CFO of SBI, as the new MD and CEO of Yes Bank. Currently, Yes Bank is owed by SBI who has a 30% stake in the company. The new approach adopted by the RBI and

SBI is a correct and bold approach. There are two ways of handling this and both mean the same thing. Either separate and take the baby out of the bath water, which is dirty or if it is dirtying the pond, you take the fish out of the pond. So, either way system has taken the business out of the bank management control and put it under the SBI, so baby is taken out of the bath water which is dirty or fish that was dirtying the pond has been taken out that is Rana Kapoor and the old management and now there is a new management. But either way this is a bold decision on part of the government and RBI. There are some risks. Is there any moral hazard? We do not see a moral hazard because this is not in odes criticism that government is socializing private sector losses. The government is not socializing private sector losses, private sector investors and the shareholder has lost everything. This is one way of doing something with the value that remains at a very small investment and protecting shareholders and banking operations and the trust in the banking system. This is not a case of socializing private sectors losses because in the private sector every investor has lost loads of money in Yes bank.

LESSONS FOR FUTURE

YES bank has now get a new team that focus on proper management of banking function in strategically proper way. Pertinently, the bank needs is strategically improved and qualified management is fulfilled for professionalize management, tighten corporate governance, and create fiercely independent supervisory boards that can keep management accountable and ensure that decisions are made solely on the basis of merit. Corporate governance must now address all aspects of enforcement, including clear roles for ombudsman and whistle-blowers. Further, boards must ensure that all environmental, social, and governance criteria are included in balance sheets, as well as that social accounting is considered. External auditors' roles must be clearly established in order to ensure the consistency and fairness of financial statements.

Independence of Supervisory Authority

Independent Directors are mainly responsible for overseeing the Board's operations and ensuring that the Board's actions and do not jeopardize the rights of minority shareholders. According to current standards, two-thirds of the members of the Audit Committee, including the Chairman, must be autonomous.

In order to ensure effective application of the functions of Board members, it is necessary that the nexus between the promoters and directors appointed in the board should be stopped. Pertinently, the experts in banking, financial services, risk management, information technology, human resources, and others should serve on boards. These experts should be clearly unbiased and have no links to the promoters or management.

Curbing Misdemeanour at Initial Stage

A tendency to make risky or suboptimal decisions for the sake of higher interest, processing fees, or collaterals is heinous for banks. One such decision could go wrong and for covering-up the decision, more risky actions are taken in similar way to retrieve the funds, resulting in a snowball effect. The more important issue is bribery, which occurs when proper procedures are not followed, and lending decisions are made in secret.

Only when a wrongdoing is brought before an investigating body (for e.g., RBI in case of YES Bank), its accountability is sought in the field. Thus, the problem should be dealt at the initial stage itself, rather than waiting for the further results for recovering the loss.

Stringent Supervision and Control Over Mishappenings

Efficient and strict monitoring cannot be underestimated. Not only should supervision be rigorous and prompt, but wrongs discovered during inspections should be treated with extreme caution. This will serve as a deterrent to anyone plotting a sneaky way to get around the system.

Moreover, it would be worthy to test a system in which, if an early warning signal is received, a completely new team of RBI inspectors takes over the inspection to ensure that any snowball effect does not grow. Such a team would be unfamiliar with the bank's management and therefore would be free of any pre-existing ties.

Well Structured Audit Functionaries

It is critical to establish an internal audit function that is well-structured at the outset. It gives management and the Board of Directors more confidence than any other external authority. The obligation to appoint external auditors that are fully impartial and their rotation in the period of every three years follows.

REGULATOR: THE RESPONSIBLE HOLDER

The regulator should have one competent investigating agency to oversee the working of the bank. The regulator must ensure that inspectors appointed to inspect the wrongdoing in a bank should nowhere be related to the management of bank.

Moreover, it is the responsibility of the regulator to pick out the instances where-in the management lacks in fulfilling its responsibilities. In case of such misdemeanour, the regulator must act immediately providing stringent actions against the management.

Further, it should be the regulator's duty to ensure that the bank's annual audit committee appoints competent and independent auditors. This will ensure that there is no window-dressing on the part of the bank

Table 1. Consolidated balance sheet

Consolidated Balance Sheet in Rs. Cr.	Mar 19	Mar-18	Mar-17	Mar-16
EQUITIES AND LIABILITIES				
SHAREHOLDER'S FUNDS	463.01	460.59	456.49	420.53
Equity Share Capital				
Total Share Capital	**463.01**	**460.59**	**456.49**	**420.53**
Reserves and Surplus	26,424.40	25,291.91	21,583.14	13,341.85
Total Reserves and Surplus	**26,424.40**	**25,291.91**	**21,583.14**	**13,341.85**
Total Share Holders Funds	**26,887.41**	**25,752.51**	**22,039.63**	**13,762.38**
Deposits	2,27,557.90	2,00,688.60	1,42,857.44	1,11,704.18
Borrowings	1,08,424.11	74,893.58	38,606.67	31,658.98
Other Liabilities and Provisions	17,990.19	11,114.96	11,555.94	8,117.08
Total Capital and Liabilities	**3,80,859.61**	**3,12,449.65**	**2,15,059.69**	**1,65,242.62**
Cash and Balances with Reserve Bank of India	10,797.74	11,425.75	6,952.07	5,776.16
Balances with Banks Money at Call and Short Notice	16,187.19	13,328.07	12,602.59	2,442.74
Investments	89,328.53	68,293.44	49,981.80	48,788.47
Advances	2,41,397.19	2,03,518.83	1,32,262.68	98,209.93
Fixed Assets	829.89	837.3	13,260.56	474.58
Other Assets	22,319.07	15,046.28	0	9,550.75
Total Assets	**3,80,859.61**	**3,12,449.65**	**2,15,059.69**	**1,65,242.62**

Source: annual report of Yes bank

Table 2. Yes bank's Profit and loss Statement

Consolidated Profit & Loss Account in Rs. Cr	Mar 19	Mar-18	Mar-17	Mar-16
INCOME				
Interest / Discount on Advances / Bills	22,918.54	15,477.85	12,209.77	9,711.48
Income from Investments	6,048.42	4,102.53	3,796.84	3,508.21
Interest on Balance with RBI and Other Inter-Bank funds	397.57	516.07	257.82	112.54
Others	259.26	172.14	160.57	201.21
Total Interest Earned	**29,623.80**	**20,268.59**	**16,425.00**	**13,533.44**
Other Income	4,675.48	5,293.15	4,217.80	2,729.42
Total Income	34,299.28	25,561.75	20,642.80	16,262.86
EXPENDITURE				
Interest Expended	19,811.29	12,529.43	10,626.53	8,965.41
Payments to and Provisions for Employees	2,538.11	2,234.66	1,840.24	1,319.78
Depreciation	305.45	232.36	172.61	111.84
Operating Expenses (excludes Employee Cost & Depreciation)	3,517.86	2,806.52	2,155.77	1,573.41
Total Operating Expenses	**6,361.43**	**5,273.54**	**4,168.61**	**3,005.03**
Provision Towards Income Tax	2,300.97	2,243.92	1,839.55	1,348.76
Provision Towards Deferred Tax	-1,661.23	-272.6	-125.97	-122.33
Other Provisions and Contingencies	5,777.56	1,554.24	794.19	536.3
Total Provisions and Contingencies	**6,417.30**	**3,525.56**	**2,507.78**	**1,762.73**
Total Expenditure	**32,590.01**	**21,328.53**	**17,302.91**	**13,733.18**
Net Profit / Loss for The Year	**1,709.27**	**4,233.22**	**3,339.89**	**2,529.69**
Net Profit / Loss After EI & Prior Year Items	**1,709.27**	**4,233.22**	**3,339.89**	**2,529.69**
Consolidated Profit/Loss After MI And Associates	**1,709.27**	**4,233.22**	**3,339.89**	**2,529.69**
Profit / Loss Brought Forward	10,369.53	7,918.96	5,520.46	4,205.59
Total Profit / Loss available for Appropriations	**12,078.80**	**12,152.18**	**8,860.35**	**6,735.28**
APPROPRIATIONS				
Transfer To / From Statutory Reserve	430.07	1,056.14	832.52	634.86
Transfer To / From Capital Reserve	101.01	65.96	108.3	73.48
Transfer To / From Investment Reserve	0.67	0	0	0
Transfer To / From Revenue And Other Reserves	53.91	0	0	0

continues on following page

Table 2. Continued

Consolidated Profit & Loss Account in Rs. Cr	Mar 19	Mar-18	Mar-17	Mar-16
Dividend and Dividend Tax for The Previous Year	750.36	0	0.56	0.32
Equity Share Dividend	0	548.81	0	420.53
Tax On Dividend	0	111.74	0	85.62
Balance Carried Over To Balance Sheet	10,742.77	10,369.53	7,918.96	5,520.46
Total Appropriations	**12,078.80**	**12,152.18**	**8,860.35**	**6,735.28**

Source: annual report of Yes bank

It seems from the past 4 years data that the profitability of the bank is good with available profit for appropriation (in Profit & loss account) and increasing balances with Banks Money at Call and Short Notice (in Balance sheet), but the suddenly the problem started, and the cause was found in the bank's cash flow as the cash flow from operating and investing activities are showing the negative balances and operating loss is itself reported by bank as under:

Table 3. Yes bank's cash flow statement

CASH FLOW OF YES BANK (in Rs. Cr.)	Mar-19	Mar-18	Mar-17	Mar-16
NET PROFIT/LOSS BEFORE EXTRAORDINARY ITEMS AND TAX	**2,349.01**	**6,204.54**	**5,053.47**	**3,756.12**
Net Cash Flow From Operating Activities	-24,573.30	-21,810.44	4,384.14	-375.62
Net Cash Used In Investing Activities	-6,293.69	-8,744.90	-4,473.87	-4,022.57
Net Cash Used From Financing Activities	33,039.32	35,747.92	11,429.21	5,059.70
Foreign Exchange Gains / Losses	58.78	6.58	-3.72	0
NET INC/DEC IN CASH AND CASH EQUIVALENTS	**2,231.11**	**5,199.16**	**11,335.75**	**661.51**
Cash And Cash Equivalents Begin of Year	24,753.82	19,554.66	8,218.90	7,557.40
Cash And Cash Equivalents End Of Year	26,984.93	24,753.82	19,554.66	8,218.90

Source: annual report of Yes bank

Figure 1. Yes bank's Gross NPA's and Provision Coverage vs other banks

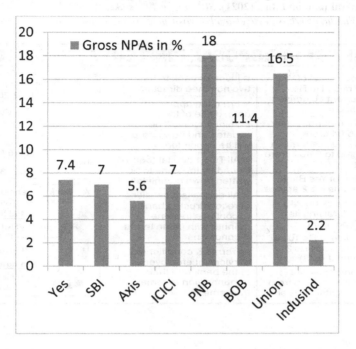

Figure 2. Yes bank's Gross NPA's and Provision Coverage vs other banks
Source Nomura Research

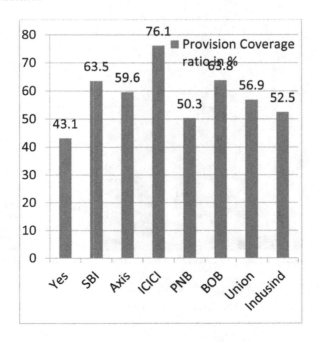

Figure 3.
Yes Bank revival plan on table. (2021). *SBI to take 49% stake, Wednesday, 09 June, from https:// www.telegraphindia.com/business/yes-bank-revival-plan-on-table/cid/1751628*

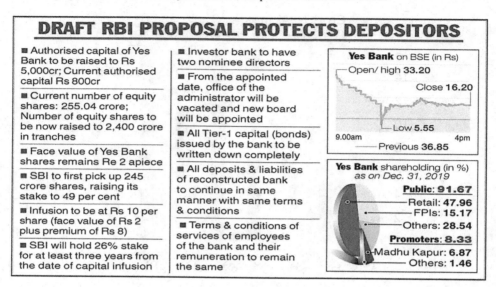

Figure 4.
Source: Yes Bank crisis: False message claims Congress-linked companies are top willful defaulters. (2021). from https://www.altnews.in/yes-bank-crisis-false-message-names-congress-linked-companies-as-top-willful-defaulters/

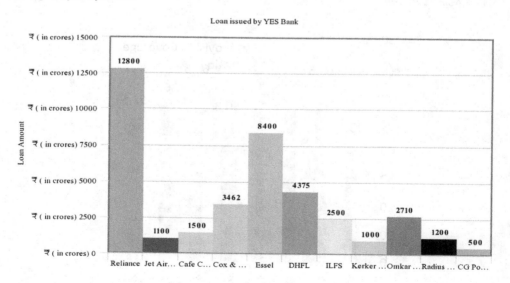

Figure 5. Top Defaulters of Yes Bank
Source: *Economic Times from https://www.altnews.in/yes-bank-crisis-false-message-names-congress-linked-companies-as-top-willful-defaulters/*

Company	Loan Amount (Rs. in crores)
Reliance (ADAG)	12800
Essel	8400
DHFL	4375
ILFS	2500
Jet Airways	1100
Kerkar Group	1000
Omkar Realtors & Developers	2710
Radius Developers	1200
CG Power	500

Figure 6.
Source: *https://www.insightsonindia.com/2020/04/01/secure-synopsis-16-march-2020/yes_bank-2/*

YES BANK JOURNEY:
FROM PEAK TO PLUNGE

1999 | Rana Kapoor, brother-in-law Ashok Kapur & Harkirat Singh partner with Dutch **Rabobank** to set up Rabo India Finance

2002 | The trio gets in-principle approval to set up a bank with support from Rabobank

2003 | Harkirat Singh is sidelined. Rana Kapoor, Ashok Kapur and Rabo promote Yes Bk

2005 | Yes Bank hits the stock market with a Rs 300-crore IPO

2017 | Yes Bank reports **divergence of Rs 6,355 crore in bad loans** — disclosed and identified by RBI

2018 | The bank's shares tank nearly 30% in Sept after RBI cuts Rana Kapoor's tenure to 3 months

2019 | The lender reports fresh divergence in FY19. New CEO Ravneet Gill announces **plans for $2-billion capital-raising**

2019 | Lenders sell Rana Kapoor's entire stake in the bank by invoking pledged shares. Kapoor had pledged the shares to finance family businesses

2019 | Yes Bank balance sheet hit by **a spate of bad loans** — IL&FS, Anil Ambani Group, CG Power, Cox & Kings, Altico, CCD, Essel Group, Essar Power, Vardaraj Cement, Radius Developers, Mantri Group

2020 | The lender's shares tank after bank reveals little-known NRIs as potential investors

Feb '20 | Yes Bank **delays financial results** for Q3

Mar 5, '20 | RBI places Yes Bank under moratorium over severe deterioration in financial condition

Figure 7.
Source: Times of India (2019) RBI sees Rs 3,277 crore divergence in Yes Bank's reported NPAs, from https://timesofindia.indiatimes.com/business/india-business/rbi-sees-rs-3277cr-divergence-in-yes-banks-reported-npas/articleshow/72133830.cms

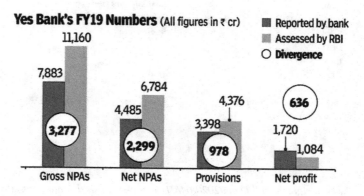

Table 4. Yes Bank Shareholding Pattern

Summary	Mar 2021	Jun 2020	Jun 2019	Jun 2018
Promoter	0%	0%	19.8%	20.0%
Holding	0%	0%	19.8%	20.0%
Pledged	0.0%	0.0%	3.64%	3.62%
Locked	0.0%	0.0%	0.0%	0.0%
FII	13.8%	1.7%	33.7%	42.5%
DII	46.7%	69.1%	17.0%	25.2%
Public	39.5%	29.2%	29.5%	12.3%
Others	0%	0%	0%	0%

Source: Annual report Yes bank, 2021

Figure 8.
Source: self-compiled from Annal report of Yes Bank

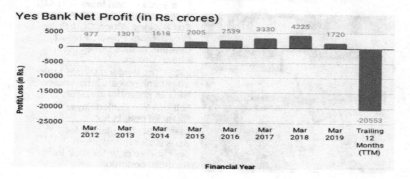

Figure 9.

Source: The economic times (2020, Mar 13) Seven investors join SBI to put over Rs 12,000 cr into Yes Bank; Prashant Kumar proposed as new CEO, from https://economictimes.indiatimes.com/industry/ banking/finance/banking/seven-investors-join-sbi-to-put-over-rs-12000-cr-into-yes-bank-prashant-kumar-proposed-as-new-ceo/articleshow/74603685.cms?from=mdr

Table 5. Key performance indicators of Yes Bank

Ratios	2017	2018	2019	2020
CASA Ratio	36.30%	36.50%	33.10%	26%
PCR Ratio	46.90%	50%	43.10%	72.70%
CET-1 ratio	11.40%	9.70%	8.40%	6.30%
CRAR ratio	17%	18.40%	16.50%	8.50%
Gross NPA	1.90%	1.40%	3.30%	16.80%
Net NPA	0.80%	0.60%	1.90%	5.03%

Source: Annual report Yes bank

Figure 10.

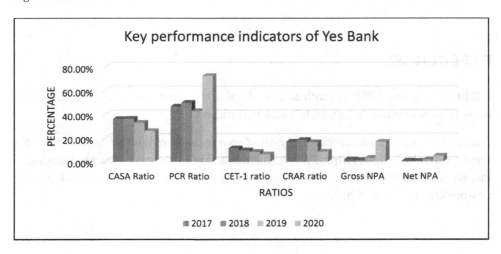

Figure 11.
Source: Namura Research

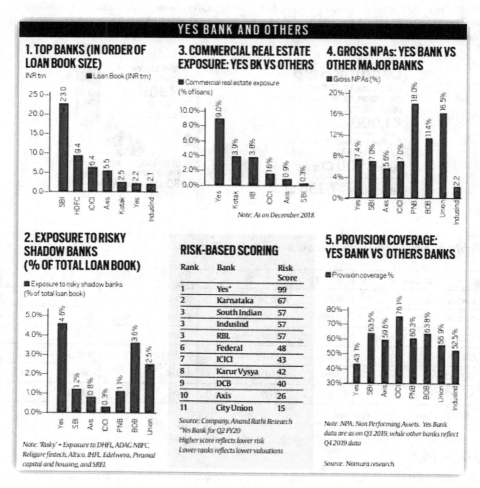

YES BANK AND OTHERS

1. TOP BANKS (IN ORDER OF LOAN BOOK SIZE)

3. COMMERCIAL REAL ESTATE EXPOSURE: YES BK VS OTHERS

Note: As on December 2018

4. GROSS NPAs: YES BANK VS OTHER MAJOR BANKS

2. EXPOSURE TO RISKY SHADOW BANKS (% OF TOTAL LOAN BOOK)

Note: 'Risky' = Exposure to DHFL, ADAG NBFC, Religare fintech, Altico, IHFL, Edelweiss, Piramal capital and housing, and SREI.

RISK-BASED SCORING

Rank	Bank	Risk Score
1	Yes*	99
2	Karnataka	67
3	South Indian	57
3	IndusInd	57
3	RBL	57
6	Federal	48
7	ICICI	43
8	Karur Vysya	42
9	DCB	40
10	Axis	26
11	City Union	15

Source: Company, Anand Rathi Research
*Yes Bank for Q2 FY20
Higher score reflects lower risk
Lower ranks reflects lower valuations

5. PROVISION COVERAGE: YES BANK VS OTHERS BANKS

Note: NPA: Non Performing Assets. Yes Bank data are as on Q3 2019, while other banks reflect Q4 2019 data

Source: Nomura research

REFERENCES

Affairscloud.com. (2020, March 23). *Yes Bank Crisis Explained* [Video]. YouTube. https://www.youtube.com/watch?v=nKmWrtk2wyI

Agarwal, M. (2020, December 31). *Fall of an ace banker! Who's Rana Kapoor, the brain behind YES Bank*. Https://Www.Businesstoday.In/. https://www.businesstoday.in/current/corporate/fall-of-an-ace-banker-who-is-rana-kapoor-the-brain-behind-yes-bank/story/397838.html

Ahuja, C. (2020, March 20). *Yes Bank fiasco and genesis of trouble with banking system*. Tehelka.

RBI Annual Report. (2020). *BSE Sensex, March 2020*. Author.

Bfsi, E. T. (2020, March 17). *Yes Bank crisis: Ten lessons to prevent bank failures in future*. https://bfsi.economictimes.indiatimes.com/news/banking/yes-bank-crisis-ten-lessons-to-prevent-bank-failures-in-future/74668041

Bhaumik, S. K., & Mukherjee, P. (2020). The Indian Banking Industry: a commentary. In P. Banerjee & F. J. Richter (Eds.), *Economic Institutions in India: Sustainability under Liberalization and Globalization. Palgrave Macmillan*.

Business Standard. (2020). *YES Bank crisis: RBI's Moratorium on lender to be lifted on March 18*. https://www.business-standard.com/article/finance/yes-bank-crisis-rbi-s-moratorium-on-lender-to-be-lifted-on-march-18-120031400188_1.html

Business Standard. (2020, March 5). *What is yes bank crisis?* https://www.business-standard.com/about/what-is-yes-bank-crisis

Business Today. (2020). *YES Bank crisis: How SBI executed a perfect 'rescue plan'*. https://www.businesstoday.in/sectors/banks/yes-bank-crisis-how-sbi-executed-a-perfect-rescue-plan/story/397777.html(March, 9)

Chakraborty, B. (2020, March 20). *Yes Bank crisis and lessons for the Indian Banking industry*. https://www.linkedin.com/pulse/yes-bank-crisis-lessons-indian-banking-industry-biplab-chakraborty/

Chouhan, V. (2016). Investigating Factors Affecting Electronic Word-of-Mouth. In Capturing, Analyzing, and Managing Word-of-Mouth in the Digital Marketplace (pp. 119-135). IGI Global. doi:10.4018/978-1-4666-9449-1.ch007

Chouhan, V., Chandra, B., Saraswat, P., & Goswami, S. (2020b). *Developing sustainable accounting framework for cement industry: evidence from India*. Finance India.

Chouhan, V., Sharma, R. B., & Goswami, S. (2020a). Factor Affecting Audit Quality: A study of the companies listed in Bombay Stock Exchange (BSE). *International Journal of Management, 11*(7), 989–999.

Chouhan, V., Sharma, R. B., Goswami, S., & Hashed, A. W. A. (2021a). Measuring challenges in adoption of sustainable environmental technologies in Indian cement industry. *Accounting, 7*(2), 339–348. doi:10.5267/j.ac.2020.11.019

Chouhan, V., Sharma, R. B., Goswami, S., & Hashed, A. W. A. (2021b). Stainable reporting: A case study of selected cement companies of India. *Accounting*, *7*(1), 151–160. doi:10.5267/j.ac.2020.10.002

Chouhan, V., Vasita, M. L., & Goswami, S. (2020c). The Impact And Role Of Social Media For Consciousness of COVID-19 pandemic, Journal of Content. *Community and Communication*, *12*(1), 250–262.

Commercial Banks in India: Growth, Challenges and Strategies/Benson Kunjukunju. (2008). New Century Pub.

Contributor, M. (2020, March 16). *Lessons from the Yes Bank saga: Eternal vigilance is the price of financial stability*. Moneycontrol. https://www.moneycontrol.com/news/business/markets/lessons-from-the-yes-bank-saga-eternal-vigilance-is-the-price-of-financial-stability-5034861.html

Dadhich, M., Chouhan, V., & Adholiya, A. (2019). Stochastic Pattern of Major Indices of Bombay Stock Exchange. *International Journal of Recent Technology and Engineering Regular Issue*, *8*(3), 6774–6779. doi:10.35940/ijrte.C6068.098319

Dattagupta, I. (2020, March 12). *Decoding the Rescue Plan for Yes Bank*. https://www.ndtv.com/opinion/decoding-the-rescue-plan-for-yes-bank-2193266

Deb, R. (2021). YES Bank fiasco: A corporate governance failure. *Decision (Washington, D.C.)*, 1–10.

Devi, P., Kumar, P., Singh, R., & Kumar, S. (2021). Multifractal detrended fluctuation analysis approach to study period of crisis of YES bank. *Nonlinear Studies*, *28*(1).

Dhruv Rathee. (2020). *Yes Bank Crisis | Explained by Dhruv Rathee* [Video]. https://youtu.be/NagvYDGL76s

Dutta, P. K. (2020, March 9). Rapid rise and free fall of Yes Bank in 10 years after co-founder died in 26/11 attack. *India Today*. https://www.indiatoday.in/news-analysis/story/yes-bank-rana-kapoor-1653955-2020-03-09

Dziobek, C., & Pazarbasioglu, C. (1998). Lessons from Systemic Bank Restructuring. Economic Issues No. 14, International Monetary Fund.

Economic Times. (2020). *Rana Kapoor, wife took Rs 307 cr. illegal gratification through bungalow deal: CBI FIR*. https://economictimes.indiatimes.com/news/politics-and-nation/cbi-files-fresh-case-against-yes-bank-founder-rana-kapoor-others/articleshow/74614279.cms?utm_source=contentofinterest&utm_medium=text&utm_campaign=cppst(March, 13)

ETBFSI. (2020, March 7). *Is customer really a king? Yes Bank's says "no."* Https:// Bfsi.Economictimes.Indiatimes.Com/. https://bfsi.economictimes.indiatimes.com/ news/banking/is-customer-really-the-king-yes-banks-feel-no/74514802

Gopinath, G. R. (2020, March 10). Beneath the 'Yes mess', some stark truths. *The Hindu.*

Hawkins, J. (1999). *Bank Restructuring in South-East Asia", included in "Bank Restructuring in Practice.* BIS Policy Papers No. 6, Bank for International Settlements. http://tehelka.com/yes-bank-fiasco-and-genesis-of-trouble-with-banking-system/

India Today. (2020). *Yes Bank crisis: From what happens to my money to will SBI be saviour, all that has happened.* https://www.indiatoday.in/business/story/ yes-bank-crisis-rbi-sbi-invest-withdrawal-limit-reason-full-roundup-developmen ts-1653193-2020-03-06

Indian Express Online. (2020, March 6). *What Is Yes Bank Crisis? Is Your Money Safe in Yes Bank?* [Video]. https://youtu.be/agIMUDKnCsM

Kautish, S. (2008). Online Banking: A Paradigm Shift. *E-Business, 9*(10), 54-59.

Kautish, S. (2013). Knowledge sharing: A contemporary review of literature in context to information systems designing. *ACADEMICIA: An International Multidisciplinary Research Journal, 3*(1), 101–114.

Kautish, S., & Thapliyal, M. P. (2013). Design of new architecture for model management systems using knowledge sharing concept. *International Journal of Computers and Applications, 62*(11), 1–25.

Khan, S., Chouhan, V., Chandra, B., & Goswami, S. (2014). Sustainable accounting reporting practices of Indian cement industry: An exploratory study. *Uncertain Supply Chain Management, 2*(1), 61–72.

Maina, E. M., Chouhan, V., & Goswami, S. (2020). Measuring Behavioral Aspect of IFRS Implementation in India And Kenya. *International Journal of Scientific & Technology Research, 9*(1), 2045–2048.

Market, C. (2020, October 23). *Yes Bank posts Q2 PAT at Rs 129 crores; NII falls 9.7% YoY.* Business Standard. https://www.business-standard.com/article/news-cm/ yes-bank-posts-q2-pat-at-rs-129-cr-nii-falls-9-7-yoy-120102301164_1.html

Mint2Save. (2020, April 7). *Yes Bank: Collapse Full Case Study | Are banks Safe in India?* [Blog Post]. https://www.mint2save.com/yes-bank-collapse-full-case-study- are-banks-safe-in-india/

Misra, U. (2020, March 10). *Explained: How Yes Bank ran into crisis.* The Indian Express. https://indianexpress.com/article/explained/how-yes-bank-ran-into-crisis-rana-kapoor-arrest-6307314/

Nair, V. (2020). *Virus Spread, Yes Bank Crisis Raise Risks For Private Banks.* Bloomberg. https://www.bloombergquint.com/business/virus-spread-yes-bank-crisis-raise-risks-for-private-banks

Pandey, A., Guha, R., Malkar, N., & Pandey, N. (2019). Marching Towards Creating Shared Value: The Case of YES Bank. *Asian Case Research Journal, 23*(02), 289–312.

P.K.D. (2020a, March 9). *Rapid rise and free fall of Yes Bank in 10 years after co-founder died in 26/11 attack.* India Today. https://www.indiatoday.in/news-analysis/story/yes-bank-rana-kapoor-1653955-2020-03-09

Pombarla, P. (2020, July 21). A Study on Yes Bank Crisis. *IOSR Journal of Business and Management (IOSR-JBM), 22*(7), 1–10. https://www.iosrjournals.org/iosr-jbm/papers/Vol22-issue7/Series-7/E2207073645.pdf

P.S.P. (2020b, July). A Study on Yes Bank Crisis. *IOSR Journal of Business and Management*, 36–45. doi:10.9790/487X-2207073645

Rai, V. (2020). *Lessons from the Yes Bank Saga in India.* ISAS Insights, No. 605. https://www.isas.nus.edu.sg/wp-content/uploads/2020/03/ISAS-Insight-605_Vinod-Rai.pdf

Ramchandani, K., & Jethwani, K. (2021). Yes bank: an untold story. *Emerald Emerging Markets Case Studies, 11*(1). doi:10.1108/EEMCS-04-2020-0123

Ray, A. (2021, January 22). *YES Bank Q3 results: Net profit rises to ₹151 crore, NII jumps to ₹2,560 cr. Mint.* https://www.livemint.com/industry/banking/yes-bank-q3-results-net-profit-rises-to-rs-151-crore-11611312884826.html

Reserve Bank of India. (1998). *Report of the Narasimham Committee on Banking Sector Reforms.* Author.

Saraswat, P. (2012). Forensic accounting: A tool to uncover the Accounting and Financial frauds, Chartered Secretary. *The Journal of Corporate Professional, XLII*(3), 281–342.

Saraswat, P. (2021, Jan.). Elements of Effective Insider Trading Regulations: A Comparative Analysis of India and US. *Niram University Law Journal.*

Saraswat, P., & Banga, J. (2012). Volatility of Sensex with respect of Union Budget of India: A Pragmatic study. *International Journal of Accounting and Financial Management Research*, 2(March), 19–31.

Sarkar, P. (2020). The crisis of yes bank ltd. International journal of multidisciplinary educational research. *Editorial Board*, 9(7), 167–175.

Singh, H. (2020, March 6). *Yes Bank Crisis: 5 Key Reasons to Know.* Jagaran Josh. https://www.jagranjosh.com/general-knowledge/reasons-behind-the-yes-bank-crisis-1583503237-1

Singh, T., & Pathak, N. (2020). Yes bank debacle: Whom to blame for investor destruction; securities exchange board of India (SEBI) or reserve bank of India (RBI)? *Journal of Critical Reviews*, 7(16), 1459–1471. https://www.researchgate.net/publication/343335828_JOURNAL_OF_CRITICAL_REVIEWS_YES_BANK_DEBACLE_WHOM_TO_BLAME_FOR_INVESTOR_DESTRUCTION_SECURITIES_EXCHANGE_BOARD_OF_INDIA_SEBI_OR_RESERVE_BANK_OF_INDIA_RBI

Sriram, R. (2020). *YES Bank crisis: Why government must fix the vulnerabilities in financial system.* Economic Times. https://economictimes.indiatimes.com/industry/banking/finance/banking/yes-bank-crisis-why-government-must-fix-the-vulnerabilities-in-financial-system/articleshow/74531257.cms?from=mdr

The Hindu. (2020). *Yes Bank crisis explained.* https://www.thehindu.com/business/yes-bank-crisis-explained/article31030273.ece.

The Hindu Net Desk. (2020, March 10). *Yes Bank crisis explained.* https://www.thehindu.com/business/yes-bank-crisis-explained/article31030273.ece

The Indian Express. (2020). *Explained: How Yes Bank ran into crisis.* https://indianexpress.com/article/explained/how-yes-bank-ran-into-crisis-rana-kapoor-arrest-6307314/

The Quint. (2021, March 4). *'A Rigged System': Rana Kapoor Wasn't Alone In The Yes Bank Crisis* [Video]. https://youtu.be/grcdbhLIC0I

The Yes Bank Crisis. (2020, March 7). *Drishti Ias.* https://www.drishtiias.com/daily-updates/daily-news-editorials/the-yes-bank-crisis

Today, I. (2020). *Yes Bank crisis: Bad loans worth Rs 20,000 crore granted on Rana Kapoor's direction.* https://www.indiatoday.in/business/story/yes-bank-crisis-rs-20-000-crore-worth-bad-loans-were-given-on-rana-kapoor-s-direction-say-ed-sources-1654280-2020-03-11

Wadhwa, R., Ramaswamy, M. K., & Fin, S. M. (2020). Impact of NPA on Profitability of Banks. *International Journal of Engineering Technology and Management Sciences*, *4*(3), 1–8.

Wikipedia Contributors. (2021). Yes Bank. In *Wikipedia*. https://en.wikipedia.org/wiki/Yes_Bank

Yes bank. (n.d.). *Annual reports*. www.yesbank.in

Yes Bank Crisis Explained by Dhruv Rathee. (2020). [Video]. *YouTube*. https://www.youtube.com/watch?v=NagvYDGL76s

Yes Bank crisis explained. (2020). *The Hindu*. https://www.thehindu. com/business/yes-bank-crisis-explained/article31030273.ece

Yes Bank crisis: Ten lessons to prevent bank failures in future. (2020, March 17). BFSI.Com.

Compilation of References

Abelló, A., & Romero, O. (2009). Online Analytical Processing. Encyclopedia of Database Systems, 20, 2731-2735.

Abraham, J., Higdon, D., Nelson, J., & Ibarra, J. (2018). Cryptocurrency price prediction using tweet volumes and sentiment analysis. *SMU Data Science Review, 1*(3), 1.

Adrian, T., & Shin, H. S. (2009). *Money, Liquidity, and Monetary Policy.* Social Science Research Network. SSRN Scholarly Paper.

Affairscloud.com. (2020, March 23). *Yes Bank Crisis Explained* [Video]. YouTube. https://www.youtube.com/watch?v=nKmWrtk2wyI

Agarwal, M. (2020, December 31). *Fall of an ace banker! Who's Rana Kapoor, the brain behind YES Bank.* Https://Www.Businesstoday.In/. https://www.businesstoday.in/current/corporate/fall-of-an-ace-banker-who-is-rana-kapoor-the-brain-behind-yes-bank/story/397838.html

Ahmad, B., Latif, S., Bilal, A. R., & Hai, M. (2019). The mediating role of career resilience on the relationship between career competency and career success: An empirical investigation. *Asia-Pacific Journal of Business Administration, 11*(3), 209–231. doi:10.1108/APJBA-04-2019-0079

Ahuja, C. (2020, March 20). *Yes Bank fiasco and genesis of trouble with banking system.* Tehelka.

Ahuja, G. (2000). The duality of collaboration: Inducements and opportunities in the formation of interfirm linkages. *Strategic Management Journal, 21*(3), 317–343. doi:10.1002/(SICI)1097-0266(200003)21:3<317::AID-SMJ90>3.0.CO;2-B

Akgün, A. E., & Keskin, H. (2014). Organisational resilience capacity and firm product innovativeness and performance. *International Journal of Production Research, 52*(23), 6918–6937. doi:10.1080/00207543.2014.910624

Akhtar, N., Perwej, A., & Perwej, Y. (2020). Data analytics and visualization using Tableau utilitarian for COVID-19 (Coronavirus). *Global Journal of Engineering and Technology Advances, 3*(2), 28-50.

Akter, S., Wamba, S. F., Gunasekaran, A., Dubey, R., & Childe, S. J. (2016). How to improve firm performance using big data analytics capability and business strategy alignment? *International Journal of Production Economics, 182*, 113–131. doi:10.1016/j.ijpe.2016.08.018

Akyildirim, E., Goncu, A., & Sensoy, A. (2021). Prediction of cryptocurrency returns using machine learning. *Annals of Operations Research*, *297*(1), 3–36. doi:10.100710479-020-03575-y

Ali, S. M., Gupta, N., Nayak, G. K., & Lenka, R. K. (2016, December). Big data visualization: Tools and challenges. In *2016 2nd International Conference on Contemporary Computing and Informatics (IC3I)* (pp. 656-660). IEEE.

Amir, E., Kirschenheiter, M., & Willard, K. (1997). The Valuation of Deferred Taxes. *Contemporary Accounting Research*, *14*(4), 597–622. doi:10.1111/j.1911-3846.1997.tb00543.x

Amir, E., & Sougiannis, T. (1999, Spring). Analysts" interpretation and investors" valuation of tax carryforwards. *Contemporary Accounting Research*, *16*(1), 1–33. doi:10.1111/j.1911-3846.1999.tb00572.x

Andolfatto, D., & Spewak, A. (2019). Whither the price of bitcoin? *Economic Synopses*, (1), 1–2.

Antoniadis, I., Tsiakiris, T., & Tsopogloy, S. (2015). Business Intelligence during times of crisis: Adoption and usage of ERP systems by SMEs. *Procedia: Social and Behavioral Sciences*, *175*(1), 299–307. doi:10.1016/j.sbspro.2015.01.1204

Assenmacher, K., & Gerlach, S. (2010). Monetary policy and financial imbalances: Facts and fiction. *Economic Policy*, *25*(63), 437–482. doi:10.1111/j.1468-0327.2010.00249.x

Atwood, T., Drake, M. S., & Myers, L. A. (2010). Book-tax conformity, earnings persistence and the association between earnings and future cash flows. *Journal of Accounting and Economics*, *50*(1), 111–125. doi:10.1016/j.jacceco.2009.11.001

Awotoye, Y., & Singh, R. (2017). Entrepreneurial Resilience, High Impact Challenges, and Firm Performance. *Journal of Management Policy and Practice*, *18*(2), 28–37.

Ayers, B. C., Laplante, S. K., & McGuire, S. T. (2010). Credit Ratings and Taxes: The Effect of Book-Tax Differences on Ratings Changes. *Contemporary Accounting Research*, *27*(2), 359–402. doi:10.1111/j.1911-3846.2010.01011.x

Badarau, C., & Popescu, A. (2015). Monetary policy and financial stability: What role for the interest rate? *International Economics and Economic Policy*, *12*(3), 359–374. doi:10.100710368-014-0307-6

Baesens, B., & van Gestel, T. (2009). *Credit Risk Management*. Oxford University Press.

Bagozzi, R. P. (2011). Measurement and meaning in information systems and organizational research: Methodological and philosophical foundations. *Management Information Systems Quarterly*, *35*(2), 261–292. doi:10.2307/23044044

Baker, W. E., & Sinkula, J. M. (1999). The Synergistic Effect of Market Orientation and Learning Orientation on Organizational Performance. *Journal of the Academy of Marketing Science*, *27*(4), 411–427. doi:10.1177/0092070399274002

Bansal, P. (2003). From Issues to Actions: The Importance of Individual Concerns and Organizational Values in Responding to Natural Environmental Issues. *Organization Science*, *14*(5), 510–527. doi:10.1287/orsc.14.5.510.16765

Baqer, K., Huang, D. Y., McCoy, D., & Weaver, N. 2016, February. Stressing out: Bitcoin "stress testing". In *International Conference on Financial Cryptography and Data Security* (pp. 3-18). Springer.

Baron, R. M., & Kenny, D. A. (1986). The Moderator-Mediator Variable Distinction in Social Psychological Research: Conceptual, Strategic, and Statistical Considerations. *Journal of Personality and Social Psychology*, *51*(6), 1173–1182. doi:10.1037/0022-3514.51.6.1173 PMID:3806354

Bartoletti, M., Pes, B., & Serusi, S. (2018, June). Data mining for detecting bitcoin ponzi schemes. In *2018 Crypto Valley Conference on Blockchain Technology (CVCBT)* (pp. 75-84). IEEE. 10.1109/CVCBT.2018.00014

Baum, S. C. (2018). Cryptocurrency Fraud: A Look Into The Frontier of Fraud (University Honors Program). Georgia Southern University.

Baur, D. G., & Hoang, L. T. (2021). A crypto safe haven against Bitcoin. *Finance Research Letters*, *38*, 101431. doi:10.1016/j.frl.2020.101431

Becker, L. T., & Gould, E. M. (2019). Microsoft Power BI: Extending excel to manipulate, analyze, and visualize diverse data. *Serials Review*, *45*(3), 184–188. doi:10.1080/00987913.2019.1644891

Beck, R. (2018). Beyond bitcoin: The rise of blockchain world. *Computer*, *51*(2), 54–58. doi:10.1109/MC.2018.1451660

Bedwell, W. L., Wildman, J. L., DiazGranados, D., Salazar, M., Kramer, W. S., & Salas, E. (2012). Collaboration at work: An integrative multilevel conceptualization. *Construct Clarity in Human Resource Management Research*, *222*(2), 128–145. doi:10.1016/j.hrmr.2011.11.007

Benchimol, J., & Fourçans, A. (2019). *Central Bank Losses and Monetary Policy Rules: A DSGE Investigation*. Social Science Research Network. SSRN Scholarly Paper.

Benedictow, A., & Roger, H. (2020). A ðnancial accelerator in the business sector of a macro-econometric model of a small open economy. *Economic Systems*, *44*(1), 100731. doi:10.1016/j.ecosys.2019.100731

Berisha Qehaja, A., Kutllovci, E., & Shiroka Pula, J. (2017). Strategic management tools and techniques: A comparative analysis of empirical studies. *Croatian Economic Survey*, *19*(1), 67–99. doi:10.15179/ces.19.1.3

Bernanke & Gertler. (1989). Agency Costs, Net Worth, and Business Fluctuations. *The American Economic Review, 79*(1), 14-31.

Bernanke, Gertler, & Gilchrist. (1999). The financial accelerator in a quantitative business cycle framework. In Handbook of Macroeconomics. Elsevier.

Bfsi, E. T. (2020, March 17). *Yes Bank crisis: Ten lessons to prevent bank failures in future.* https://bfsi.economictimes.indiatimes.com/news/banking/yes-bank-crisis-ten-lessons-to-prevent-bank-failures-in-future/74668041

Bhalla, S. S. (2011). Euro and the Yuan: Different peas in the same pod. *Comparative Economic Studies, 53*(3), 355–381. doi:10.1057/ces.2011.20

Bhattacharyya, S., Jha, S., Tharakunnel, K., & Westland, J. C. (2011). Data mining for credit card fraud: A comparative study. *Decision Support Systems, 50*(3), 602–613. doi:10.1016/j.dss.2010.08.008

Bhaumik, S. K., & Mukherjee, P. (2020). The Indian Banking Industry: a commentary. In P. Banerjee & F. J. Richter (Eds.), *Economic Institutions in India: Sustainability under Liberalization and Globalization. Palgrave Macmillan.*

Blanco, V., Guisande, M. A., Sánchez, M. T., Otero, P., & Vázquez, F. L. (2019). Spanish validation of the 10-item Connor–Davidson Resilience Scale (CD-RISC 10) with non-professional caregivers. *Aging & Mental Health, 23*(2), 183–188. doi:10.1080/13607863.2017.1399340 PMID:29116825

Boivin, J., Kiley, M. T., & Mishkin, F. S. (2010). *How Has the Monetary Transmission Mechanism Evolved Over Time?* Social Science Research Network. SSRN Scholarly Paper. doi:10.3386/w15879

Borio, C., & Zhu, H. (2012). Capital regulation, risk-taking, and monetary policy: A missing link in the transmission mechanism? *Journal of Financial Stability, 8*(4), 236–251. doi:10.1016/j.jfs.2011.12.003

Bowen, D. E., & Hallowell, R. (2002). Suppose we took service seriously? An introduction to the special issue. *The Academy of Management Executive, 16*(4), 69–72. doi:10.5465/ame.2002.8951329

Bradshaw, A. (2012). *Putting Value Alignment to Work to Drive Positive Organizational Outcomes.* DeGarmo Group.

Branicki, L. J., Sullivan-Taylor, B., & Livschitz, S. R. (2018). How entrepreneurial resilience generates resilient SMEs. *International Journal of Entrepreneurial Behaviour & Research, 24*(7), 1244–1263. doi:10.1108/IJEBR-11-2016-0396

Brázdik & Marsal. (2011). *Survey of research on financial sector modeling within DSGE models: what central banks can learn from it.* Available at SSRN 2274689.

Brazdik, F., Hlavacek, M., & Maršál, A. (2012). Survey of research on financial sector modeling within DSGE models: What central banks can learn from it. Finance a Uver - *Czech. Journal of Economics and Finance, 62,* 252–277.

Bullough, A., Renko, M., & Myatt, T. (2014). Danger zone entrepreneurs: The importance of resilience and self-efficacy for entrepreneurial intentions. *Entrepreneurship Theory and Practice, 38*(3), 473–499. doi:10.1111/etap.12006

Burgstahler, D. C., Elliott, W. B., & Hanlon, M. (2002). *How Firms Avoid Losses: Evidence of Use of the Net Deferred Tax Asset Account.* Academic Press.

Busacca, L. A., Beebe, R. S., & Toman, S. M. (2011). Life and Work Values of Counselor Trainees: A National Survey. *The Career Development Quarterly, 59*(1), 2–18. doi:10.1002/j.2161-0045.2010. tb00126.x

Busch, T. (2011). Organizational adaptation to disruptions in the natural environment: The case of climate change. *Scandinavian Journal of Management, 27*(4), 389–404. doi:10.1016/j. scaman.2010.12.010

Business Architecture Guild. (2018). *The business architecture quick guide: A brief guide for gamechangers.* Meghan-Kiffer Press.

Business Standard. (2020). *YES Bank crisis: RBI's Moratorium on lender to be lifted on March 18.* https://www.business-standard.com/article/finance/yes-bank-crisis-rbi-s-moratorium-on-lender-to-be-lifted-on-march-18-120031400188_1.html

Business Standard. (2020, March 5). *What is yes bank crisis?* https://www.business-standard. com/about/what-is-yes-bank-crisis

Business Today. (2020). *YES Bank crisis: How SBI executed a perfect 'rescue plan'.* https:// www.businesstoday.in/sectors/banks/yes-bank-crisis-how-sbi-executed-a-perfect-rescue-plan/ story/397777.html(March, 9)

Calantone, R. J., Cavusgil, S. T., & Zhao, Y. (2002). Learning orientation, firm innovation capability, and firm performance. *International Journal of Research in Marketing, 31*(6), 515–524.

Calvo, G. A. (1983). Staggered prices in a utility-maximizing framework. *Journal of Monetary Economics, 12*(3), 383–398. doi:10.1016/0304-3932(83)90060-0

Cannon-Bowers, J. A., & Salas, E. (2001). Reflections on shared cognition. *Journal of Organizational Behavior, 22*(2), 195–202. doi:10.1002/job.82

Carlsten, M., Kalodner, H., Weinberg, S. M., & Narayanan, A. (2016, October). On the instability of bitcoin without the block reward. In *Proceedings of the 2016 ACM SIGSAC Conference on Computer and Communications Security* (pp. 154-167). 10.1145/2976749.2978408

Carlstrom, C. T., Fuerst, T. S., & Paustian, M. (2009). Inflation Persistence, Monetary Policy, and the Great Moderation. *Journal of Money, Credit and Banking, 41*(4), 767–786. doi:10.1111/ j.1538-4616.2009.00231.x

Cavalcante, L. R. (2020). Abrangência geográfica das políticas de desenvolvimento regional no Brasil. *Revista Brasileira de Gestão e Desenvolvimento Regional, 16*(2), 407–420.

Cellini, R., & Cuccia, T. (2019). Do behaviours in cultural markets affect economic resilience? An analysis of Italian regions. *European Planning Studies, 27*(4), 784–801. doi:10.1080/0965 4313.2019.1568397

Cermak, V. (2017). Can bitcoin become a viable alternative to fiat currencies? An empirical analysis of bitcoin's volatility based on a GARCH model. *An Empirical Analysis of Bitcoin's Volatility Based on a GARCH Model.*

Céspedes, L. F., Chang, R., & Velascode, A. (2017). Financial intermediation, real exchange rates, and unconventional policies in an open economy. *Journal of International Economics, 108*(1), 76–86. doi:10.1016/j.jinteco.2016.12.012

Chaim, P., & Laurini, M. P. (2019). Is Bitcoin a bubble? *Physica A, 517,* 222–232. doi:10.1016/j.physa.2018.11.031

Chakraborty, B. (2020, March 20). *Yes Bank crisis and lessons for the Indian Banking industry.* https://www.linkedin.com/pulse/yes-bank-crisis-lessons-indian-banking-industry-biplab-chakraborty/

Cheah, E. T., & Fry, J. (2015). Speculative bubbles in Bitcoin markets? An empirical investigation into the fundamental value of Bitcoin. *Economics Letters, 130,* 32–36. doi:10.1016/j.econlet.2015.02.029

Chen, Y. L., Kuo, M. H., Wu, S. Y., & Tang, K. (2009). Discovering recency, frequency, and monetary (RFM) sequential patterns from customers' purchasing data. *Electronic Commerce Research and Applications, 8*(5), 241–251. doi:10.1016/j.elerap.2009.03.002

Chouhan, V. (2016). Investigating Factors Affecting Electronic Word-of-Mouth. In Capturing, Analyzing, and Managing Word-of-Mouth in the Digital Marketplace (pp. 119-135). IGI Global. doi:10.4018/978-1-4666-9449-1.ch007

Chouhan, V., Chandra, B., Saraswat, P., & Goswami, S. (2020b). *Developing sustainable accounting framework for cement industry: evidence from India.* Finance India.

Chouhan, V., Sharma, R. B., & Goswami, S. (2020a). Factor Affecting Audit Quality: A study of the companies listed in Bombay Stock Exchange (BSE). *International Journal of Management, 11*(7), 989–999.

Chouhan, V., Sharma, R. B., Goswami, S., & Hashed, A. W. A. (2021a). Measuring challenges in adoption of sustainable environmental technologies in Indian cement industry. *Accounting, 7*(2), 339–348. doi:10.5267/j.ac.2020.11.019

Chouhan, V., Sharma, R. B., Goswami, S., & Hashed, A. W. A. (2021b). Stainable reporting: A case study of selected cement companies of India. *Accounting, 7*(1), 151–160. doi:10.5267/j.ac.2020.10.002

Chouhan, V., Vasita, M. L., & Goswami, S. (2020c). The Impact And Role Of Social Media For Consciousness of COVID-19 pandemic, Journal of Content. *Community and Communication, 12*(1), 250–262.

Christensen, I., & Dib, A. (2008). The financial accelerator in an Estimated New Keynesian model. *Review of Economic Dynamics, 11*(1), 155–178. doi:10.1016/j.red.2007.04.006

Chu, J., Chan, S., Nadarajah, S., & Osterrieder, J. (2017). GARCH modelling of cryptocurrencies. *Journal of Risk and Financial Management*, *10*(4), 17. doi:10.3390/jrfm10040017

Claus, I., & Krippner, L. (2019). Contemporary Topics in Finance: A Collection of Literature Surveys. Wiley. *Business Economics (Cleveland, Ohio).*

Cloudera. (n.d.). *Nissan | Customer Success | Cloudera*. Retrieved 28 January 2021, from https://www.cloudera.com/about/customers/nissan.html

Cohen, D. G., & Nair, S. (2017). Measuring the Middle: The Use of Social Network Analysis in Middle Management Research. In S. W. Floyd (Ed.), *Middle Management Strategy Process Research*. Edward Elgar Publishing Ltd. doi:10.4337/9781783473250.00024

Cohen, J. (1992). Statistical power analysis. *Current Directions in Psychological Science*, *1*(3), 98–101. doi:10.1111/1467-8721.ep10768783

Colley, R., Rue, J., Valencia, A., & Volkan, A. (2007). Deferred Taxes in the Context of the Unit Problem. *Journal of Finance and Accountancy.*

Commercial Banks in India: Growth, Challenges and Strategies/Benson Kunjukunju. (2008). New Century Pub.

Connor, K. M., & Davidson, J. R. T. (2003). Development of a new Resilience scale: The Connor-Davidson Resilience scale (CD-RISC). *Depression and Anxiety*, *18*(2), 76–82. doi:10.1002/da.10113 PMID:12964174

Continuous Integration. (2021, March 3). Retrieved from /https://www.agilealliance.org/glossary/continuous-integration/

Contributor, M. (2020, March 16). *Lessons from the Yes Bank saga: Eternal vigilance is the price of financial stability*. Moneycontrol. https://www.moneycontrol.com/news/business/markets/lessons-from-the-yes-bank-saga-eternal-vigilance-is-the-price-of-financial-stability-5034861.html

Copeland, L., Edberg, D., Panorska, A. K., & Wendel, J. (2012). Applying business intelligence concepts to Medicaid claim fraud detection. *Journal of Information Systems Applied Research*, *5*(1), 1–14.

Corbet, S., Lucey, B., Peat, M., & Vigne, S. (2018). Bitcoin futures—What use are they? *Economics Letters*, *172*, 23–27. doi:10.1016/j.econlet.2018.07.031

Cordon-Pozo, E., Garcia-Morales, V. J., & Aragon-Correa, J. A. (2006). Inter-departmental collaboration and new product development success: A study on the collaboration between marketing and R&D in Spanish high-technology firms. *International Journal of Technology Management*, *35*(1–4), 52–79. doi:10.1504/IJTM.2006.009229

Corner, P. D., Singh, S., & Pavlovich, K. (2017). Entrepreneurial resilience and venture failure. *International Small Business Journal: Researching Entrepreneurship*, *35*(6), 687–708. doi:10.1177/0266242616685604

Cox, Ingersoll, & Ross. (1985). A Theory of the Term Structure of Interest Rates. *Econometrica*, *53*(2), 385–407. doi:10.2307/1911242

Cox, J. C., Ross, S. A., & Rubinstein, M. (1979). Option pricing: A simplified approach. *Journal of Financial Economics*, *7*(3), 229–263. doi:10.1016/0304-405X(79)90015-1

Crabtree, A., & Maher, J. J. (2009). The Influence of Differences in Taxable Income and Book Income on the Bond Credit Market. *The Journal of the American Taxation Association*, *31*(1), 75–99. doi:10.2308/jata.2009.31.1.75

Criddle, C. (2021). *Bitcoin consumes 'more electricity than Argentina'*. Retrieved 1 May 2021, from https://www.bbc.co.uk/news/technology-56012952

Cross, R. L., Singer, J., Colella, S., Thomas, R. J., & Silverstone, Y. (2010). *The Organizational Network Fieldbook: Best Practices, Techniques and Exercises to Drive Organizational Innovation and Performance*. Jossey-Bass.

Cross, R., Borgatti, S. P., & Parker, A. (2002). Making Invisible Work Visible: Using Social Network Analysis to Support Strategic Collaboration. *California Management Review*, *44*(2), 25–46. doi:10.2307/41166121

Cross, R., Kase, R., Kilduff, M., & King, Z. (2013). Bridging the Gap between Research and Practice in Organizational Network Analysis: A Conversation between Rob Cross and Martin Kilduff. *Human Resource Management*, *52*(4), 627–644. doi:10.1002/hrm.21545

Cuijpers, M., Guenter, H., & Hussinger, K. (2011). Costs and Benefits of Inter-Departmental Innovation Collaboratio. *Research Policy*, *40*(4), 565–575. doi:10.1016/j.respol.2010.12.004

Cunningham, J., & Mcguire, D. (2019). Business support and training in minority-ethnic, family-run firms: The case of SMEs in Scotland. *Human Resource Development International*, *22*(5), 526–552. doi:10.1080/13678868.2019.1608124

Cúrdia, V., & Woodford, M. (2010). Credit Spreads and Monetary Policy. *Journal of Money, Credit and Banking*, *42*(s1), 3–35. doi:10.1111/j.1538-4616.2010.00328.x

Dadhich, M., Chouhan, V., & Adholiya, A. (2019). Stochastic Pattern of Major Indices of Bombay Stock Exchange. *International Journal of Recent Technology and Engineering Regular Issue*, *8*(3), 6774–6779. doi:10.35940/ijrte.C6068.098319

Dattagupta, I. (2020, March 12). *Decoding the Rescue Plan for Yes Bank*. https://www.ndtv.com/opinion/decoding-the-rescue-plan-for-yes-bank-2193266

Davenport, T. H., & Dyché, J. (2013). Big data in big companies. *International Institute for Analytics*, *3*, 1–31.

De Vries, T. (2018). *Market Consistent Valuation of Deferred Taxes* (MSc thesis). Technical University Delft.

De Walque, G., Pierrard, O., & Rouabah, A. (2010). Financial (in) stability, supervision and liquidity injections: A dynamic general equilibrium approach. *Economic Journal (London)*, *120*(549), 1234–1261. doi:10.1111/j.1468-0297.2010.02383.x

Deb, R. (2021). YES Bank fiasco: A corporate governance failure. *Decision (Washington, D.C.)*, 1–10.

Deloitte Insights. (2018). *2018 Global Human Capital Trends report*. Author.

Deloitte. (2016). *Organizational Network Analysis Gain insight, drive smart*. Author.

Dempsey, J. (2009). Nurses values, attitudes and behavior related to falls prevention. *Journal of Clinical Nursing*, *18*(6), 838–848. doi:10.1111/j.1365-2702.2008.02687.x PMID:19239663

Dervitsiotis, K. (2003). The pursuit of sustainable business excellence: Guiding transformation for effective organizational change. *Total Quality Management & Business Excellence*, *14*(3), 251–267. doi:10.1080/1478336032000046599

Devi, P., Kumar, P., Singh, R., & Kumar, S. (2021). Multifractal detrended fluctuation analysis approach to study period of crisis of YES bank. *Nonlinear Studies*, *28*(1).

Dezyre. (2021). *How Uber uses data science to reinvent transportation?* Retrieved 28 February 2021, from https://www.dezyre.com/article/how-uber-uses-data-science-to-reinvent-transportation/290

Dhruv Rathee. (2020). *Yes Bank Crisis | Explained by Dhruv Rathee* [Video]. https://youtu.be/NagvYDGL76s

Di Lauro, S., Tursunbayeva, A., Antonelli, G., & Martinez, M. (2018). Measuring organizational identity via LinkedIn: The role played by employees' tenure, type of employment contract and age. *Studi Organizzativi*, *2*, 114–129.

Diadiushkin, A., Sandkuhl, K., & Maiatin, A. (2019). Fraud Detection in Payments Transactions: Overview of Existing Approaches and Usage for Instant Payments. *Complex Systems Informatics and Modeling Quarterly*, (20), 72–88. doi:10.7250/csimq.2019-20.04

Diamond, M., & Mattia, A. (2017). Data visualization: An exploratory study into the software tools used by businesses. *Journal of Instructional Pedagogies, 18*.

Diamond, D. W., & Dybvig, P. H. (1983). Bank Runs, Deposit Insurance, and Liquidity. *Journal of Political Economy*, *91*(3), 401–419. doi:10.1086/261155

Drehmann, M. (2010). Countercyclical Capital Buffers: Exploring Options. *SSRN Electronic Journal*. https://www.ssrn.com/abstract=1648946

Duchek, S. (2018). Entrepreneurial resilience: A biographical analysis of successful entrepreneurs. *The International Entrepreneurship and Management Journal*, *14*(2), 429–455. doi:10.100711365-017-0467-2

Dukeov, I., Bergman, J. P., Heilmann, P., & Nasledov, A. (2020). Impact of a firm's commitment to learning and open-mindedness on its organizational innovation among Russian manufacturing firms. *Baltic Journal of Management*, 15(4), 551–569. doi:10.1108/BJM-04-2019-0128

Duncan, A., & Nolan, C. (2018). Financial Frictions in Macroeconomic Models. In *Oxford Research Encyclopedia of Economics and Finance*. Oxford University Press. doi:10.1093/acrefore/9780190625979.013.168

Dutta, P. K. (2020, March 9). Rapid rise and free fall of Yes Bank in 10 years after co-founder died in 26/11 attack. *India Today*. https://www.indiatoday.in/news-analysis/story/yes-bank-rana-kapoor-1653955-2020-03-09

Dziobek, C., & Pazarbasioglu, C. (1998). Lessons from Systemic Bank Restructuring. Economic Issues No. 14, International Monetary Fund.

Economic Times. (2020). *Rana Kapoor, wife took Rs 307 cr. illegal gratification through bungalow deal: CBI FIR.* https://economictimes.indiatimes.com/news/politics-and-nation/cbi-files-fresh-case-against-yes-bank-founder-rana-kapoor-others/articleshow/74614279.cms?utm_source=contentofinterest&utm_medium=text&utm_campaign=cppst(March, 13)

Edge Analytics. (n.d.). *Edge Analytics Northern Powergrid: Utility Planning | Edge Analytics.* Retrieved 18 March 2020, from https://edgeanalytics.co.uk/northern-powergrid/

Edwards, A. (2011). *Does the Deferred Tax Asset Valuation Allowance Signal Firm Creditworthiness? Working chapter.* University of Toronto.

Ehrmann, M., & Worms, A. (2004). Bank Networks and Monetary Policy Transmission. *Journal of the European Economic Association*, 2(6), 1148–1171. doi:10.1162/1542476042813904

Eichorn, F. L. (2005). *Who owns the data? Using internal customer relationship management to improve business and IT integration.* Tate Publishing.

Eijdenberg, E. L., Thompson, N. A., Verduijn, K., & Essers, C. (2019). Entrepreneurial activities in a developing country: An institutional theory perspective. *International Journal of Entrepreneurial Behaviour & Research*, 25(3), 414–432. doi:10.1108/IJEBR-12-2016-0418

Ermilov, D., Panov, M., & Yanovich, Y. (2017, December). Automatic bitcoin address clustering. In *2017 16th IEEE International Conference on Machine Learning and Applications (ICMLA)* (pp. 461-466). IEEE. 10.1109/ICMLA.2017.0-118

ETBFSI. (2020, March 7). *Is customer really a king? Yes Bank's says "no."* Https://Bfsi.Economictimes.Indiatimes.Com/. https://bfsi.economictimes.indiatimes.com/news/banking/is-customer-really-the-king-yes-banks-feel-no/74514802

Evelson, B., McNabb, K., Karel, R., & Barnett, J. (2007). It's time to reinvent your BI strategy. *Intelligent Enterprise*.

Everest, G. C. (1976). *Basic data structure models explained with a common example. Reprinted from Computing Systems 1976. In Proceedings Fifth Texas Conference on Computing Systems. Austin, TX*: IEEE Computer Society Publications Office. https://www.researchgate.net/profile/Gordon_Everest/publication/291448084_BASIC_DATA_STRUCTURE_MODELS_EXPLAINED_WITH_A_COMMON_EXAMPLE/links/57affb4b08ae95f9d8f1ddc4/BASIC-DATA-STRUCTURE-MODELS-EXPLAINED-WITH-A-COMMON-EXAMPLE.pdf

Eyal, I., & Sirer, E. G. (2014, March). Majority is not enough: Bitcoin mining is vulnerable. In *International conference on financial cryptography and data security* (pp. 436-454). Springer. 10.1007/978-3-662-45472-5_28

Fahr, S., Motto, R., Rostagno, M., Smets, F., & Tristani, O. (2013). A monetary policy strategy in good and bad times: Lessons from the recent past. *Economic Policy*, *28*(74), 243–288. doi:10.1111/1468-0327.12008

Farrokhi, V., & Pokoradi, L. (2012). The necessities for building a model to evaluate Business Intelligence projects-Literature Review. *The International Journal of Computer Science & Engineering Survey*, *3*(2), 1–10. doi:10.5121/ijcses.2012.3201

Feng, C., & Niu, J. (2019, July). Selfish mining in ethereum. In *2019 IEEE 39th International Conference on Distributed Computing Systems (ICDCS)* (pp. 1306-1316). IEEE. 10.1109/ICDCS.2019.00131

Fitzgerald, G. A., & Desjardins, N. M. (2004). Organizational Values and Their Relation to Organizational Performance Outcomes. *Atlantic Journal of Communication*, *12*(3), 121–145. doi:10.120715456889ajc1203_1

Flourish Studio [Computer software]. (2020). Retrieved from https://public.flourish.studio/visualisation/4581015

Foley, É., & Guillemette, M. G. (2010). What is business intelligence? *International Journal of Business Intelligence Research*, *1*(4), 1–28. doi:10.4018/jbir.2010100101

Fornell, C., & Larcker, D. F. (1981). Evaluating Structural Equation Models with Unobservable Variables and Measurement Error. *JMR, Journal of Marketing Research*, *18*(1), 39–50. doi:10.1177/002224378101800104

Foundations for Evidence-Based Policymaking Act of. 2018, H.R. 4174, 115th Cong. (2017). https://www.congress.gov/bill/115th-congress/house-bill/4174

Froot, K. A., Scharfstein, D. S., & Stein, J. C. (1993). Risk management: Coordinating corporate investment and financing policies. *The Journal of Finance*, *48*(5), 1629–1658. doi:10.1111/j.1540-6261.1993.tb05123.x

Gahan, P., & Abeysekera, L. (2009). What shapes an individual's work values? An integrated model of the relationship between work values, national culture and self-construal. *International Journal of Human Resource Management*, *20*(1), 126–147. doi:10.1080/09585190802528524

Gallemore, J. (2011). *Deferred Tax Assets and Bank Regulatory Capital: Working chapter.* University of North Carolina.

Gambacorta & Signoretti. (2013). *Should Monetary Policy Lean against the Wind? An Analysis Based on a DSGE Model with Banking.* Bank of Italy, Economic Research, and International Relations Area.

Gartner. (2021). *Definition of Business Intelligence (BI) Services - Gartner Information Technology Glossary.* Retrieved 19 February 2021, from https://www.gartner.com/en/information-technology/glossary/business-intelligence-bi-services

Gartner. (2021). *Gartner Glossary.* Retrieved 19 February 2021, from https://www.gartner.com/en/information-technology/glossary/bi-platforms

Gbosbal, S., & Kim, S. K. (1986). Building effective intelligence systems for competitive advantage. *Sloan Management Review, 28*(1), 49.

GeorgoulaI.PournarakisD.BilanakosC.SotiropoulosD.GiaglisG. M. (2015). Using time-series and sentiment analysis to detect the determinants of bitcoin prices. *Available at* SSRN 2607167. doi:10.2139srn.2607167

Gertler, M., Kiyotaki, N., & Prestipino, A. (2016). Wholesale Banking and Bank Runs in Macroeconomic Modeling of Financial Crises. In Handbook of Macroeconomics. Elsevier.

Gertler, M., & Karadi, P. (2011). A Model of Unconventional Monetary Policy. *Journal of Monetary Economics, 58*(1), 17–34. doi:10.1016/j.jmoneco.2010.10.004

Gertler, M., & Kiyotaki, N. (2015). Banking, Liquidity, and Bank Runs in an Infinite Horizon Economy. *The American Economic Review, 105*(7), 2011–2043. doi:10.1257/aer.20130665

Giannakis, E., & Bruggeman, A. (2017). Determinants of regional resilience to economic crisis: A European perspective. *European Planning Studies, 25*(8), 1394–1415. doi:10.1080/0965431 3.2017.1319464

Gilchrist & Zakrajšek. (2011). *Credit Spreads and Business Cycle Fluctuations. National Bureau of Economic Research.* Working Paper.

Gladden, M. E. (2015). Cryptocurrency with a conscience: Using artificial intelligence to develop money that advances human ethical values. *Annales. Etyka w życiu gospodarczym, 18*(4).

Glaser, B. G., & Strauss, A. L. (1967). *The Discovery of Grounded Theory: Strategies for Qualitative Research.* Aldine Pub. Co.

Godin, M. (2018). *3 Unbelievable Amazon Success Stories.* Retrieved 3 January 2021, from https://crazylister.com/blog/amazing-amazon-success-stories/

Goodfriend & McCallum. (2007). *Banking and Interest Rates in Monetary Policy Analysis: A Quantitative Exploration.* National Bureau of Economic Research. Working Paper.

Goodkind, A. L., Jones, B. A., & Berrens, R. P. (2020). Cryptodamages: Monetary value estimates of the air pollution and human health impacts of cryptocurrency mining. *Energy Research & Social Science*, *59*(1), 101281. doi:10.1016/j.erss.2019.101281

Gopinath, G. R. (2020, March 10). Beneath the 'Yes mess', some stark truths. *The Hindu.*

Government Performance and Results Act, S. 20, 103rd Cong. (1993). https://www.congress.gov/bill/103rd-congress/senate-bill/20

Green, D. (2018). The role of Organisational Network Analysis in People Analytics. *LinkedIn.* https://www.linkedin.com/pulse/role-organisational-network-analysis-people-analytics-david-green/

Grover, V., Chiang, R. H., Liang, T. P., & Zhang, D. (2018). Creating strategic business value from big data analytics: A research framework. *Journal of Management Information Systems*, *35*(2), 388–423. doi:10.1080/07421222.2018.1451951

Grundy, T. (2006). Rethinking and reinventing Michael Porter's five forces model. *Strategic Change*, *15*(5), 213–229. doi:10.1002/jsc.764

Guerard, J., Wang, Z., & Xu, G. (2019). *Portfolio and Investment Analysis with SAS: Financial Modeling Techniques for Optimization.* SAS Institute.

Guo, T., Bifet, A., & Antulov-Fantulin, N. (2018, November). Bitcoin volatility forecasting with a glimpse into buy and sell orders. In 2018 IEEE international conference on data mining (ICDM) (pp. 989-994). IEEE. doi:10.1109/ICDM.2018.00123

Hair, J. F., Black, W. C., Babin, B. J., Anderson, R. E., & Tatham, R. L. (2009). *Análise multivariada de dados. 6.* Bookman.

Hamel, G., & Välikangas, L. (2003). En busca de la resiliencia. *Harvard Business Review*, *81*(9), 40–52. PMID:12964393

Hammersland, R. (2017). The Financial accelerator and the Real economy: evidence using a data-based procedure of simultaneous structural model design. *Proceedings ITISE 2017*, 1007–1034.

Hammersland, R., & Træe, C. B. (2014). The financial accelerator and the real Economy: A small macro-econometric model for Norway with financial frictions. *Economic Modelling*, *36*, 517–537. doi:10.1016/j.econmod.2013.04.051

Hanid, M., Siriwardena, M., & Koskela, L. (2011, September). What are the significant issues in cost management? In *RICS Construction and Property Conference* (p. 738). Academic Press.

Hanlon, M., & Shevlin, T. (2005). *Bank-Tax Conformity for Corporate Income: An Introduction to the Issues.* Academic Press.

HarveyC. R. (2014). Bitcoin myths and facts. Available at SSRN 2479670.

Hasan, M. M., Popp, J., & Oláh, J. (2020). Current landscape and influence of big data on finance. *Journal of Big Data*, *7*(1), 1–17. doi:10.118640537-020-00291-z

Hawkins, J. (1999). *Bank Restructuring in South-East Asia", included in "Bank Restructuring in Practice*. BIS Policy Papers No. 6, Bank for International Settlements.http://tehelka.com/yes-bank-fiasco-and-genesis-of-trouble-with-banking-system/

Hayes, A. F. (2015). An Index and Test of Linear Moderated Mediation. *Multivariate Behavioral Research, 50*(1), 1–22. doi:10.1080/00273171.2014.962683 PMID:26609740

Helfert, E. A., & Helfert, E. A. (2001). *Financial analysis: tools and techniques: a guide for managers*. McGraw-Hill.

Herbane, B. (2013). Exploring crisis management in uk small- and medium-sized enterprises. *Journal of Contingencies and Crisis Management, 21*(2), 82–95. doi:10.1111/1468-5973.12006

Herbane, B. (2019). Rethinking organizational resilience and strategic renewal in SMEs. *Entrepreneurship and Regional Development, 31*(5–6), 476–495. doi:10.1080/08985626.2018.1541594

Hindle, G. A., & Vidgen, R. (2018). Developing a business analytics methodology: A case study in the foodbank sector. *European Journal of Operational Research, 268*(3), 836–851. doi:10.1016/j.ejor.2017.06.031

Hogan, R., & Huerta, D. (2019). The impact of gender and ethnic diversity on REIT operating performance. *Managerial Finance, 45*(1), 72–84. doi:10.1108/MF-02-2018-0064

Hogg, R. V. (2004). Introduction to mathematical statistics (6th ed.). Upper Saddle River, NJ: Prentice Hall.

Ho, J. K. K. (2014). Formulation of a Systemic PEST analysis for strategic analysis. *European Academic Research, 2*(5), 6478–6492.

Homocianu, D., & Airinei, D. (2014). Business Intelligence facilities with applications in audit and financial reporting. *Financial Audit*.

Iacoviello, M. (2005). House Prices, Borrowing Constraints, and Monetary Policy in the Business Cycle. *The American Economic Review, 95*(3), 739–764. doi:10.1257/0002828054201477

Iacoviello, M., & Minetti, R. (2008). The credit channel of monetary policy: Evidence from the housing market. *Journal of Macroeconomics, 30*(1), 69–96. doi:10.1016/j.jmacro.2006.12.001

IBGE. (n.d.). *Cidades e Estados*. Disponível em: www.ibge.gov.br

IBM. (2013). *IBM helps transform Thames Water using Big Data Analytics in preparation for future growth*. Retrieved 9 January 2021, from https://newsroom.ibm.com/2013-05-16-IBM-helps-transform-Thames-Water-using-Big-Data-Analytics-in-preparation-for-future-growth

India Today. (2020). *Yes Bank crisis: From what happens to my money to will SBI be saviour, all that has happened*. https://www.indiatoday.in/business/story/yes-bank-crisis-rbi-sbi-invest-withdrawal-limit-reason-full-roundup-developments-1653193-2020-03-06

Indian Express Online. (2020, March 6). *What Is Yes Bank Crisis? Is Your Money Safe in Yes Bank?* [Video]. https://youtu.be/agIMUDKnCsM

Irani, R. M., Iyer, R., & Meisenzahl, R. R. (2018). *The Rise of Shadow Banking: Evidence from Capital Regulation.* Finance and Economics Discussion Series Divisions of Research & Statistics and Monetary Affairs Federal Reserve Board.

Işı, K. (2013). Business intelligence success: The roles of BI capabilities and decision environments. *Information & Management*, *50*(1), 13–23. doi:10.1016/j.im.2012.12.001

Isik, O., Jones, M. C., & Sidorova, A. (2011). Business intelligence (BI) success and the role of BI capabilities. *Intelligent Systems in Accounting, Finance & Management*, *18*(4), 161–176. doi:10.1002/isaf.329

Islami, X., Mustafa, N., & Latkovikj, M. T. (2020). Linking Porter's generic strategies to firm performance. *Future Business Journal*, *6*(1), 1–15. doi:10.118643093-020-0009-1

Jain, A. (2017). Big Data for Supply Chain Management: An Insight to the Analytical Aspects of Tableau & Power BI. *International Journal of Scientific Research*, *6*(10), 1–5.

Jang, H., & Lee, J. (2017). An empirical study on modeling and prediction of bitcoin prices with bayesian neural networks based on blockchain information. *IEEE Access: Practical Innovations, Open Solutions*, *6*, 5427–5437. doi:10.1109/ACCESS.2017.2779181

Jaworski, B. J., & Kohli, A. K. (1993). Market Orientation: Antrcendent and Consequances. *Journal of Marketing*, *57*(3), 53–70. doi:10.1177/002224299305700304

Ji, S., Kim, J., & Im, H. (2019). A comparative study of bitcoin price prediction using deep learning. *Mathematics*, *7*(10), 898. doi:10.3390/math7100898

Jourdan, M., Blandin, S., Wynter, L., & Deshpande, P. (2019). A probabilistic model of the bitcoin blockchain. In *Proceedings of the IEEE/CVF Conference on Computer Vision and Pattern Recognition Workshops* (pp. 1-11). 10.1109/CVPRW.2019.00337

Jung, E., Le Tilly, M., Gehani, A., & Ge, Y. (2019, July). Data mining-based ethereum fraud detection. In *2019 IEEE International Conference on Blockchain (Blockchain)* (pp. 266-273). IEEE. 10.1109/Blockchain.2019.00042

Kabanoff, B., Waldersee, R., & Cohen, M. (1995). Espoused Values and Organizational Change Themes. *Academy of Management Journal*, *38*(4), 1075–1104.

Kara, G. I. (2016). *Bank Capital Regulations around the World: What Explains the Differences?* Finance and Economics Discussion Series 2016-057. Washington, DC: Board of Governors of the Federal Reserve System. doi:10.17016/feds.2016.057

Karmelavicius, J., & Ramanauskas, T. (2019). Bank credit and money creation in a DSGE model of a small open economy. *Baltic Journal of Economics*, *19*(2), 296–333. doi:10.1080/140609 9X.2019.1640958

Kaur, G. (2019). *Development of Business Intelligence Outlier and financial crime analytics system for predicting and managing fraud in financial payment services.* Available at: http://www.cs.stir.ac.uk/courses/ITNP097/PastProjects/exemplars/Guneet_Kaur.pdf

Kautish, S. (2008). Online Banking: A Paradigm Shift. *E-Business, 9*(10), 54-59.

Kautish, S. (2008). Online Banking: A Paradigm Shift. *E-Business, 9*(10), 54–59.

Kautish, S. (2008). Online Banking: A Paradigm Shift. E-Business. *ICFAI Publication, Hyderabad, 9*(10), 54–59.

Kautish, S. (2013). Knowledge sharing: A contemporary review of literature in context to information systems designing. *ACADEMICIA: An International Multidisciplinary Research Journal, 3*(1), 101–114.

Kautish, S., & Thapliyal, M. P. (2012). Concept of Decision Support Systems in relation with Knowledge Management–Fundamentals, theories, frameworks and practices. *International Journal of Application or Innovation in Engineering & Management, 1*(2), 9.

Kautish, S., & Thapliyal, M. P. (2013). Design of new architecture for model management systems using knowledge sharing concept. *International Journal of Computers and Applications, 62*(11), 1–25.

Kearns, K. P. (1992). From comparative advantage to damage control: Clarifying strategic issues using SWOT analysis. *Nonprofit Management & Leadership, 3*(1), 3–22. doi:10.1002/nml.4130030103

Kelly, K., & Schaefer, A. (2014). *Creating a Collaborative Organizational Culture.* UNC Executive Development.

Kerzner, H. (2017). *Project management metrics, KPIs, and dashboards: a guide to measuring and monitoring project performance.* John Wiley & Sons. doi:10.1002/9781119427599

Khan, R. A., & Quadri, S. M. K. (2014). Business intelligence: An integrated approach. *International Journal of Management and Innovation, 6*(2), 21.

Khan, S., Chouhan, V., Chandra, B., & Goswami, S. (2014). Sustainable accounting reporting practices of Indian cement industry: An exploratory study. *Uncertain Supply Chain Management, 2*(1), 61–72.

Kidron, A. (1978). Work Values and Organizational Commitment. *Academy of Management Journal, 21*(2), 239–247. PMID:10308606

Kim, D., & Santomero, A. M. (1988). Risk in banking and capital regulation. *The Journal of Finance, 43*(December), 1219–1233. doi:10.1111/j.1540-6261.1988.tb03966.x

Kinderis, M., Bezbradica, M., & Crane, M. (2018). *Bitcoin currency fluctuation.* Academic Press.

Kitchenham, A. (2010). Mixed methods in case study research. In A. J. Mills, G. Durepos, & E. Wiebe (Eds.), *Encyclopedia of case study research* (pp. 562–564). SAGE Publications, Inc.

Kiyotaki, N., & Moore, J. (1997). Credit Cycles. *Journal of Political Economy, 105*(2), 211–248. doi:10.1086/262072

Klein, T., Thu, H. P., & Walther, T. (2018). Bitcoin is not the New Gold–A comparison of volatility, correlation, and portfolio performance. *International Review of Financial Analysis, 59*, 105–116. doi:10.1016/j.irfa.2018.07.010

Kohli, A. K., & Jaworski, B. (1990). J. Market orientation: The construct, research propositions, and managerial implications. *Journal of Marketing, 54*(2), 1–18. doi:10.1177/002224299005400201

Korber, S., & Mcnaughton, R. B. (2018). Resilience and entrepreneurship: A systematic literature review. *International Journal of Entrepreneurial Behaviour & Research, 24*(7), 1129–1154. doi:10.1108/IJEBR-10-2016-0356

Kotter, J. P. (2012). *Leading change.* Harvard Business Review Press.

Kristof-Brown, A. L., Zimmerman, R. D., & Johnson, E. C. (2005). Consequences of individuals' fit at work: A meta-analysis of person–job, person–organization, person–group, and person–supervisor fit. *Personnel Psychology, 58*(2), 281–342. doi:10.1111/j.1744-6570.2005.00672.x

Krylov, S. (2015). Applied strategic financial analysis within strategic management of organization finance. *European Journal of Business and Management, 7*(15), 1–16.

Kudyba, S. (2014). *Big data, mining, and analytics: components of strategic decision making.* CRC Press. doi:10.1201/b16666

Kunc, M. (2018). *Strategic analytics: integrating management science and strategy.* John Wiley & Sons. doi:10.1002/9781119519638

Lauridsen, L. S., Willert, M. V., Eskildsen, A., & Christiansen, D. H. (2017). Cross-cultural adaptation and validation of the Danish 10-item Connor-Davidson Resilience Scale among hospital staff. *Scandinavian Journal of Public Health, 45*(6), 654–657. doi:10.1177/1403494817721056 PMID:28707513

Laux, R. C. (2013). *The Association between Deferred Tax Assets and Liabilities and Future Tax Payments. SSRN.* Electronic Journal.

Lee, N., Sameen, H., & Cowling, M. (2015). Access to finance for innovative SMEs since the financial crisis. *Research Policy, 44*(2), 370–380. doi:10.1016/j.respol.2014.09.008

Lee, T.-S., & Tsai, H.-J. (2005). The effects of business operation mode on market orientation, learning orientation and innovativeness. *Industrial Management & Data Systems, 105*(3), 325–348. doi:10.1108/02635570510590147

Levenson, A. (2015). *Strategic analytics: Advancing strategy execution and organizational effectiveness.* Berrett-Koehler Publishers.

Liebau, D., & Schueffel, P. (2019). Cryptocurrencies & initial coin offerings: Are they scams?-an empirical study. *The Journal of The British Blockchain Association, 2*(1), 7749. doi:10.31585/jbba-2-1-(5)2019

Liu, Y., Li, R., Liu, X., Wang, J., Zhang, L., Tang, C., & Kang, H. (2017, October). An efficient method to enhance Bitcoin wallet security. In *2017 11th IEEE International Conference on Anti-counterfeiting, Security, and Identification (ASID)* (pp. 26-29). IEEE. 10.1109/ICASID.2017.8285737

Liu, Z. (2010). Strategic financial management in small and medium-sized enterprises. *International Journal of Business and Management, 5*(2), 132. doi:10.5539/ijbm.v5n2p132

Li, W., Cao, M., Wang, Y., Tang, C., & Lin, F. (2020). Mining pool game model and Nash equilibrium analysis for PoW-based blockchain networks. *IEEE Access: Practical Innovations, Open Solutions, 8*, 101049–101060. doi:10.1109/ACCESS.2020.2997996

Lucas, H. C. Jr, & Goh, J. M. (2009). Disruptive technology: How Kodak missed the digital photography revolution. *The Journal of Strategic Information Systems, 18*(1), 46–55. doi:10.1016/j.jsis.2009.01.002

Lukić, Z. (2017). The art of company financial modelling. *Croatian Operational Research Review, 8*(2), 409–427. doi:10.17535/crorr.2017.0026

Maina, E. M., Chouhan, V., & Goswami, S. (2020). Measuring Behavioral Aspect of IFRS Implementation in India And Kenya. *International Journal of Scientific & Technology Research, 9*(1), 2045–2048.

Malliaris, A. G. (2020). *Asset Price Bubbles and Central Bank Policies: The Crash of the 'Jackson Hole Consensus.* Oxford University Press.

Maney, K. (2003). *The maverick and his machine: Thomas Watson, Sr. and the making of IBM.* John Wiley & Sons.

Marius, G., Aref, M., & Bilal, H. (2009). Real time online analytical processing for business intelligence. *UPB Scientific Bulletin, Series C. Electrical Engineering, 71*(3), 79–88.

Market, C. (2020, October 23). *Yes Bank posts Q2 PAT at Rs 129 crores; NII falls 9.7% YoY.* Business Standard. https://www.business-standard.com/article/news-cm/yes-bank-posts-q2-pat-at-rs-129-cr-nii-falls-9-7-yoy-120102301164_1.html

Marôco, J. (2010). *Análise de Equações Estruturais: Fundamentos teóricos, Software & Aplicações.* ReportNumber.

Mazzocchi, M. (2008). *Statistics for Employee Values.* Sage.

McCunn, P. (1998). The balanced scorecard…the eleventh commandment. *Management Accounting, 76*(11), 34–36.

McDonald, P., & Gandz, J. (1991). Identification of values relevant to business research. *Human Resource Management*, *30*(2), 217–236. doi:10.1002/hrm.3930300205

Meglino, B. M., Ravlin, E. C., & Adkins, C. L. (1989). A work values approach to corporate culture: A field test of the value congruence process and its relationship to individual outcomes. *The Journal of Applied Psychology*, *74*(3), 424–432. doi:10.1037/0021-9010.74.3.424

Melnyk, S. A., Stewart, D. M., & Swink, M. (2004). Metrics and performance measurement in operations management: Dealing with the metrics maze. *Journal of Operations Management*, *22*(3), 209–217. doi:10.1016/j.jom.2004.01.004

Meynkhard, A. (2019). Fair market value of bitcoin: Halving effect. *Investment Management and Financial Innovations*, *16*(4), 72–85. doi:10.21511/imfi.16(4).2019.07

Mierau, J. O., & Mink, M. (2018). A Descriptive Model of Banking and Aggregate Demand. *De Economist*, *166*(2), 207–237. doi:10.100710645-018-9320-4

Mikhaylov, A. (2020). Cryptocurrency Market Analysis from the Open Innovation Perspective. *Journal of Open Innovation*, *6*(4), 197. doi:10.3390/joitmc6040197

Mint2Save. (2020, April 7). *Yes Bank: Collapse Full Case Study | Are banks Safe in India?* [Blog Post]. https://www.mint2save.com/yes-bank-collapse-full-case-study-are-banks-safe-in-india/

Miroljub, L., & Labus, M. (2019). Monetary Transmission Channels in DSGE Models: Decomposition of Impulse Response Functions Approach. *Computational Economics*, *53*(1), 27–50. doi:10.100710614-017-9717-1

Mishkin, F. S. (1996). *The Channels of Monetary Transmission: Lessons for Monetary Policy*. National Bureau of Economic Research. Working Paper.

Mishkin, F. S. (1995). Symposium on the Monetary Transmission Mechanism. *The Journal of Economic Perspectives*, *9*(4), 3–10. doi:10.1257/jep.9.4.3

Misra, U. (2020, March 10). *Explained: How Yes Bank ran into crisis*. The Indian Express. https://indianexpress.com/article/explained/how-yes-bank-ran-into-crisis-rana-kapoor-arrest-6307314/

Modigliani, F., & Miller, M. H. (1958). The Cost of Capital, Corporation Finance and the Theory of Investment. *The American Economic Review*, *48*(3), 261–297.

Monamo, P. M., Marivate, V., & Twala, B. (2016, December). A multifaceted approach to Bitcoin fraud detection: Global and local outliers. In *2016 15th IEEE International Conference on Machine Learning and Applications (ICMLA)* (pp. 188-194). IEEE.

Moodys Research Report. (2015). https://www.moodys.com/research/Moodys-Reliance-on-global-banks-deferred-tax-assets-poses-potential--PR_340219

Morabito, V. (2015). Big data and analytics for competitive advantage. In *Big Data and Analytics* (pp. 3–22). Springer. doi:10.1007/978-3-319-10665-6_1

Moshirian, F. (2007). Global financial services and a global single currency. *Journal of Banking & Finance, 31*(1), 3–9. doi:10.1016/j.jbankfin.2006.07.001

Muhammad, G., Ibrahim, J., Bhatti, Z., & Waqas, A. (2014). Business intelligence as a knowledge management tool in providing financial consultancy services. *American Journal of Information Systems, 2*(2), 26–32.

Nair, V. (2020). *Virus Spread, Yes Bank Crisis Raise Risks For Private Banks*. Bloomberg. https://www.bloombergquint.com/business/virus-spread-yes-bank-crisis-raise-risks-for-private-banks

Nair, V. R. (2015). Customer Acquisition and Retention Strategies in Financial Services. *Journal of Indian Management, 1*(1), 21–25.

Nazier, M. M., Khedr, A., & Haggag, M. (2013). Business Intelligence and its role to enhance Corporate Performance Management. *International Journal of Management & Information Technology, 3*(3), 8–15. doi:10.24297/ijmit.v3i3.1745

Neeley, T. (2017). How to Successfully Work Across Countries, Languages, and Cultures. *Harvard Business Review*.

Nelson, P. (2019). *Six Big Data Use Cases for Modern Business | Accenture*. Retrieved 11 January 2021, from https://www.accenture.com/us-en/blogs/search-and-content-analytics-blog/big-data-use-cases-business

Nybakk, E. (2018). *SAS® Credit Scoring for Banking – An Integrated Solution from Data Capture to Insight*. Capgemini. Retrieved from https://www.sas.com/content/dam/SAS/support/en/sas-global-forum-proceedings/2018/2751-2018.pdf

O'Brien, A. D., & Stone, D. N. (2020). Yes, You Can Import, Analyze, and Create Dashboards and Storyboards in Tableau! The GBI Case. *Journal of Emerging Technologies in Accounting, 17*(1), 21–31. doi:10.2308/jeta-52760

O'Brien, F. A., & Dyson, R. G. (2007). *Supporting strategy: Frameworks, methods and models*. John Wiley & Sons.

Olszak, C. M. (2016). Toward better understanding and use of Business Intelligence in organizations. *Information Systems Management, 33*(2), 105–123. doi:10.1080/10580530.2016.1155946

Orphanides, A., & Williams, J. (2007). Robust monetary policy with imperfect knowledge. *Journal of Monetary Economics, 54*(5), 1406–1435. doi:10.1016/j.jmoneco.2007.06.005

Özemre, M., & Kabadurmus, O. (2020). A big data analytics based methodology for strategic decision making. *Journal of Enterprise Information Management*.

P.K.D. (2020a, March 9). *Rapid rise and free fall of Yes Bank in 10 years after co-founder died in 26/11 attack*. India Today. https://www.indiatoday.in/news-analysis/story/yes-bank-rana-kapoor-1653955-2020-03-09

P.S.P. (2020b, July). A Study on Yes Bank Crisis. *IOSR Journal of Business and Management*, 36–45. doi:10.9790/487X-2207073645

Pandey, A., Guha, R., Malkar, N., & Pandey, N. (2019). Marching Towards Creating Shared Value: The Case of YES Bank. *Asian Case Research Journal*, *23*(02), 289–312.

Peng, Y., Albuquerque, P. H. M., de Sá, J. M. C., Padula, A. J. A., & Montenegro, M. R. (2018). The best of two worlds: Forecasting high frequency volatility for cryptocurrencies and traditional currencies with Support Vector Regression. *Expert Systems with Applications*, *97*, 177–192. doi:10.1016/j.eswa.2017.12.004

Pérez-López, M. C., González-López, M. J., & Rodríguez-Ariza, L. (2016). Competencies for entrepreneurship as a career option in a challenging employment environment. *Career Development International*, *21*(3), 214–229. doi:10.1108/CDI-07-2015-0102

Petty, R. (2007). *Nissan: Success Story of a Dramatic Turnaround*. Retrieved 16 January 2021, from https://www.capgemini.com/fr-fr/ressources/nissan-success-story-of-a-dramatic-turnaround/

Phan, L., Li, S., & Mentzer, K. (2019). Blockchain technology and the current discussion on fraud. *Computer Information Systems Journal Articles*.

Pokharel, B. (2011). Customer relationship management: Related theories, challenges and application in banking sector. *Banking Journal*, *1*(1), 19–28. doi:10.3126/bj.v1i1.5140

Pombarla, P. (2020, July 21). A Study on Yes Bank Crisis. *IOSR Journal of Business and Management (IOSR-JBM)*, *22*(7), 1–10. https://www.iosrjournals.org/iosr-jbm/papers/Vol22-issue7/Series-7/E2207073645.pdf

Portal da Indústria. (n.d.). *Perfil da indústria nos estados*. Disponível em: www.portaldaindustria.com.br

Porter, M. E., & Advantage, C. (1985). Creating and sustaining superior performance. *Competitive Advantage*, *167*, 167-206.

Poterba, J. M., Rao, N. S., & Seidman, J. K. (2011). Deferred tax positions and incentives for corporate behavior around corporate tax changes. *National Tax Journal*, *64*(1), 27–57. doi:10.17310/ntj.2011.1.02

Powell, B. (2018). *Mastering Microsoft Power BI: expert techniques for effective data analytics and business intelligence*. Packt Publishing Ltd.

Powell, T. C. (1995). Total quality management as competitive advantage: A review and empirical study. *Strategic Management Journal*, *16*(1), 15–37. doi:10.1002mj.4250160105

Preacher, K. J., & Hayes, A. F. (2004). SPSS and SAS procedures for estimating indirect effects in simple mediation models. *Behavior Research Methods, Instruments, & Computers*, *36*(4), 717–731. doi:10.3758/BF03206553 PMID:15641418

Preacher, K. J., Rucker, D. D., & Hayes, A. F. (2007). Addressing moderated mediation hypotheses: Theory, methods, and prescriptions. *Multivariate Behavioral Research*, *42*(1), 185–227. doi:10.1080/00273170701341316 PMID:26821081

Priest, D., & Hull, A. (2007, February 18). Soldiers face neglect, frustration at Army's top medical facility. *Washington Post*. https://www.washingtonpost.com/archive/politics/2007/02/18/soldiers-face-neglect-frustration-at-armys-top-medical-facility/c0c4b3e4-fb22-4df6-9ac9-c602d41c5bda/

Pröllochs, N., & Feuerriegel, S. (2020). Business analytics for strategic management: Identifying and assessing corporate challenges via topic modeling. *Information & Management*, *57*(1), 103070. doi:10.1016/j.im.2018.05.003

Rahman, M., & Mendy, J. (2019). Evaluating people-related resilience and non-resilience barriers of SMEs' internationalisation: A developing country perspective. *The International Journal of Organizational Analysis*, *27*(2), 225–240. doi:10.1108/IJOA-02-2018-1361

Rai, V. (2020). *Lessons from the Yes Bank Saga in India*. ISAS Insights, No. 605. https://www.isas.nus.edu.sg/wp-content/uploads/2020/03/ISAS-Insight-605_Vinod-Rai.pdf

Ramchandani, K., & Jethwani, K. (2021). Yes bank: an untold story. *Emerald Emerging Markets Case Studies*, *11*(1). doi:10.1108/EEMCS-04-2020-0123

Ranjan, J. (2009). Business intelligence: Concepts, components, techniques and benefits. *Journal of Theoretical and Applied Information Technology*, *9*(1), 60–70.

Ranneberg, A. (2016). Bank Leverage Cycles and the External Finance Premium. *Journal of Money, Credit and Banking*, *48*(8), 1569–1612. doi:10.1111/jmcb.12359

Rao, G. K., & Kumar, R. (2011). Framework to integrate business intelligence and knowledge management in the banking industry. *Review of Business and Technology Research*, *4*(1), 1–14.

Rao, M. C., & Rao, K. P. (2009). Inventory turnover ratio as a supply chain performance measure. *Serbian Journal of Management*, *4*(1), 41–50.

Rasmussen, N. H., Goldy, P. S., & Solli, P. O. (2002). *Financial business intelligence: trends, technology, software selection, and implementation*. John Wiley & Sons.

Ray, A. (2021, January 22). *YES Bank Q3 results: Net profit rises to ₹151 crore, NII jumps to ₹2,560 cr. Mint*. https://www.livemint.com/industry/banking/yes-bank-q3-results-net-profit-rises-to-rs-151-crore-11611312884826.html

RBI Annual Report. (2020). *BSE Sensex, March 2020*. Author.

Reilly, D. (2009, Jan. 28). Citi, BofA Show Investors Can't Bank on Capital. *Bloomberg*, p. 1.

Reserve Bank of India. (1998). *Report of the Narasimham Committee on Banking Sector Reforms*. Author.

Richards, G., Yeoh, W., Chong, A. Y. L., & Popovič, A. (2019). Business intelligence effectiveness and corporate performance management: An empirical analysis. *Journal of Computer Information Systems*, *59*(2), 188–196. doi:10.1080/08874417.2017.1334244

Rivard, K., & Cogswell, D. (2004). Are you drowning in BI reports? Using analytical dashboards to cut through the clutter. *Information & Management*, *14*(4), 26.

Rizardi, B. (2020, December 8). Solving complex problems in the public sector. *Apolitical*. https://apolitical.co/en/solution_article/solving-complex-problems-in-the-public-sector

Rocha, S., Bernardino, J., Pedrosa, I., & Ferreira, I. (2017, April). Dashboards and indicators for a BI healthcare system. In *World Conference on Information Systems and Technologies* (pp. 81-90). Springer. 10.1007/978-3-319-56535-4_8

Rodrigues, T. C., Montibeller, G., Oliveira, M. D., & Costa, C. A. B. (2017). Modelling multicriteria value interactions with reasoning maps. *European Journal of Operational Research*, *258*(3), 1054–1071. doi:10.1016/j.ejor.2016.09.047

Ryan, S. (2007). *Financial Instruments and Institutions: Accounting and Disclosure Rules* (2nd ed.). John Wilen & Sons.

Sabry, F., Labda, W., Erbad, A., & Malluhi, Q. (2020). Cryptocurrencies and Artificial Intelligence: Challenges and Opportunities. *IEEE Access: Practical Innovations, Open Solutions*, *8*, 175840–175858. doi:10.1109/ACCESS.2020.3025211

Salisu, I., Hashim, N., Mashi, M. S., & Aliyu, H. G. (2020). Perseverance of effort and consistency of interest for entrepreneurial career success: Does resilience matter? *Journal of Entrepreneurship in Emerging Economies*, *12*(2), 279–304. doi:10.1108/JEEE-02-2019-0025

Sandner, P. G., Gross, J., Schulden, P., & Grale, L. (2020). The Digital Programmable Euro, Libra and CBDC: Implications for European Banks. *Libra and CBDC: Implications for European Banks*.

Sansing, R. C., & Guenther, D. A. (n.d.). *The Valuation Relevance of Reversing Deferred Tax Liabilities*. Academic Press.

Santoro, G., Messeni-Petruzzelli, A., & Del Giudice, M. (2020). Searching for resilience: The impact of employee-level and entrepreneur-level resilience on firm performance in small family firms. *Small Business Economics*, 1–17. doi:10.100711187-020-00319-x

Santos-Vijande, M. L., & Álvarez-González, L. I. (2007). Innovativeness and organizational innovation in total quality oriented firms: The moderating role of market turbulence. *Technovation*, *27*(9), 514–532. doi:10.1016/j.technovation.2007.05.014

Saraswat, P. (2021, Jan.). Elements of Effective Insider Trading Regulations: A Comparative Analysis of India and US. *Niram University Law Journal*.

Saraswat, P. (2012). Forensic accounting: A tool to uncover the Accounting and Financial frauds, Chartered Secretary. *The Journal of Corporate Professional*, *XLII*(3), 281–342.

Saraswat, P., & Banga, J. (2012). Volatility of Sensex with respect of Union Budget of India: A Pragmatic study. *International Journal of Accounting and Financial Management Research*, 2(March), 19–31.

Sarkar, P. (2020). The crisis of yes bank ltd. International journal of multidisciplinary educational research. *Editorial Board*, 9(7), 167–175.

SAS. (2014). *SAS® Financial Crimes Suite*. Retrieved from https://www.sas.com/content/dam/SAS/en_us/doc/productbrief/sas-financial-crimes-suite-106022.pdf

Sayadi, S., Rejeb, S. B., & Choukair, Z. 2019, June. Anomaly detection model over blockchain electronic transactions. In 2019 15th International Wireless Communications & Mobile Computing Conference (IWCMC) (pp. 895-900). IEEE.

Schick, A., Frolick, M., & Ariyachandra, T. (2012). Competing with BI and analytics at monster worldwide. *International Journal of Business Intelligence Research*, 3(3), 29–41. doi:10.4018/jbir.2012070103

Schmidt, G., & Wilhelm, W. E. (2000). Strategic, tactical and operational decisions in multi-national logistics networks: A review and discussion of modelling issues. *International Journal of Production Research*, 38(7), 1501–1523. doi:10.1080/002075400188690

Schularick, M., & Taylor, A. M. (2012). Credit Booms Gone Bust: Monetary Policy, Leverage Cycles, and Financial Crises, 1870-2008. *The American Economic Review*, 102(2), 1029–1061. doi:10.1257/aer.102.2.1029

Scott, B., & McGoldrick, M. (2018). Financial intelligence and financial investigation: Opportunities and challenges. *Journal of Policing. Intelligence and Counter-Terrorism*, 13(3), 301–315. doi:10.1080/18335330.2018.1482563

Seetharaman, A., Saravanan, A. S., Patwa, N., & Mehta, J. (2017). Impact of Bitcoin as a world currency. *Accounting and Finance Research*, 6(2), 230–246. doi:10.5430/afr.v6n2p230

Senge, P. M. (1992). Mental models. Planning Review, 20(2), 4–44.

Senge, P. (2006). *Peter Senge the Fifth Discipline*. Doubleday Currency.

Senthuran, G., & Halgamuge, M. N. (2019). Prediction of Cryptocurrency Market Price Using Deep Learning and Blockchain Information. *Essentials of Blockchain Technology*, 349.

Sergi, F. (n.d.). L'histoire (faussement) naïve des modèles. *DSGE*, 42.

Sharma, R. S., & Djiaw, V. (2011). Realising the strategic impact of business intelligence tools. *Vine*, 41(2), 113–131. doi:10.1108/03055721111134772

Simmerly, R. G. (1987). *Strategic Planning and Leadership in Continuing Education*. Jossey-Bass Publishers.

Sin, E., & Wang, L. (2017, July). Bitcoin price prediction using ensembles of neural networks. In *2017 13th International conference on natural computation, fuzzy systems and knowledge discovery (ICNC-FSKD)* (pp. 666-671). IEEE. 10.1109/FSKD.2017.8393351

Singh, H. (2020, March 6). *Yes Bank Crisis: 5 Key Reasons to Know*. Jagaran Josh. https://www.jagranjosh.com/general-knowledge/reasons-behind-the-yes-bank-crisis-1583503237-1

Singh, T., & Pathak, N. (2020). Yes bank debacle: Whom to blame for investor destruction; securities exchange board of India (SEBI) or reserve bank of India (RBI)? *Journal of Critical Reviews*, *7*(16), 1459–1471. https://www.researchgate.net/publication/343335828_JOURNAL_OF_CRITICAL_REVIEWS_YES_BANK_DEBACLE_WHOM_TO_BLAME_FOR_INVESTOR_DESTRUCTION_SECURITIES_EXCHANGE_BOARD_OF_INDIA_SEBI_OR_RESERVE_BANK_OF_INDIA_RBI

Sinkula, J. M., Baker, W. E., & Noordewier, T. (1997). A framework for market-based organizational learning: Linking values, knowledge, and behavior. *Journal of the Academy of Marketing Science*, *25*(4), 305–318. doi:10.1177/0092070397254003

Skole, D., & Tucker, C. (1993). Tropical deforestation and habitat fragmentation in the Amazon: Satellite data from 1978 to 1988. *Science*, *260*(21), 1905–1910. doi:10.1126cience.260.5116.1905 PMID:17836720

Smales, L. A. (2019). Bitcoin as a safe haven: Is it even worth considering? *Finance Research Letters*, *30*, 385–393. doi:10.1016/j.frl.2018.11.002

Smets, F. (2014). Financial Stability and Monetary Policy: How Closely Interlinked? *International Journal of Central Banking*, *10*(2), 263–300.

Smets, F., & Wouters, R. (2007). Shocks and Frictions in US Business Cycles: A Bayesian DSGE Approach. *The American Economic Review*, *97*(3), 586–606. doi:10.1257/aer.97.3.586

Sriram, R. (2020). *YES Bank crisis: Why government must fix the vulnerabilities in financial system*. Economic Times. https://economictimes.indiatimes.com/ industry/banking/finance/banking/yes-bank-crisis-why-government-must-fix-the-vulnerabilities-in-financial-system/articleshow/74531257.cms?from=mdr

Stackowiak, R., Rayman, J., & Greenwald, R. (2007). *Oracle data warehousing & business intelligence SO*. John Wiley & Sons.

Statista. (2019). *U.S. Amazon Prime subscribers 2019 | Statista*. Retrieved 13 February 2021, from https://www.statista.com/statistics/546894/number-of-amazon-prime-paying-members/

Statista. (2021). *Number of crypto coins 2013-2021 | Statista*. Retrieved 22 March 2021, from https://www.statista.com/statistics/863917/number-crypto-coins-tokens/#:~:text=How%20many%20cryptocurrencies%20are%20there,of%20digital%20coins%20in%202013

Stiglitz, J. E. (2017). *Where Modern Macroeconomics Went Wrong*. National Bureau of Economic Research. Working Paper.

Stratta, G. (2017). *Lo storytelling come strumento per il cambiamento organizzativo: l'esperienza Enel*. Paper presented at the ASSIOA Winter School, Narratives in Organizational Research, Italy.

Svensson, L. E. O. (2016). *Cost-Benefit Analysis of Leaning Against the Wind*. National Bureau of Economic Research. Working Paper.

Tabassum, N., Shafique, S., Konstantopoulou, A., & Arslan, A. (2019). Antecedents of women managers' resilience: Conceptual discussion and implications for HRM. *The International Journal of Organizational Analysis*, *27*(2), 241–268. doi:10.1108/IJOA-07-2018-1476

Tanwar, R. (2013). Porter's generic competitive strategies. *Journal of Business and Management*, *15*(1), 11–17.

Taylor, J. B. (1993). Discretion versus Policy Rules in Practice. *Carnegie-Rochester Conference Series on Public Policy*, *39*, 195–214. doi:10.1016/0167-2231(93)90009-L

TCS. (2014). *Business Intelligence in Finance & Accounting: Foundation for an Agile Enterprise*. Tata Consultancy Services. Retrieved from https://www.iqpc.com/media/1000431/50415.pdf

The Business Dictionary. (2019). *Organizational culture*. http://www.businessdictionary.com/definition/organizational-culture.html

The Hindu Net Desk. (2020, March 10). *Yes Bank crisis explained*. https://www.thehindu.com/business/yes-bank-crisis-explained/article31030273.ece

The Hindu. (2020). *Yes Bank crisis explained*. https://www.thehindu.com/business/yes-bank-crisis-explained/article31030273.ece.

The Indian Express. (2020). *Explained: How Yes Bank ran into crisis*. https://indianexpress.com/article/explained/how-yes-bank-ran-into-crisis-rana-kapoor-arrest-6307314/

The Quint. (2021, March 4). *'A Rigged System': Rana Kapoor Wasn't Alone In The Yes Bank Crisis* [Video]. https://youtu.be/grcdbhLIC0I

The Yes Bank Crisis. (2020, March 7). *Drishti Ias*. https://www.drishtiias.com/daily-updates/daily-news-editorials/the-yes-bank-crisis

Thurlby, B. (1998). Competitive forces are also subject to change. *Management Decision*, *36*(1), 19–24. doi:10.1108/00251749810199202

Tichy, N. L., Tushman, M. L., & Fombrun, C. (1979). Social Network Analysis for Organizations. *Academy of Management Review*, *4*(4), 507–520. doi:10.5465/amr.1979.4498309

Tobin, J. (1969). A General Equilibrium Approach To Monetary Theory. *Journal of Money, Credit and Banking*, *1*(1), 15–29. doi:10.2307/1991374

Today, I. (2020). *Yes Bank crisis: Bad loans worth Rs 20,000 crore granted on Rana Kapoor's direction*. https://www.indiatoday.in/business/story/yes-bank-crisis-rs-20-000-crore-worth-bad-loans-were-given-on-rana-kapoor-s-direction-say-ed-sources-1654280-2020-03-11

Totterdell, P., Wall, P., Holman, D., Diamond, H., & Epitropaki, O. (2004). Affect Networks: A Structural Analysis of the Relationship Between Work Ties and Job-Related Affect. *The Journal of Applied Psychology*, *89*(5), 854–867. doi:10.1037/0021-9010.89.5.854 PMID:15506865

Toyoda, K., Mathiopoulos, P. T., & Ohtsuki, T. (2019). A novel methodology for hyip operators' bitcoin addresses identification. *IEEE Access: Practical Innovations, Open Solutions*, *7*, 74835–74848. doi:10.1109/ACCESS.2019.2921087

Trautman, L. J. (2014). Virtual currencies; Bitcoin & what now after Liberty Reserve, Silk Road, and Mt. Gox? *Richmond Journal of Law and Technology*, *20*(4), 1–11.

Tursunbayeva, A., Di Lauro, S., & Pagliari, C. (2018). People analytics—A scoping review of conceptual boundaries and value propositions. *International Journal of Information Management*, *43*, 224–247. doi:10.1016/j.ijinfomgt.2018.08.002

Ueda, Y., & Ohzono, Y. (2012). Effect of Work Values on Work Outcomes: Investigating Differences between Job Categories. *International Journal of Business Administration*, *3*(2), •••. doi:10.5430/ijba.v3n2p98

Vahdati, H., Nejad, S. H., & Shahsiah, N. (2018). Generic Competitive Strategies toward Achieving Sustainable and Dynamic Competitive Advantage. *Revista Espacios, 39*(13).

Valahu, A., & Devraj, J. (2014). *Accenture to Help Thames Water Prove the Benefits of Smart Monitoring Capabilities*. Retrieved 5 February 2021, from https://newsroom.accenture.com/industries/utilities/accenture-to-help-thames-water-prove-the-benefits-of-smart-monitoring-capabilities.htm

Van Rooyen, M. (2005). *A strategic analytics methodology* (Doctoral dissertation).

Vasek, M., & Moore, T. (2015, January). There's no free lunch, even using Bitcoin: Tracking the popularity and profits of virtual currency scams. In *International conference on financial cryptography and data security* (pp. 44-61). Springer. 10.1007/978-3-662-47854-7_4

Verona, Martins, & Drumond. (2017). Financial Shocks, Financial Stability, and Optimal Taylor Rules. *Journal of Macroeconomics, 54*(PB), 187-207.

Vieira, V. A. (2009). Moderação, mediação, moderadora-mediadora e efeitos indiretos em modelagem de equações estruturais: uma aplicação no modelo de desconfirmação de expectativas. Revista de Administração - RAUSP, 44(1), 17–33.

Vieira, P. R. (2011). *Análise Multivariada com uso do SPSS*. Ciência Moderna Ltda.

Vranken, H. (2017). Sustainability of bitcoin and blockchains. *Current Opinion in Environmental Sustainability*, *28*, 1–9. doi:10.1016/j.cosust.2017.04.011

Wadhwa, R., Ramaswamy, M. K., & Fin, S. M. (2020). Impact of NPA on Profitability of Banks. *International Journal of Engineering Technology and Management Sciences*, *4*(3), 1–8.

Wang, T., Liew, S. C., & Zhang, S. (2019). *When blockchain meets AI: Optimal mining strategy achieved by machine learning.* arXiv preprint arXiv:1911.12942.

Wang, C. Y. P., Chen, M. H., Hyde, B., & Hsieh, L. (2010). Chinese employees' work values and turnover intensions in multinational companies: The mediating effect of pay satisfaction. *Social Behavior and Personality*, *38*(7), 871–894. doi:10.2224bp.2010.38.7.871

Wardley, S. (2015, February 2). An introduction to Wardley (value chain) mapping. *Bits or Pieces?* https://blog.gardeviance.org/2015/02/an-introduction-to-wardley-value-chain.html

Warr, P. (2008). Work values: Some demographic and cultural correlates. *Journal of Occupational and Organizational Psychology*, *81*(4), 751–775. doi:10.1348/096317907X263638

Welsh, R., Glenna, L., Lacy, W., & Biscotti, D. (2008). Close enough but not too far: Assessing the effects of university–industry research relationships and the rise of academic capitalism, *Special Section Knowledge Dynamics out of Balance: Knowledge Biased, Skewed and Unmatched*, *37*(10), 1854–1864.

What is extreme programming (XP)? (2019, September 24). Retrieved from https://www.agilealliance.org/glossary/xp/

White, B. (1996). Developing products and their rhetoric from a single hierarchical model. *STC Proceedings, Theory and Research*, 223-224.

White, B. (2005, April/May). Using a hierarchical process design. *Capital Letter*, *45*(1), 7-16.

White, B., & Martin, B. (2020a, June 30). How to connect the dots between work and the organization's mission. *Apolitical*. https://apolitical.co/en/solution_article/how-to-connect-dots-between-work-and-organisations-mission

White, B., & Martin, B. (2020b, December 11). Not meeting your goals? Use a value network. *Apolitical*. https://apolitical.co/en/solution_article/not-meeting-your-goals-use-a-value-network

Wikipedia Contributors. (2021). Yes Bank. In *Wikipedia*. https://en.wikipedia.org/wiki/Yes_Bank

Williams, G. (2011). Descriptive and predictive analytics. In *Data Mining with Rattle and R* (pp. 171–177). Springer. doi:10.1007/978-1-4419-9890-3_8

Wooden, M., & Harding, D. (1998). Recruitment practices in the private sector: Results from a national survey of employers. *Asia Pacific Journal of Human Resources*, *36*(2), 73–87. doi:10.1177/103841119803600207

Woodford, M. (2012). *Inflation Targeting and Financial Stability*. National Bureau of Economic Research, Inc. NBER Working Paper.

Yap, B. W., Ong, S. H., & Husain, N. H. M. (2011). Using data mining to improve assessment of creditworthiness via credit scoring models. *Expert Systems with Applications*, *38*(10), 13274–13283. doi:10.1016/j.eswa.2011.04.147

Yermack, D. (2015). Is Bitcoin a real currency? An economic appraisal. In *Handbook of digital currency* (pp. 31–43). Academic Press. doi:10.1016/B978-0-12-802117-0.00002-3

Yerpude, S., & Singhal, T. K. (2017). Internet of Things and its impact on Business Analytics. *Indian Journal of Science and Technology*, *10*(5), 1–6. doi:10.17485/ijst/2017/v10i5/109348

Yes Bank Crisis Explained by Dhruv Rathee. (2020). [Video]. *YouTube*. https://www.youtube.com/watch?v=NagvYDGL76s

Yes Bank crisis explained. (2020). *The Hindu*. https://www.thehindu.com/business/yes-bank-crisis-explained/article31030273.ece

Yes Bank crisis: Ten lessons to prevent bank failures in future. (2020, March 17). BFSI.Com.

Yes bank. (n.d.). *Annual reports*. www.yesbank.in

Zeng, L., Xu, L., Shi, Z., Wang, M., & Wu, W. (2006, October). Techniques, process, and enterprise solutions of business intelligence. In *2006 IEEE International Conference on Systems, Man and Cybernetics* (Vol. 6, pp. 4722-4726). IEEE. 10.1109/ICSMC.2006.385050

About the Contributors

Sandeep Kautish is working as Professor & Dean-Academics with LBEF Campus, Kathmandu Nepal running in academic collaboration with Asia Pacific University of Technology & Innovation Malaysia. He is an academician by choice and backed with 17+ Years of work experience in academics including over 06 years in academic administration in various institutions of India and abroad. He has meritorious academic records throughout his academic career. He earned his bachelors, masters and doctorate degree in Computer Science on Intelligent Systems in Social Networks. He holds PG Diploma in Management also. His areas of research interest are Business Analytics, Machine Learning, Data Mining, and Information Systems. He has 40+ publications in his account and his research works has been published in reputed journals with high impact factor and SCI/SCIE/Scopus/WoS indexing. His research papers can be found at Computer Standards & Interfaces (SCI, Elsevier), Journal of Ambient Intelligence and Humanized Computing (SCIE, Springer). Also, he has authored/edited more than 07 books with reputed publishers i.e. Springer, Elsevier, Scrivener Wiley, De Gruyter, and IGI Global. He has been invited as Keynote Speaker at VIT Vellore (QS ranking with 801-1000) in 2019 for an International Virtual Conference. He filed one patent in the field of Solar Energy equipment using Artificial Intelligence in 2019. He is an editorial member/reviewer of various reputed SCI/SCIE journals i.e. Computer Communications (Elsevier), ACM Transactions on Internet Technology, Cluster Computing (Springer), Neural Computing and Applications (Springer), Journal of Intelligent Manufacturing (Springer), Multimedia Tools & Applications (Springer), Computational Intelligence (Wiley), Australasian Journal of Information Systems (AJIS, International Journal of Decision Support System Technology (IGI Global USA), International Journal of Image Mining (Inderscience). He has supervised one PhD in Computer Science as a co-supervisor at Bharathiar University Coimbatore. Presently two doctoral scholars are pursuing their PhD under his supervision in different application areas of Machine Learning. He is a recognized academician as Session Chair/ PhD thesis examiner at various international universities of reputes i.e. University of Kufa, University of Babylon, Polytechnic University of the Philippines (PUP),

University of Madras, Anna University Chennai, Savitribai Phule Pune University, M.S. University, Tirunelveli, and various other Technical Universities. (Google Scholar - https://scholar.google.co.in/citations?user=O3mUpVQAAAAJ&hl=en; Linkedin Profile - https://www.linkedin.com/in/sandeep-k-40316b20/; ORCID Profile - https://orcid.org/0000-0001-5120-5741; More details about the academic profile can be found at www.sandeepkautish.com.)

* * *

Shivani Agarwal is an Assistant Professor in KIET School of Management at KIET Group of Institutions, Ghaziabad, India. She has earned her PhD from Indian Institute of Technology (IIT, Roorkee) in Management. Prior to his current role, she was associated with Institute of Technology & Science, Ghaziabad, UP, India, HRIT Group of Institutions, Ghaziabad, UP, India; IIT Roorkee, UK, India and Center for Management Development, Modinagar, UP. She has authored or co-authored more than 10 research articles that are published in journals, books and conference proceedings. She teaches graduate & post graduate level courses in management. She is the Book Series Editor of Information Technology, Management & Operations Research Practices, CRC Press, Taylor & Francis Group, USA, She is guest editor with IGI-Global, USA. She can be contacted at jindal.shivani24@gmail.com

Gilda Antonelli (BSc, PhD) is a professor of Organizational Design and Human Resources Management at the Law, Economics, Management and Quantitative Methods Department of University of Sannio, Italy. Her research focuses on innovation and change management at different organizational levels (individual, team, organization and network), and on organizational identity issues. She is now focused on studying organizational change driven by Human Research Analytics methods. She is responsible for several research funds and she is a member of the Italian Association for Organizational Studies.

Salha Ben Salem is a PhD student at the Faculty of Economics and Management of Sousse, University of Sousse; and researcher at the Financial Development and Innovation Research Unit (DEFI) -Tunis. She spent three years of professional experience in the Faculty of Economics and Management of Mahdia-Tunisia, Higher Institute of Technologies, Mahdia-Tunisia, and higher institute of applied languages Moknine-Tunisia. She has national and international training and Scientific formation. She practiced the software Eviews, Stata, Matlab, DynareShe has four scientific articles and two book chapters. Her field of research is on Monetary policy, banking sector vulnerability, Financial frictions, DSGE models, Financial Economics, banking system stress, Big Data.

Marcelo Carneiro graduated in Computer Engineering from the Federal University of Pará (2008 - 2014). Specialization in computer networks by Escola Superior Aberta do Brasil - ESAB (2017-2018). He is an information technology analyst at UFPA-Universidade Federal do Pará (2017- current), acting as coordinator of the information technology division of the Institute of Geosciences (2018-current). Master's student of the Graduate Program in Administration at UFPA.

Vineet Chouhan is currently working as Assistant Professor, at Sir Padampat Singhania University, Udaipur. He holds a Ph.D., M. Com (ABST), MBA-FM, UGC-NET (Commerce and Management), RPSC SLET. He is having 18 years of experience in the field of Accounting, Finance, and Research at various reputed colleges of Rajasthan and Gujarat-India. He has successfully completed 4 funded Research projects and Two Industrial Consultancy projects. He is the sole author of 3 books including one reference book and first co-author of 11 books at the university level on the subject of Financial Accounting, Activity Based Costing, Sustainable Accounting Reporting, and GST. He has got above 82 research papers published in National and International journals and presented papers and attended over 60 Conferences/Seminars.

Stefano Di Lauro (PhD, Doctor Europaeus) is a Postdoctoral Researcher at the University of Sannio. He teaches Organization studies related topics at the University of Sannio and University of Molise. He recently completed his PhD in Management (focused on Organizational Identity, Corporate Identity and Social Media) at the University of Naples Federico II. During his PhD, he was a visiting researcher at the Business School of the University of Edinburgh.

Rodrigo Guerra is a PhD in Administration from the Pontifical Catholic University of Rio Grande do Sul, PUCRS, Brazil, with a wide association with the University of Caxias do Sul, UCS, Brazil (2017). He holds a Master's Degree in Production Engineering (2005) from the Federal University of Paraíba (UFPB), Specialist in Quality and Productivity Management (2002) from UFPB, Specialist in Business Logistics (2003) from Potigua University (UNP) and Graduated in Administration (2001)) by UFPB. He is currently an adjunct professor at UFSM-Federal University of Santa Maria / RS, linked to the Department of Administrative Sciences. He is a permanent professor at the PPGAD-Graduate Program in Administration at UFPA (Federal University of Pará), research line: Strategy and Competitiveness in Organizations. He is interested in the following themes: Organizational strategies, Entrepreneurship and Innovation, Organizational ambidexterity, Entrepreneurial resilience, and Performance.

Guneet Kaur is a certified credit and securities analyst. She is Msc Fintech graduate (with distinction) from the University of Stirling, Scotland, United Kingdom. Prior to Msc, she has also done MBA from GNDU (gold medal) and has worked as a global client and partner business manager with Singapore based MNC. Currently, she is working as Fintech Innovator at the University of Stirling Innovation Park Ltd and as a research fellow at Digital Euro Association. She has written various conference papers and has authored a book titled 'The Magic Of Compounding'. She was the Finalist of Women in STEM-Lovelace Colloquium that was held in 2019 at the University of Salford, UK and Royal Bank of Scotland's Hackathon in 2019. Her expertise includes financial modelling, quantitative analysis, academic research, business valuation, business analysis, data visualization and financial fraud and AML analysis.

Moez Labidi is Professor of International Finance and Monetary Policy at Faculty of Economics and Management of Mahdia, University of Monastir, and a Research Director to the research Unit "Développement Financier et Innovation" (DEFI) at Higher School of Economic and Commercial Sciences of Tunis. Tunisia. Her main research interests are in monetary policy, banking sector, financial inclusion, macro-prudential policy, Financial financial instability. Between 2011 and 2012 Moez Labidi was a Member of the Board of directors of the Central bank of Tunisia. In 2015 he joined the Council of Economic Analysis (Government Presidency). Between 2016 and February 2020 he was a Member of Stock Index Committee (Tunisian Stock Exchange). Between 2016 and 2018 Moez Labidi was the Advisor to the Minister of Finance in charge of Financial Reforms Implementation. Since January 2020 he is a member of the License Banking Commission of the Central Bank of Tunisia.

Nadia Mansour is an assistant at The University of Sousse- Tunisia, and a visiting researcher at the University of Salamanca- Spain. Dr. MANSOUR research interests focus on Banking, macroeconomic, DSGE, Big Data, Business Tourism, and Innovation. She is an academic member and ambassador of Communication Institute of Greece, a committee member of indexed conferences, editorial Board Member of Taylor & Francis, IGI GLOBAL, and Springer, a reviewer in IGI Global, Emerald, and Wiley. Dr. MANSOUR has presented various scientific papers in international (France, Morocco, USA, Turkey…) and national conferences. She is also a keynote speaker and session chair in several conferences in (Turkey, India UAE…). She has several published articles in ranked journals and chapters (IGI Global & Palgrave Macmillan) as well as edited books (Taylor & Francis, Springer).

Beth Archibald Martin received her BA in French and MA in Secondary Education from West Virginia University. She writes and presents on aspects of user experience, strategic planning, performance measurement, and online learning. In addition to more than 25 years as a practitioner in the public and private sectors, she teaches at the Maryland Institute College of Art.

Nathália Nogueira is a Master's student of the Graduate Program (PPGAD) in Administration at the Federal University of Pará - UFPA. Specialist in Communication and Public Speaking at Faculdade Futura (2020). Bachelor in Trilingual Executive Secretariat from the State University of Pará - UEPA (2012). She is interested in the following topics: Strategy, Entrepreneurship, Organizational Behavior and Performance.

Pranav Saraswat is currently working as Associate Professor at MIT World Peace University, Pune, India. He holds a Ph.D., MBA, M. Com (ABST), UGC NET with 16 years of experience in the field of Accounting, Finance, and Research at reputed institutions of India. He has got more than 20 research papers published in National and International journals of repute and presented papers in more than 30 Conferences/Seminars.

Nuno Souto graduated in aerospace engineering - avionics branch, in 2000 in Instituto Superior Técnico, Lisbon, Portugal and received his Ph.D. in 2006 . From November 2000 to January 2002 he worked as a researcher in the field of automatic speech recognition for Instituto de Engenharia e Sistemas de Computadores, Lisbon Portugal. He joined the ISCTE- University Institute of Lisbon, as an assistant professor in 2006. He is a researcher at IT (Instituto de Telecomunicações), Portugal, since 2002 and has been involved in several international research projects and many national projects. His research interests include wireless networks, signal processing for communications, OFDM, single carrier transmission with frequency domain equalization, channel coding, modulation, channel estimation, synchronization, MIMO schemes, wireless sensor networks, unmanned aerial vehicles, application of algorithms and performance analysis methods used in Telecommunications to areas of Economy/Finance.

Aizhan Tursunbayeva (PhD, Doctor Europaeus, GRP) is an Assistant Professor at the University of Twente. Her previous professional roles include Management Consultant at KPMG Advisory (Healthcare Division) and HR Manager at HSBC Bank. Her research lies at the intersection of HRM, Technology, Innovation, and healthcare. She has published in a range of journals including Information Technology & People, Journal of the American Medical Informatics Association, and Management Learning.

Basil White is a policy analyst at the U.S. Department of Veterans Affairs in Washington, DC, in the Office of Policy and Interagency Collaboration. He has a Project Management Professional certification from the Project Management Institute, and is a fellow of the Partnership for Public Service's Excellence in Government Fellowship. He has an M.A. in Science Writing from Johns Hopkins University, and a B.A. in Technical Writing and Experimental Psychology from the University of Memphis.

Ryan Wold earned a Bachelor's in Communications and a Master's in Public Administration. He has consulted with small-businesses, large enterprises, and fast-paced startups as a Software Engineer and Product Manager. He has worked in the public sector at the local, county, state, and federal levels.

Samir Yerpude is presently working as an Deputy General Manager with one of the largest automobile manufacturing company of India, Tata Motors Ltd. He has various research publications to his credit and his research areas are Internet of Things and Business Analytics. He holds Masters Degrees (MBA) in Operations and Engineering Degree in Mechanical. Completed IIM Ahmedabad courses in IT Strategy Management and Customer Relations Management. He also possesses Post-graduate diploma in Material Management and Business Management apart from a Diploma in Mechanical Engineering. Honors and Awards: - Winner - CSI Award (National Award) for Excellence in Information Technology - Awarded Best Business Relationship Manager at Tata Motors - Awarded Best Project Award - Warehouse Management Implementation - ACES Award awarded by Tata Motors CFO for the CRM Application maintenance domain. - Champion Award for the After Market in IT Domain.

Index

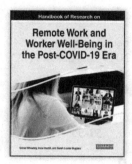
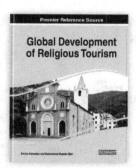

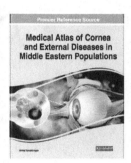

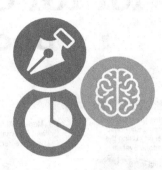

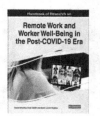

Printed in the United States
by Baker & Taylor Publisher Services